Clark County Washington
Cemetery Records

Brush Prairie
Hawk (or Fairchild)
Yacolt
Page (or Red Rock)
Sunnyside
Finn Hill
Sifton
Fern Prairie
St. John's Catholic
Hurt Road
Crawford
Gravel Point
Wilson Bridge
Northwood Park
Memory Memorial Park

Volume Five

Clark County Genealogical Society

Copies of this book may be purchased from:

Clark County Genealogical Society
P.O. Box 5249
Vancouver Washington 98668-5249

for $17.50 + $3.00 postage
Washington residents add 7.7% sales tax

ISBN 1-892685-05-1

TABLE OF CONTENTS

***

NAMES & NUMBERS OF CLARK COUNTY CEMETERIES AS SHOWN ON MAP

1. Post Military Cemetery (Vol. 3)
2. St. James Cemetery (Vol. 2)
3. Old City Cemetery (Vol. 1)
4. Park Hill Cemetery
5. Evergreen Memorial Gardens
6. Fisher Cemetery (Vol. 2)
7. Knight Family Cemetery
8. Camas Cemetery
9. Dead Lake Cemetery (Vol. 3)
10. Washougal Cemetery (Vol. 4)
11. Washougal Catholic Cemetery (Vol. 3)
12. Sunnyside Memorial Cemetery
13. Fern Prairie Cemetery
14. Livingston [or Shanghai] Cemetery
           (Vol. 4)
15. Sifton Cemetery
16. Brush Prairie Cemetery
17. St. John's Catholic Cemetery
18. Wilson Bridge Cemetery
19. Memory Memorial Park
20. Salmon Creek Methodist Cemetery
           (Vol. 2)
21. St. John Lutheran Cemetery (Vol. 2)
22. Northwood Park Cemetery
23. Sara Union Cemetery (Vol. 3)
24. Elim Lutheran Cemetery (Vol. 4)

25. Bethel Lutheran Cemetery
           (Vol. 3)
26. Finn Hill Cemetery
27. Gravel Point Cemetery
28. Venersberg Cemetery (Vol. 4)
29. Crawford [or Kumtux] Cemetery
30. Sacred Heart [or Dublin]
           Cemetery (Vol. 4)
31. Lewisville Cemetery (Vol. 4)
32. Pioneer Cemetery (Vol. 2)
33. St. Mary's Catholic Cemetery
           (Vol. 3)
34. Bethel Methodist Cemetery
           (Vol. 3)
35. Ridgefield Cemetery (Vol. 3)
36. Fairchld [or Hawk] Cemetery
37. Page [or Red Rock] Cemetery
38. Gardner [or Hayes] Cemetery
           (Vol. 4)
39. Hurt Road Cemetery
40. Mt. Zion I.O.O.F. Cemetery
           (Vol. 3)
41. Highland Lutheran Cemetery
           (Vol. 3)
42. Mountain View Cemetery
           (Vol. 4)
43. Yacolt Cemetery
44. Amboy Cemetery (Vol. 4)
45. Chelatchie Prairie Cemetery
           (Vol. 3)
46. Columbia Tie Road Cemetery
47. Buncombe Hollow Cemetery
           (Vol. 4)
48. Indian Burial Grounds

49. John Pollock Gravesite

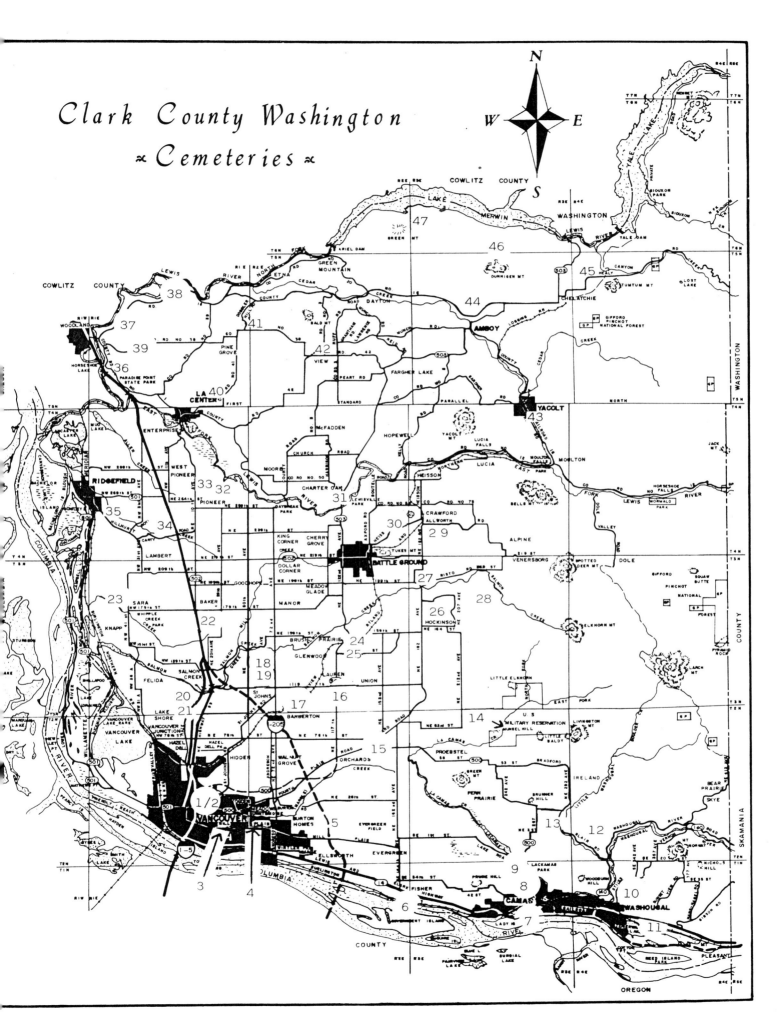

Clark County Washington
~ Cemeteries ~

M	ABELS	Winfield S. Abels, 1901 - 1939
N	AHLQUIST	Annie S. Ahlquist, 1887 - 1971
N	AHLQUIST	Harry R. Ahlquist, 1882 - 1953
N	AHLQUIST	William H. Ahlquist, Dad, 1910 - 1978
S	ALINGER	Ivar A. Alinger, Father, 1885 - 1957
	ALINGER	Larry Dave Alinger, (age 42, Apr 7, 1941, Vancouver, WA, May 22, 1983, Portland, OR, Res.: Portland, OR, Graveside service Thursday, May 26, at Brush Prairie Cemetery. Batman's Parkrose Mortuary, Portland, OR, Obit - The Columbian)
S	ALINGER	Lydia K. Alinger, Mother, 1891 - 1940
M	ALLMAN	E. A. Allman, Born Oct 14, 1863 - Died Jan 8, 1912
M	ALLMAN	G. W. Allman, Born Feb 17, 1854 - Died Dec 31, 1908
N	ALTIZER	Arnold Altizer, Son, 1898 - 1937
N	ALTIZER	Ellen M. Altizer, 1877 - 1977
N	ALTIZER	Grace Altizer, Daughter, 1895 - 1896
M	ANDERSON	Charles F. Anderson, Sept 14, 1874 - Nov 29, 1950
M	ANDERSON	Emil F. Anderson, 1882 - 1954
N	ANDERSON	Lettie V. Anderson, 1870 - 1953
M	ANDERSON	Marie C. Anderson, 1884 - 1963
N	ANDERSON	May Belle Anderson, 1875 - 1963
N	ANDERSON	Ray G. Anderson, 1873 - 19__
S	ANDRUS	Arthur G. Andrus, Husband, 1874 - 1950
S	APROZEAN	Alexandrea Aprozean, Mother, 1877 - 1965
S	APROZEAN	Vasile Aprozean, Father, 1864 - 1935
N	ATKINS	Elmer J. Atkins, 1879 - 1968
N	ATKINS	Everett E. Atkins, 1905 - 1964
N	ATKINS	Lloyd E. Atkins, U S Air Force, W W 2, Dec 11, 1907 - Aug 24, 1975

BRUSH PRAIRIE CEMETERY

ATKINS   (Muriel A. Atkins, Age 44, Nov 12, 1942, Nippawin, Saskatchewan, Apr 7, 1987, at home, Brush Prairie, WA. Res: Brush Prairie, WA. Widower: Gary, at home. Father & stepmother: Eugene & Dorothy Holt, LaCenter. Son: David, at home. Daughter: Lanelle Spencer, Vancouver. Sisters: Pauline Fjellgaard, Prince George, BC; Dianne Watermeier and Gail Bevard, both of Vancouver. Funeral Saturday, Apr 11, 1987, at Layne's Funeral Home Chapel. Inurnment in Brush Prairie Cemetery. Obit - The Columbian)

N   ATKINS   Myrtle S. Atkins,   1879 - 1952

S   AULDRIDGE   Laura A. Auldridge,   1875 - 1946

S   AULDRIDGE   Harry G. Auldridge,   1873 - 1953

M   AUSTIN   Chester A. Austin,   1886 - 1976

M   AUSTIN   Gertrude L. Austin,   1888 - 1977

M   AUSTIN   Morton F. Austin,   1883 - 1961

M   AUSTIN   Olive M. Austin,   1885 - 1955

S   AXFORD   Anna Betts Axford, Mother,   1895 - 1958

M   BABCOCK   James H. Babcock,   1889 - 1956

M   BABCOCK   Lillian G. Babcock,   1899 - ____

S   BAILEY   Edward Ray Bailey,   1908 - 1930

BAILEY   (Stewart P. Bailey, Age 70, Jun 9, 1913, Altadena, CA - Jan 20, 1984, Gresham, OR. Res: Vancouver, WA, Husband of Emma L. Bailey, at home. Services Tues., Jan 24, at Vancouver Funeral Chapel. Interment in Brush Prairie Cemetery. Vancouver Funeral Chapel. Obit - The Columbian)

M   BAKER   Fremont H. Baker,   Oct 29, 1890 - Mar 14, 1977, BELOVED HUSBAND

N   BAKER   Isaac Baker,   1858 - 1945

N   BAKER   Martha Baker, Wife of William Baker, Born Jan 7, 1832 - Died Jan 3, 1888. The Gift of God Is Eternal Life Through Jesus Christ Our Lord

M   BAKER   Phebe A. (Britch) Baker, BELOVED WIFE, Dec 4, 1891 - Aug 28, 1973, (M 62 y, 16 d, 6 ch, 14 grch, 26 grgrch)

N   BAKER   Thurston Baker, Son of Wm. & Martha Baker, B. 22 Jul 1874 - D. Dec 13, 1879

N   BAKER   Wm. Baker, Co. F. 25 Missouri Inf.

N   BAKER   Wm. H. Baker, Son of Wm. & Martha Baker, B. May 20, 1871 - D. Dec 21, 1879   2

N	BAKER	Zimmerman Baker, Baby, 1880 - 1880
S	BAKKE	Albert A. Bakke, 1873 - 1943
S	BAKKE	Mina Bakke, 1878 - 1949
S	BALKE	Francilla May Balke, Sep 9, 1939 - Sep 22, 1939
S	BALKE	John Elmer Balke, Dec 31, 1939
S	BANTA	Hattie M. Banta, MOTHER, 1892 - 1938
S	BANTA	William Banta, FATHER, 1889 - 1928
N	BARNRENT	Florence Barnrent, 1929 - 1975
N	BATCHELOR	Edward R. Batchelor, FATHER, 1909 - 1952
	BATCHELDER	(Verna Batchelder, Age 89, Apr 23, 1894 - Feb 8, 1984. Res: Battle Ground, WA. Graveside service Monday, Feb 13, at Brush Prairie Cem., Layne's Funeral Home. Obit - The Columbian)
S	BAYLEY	Ben W. Bayley, 1866 - 1957
S	BAYLEY	Flora E. Bayley, 1871 - 1939
S	BAYLEY	Leslie Bayley, 1900 - 1947
M	BECKMANN	Emil Beckmann, AT REST, 1851 - 1912
M	BEELER	Eddie Claire Beeler, BABY, 1937 - 1938
N	BEGAU	Christian C. Begau, 1888 - 1961
N	BEGAU	Lydia M. Begau, 1883 - 1956
M	BELL	Amanda C. Bell, 1844 - 1928
M	BELL	Ben J. Bell, 1872 - 1929
M	BELL	John S. Bell, GONE BUT NOT FORGOTTEN, 1843 - 1911
M	BELL	Lizzie Ellen Bell, Mar 22, 1862 - Jan 28, 1886
M	BELL	Olive D. Bell, 1874 - 1961
N	BENNETT	Allen E. Bennett, 1917 - 1965
N	BENNETT	Blanche G. Bennett, 1914 - 1966
N	BENNETT	Edith A. Bennett, Mother, 1899 - 1958
N	BENNETT	J. J. Bennett, "Red", Father, 1899 - 1962

M   BENNETT   Zoah M. Bennett, Mother, 1879 - 1963

N   BENSON   Elizabeth Benson, 1909 - 1972

N   BENSON   James Benson, 1906 - ____

M   BENSON   Ralph J. Benson, Father, 1878 - 1972

M   BENSON   Ruth R. Benson, Mother, 1889 - 1973

N   BERRY   Aileen A. Berry, (Eastern Star Emblem), 1930 - 1977

M   BERRY   Minnie Olive Berry, 1955 - 1914

N   BERRY   Robert E. Berry, (Masonie Emblem), 1920 - ____

N   BESLANOIWITCH   Kent W. Beslanoiwitch, BELOVED SON, 1955 - 1966

M   BETHJE   Wayne E. Bethje, THE LORD IS MY SHEPHERD, 1945 - 1954

S   BETTERS   Arlene M. Betters, 1912 - 1937

S   BETTS   Chas. Beecher Betts, Son, 1919 - 1941

S   BETTS   Earl Ray, Father, 1888 - 1943

M   BILLS   Ira P. Bills, 1887 - 1960

M   BILLS   Ira G. Bills, 1845 - 1923

N   BIRMINGHAM   Blanche C. Birmingham, In Gods Care, 1913 - 1976

S   BIRMINGHAM   David Birmingham, 1938

N   BIRMINGHAM   Murray G. Birmingham, 1911 - ____

M   BISSELL   Arnold L. Bissell, AT REST, D. Mar 25, 1919 - age 77 y

M   BLACKBURN   Henry B. Blackburn, Dearest Dad, 1878 - 1968

M   BLACKBURN   Sophia C. Blackburn, Our Beloved Mother, 1883 - 1953

M   BLACKETER   Albert Blacketer, 1879 - 1929

M   BLACKETER   Julia Ann Blacketer, 1882 - 1968

M   BLACKETER   Minnie L. Blacketer, 1913 - 1913

N   BLIVEN   Anna Janet Bliven, 1884 - 1972

N   BODEL   Alice Penden Bodel, 1884 - 1944

M   BONE   Alice M. Bone,   A precious one from us has gone,
A voice we love is stilled,
A place is vacant in our home,
Which never will be filled,
God in his wisdom has recalled,
The bone his love had given,
And tho her body must lie here,
The soul is safe in Heaven.
Sep 22, 1868 - Dec 24, 1888

M   BONE   Harvey Bone, Son of J. M. and S. M. Bone, Dec 21, 1880 - Jan 3, 1885

M   BONE   J. M. Bone,   BLESSED ARE THE PURE IN HEART FOR THEY SHALL SEE GOD,
Jul 3, 1857 - Nov 3, 1884

M   BONE   Pearl Tripper Bone,   1893 - 1975

M   BONE   Rachel Bone, Wife of Joseph, Dec 19, 1839 - Mar 25, 1896

M   BONE   Willis P. Bone,   Beautiful spirit, free from all stain,
Ours the healing the sorrow and pain,
Thine is the glory and infinite gain,
Thy slumber is rest
Born Nov 6, 1866 - Died Dec 31, 1908

M   BONE   Willis P. Bone,   A precious one from us has gone,
A voice we love is stilled,
A place is vacant in our home,
Which never will be filled,
God in his wisdom has recalled,
The bone his love has given,
And tho his body must lie here,
The soul is safe in Heaven.
Nov 6, 1866 - _____

N   BONHAM   Cenith D. Bonham,   1888 - 1964

N   BONHAM   Welcome H. Bonham,   1877 - 1964

S   BORDEN   M. A. Borden,   1881 - 1922

S   BORDON   Anna Bordon,   1861 - 1943

S   BORDON   James L. Bordon,   1886 - 1955

S   BORDON   Merta G. Bordon,   1881 - 1945

M   BOTTON   Gladys G. Botton,   1896 - 1970

M   BOYD   Mary E. Boyd,   1861 - 1936

M   BOYD   Robert C. Boyd,   Feb 23, 1914 - Oct 13, 1923

M   BOYD   Robert Boyd, Jr.,   1881 - 1915

M   BOYD   Robert Boyd, Sr.,   1854 - 1934

M   BOYSE   Charles S. Boyse, BELOVED,   1905 - 1960

S   BRIGHT   Catherine Bright,   1850 - 1936

M   BROOKS   Jessie Brooks, IN LOVING MEMORY,   Jan 31, 1824 - Jan 29, 1899

S   BROOKSHIRE   David Brookshire,   illegible - 1938

N   BROSI   Otto W. Brosi,   Feb 1, 1876 - Sep 15, 1904

N   BROWN   Andrew Brown, Son of A. & O. Brown, SUFFER LITTLE CHILDREN TO
              COME UNTO ME,   Dec 24, 1883 - Jan 9, 1886

S   BROWN   Charles Brown,   Sep 1955

N   BROWN   Iva G. Brown, Daughter of A. & O. Brown, She was but as a smile,
              Which Glistens in a tear, Seen but a little while, But oh
              how loved, How dear

M   BROWN   Nellie I. Brown,   1881 - 1954

N   BROWN   Steve F. Brown, "Sandy", HUSBAND AND SON,   Sep 30, 1950 - Jan
              30, 1978

N   BROWN   Vivian V. Brown, Daughter of A. & O. Brown, OF SUCH IS THE KING-
              DOM OF HEAVEN,   Mar 2, 1886 - Oct 27, 1886

M   BRUETGEMAN   Sara K. Bruetgeman,   1862 - 1950

M   BRULEY   Earl N. Bruley,   Nov 8, 1911 - Nov 12, 1932

S   BRULEY   Ellsworth H. Bruley,   1923 - 1929

M   BRULEY   Michael Vane Bruley, Our Son & Brother, In Gods Care,   1953 -
              1970

S   BUDD   James E. Budd,   1884 - 1946

S   BUDD   Lloyd I. Budd, Together Forever,   1893 - 1965

M   BUDD   Nellie Budd, Mother,   1864 - 1940

N   BURDOIN   Frank Burdoin,   Jun 18, 1864 - Dec 9, 1955

N   BURDOIN   Mattie Burdoin,   1869 - 1966

M   BURKEY   Danton J. Burkey, U S Air Force, W W 2,   1916 - 1976

S   BURNETT   Charles H. Burnett,   1880 - 1929

S	BURNETT	Ida G. Burnett, 1888 - 1939
S	BURNETT	Naomi R. Burnett, 1925 - 1942
M	BUSWELL	Jake Buswell, 1878 - 1918
M	CALVERT	Vernon C. Calvert, 1892 - 1950
M	CAMPBELL	Anna V. Campbell, 1901 - 1966
M	CAMPBELL	Arthur Campbell, 1855 - 1922
M	CAMPBELL	Arthur H. Campbell, 1897 - 1952
M	CAMPBELL	Baby Campbell, 1919 - 1919
M	CAMPBELL	Carrie F. Campbell, 1893 - 1974
M	CAMPBELL	Ernest E. Campbell, 1890 - 1967
M	CAMPBELL	Erma G. Campbell, Our Darling, Dec 2, 1914 - Dec 26, 1929
M	CAMPBELL	Frank A. Campbell, Sr., Washington, Cook U S Army, W W I, Apr 12, 1887 - Feb 11, 1970
M	CAMPBELL	Fred G. Campbell, Illinois, Sgt. Co. K, 22 Engr, W W I, Aug 7, 1896 - Jan 22, 1963
M	CAMPBELL	Hilda T. Campbell, Wife & Mother, 1899 - 1972
M	CAMPBELL	Susan J. Campbell, 1867 - 1939
M	CAMPBELL	Wallace W. Campbell, Sgt U S Army, 1921 - 1975
N	CANNELL	Francis Gray Cannell, Mom, 1908 - 1978 (Eastern Star emblem)
M	CAPLES	Anna Marie, 1875 - 1936
M	CAPLES	Charles William Caples, 1865 - 1944
M	CAPLES	Herbert L. Caples, 1912 - 1934
N	CARBOROUGH	Lou T. Carborough, 1884 - 19___
N	CARBOROUGH	Webb R. Carborough, 1885 - 1960

CARLSON (Edna H. Carlson, Age 78, May 21, 1908, Springfield, IL, Nov 18, 1986, Cancer. Res: Vancouver. Sons: Greg Brown and Mike Amis, both of Portland. Daughters, Nancy Clark of LaCenter; Sandra Wing of Battle Ground, and Judy Cutter of Anchorage, AK. Brother: Kenneth Miller, CA; sister: Freda Grove, Lake Oswego, OR. Preceded in death by her husband, Leonard, in 1966. Funeral Sat., Nov. 22, Layne's Funeral Home. Burial Brush Prairie Cem. Obit - The Columbian

	CARLSON	Gust Carlson,	1870 - 1948
S	CARR	Mary Ellen Carr,	1878 - 1951
S	CARR	Ted Carr,	1891 - 1971
S	CAUGHLEY	Ella M. Caughley	1895 - 1973
S	CAULEY	Lyle L. Cauley,	1903 - 1941
M	CHANEY	Cora C. Chaney,	1881 - 1959
M	CHANEY	John W. Chaney,	1883 - 1956
M	CHANNING	Ruth L. Channing,	1895 - 1954
N	CHAPMAN	Rev. Marvel Chapman, Father,	1911 - 1955
N	CHARLSON	Shirley L. Charlson,	1921 - 1961
S	CHRISTIANS	John A. Christians,	1861 - 1939
S	CHRISTIANS	Margaret M. Christians,	1871 - 1946
S	CIRCLE	Abbie L. Circle,	1885 - 1974
S	CIRCLE	Elmer M. Circle,	1876 - 1931
N	CLARK	Alvin Clark,	Aug 25, 1880 - Dec 3, 1955 age 75 y. 3 m. 8d.

Inscription illegible

N	CLARK	Annie M. Clark,	1886 - 1871
M	CLARK	Carrie E. Clark,	1876 - 1965
N	CLARK	Cephas B. Clark,	1855 - 1875
N	CLARK	Effariah Clark, Wife of Alvin,	May 28, 1816 - Jun 22, 1895
S	CLARK	Electa Clark, AT REST,	1835 - 1922
N	CLARK	Elizabeth V. Clark,	1834 - 1891
N	CLARK	Emery C. Clark,	1872 - 1892
M	CLARK	Gibbs G. Clark,	1870 - 1956
N	CLARK	Grant L. Clark,	1884 - 1959
N	CLARK	John Jay Clark,	1815 - 1902
N	CLARK	Miner P. Clark,	1856 - 1888

BRUSH PRAIRIE CEMETERY

N CLARK Nellie E. Clark, 1875 - 1889

N CLARK Rhoda A. Clark, 1878 - 1891

N CLARK Riley H. Clark, 1861 - 1888

N CLARK Vesta E. Clark, 1893 - 1952

S CLARY John J. Clary, 1870 - 1943

M COLBY Ernest A. Colby, Father & Grandfather, 1858 - 1952

S COLE Fannie Cole, 1868 - 1937

S COLE John Cole, 1862 - 1937

N COLEMAN John R. Coleman, Father, 1899 - 1976

N COLEMAN (Thelma Coleman, Age 82, Nov 18, 1902, Charlston, IL., Feb 4,
            1985, Battle Ground, WA. Res: Brush Prairie, Hockinson,
            WA area. Preceded in death by her husband, John, in Mar
            1976. ..... Funeral Thursday, Feb 7, at Vancouver Funeral
            Chapel. Interment at Brush Prairie Cem. VFC. Obit - The
            Columbian)

M COLLINS Nancy A. Collins, Mother, 1883 - 1960

M COLLINS Stuart G. Collins, Father, 1876 - 1965

M CONDON Denise E. Condon, Our Daughter, Mar 14, 1971

N CONDON Emma E. Condon, MOM, 1898 - 1962

N CONDON Frank W. Condon, DAD, 1892 - 1976

M CONE Mary Louise Cone, 1889 - 1965

S CONNER Hazel Conner, DAUGHTER, 1918 - 1933

N CONNER John H. Conner, FATHER, 1911 - 1972

S CONNER Margaret E. Conner, MOTHER, 1877 - 1954

M CONNER Julias Conner, DAD, 1875 - 1955

S CONSTABLE Baby Constable, 1952

   COOK (Larry Leeroy Cook, Age 28, Auto accident. May 15, 1957, Hillsboro
         OR, May 3 1986. Clark Co., WA. (3 miles w. of Battle
         Ground). Currently Res: California. Mother: Sharon Mayers,
         Battle Ground, Bros: Delton Bellomy, Brush Prairie; Ray
         Cook, Battle Ground; Brian Holmgren, Brush Prairie; (cont.)

COOK (cont.) Brett Holmgren, Brush Prairie, Ron Cook, Battle Ground,
Sister: Debbie Cook, Battle Ground. G-Parents: Delma
Bellomy, Battle Ground; Mr./Mrs. Al Holmgren, Brush
Prairie. Burial: Brush Prairie Cem. Evergreen Staples
Fun. Chapel, Obit - The Columbian)

N   COOP   Anna Pearl Coop, Dau of G & L,   1900 - 1902

N   COOP   Arthene M. Coop, In Memory Of Granny,   1904 - 1977

N   COOP   Charles C. Coop, FATHER,   1847 - 1930

N   COOP   Ira Coop,   1887 - 1904

N   COOP   Irene P. Coop, MOTHER,   1861 - 1909

M   COOP   Thomas Willard Coop,   Oct 25, 1875 - Nov 11, 1963

M   CORNELIUS   Rhoda J. Cornelius,   1893 - 1978

M   CORNELIUS   William Cornelius,   1893 - 1958

N   COURSER   K. Pearl Courser,   1882 - 1966

M   COURTION   Bonnie Jeanne Courtion,   1939 - 1971

M   COURTION   Clarence C. Courtion,   1901 - 1905

M   COURTION   Edward C. Courtion,   1876 - 1968

M   COURTION   Vena S. Courtion,   1882 - 1968

COX   (Charles R. Cox, Age 74. Sep 25, 1912, Belfield County, North
Dakota. - Oct 9, 1986, Cancer. Husb/of Verdelle, at home.
Res: Battle Ground, WA....... Funeral Tuesday, Oct 14, at
Layne's Funeral Home. Burial in Brush Prairie Cem. Layne's
Fun. Home. Obit - The Columbian)

S   COWLEY   Caroline S. Cowley,   1866 - 1948

M   COX   Ruby B. Cox, Mother,   1877 - 1968

M   CRAIK   Emma Craik, Mother,   1891 - 1975

M   CRAIK   Wilfred E. Craik, Father,   1887 - 1971

M   CROSS   Joy A. Cross, FATHER,   1903 - 1955

M   CUNDIFF   Susie Mickey Cundiff,   1908 - 1933

M   CURRY   James Curry,   Nov 17, 1859 - Jun 26, 1908

M   CURRY   Naomi Curry, MOTHER,   1866 - 1931

M   CURRY   Robert R. Curry, BROTHER,   1889 - 1922

M   DALY   Daisy B. Daly,   Born Aug 22, 1874 - Died Nov 18, 1908,   Gone But Not Forgotten, Not My Will But Thine Be Done

M   DALY   Edson Daly, Father, Nov 3, 1833 - May 8, 1907

M   DALY   Eunice Daly, His Wife (Edson Daly), Sep 26, 1836 - Apr 26, 1912

M   DALY   John E. Daly,   1880 - 1923

M   DALY   Lloyd Daly,   1906 - 1945

S   DANIL   4 years

S   DAUGHERTY   Daniel E. Daugherty,   1863 - 1934

S   DAUGHERTY   Sarah N. Daugherty,   1873 - 1973

M   DAUGHTY   Willard L. Daughty, Washington, Marine Corp.,   1907 - 1953

S   DAVIS   Burton Davis,   1885 - 1968

DAVIS   (Eva H. Davis. Age 62, Oct 8, 1922, Alden, Iowa - May 7, 1985, Vancouver, WA. Res: Battle Ground, WA, wife of Ralph, at home..... Funeral Saturday, May 11, at Layne's Funeral Home Chapel. Burial at Brush Prairie Cem. LFC, Obit - The Columbian)

DAVIS   (Nida Geraldine Davis. Age 83. Sep 15, 1901, Fruitland, WA - Feb 11, 1985, at home, Battle Ground, WA. ..... Funeral Thursday at Layne's Funeral Home Chapel. Burial in Brush Prairie Cem. Obit - The Columbian)

M   DAVIS   John Davis, AT REST,   1877 - 1951

M   DAVIS   Leo L. Davis,   1907 - 1973

M   DAVIS   Minnie Davis, AT REST,   1873 - 1941

M   DAVIS   Myrtle B. Davis,   1912 - _____

M   DAVIS   Ralph Clifford Davis,   1930 - 1956

DAVIS   (Ralph F. Davis. Age 65. Probable stroke. Apr 3, 1920, Salem, OR - Oct 9, 1985, at home, Battle Ground, WA. Preceded in death by his wife, Eva H. in 1985. Funeral Saturday, Oct 12, at Layne's Funeral Home Chapel. Burial in Brush Prairie Cem. Obit - The Columbian)

N   DEITRICH   Cora F. Deitrich,   Jun 17, 1868 - Jun 5, 1871

N   DEITRICH   Elizabeth J. Deitrich,   1839 - 1933

M   DEITRICK   Frederick Deitrick,   D. Jul 14, 1889, age 79 y

M   DEITRICH   Frederick W. Deitrich,   1886 - 1928

N   DEITRECH   Hannah M. Deitrech, Jun 28, 1864 - Jun 5, 1871

N   DEITRICH   Isaac Deitrich,   1835 - 1906

N   DEITRICH   James A. Deitrich,   1885 - 1908

N   DEITRICH   Lillian U. Deitrich,   Mar 6, 1866 - Jun 5, 1871

M   DEITRICK   Margaret Deitrick,   D. Jul 13, 1890 - age 83 y

N   DEITRICH   William H. Deitrich,   1881 - 1904

S   DENNIS   Caroline M. Dennis,   1879 - 1923

      DENNY   (Elsie Fullerton Denny. Age 91. Oct 28, 1893, Vancouver, WA. - Jan 24, 1985, Vancouver, WA. Husband: Dimner Denny, at home........ Graveside service Monday, Jan 28, 1985, at Brush Prairie Cem. VFC. Obit - The Columbian)

S   DEPUTY   Isabel H. Deputy,   1876 - 1956

S   DEPUTY   John E. Deputy,   1874 - 1935

S   DESHLER   Edward B. Deshler, In Memory of,   1875 - 1939

M   DEWEY   Jo Ann Dewey, In Loving Memory From Her Friends,   1931 - 1950

      DEWEY   (Noble Clyde Dewey. Age 96. Sep 8, 1886, Maynard, Iowa - Aug 17, 1983, Portland, OR. Husband of Anna Dewey. ..... Funeral Monday, Aug 22, at Meadow Glade Seventh-day Adventist Church. Burial in Brush Prairie Cem. Layne's Funeral Home. Obit - The Columbian) U S Army, W W I

M   DILLON   Laura A. Dillon, Sister,   1862 - 1931

M   DILLON   William H. Dillon, In Memory Of:,   1854 - 1935

S   DISBROW   Arthur Disbrow, Father,   1862 - 1940

N   DIXON   Joseph Orin Dixon, Nebraska CGM U S Navy W W II, Jun 15, 1920 - Mar 13, 1974

S   DOIDGE   Mable E. Doidge, Mother,   1885 - 1940

M   DONALDSON   Muriel Donaldson,   1955 - 1957

M   DOUGHTY   Frances Doughty,   1909 - 1970

M   DOUGHTY   Mae E. Daughty, MOTHER,   1889 - 1956

S   DOUGHERTY   John Dougherty, FATHER, 1879 - 1950

S   DOUGHERTY   Lotta Dougherty, 1882 - 1951

N   DOUGLAS   Nadine Leslie Douglas, MOTHER, 1922 - 1973

N   DRESSER   Eddie Dresser, 1872 - 1873

     DUNN   (Charles V. Dunn. Age 82. Oct 10, 1902, Elliot, Ark - Jan 16, 1985, Vancouver, WA. Husband of Iva, at home .... Funeral Saturday, Jan 19, at Layne's Funeral Home Chapel. Burial in Brush Prairie Cem. LFC. Obit - The Columbian)

M   DUNNING   Alvie Dunning, 1857 - 1911 BELOVED FATHER

M   DUNNING   Mary Dunning, 1861 - 1906 BELOVED MOTHER

M   DUPUIS   Gerald Lee DuPuis, 1938 - 1946

S   DURKEE   Elbert Durkee, 1852 - 1932

M   EARLE   Mary Faye Earle, Sister, 1905 - 1968

S   ECKTON   Arthur W. Eckton, 1892 - 1970

S   ECKTON   Edgar J. Eckton, In Memory Of; 1895 - 1945

S   ECKTON   Gundrun Eckton, 1906 - 1980

S   ECKTON   Henry B. Eckton, ABSENT FROM THE BODY, PRESENT WITH THE LORD, 1864 - 1935

S   ECKTON   Mary L. Eckton, MOTHER, IN THEE OH LORD HAVE I PUT MY TRUST, 1869 - 1946

S   ECKTON   Wilson H. Eckton, Washington, Tech 5th Class U S Army, W W 2 Apr 10, 1903 - Dec 16, 1971

M   EDNER   Alice E. Edner, 1860 - 1936

M   EDNER   Clara V. Edner, Mother, 1856 - 1915

M   EDNER   Edson H. Edner, 1879 - 1928

M   EDNER   Henry M. Edner, 1857 - 1923

     EDWARDS   (Allan L. Edwards. Age 73. Jul 3, 1910, Lewiston, Idaho - Sep 29, 1983, Vancouver, WA. Husband of Clara E. Edwards, at home. ..... Graveside service Monday, Oct 3, at Brush Prairie Cem. Hamilton-Mylan Funeral Home. Obit - The Columbian)

S   EDWARD   James P. Edward, 1884 - 1931

M   EDWARDS   Avis P. Edwards, Mother,   1915 - _____

M   EDWARDS   Koyce C. Edwards,   Father,   Forever Ours,   1912 - 1970

N   ELLSWORTH   Kathy R. Ellsworth,   illegible - 1955

S   EMERY   Irwin W. Emery,   AT REST,   1856 - 1930

S   EMERY   Kitty L. Emery,   1857 - 1939

S   EMERY   Leila B. Emery,   1883 - 1949

M   ENGVALL   Hulda S. Engvall BABY,   1878 - 1888

M   EVALT   Edward Evalt,   FATHER,   1903 - 1955

N   EVALT   Milton H. Evalt,   1932- 1977

M   EVES   Anna Pearl Eves,   MOTHER,   1898 - 1953

      EVES   (James Sylvester Eves, Age 89.   Nov 28, 1895, in Battle Ground, WA, - Sep 26, Tacoma, WA.   Res: Vancouver, WA. ..... Graveside service Tuesday, Oct 1, at Brush Prairie Cem.   VFC.   Obit - The Columbian)   U S ARMY   W W I

S   FAGG   Hattie L. Fagg,   Mother,   1872 - 1944

S   FAGG   Phillip S. Fagg,   1865 - 1948

S   FAGG   Stephen D. Fagg,   1863 - 1953

S   FARIS   Agnes G. Faris,   July 26, 1870 - Jul 17, 1951

S   FARIS   George H. Faris,   May 1, 1862 - Jul 14, 1953

N   FARLEY   Alfred E. Farley,   1908 - 1978

S   FARLEY   Esie? Era? Bessie? Vera?,   1934 - 1935

S   FERGUSON   Mable Ferguson,   1896 - 1969

S   FERGUSON   Roy Ferguson,   1894 - 1971

N   FILPPULA   Eli V. Filppula,   1887 - 1976

M   FISHER   Muriel Fisher,   1896 - 1977

M   FITZGERALD   Bessie Manley Fitzgerald,   1906 - 1926

S   FITZPATRICK   Charles H. Fitzpatrick,   1884 - 1971

S   FITZPATRICK   Martha J. Fitzpatrick,   1893 - 19___

M   FLECK   Ida M. Fleck,   1890 - _____ ,   IN THEE HAVE I PUT MY TRUST

M   FLECK   James S. Fleck,   1883 - 1977,   IN THEE HAVE I PUT MY TRUST

N   FLOCK   Edith I. Flock,   1901 - 1958

N   FOLKERSON   Howard Folkerson,   Son,   1891 - 1971

N   FOLKERSON   Phebe A. Folkerson,   Mother,   1865 - 1953

M   FOLSTROM   Ada Grace Folstrom,   Mother,   1924 - 1976

        FOSTER   (Edith G. Foster. Age 84. Feb 10, 1901, Hayes, WA - Jul 23, 1985, Vancouver, WA. .... Graveside service Friday, Jul 26, at Brush Prairie Cem. Hamilton-Mylan Funeral Home. Obit - The Columbian)

N   FREDRICKSON   Anna Fredrickson,   1877 - 1965

N   FREDRICKSON   Thomas Fredrickson,   1875 - 1956

N   FREEMAN   Bertha Freeman,   In Loving Memory,   1886 - 1953

N   FREEMAN   Matt Freeman,   1883 - 1951

S   FRIEZE   A. J. Frieze,   1860 - 1945

N   FRITZ   Ricki Fritz,   1962 - 1980

        FROST   (Helen M. Frost. Age 71. Oct 13, 1914, Havre, MT - Feb 17, 1986, Battle Ground, WA. Widower: Jack, at home. Mother: Sarah King, Battle Ground. Son: Ron Field, Denver, CO. Brothers: Elton King, Spokane and Harold King, Battle Ground, Sister: Gwen Pierce, Battle Ground. Funeral Monday, Feb 24, at Layne's Funeral Home Chapel. Burial in Brush Prairie Cem. Obit - The Columbian)

M   FULLERTON   Elsie M. Fullerton,   1893 - 19___

M   FULLERTON   Jack N. Fullerton,   "Daddy",   1914 - 1978

M   FULLERTON   Harold J. Fullerton,   1890 - 1951

M   FULLWOOD   Callie Fullwood,   1843 - 1907

S   FUSON   Troy B. Fuson,   1903 - 1963

N   GAREN   Anna Garen,   1882 - 1955

M   GARREAN   Emma W. Garrean,   MOM,   1875 - 1956

S   GARRETT   Samuel K. Garrett,   Father,   1874 - 1944

S   GASAWAY   Douglas K. Gasaway,   IN LOVING MEMORY,   1886 - 1971

GASAWAY (M. Robena Gasaway. Age 98. Aug 20, 1888, Battle Ground, WA
Sep 18, 1986, Vancouver, WA. Res: Battle Ground, WA.
Dau. of homesteaders: George and Mary Gasaway...... Grave-
side services Saturday, Sep 20, at Brush Prairie Cem.
EFC/EFH Obit - The Columbian)

M GASAWAY Winfield S. Gasaway, 1873 - 1921

M GASSAWAY Florence M. Gassaway, Died Jan 1, 1883, Aged 2 1/2 yrs.

M GASSAWAY George W. Gassaway, Father, 1838 - 1903 (Feb 28)

M GASSAWAY Mary E. Gassaway, Mother, 1848 - 1941

M GASSAWAY Walter J. Gassaway, 1871 - 1904

M GELL Sarah O. Gell, wife of Wm. H., NOT MY WILL, BUT THINE BE DONE,
Dec 15, 1862 - Jun 26, 1921

M GELL William H. Gell, NOT MY WILL, BUT THINE BE DONE, May 30, 1854 -
Jan 14, 1916

S GERBING Joseph Gerbing, 1848 - 1923

M GERTRUDE Ella Gertrude, 1851 - 1917

S GIBSON Clara E. Gibson, Mother, 1865 - 1942

S GIBSON Martin E. Gibson, Father, 1865 - 1944

M GIBSON Sadie Pearl Gibson, 1891 - 1980

M GIBSON Walter W. Gibson, 1895 - 1976

S GIFFT Ora I. Gifft, 1891 - 1978

S GIFFT Robert B. Gifft, 1887 - 1947

S GILDERSLEVE Hattie J. Gildersleve, Mother, Dec 16, 1865 - Aug 27,
1939

S GILDERSLEVE John F. Gildersleve, Father, Apr 11, 1860 - Feb 22, 1948

M GILES Alvin H. Giles, 1874 - 1955

M GILES Effie A. Giles, 1882 - 1964

S GILHAM Jannet A. Gilham, 1867 - 1956

S GILHAM Milo C. Gilham, 1858 - 1922

M GILLIS Clara A. Gillis, Mother, 1905 - 1975

N GILROY Maggie P. Gilroy, Apr 11, 1869 - Dec 26, 1937

S   GIMMER   Gust Gimmer, 1860 - 1942

S   GOODNIGHT   Edward Goodnight, PAPA,   1855 - 1933

N   GOODNIGHT   Mary E. Goodnight, Daughter of Wm & N.,   Mar 4, 1877 - Jul 18, 1880

N   GOODNIGHT   Nancy Jane Goodnight, wife of William, 1844 - 1922

M   GOODNIGHT   Roy Goodnight, 1890 - 1943

N   GOODNIGHT   William Goodnight, 1834 - 1909

S   GRAHAM   Elmer S. Graham, FATHER, 1871 - 1931

S   GRAHAM   Ethel F. Graham, MOTHER, 1885 - 1977

S   GRAVEN   Add Graven, 1867 - 1941

M   GROAT   Agnes Bartholemew Groat, 1866 - 1951

M   GROAT   Cameron Thomas Groat, 1857 - 1930

N   GROAT   Erma H. Groat, In Loving Memory, 1904 - 1970

S   GROAT   George H. Groat, 1864 - 1929

S   GROAT   Herman L. Groat, 1888 - 1943

M   GROAT   illegible, B. 1869, N Y, AT REST, rest illegible

M   GROAT   Jeremiah L. Groat, 1826 - 1904

M   GROAT   John Byron, 1860 - 1919

S   GROAT   Lillie Groat, 1900 - 1965

N   GROAT   Lloyd, In Loving Memory, 1900 - 1953

M   GROAT   Mary Ann Groat, 1834 - 1916

M   GROAT   Mary E. Groat, 1864 - 1898

S   GROAT   Minore E. Groat, 1891 - 1943

S   GROAT   Phoebe C. Groat, 1858 - 1937

M   GROAT   Raymond, 1889 - 1925

M   GROAT   Roy Vernon, 1885 - 1886

N   GROAT   Uriah D. Groat, Died Apr 1, 1901, Aged 72 yrs. 8 Mos. 3 Das.

S   GULBERG   Andrew B. Gulberg, 1865 - 1939

S HAACKE George Haacke, FATHER, 1861 - 1941

M HAACKE George W. Haacke, Oregon SC2 U S Navy, W W II, Feb 11, 1906 -
                Jul 2, 1971

S HAACKE Leodiga M. Haacke, Daughter, 1895 - 1971

M HAACKE Mary L. Haacke, May 6, 1906 - Jun 12, 1976

S HAACKE Myrtle A. Haacke, Mother, 1873 - 1946

N HAFVARGREN John A. Hafvargren, Born in Ranlnow Lady, Finland, HE
                DIED IN FAITH IN JESUS CHRIST, Jun 11, 1849 - Feb 14,
                1878

N HAILS Earnest Roy Hails, Tech Sgt U S A F, W W 2 - Korea, May 8, 1924
              - Feb 18, 1978

M HALE Charles L. Hale, Jul 8, 1899 - May 14, 1971

S HALE Elfa E. Hale, Dad

S HALE George E. Hale, FATHER, 1864 - 1945

S HALE George P. Hale, HUSBAND AND FATHER, 1912 - 1965

S HALE Litha B. Hale, Mom, 1887 - 1969

S HALE Silas Dick V. Hale, Washington MECH 48 Co. 166 DEPOT BRIG, W W I,
            Feb 14, 1888 - Dec 22, 1960

M HALE Zella L. Hale, Feb 9, 1900 - _____

M HALL Eslum M. Hall, Jul 26 1824 - Mar 5, 1888, Father

M HALL Mary Hall, Mother, Sep 30, 1840 - May 21, 1929

M HALL Missouri T. Hall, Mother, 1876 - 1947

M HALL Watt A. Hall, Father, 1874 - 1916

N HALMGREN Larry L. Halmgren, 1937 - 1971

M HAMPTON Nellie V. Hampton, 1906 - 19___

M HANEY Nettie Haney, Mother, 1879 - 1963

M HANKOLA Eino Hankola, 1910 - 1976

M HANNULA Alarick Hannula, 1880 - 19___

M HANNULA Minnie Hannula, 1887 - 1959

M HANSBROUGH Glenn A. Hansbrough, Asleep In Jesus, Feb 22, 1891 - Mar
            23, 1908

M   HANSBROUGH   Mary Elizabeth Hansbrough,   Mother,   1863 - 1955

S   HANSEN   Earl E. Hansen

M   HARADEN   James A. Haraden   1879 - 1965

M   HARADEN   Janet W. Haraden   1879 - 1968

M   HARDY   Lester P. Hardy,   1884 - 1953

M   HARPER   Clifford Alton Harper, Jr.,   Washington, A M S 3 U S Navy, "Red
              Bird", Vietnam,   Dec 9, 1951 - Sep 7, 1973

M   HARPER   Clifford A. Harper,   O M I U S Navy, W W 2, Korea,   1925 - 1976

M   HARPER   Daisy V. Harper,   1881 - 1950

M   HARPER   Edward V. Harper,   1883 - 1962

M   HARPER   Susan Gail Harper,   In Loving Memory,   The Lord Is My Shepherd,
              1856 - 1968

M   HARPOLE   Sarah L. Harpole,   1881 - 1918

N   HARRIS   Infant Daughters Harris,   Infant Daus. of Henry & Luella Harris,
              Died May 28, 1891

N   HARRIS   Lincoln M. Harris, Jr., Washington, Pvt U S Army,   Nov 4, 1928 -
              Jul 19, 1955

S   HASH   Addison Hash,   1849 - 1928

S   HARRISON   James B. Harrison,   1876 - 1934

S   HARRISON   Mary Jane Harrison,   Jun 4, 1928

S   HARRISON   Susann F. Harrison,   1878 - 1956

S   HARRISON   Weldon Harrison, Dad,   1902 - 1961

M   HARTE   George W. Harte,   1883 - 1908

S   HASH   Elizabeth Hash,   1852 - 1928

M   HASLETT   William Haslett,   1865 - 1951

     HAWTHORN   (Franklin A. Hawthorn. Age 68. Apr 28, 1917, Tulare, CA,
              May 7, 1985, Vancouver, WA. Res: Battle Ground, WA.
              Husband of Florence, at home...... Graveside service Thur.
              May 9, at Brush Prairie Cem., Layne's Funeral Home. Obit
              The Columbian)

S   HEATH   Melvin E. Heath,   1870 - 1938

BRUSH PRAIRIE CEMETERY

M HEATH Miland L. Heath, 1964 - 1967

S HEATH Myrtle E. Heath, 1886 - 1972

M HEINO Hattie A. Heino, 1885 - 1952

S HELZER Gertrude Helzer, Mother, 1890 - 1947

S HELZER Johanna Helzer, Grandmother, 1885 - 1952

S HENDRICKS Caroline Hendricks, 1846 - 1941

S HENDRICKSON Frances Hendrickson, 1870 - 1950

S HENDRICKSON George W. Hendrickson, 1888 - 1970

M HENKEL Jake Henkel, 1907 - 1972

N HENRIKSON Gustave A. Henrikson, Dec 16, 1855 - Aug 15, 1935

M HEPPENHEIMER Hedwig Heppenheimer, OUR GRANDMAMA, Apr 30, 1892 - Feb 13, 1973

S HERMAN Harvey M. Herman, 1867 - 1962

S HERMAN Lillie M. Herman, MOTHER, 1866 - 1936

M HESSEY Mary P. Hessey, 1908 - 1974

S HILL Anna Hill, MOTHER, 1869 - 1962

S HILL Issac Hill, FATHER, 1871 - 1953

S HILL Jalmer Isaac Hill, Born Tarson City, Alaska, Jun 30, 1900 - May 15, 1925

M HILL Susanna A. Hill, Born Sep 7, 1909 - Age 2 Wks., Our Loved One

HIXON (Helen A. Hixon, Nov. 8, 1917, Moose Lake, MN. Dec 4, 1985, Vancouver, WA. Res: Battle Ground, was wife of Lee H., at home. .... Funeral Monday, Dec 9, at the Faith Church of the Nazarene. Burial in Brush Prairie Cem. Layne's Funeral Home. Obit - The Columbian)

N HOCKINSON Alma M. Hockinson, 1905 - 1974

M HOCKINSON August G. Hockinson, 1860 - 1947

M HOCKINSON Herbert, 1896 - 1908

M HOCKINSON Ima H. Hockinson, 1894 - 1910

M HOCKINSON Julia A. Hockinson, 1873 - 1957

BRUSH PRAIRIE CEMETERY

N   HOCKINSON   Walter G. Hockinson,   1902 - 19___

S   HOFFMEISTER   Ralph M. Hoffmeister, Father,   1907 - 1943

M   HOGE   Oscar P. Hoge, Beloved Husband, My Dear Oscar At Rest, The Lord
Is My Shepherd,   1894 - 1970

N   HOLBROOK   Jesse Holbrook, Born Jul 7, 1826 - Died Oct 16, 1895, There
Is One Who Is Sleeping In Faith And Love, With Love That
Is Treasured In Heaven Above, Father

N   HOLBROOK   W. H. Holbrook,   1878 - 1937

S   HOLDER   Lonnin G. Holder,   1951

    HOLLIN   (Ruth Amanda Hollin. Age 82. Aug 14, 1900, in Minnesota - Jul
13, 1983, Sheridan, OR. Res: Sheridan, OR, formerly of
Clark Co. ,,,,,,,,, Graveside service Saturday, Jul 16, at
Brush Prairie Cem., Layne's Funeral Home. Obit - The
Columbian)

M   HOLMGREN   Anna Helen Holmgren,   May 27, 1881 - Jan 10, 1932

M   HOLMGREN   Peter Holmgren,   Feb 28, 1871 - Nov 7, 1943

M   HOLMGRENS   The Baby Holmgrens

M   HOLMGREN   (Victor L. Holmgren. Age 59. Sep 13, 1923, Vancouver, WA.,
Feb 23, 1983, Portland, OR. Res: Coos Bay, OR.) U S Army
W W II, (..... Graveside service Sat., Feb 26, at Brush
Prairie Cem., Layne's Funeral Home. Obit - The Columbian)

S   HOLT   Baby Boy Holt,   Sep 26, 1960

M   HOLT   Eugene D. Holt, FATHER,   1916 - _____

M   HOLT   Theresa S. Holt, MOTHER,   1920 - 1969

    HOLTER   (Ruth M. Holter. Age 78. Stroke Dec 27, 1908, The Dalles, OR -
Aug 25, 1987, Portland, OR. Res: Vancouver, WA. Pre-
ceded in death by her husband, Clarence, in 1974. .....
Graveside service Saturday, Aug 29, at Brush Prairie Cem.
A memorial service at the Fourth Plain Church of the
Nazarene. Layne's Funeral Home Chapel. Obit - The Colum-
bian)

N   HONGELL   Andrew Hongell, B. Feb 28, 1847 - D. Apr 2, 1907, Father unto
Thy hands I commit my spirit

N   HONGELL   Andrew E. Hongell, Dad,   1881 - 1967

N   HONGELL   Helena S. Hongell, B. Jun 24, 1849 - D. Jan 14, 1927

N   HONGELL   May T. Hongell, Mom, Married Jun 26, 1930,   1891 - 1963

21

M   HONKALA   Hilda Honkala,   1907 - 1974

M   HOSENEY   May R. Hoseney,   D. 1916

M   HOSENEY   (Otto W. "Bud" Hoseney. Age 77. Sep 17, 1906, Charleston, IL-
May 29, 1984, Portland, OR. Res: Vancouver, WA. Husb.
of Evelyn Hoseney, at home. ...... Funeral Monday, Jun 4,
at Memorial Gardesn Funeral Chapel. Interment at Brush
Prairie Cem., M G M, Obit - The Columbian)

M   HOSENEY   John R. Hoseney,   D. 1947

M   HOSENY   James I. Hoseny, Father,   1874 - 1958

M   HOSENY   Minnie B. Hoseny, Mother,   1878 - 1960

N   HOSTIKKA   Theodore E. Hostikka,   1910 - 1966

N   HOSTIKKA   Victoria E. Hostikka,   1917 - _____

M   HOTTMAN   Tivis F. Hottman, Son of C. E. & E. S.,   Apr 19, 1890 - Nov
30, 1908

M   HOUSE   Clara E. House,   1870 - 1962

M   HOUSE   Lewis D. House,   1868 - 1947

M   HOUSE   Wesley House, At Rest, Father, Feb 20, 1834 - Feb 11, 1909

S   HOUSEMAN   Clara Houseman,   1922 - 1924

M   HOUTER   Clarence Houter,   MY DEAR OSCAR AT REST,   1903 - 1974

S   HOVER   George A. Hover, FATHER,   1859 - 1930

S   HOVER   Louisa W. Hover, MOTHER,   1863 - 1935

N   HOWARD   Adrain E. Howard,   1884 - 1963

N   HOWARD   Anna M. Howard,   1894 - 1963

     HOWARD   (Anna Margaret Howard. Age 91. Dec 4, 1894, Hockinson, WA -
Nov 11, 1986, Battle Ground, WA. ...... Graveside service
Thursday, Nov 11, at Brush Prairie, WA. VFC. Obit - The
Columbian)

S   HOWARD   Bret R. Howard, FATHER,   1887 - 1957

S   HOWARD   Cecil Clyde Howard, Pvt S A T C, State College of WA, Jan 24,
1924

N   HOWARD   Nancy Howard, MOTHER, AT REST,   1861 - 1918

M HOWARD   Sarah E. Howard, Mother, Peace Through Christ Is Mine, 1863 -
         1949

M HOYES   Frederick R. Hoyes,   Mar 5, 1897 - May 9, 1913

M HOYES   Rebecca Hoyes,   Nov 22, 1867 - Mar 6, 1911

M HOYES   William A. Hoyes, Born Apr 6, 1887

M HOYES   William Hoyes,   Feb 3, 1850 - Dec 2, 1915

M HUBER   Clayton Davis Huber,   1874 - 1931

M HUBER   Lola Deitderich Huber,   1901 - 1937

M HUBER   Margaret C. Huber,   1884 - 1966

S HUGH   Jeremiah J. Hugh, (Masonic emblem)   1850 - 1925

M HULL   Alta M. Hull,   1891 - 1919

M HULL   Ernest Hull,   1884 - 1918

M HUMPHREY   Sarah L. Humphrey, WIFE,   1882 - 1962

M HUMPHREY   Wiley L. Humphrey,   1886 - 1960

M HUMPHREYS   Norman E. Humphreys, HUSBAND,   1910 - 1975

N HUNGERFORD   Celia A. Hungerford, Mother,   1882 - 1970

M HUNTLEY   Daisy A. Huntley, Mother,   1875 - 1959

N HURT   Mary M. Hurt, In Loving Memory, Oct 13, 1842 - May 10, 1886

M IRWIN   Martha J. Irwin,   Mother,   Mar 14, 1838 - Feb 23, 1911

N ISAACSON   Edwin W. Isaacson, Washington WT2 U S N R, W W II, May 18,
         1918 - Dec 27, 1971

N ISAACSON   Saima Isaacson, Mother,   1896 - 1953

S JACKSON   Dr. John Jackson,   1881 - 1948

S JACKSON   Mary Jackson,   1888 - 1978

N JACOBSEN   Anna M. K. Jacobsen, His Wife (Jacob Jacobsen), We shall
         sleep but not forever, We shall meet to part no never,
         On the Resurrection Morn,   1843 - 1928

N JACOBSEN   Jacob Jacobsen,   1844 - 1920

N JACOBSEN Pauline Jacobsen

N JACOBSEN Tilda Jacobsen

N JAMES Helena C. James, In Loving Memory Of Mom, 1885 - 1975

S JENNY Anna Jenny, 1872 - 1942

S JENNY Casper Jenny, 1857 - 1942

S JENNY Daniel Jenny, BROTHER, 1901 - 1929

JESKE (Samuel M. Jeske. Age 20. Aug 19, 1965, Minneapolis - Mar 20, 1986, Salem, OR. Res: Vanc., WA. Father: Samuel M. Jeske, Hermiston, OR, Mother: Julee Giesinger, Vanc., WA. Sis: Stephanie Jeske, Vanc., WA. 1/2 Sis: Sarah Jeske, Hermiston. Grandparents: Mars Jeske, Jamestown, N.D.; Evelyn Telken, Virginia; Gilbert & Hildegard Sodawasser, Courtenay, N.D. Funeral Saturday, Mar 22, at New Heights Baptist Church. Burial in Brush Prairie Cem. Vanc. Fun. Chapel. Obit - The Columbian)

N JOHNS Zertha Y. Johns, MOTHER, 1897 - 1972

M JOHNSON August Johnson, At Rest, Oct 1, 1855 - Feb 9, 1920

M JOHNSON Carl R. Johnson, Nov 3, 1887 - Nov 15, 1940

M JOHNSON Cora A. Johnson, MOTHER, 1867 - 1904

M JOHNSON Cora A. Johnson, 1904 - 1905

M JOHNSON Clarence B. Johnson, 1907 - 1980

M JOHNSON Donald B. Johnson, May 5, 1917 - Feb 12, 1918

JOHNSON (G. Gordon Johnson, Age 64. Apr 2, 1919, Brush Prairie, WA. Aug 16, 1983, Portland, OR. Res: Vancouver, WA) U S ARMY W W II (..... Funeral Friday, Aug 19, at Vancouver Funeral Chapel. Interment at Brush Prairie Cem., VFC. Obit - The Columbian)

JOHNSON (Hortense Mildred Johnson. Age 72. May 3, 1911, Springfield, MO - Apr 26, 1984. Cancer. Res: Battle Ground, WA. ..... Funeral today, Friday, Apr 27, at Brush Prairie Cem. Layne's Funeral Home. Obit - The Columbian)

M JOHNSON Jessie E. Johnson, FATHER, 1861 - 1933

M JOHNSON Joseph E. Johnson, 1881 - 1974

N JOHNSON Loran F. Johnson, 1909 - 1955

M JOHNSON Mattie L. Johnson, 1879 - 1951

BRUSH PRAIRIE CEMETERY

M JOHNSON Rachel L. Johnson, 1912 - _____

M JOHNSON Vendela C. Johnson, His Wife (August Johnson), Sep 13, 1862
  - Oct 8, 1940

S JONER Esther Joner, OUR BABY, Jun 10, 1939 - Oct 6, 1939

S JONES Carolyn Jones, 1941 - 1944

M JONES Hattie M. Jones, 1870 - 1940

M JONES Ralph D. Jones, 1963

S KAY Dale L. Kay, Nov 26, 1913 - Aug 1, 1935

N KAY Maud M. Kay, MOTHER, Aug 23, 1884 - Jun 14, 1956

S KAYS James Kays, 1847 - 1936

S KAYS Susan C. Kays 1846 - 1930

N KELLY Virginia P. Kelly, Mother, GrandMother, 1917 - 1977

M KELSEY George W. Kelsey, Father, 1852 - 1938

S KENNETT George Edw. Kennett, Father, 1878 - 1953

S KEYS Evalyn S. Keys, 1879 - 1938

S KING Ellis G. King, 1885 - 1967

S KING Robert L. King, Washington, TECH SGT. 136 INF, W W II, BSM,
  Jul 5, 1925 - Sep 28, 1947

S KING Sarah A. King, 1889 - 19___

  KING (Sarah Ann King. Age 96. Jul 8, 1889, Vernon Center, MN - Mar 8,
  1986, at home. Battle Ground, WA. Sons: Elton King, Spo-
  kane, and Harold King, Battle Ground. Daughter: Gwen
  Pierce, Battle Ground. Funeral Wednesday, Mar 12, at
  Meadow Glade Seventh-Day Adventist Church. Burial in
  Brush Prairie Cem., Layne's Funeral Home. Obit - The
  Columbian)

N KINZER James Boin Kinzer, 1896 - 1956

N KINZER Sonoma Belle Kinzer, 1899 - 1959

S KNECHTGES Edmond V. Knechtges, Father, 1879 - 1929

S KNECHTGES J. Blanche Knechtges, Mother, 1881 - 1938

S KNOPF Louisa B. Knopf, 1886 - 1939

M   KORPELA   Kalle Kustaa Korpela,   1905 - 1939

M   KOSKI   Arvid E. Koski, Husband,   1905 - 1974

M   KOSKI   Jalmer M. Koski,   1899 - 1971

N   KOSKI   William Koski, Tassc lepaa rakas michem, Jan 11, 1864 - Jul 17, 1905. Rakka anlsuille Luskau mon VHM mein ia sa pally nyi Hamkanioiku orman Krisni Ksen ja nukk u Herran nimeen

N   KOSKI   William Koski, TASSC LEPAA PAKAS MEINENL RAKKAANI SURU LUSKAINNON VIIM MEIN LASSA PACTTY NYT. HANKANIOIKUORNAN. KRISU KSEN JA NUKKUI HERRAN RIMEEN. Jan 11, 1864 - Jul 17, 1905

M   KRASKEY   Minnie L. Kraskey, MOTHER,   1903 - 1959

M   KRAVEN   Opal M. Kraven, 1901 - 1967

N   KRAY   Belle Pender Kray,   1881 - 1958

N   KURVEL   Karl Kurvel, VAATA MINA OLEN SINUGA ALATI,   Mar 10, 1897 - Aug 15, 1966

M   LACY   Elmer Lacy,   1913 - 1971

S   LADDUSAW   Anna B. Laddusaw,   1871 - 1939

S   LADDUSAW   John L. Laddusaw,   1861 - 1940

N   LAGLER   Ray E. Lagler,   1922 - 1979

S   LAHY   Hilda S. Lahy,   1863 - 1950

S   LAHY   Matt W. Lahy,   1861 - 1945

M   LAMPING   James L. Lamping, Dad,   1890 - 1969

M   LAMPING   Marjorie O. Lamping, Mom,   1898 - 1971

N   LARSEN   George W. Larsen,   1910 - _____

N   LARSEN   Hans C. Larsen,   1885 - 1959

N   LARSEN   Margaret S. Larsen,   1902 - 1977

N   LARSEN   Natallia C. Larsen,   1887 - 1958

N   LARSON   Bertha E. Larson, MOTHER AND SISTER,   1905 - 1979

M   LARSON   Carl H. Larson,   1885 - 1969

M   LARSON   Dorothy C. Larson,   1885 - 1959

BRUSH PRAIRIE CEMETERY

M   LARSON   Elizabeth E. Larson,   1884 - 1963

M   LARSON   Richard A. Larson,   1880 - 1958

S   LASHIER   Mary A. Lashier,   1867 - 1971

S   LASHIER   Harold L. Lashier, M. D.,   At Rest,   1901 - 1963

S   LASHIER   Walter H. Lashier,   At Rest,   Here Lies A Woodman Of The World,   1860 - 1921

M   LAURENT   Thomas J. Laurent,   1965 - 1965

S   LAWRENCE   Belle S. Lawrence,   1903 - 19___

M   LAWRENCE   Jesse M. Lawrence,   1862 - 1937

S   LAWRENCE   Linley E. Lawrence, Washington Pfc. Co. H 102 Inf. W W I PH,   Jan 17, 1898 - Nov 29, 1970

M   LEACH   Charles F. Leach,   1901 - 1976

S   LENNEY   Cecilia A. Lenney,   1900 - 1963

S   LENNEY   Cora A. Lenney,   1879 - 1963

S   LENNEY   Cristal Alice Lenney,   1905 - 1927

M   LEVELL   Harry Levell,   1888 - 1911

M   LEVELL   James P. Levell, FATHER,   1855 - 1936

M   LEVELL   Jane M. Levell, MOTHER,   1859 - 1942

M   LIGHTFOOT   Clara Lightfoot, MOTHER,   1878 - 1950

M   LIGHTFOOT   William M. Lightfoot, FATHER,   1871 - 1950

M   LINDH   M. B. Lindh, In Loving Memory,   1879 - 1933

N   LINDI   Eddie E. Lindi,   1925 - _____

N   LINDI   Mamie E. Lindi,   1926 - 1973

M   LINDQUIST   Henry H. Lindquist, SON,   1909 - 1921

M   LINDQUIST   Jolin Otto Lindquist, FATHER,   1856 - 1933

S   LUNDQUIST   Elizabeth Lundquist, MOTHER,   1876 - 1936

S   LINK   Robert J. Link, AT REST,   1883 - 1944

M   LONG   Curtis Long,   1849 - 1919

M LONG Zelma Leo Long, 1929 - 1929

S LOSEY Lafayette E. Losey, 1861 - 1938

S LOSEY Leon G. Losey, 1898 - 1975

S LUND Eric Lund, 1883 - 1955

S LUNDKUIST John Lundkuist, 1871 - 1943

S LUOKO Gust J. Luoko, AT REST, 1850 - 1924

M LYONS Cordelia Lyons, THE FAIREST FLOWER WE FONDLY LOVE HOW SOON IT FADES AND DIES, Feb 9, 1890 - Mar 19, 1890

M LYONS Costello Lyons, 1854 - 1947

M LYONS Evalyn Maril Lyons, A BUD PLUCKED FROM EARTH TO BLOOM IN HEAVEN, Mar 16, 1896 - Oct 29, 1902

M LYONS Mary E. Lyons, 1868 - 1947

S MABRY William H. Mabry, 1867 - 1942

M MAC DONALD Alexander A. Mac Donald, 1882 - 1973

M MACDONALD Lillie Oliva MacDonald, 1887 - 1943

S MACK James Henry Mack, Washington Pvt. U S Army, W W I, Oct 16, 1888 - Feb 21, 1972

S MACK Randall J. Mack, 1929 - 1944

S MACK Sarah Grace Mack, Grandma, Dec 1, 1892 - Jul 29, 1974

N MADDOX Edward H. Maddox, 1897 - 1964

 MADDOX (Helen R. Maddox. Mar 18, 1903, Kjer'sem, Norway - Nov 13, 1986, at home. Clark County, WA., resident. Preceded in death by her husband, Edward, in 1964. Sons: Norman of Brush Prairie; Clifford of Lilliwaup. Daughter: Shirley Lyness, Vancouver. Brother: Art Johnson, Vancouver. Sisters: Anna Anderson, Newport, OR, and Clara Bolen, Portland, OR. Graveside service Monday, Nov 17, at Brush Prairie Cem. Hamilton-Mylan Funeral Home. Obit - The Columbian)

M MANLEY Ethel Ellen Manley, Jun 5, 1884 - Jun 23, 1968

M MANLEY William Manley, Sep 24, 1877 - Oct 31, 1940

M MANLEY William Manley, Jr., 1916 - 1917

M MANNING Martha A. Manning, Wife, 1861 - 1939

BRUSH PRAIRIE CEMETERY

S   MARSH   Arlene Carrie Marsh,   1926 - 1926

M   MARSH   Eva May Marsh, MOTHER,   1885 - 1958

M   MARSH   George M. Marsh, FATHER,   1870 - 1959

S   MARSH   Harold J. Marsh,   1896 - 1936

S   MARSH   Johnnie Marsh,   1928 - 1937

S   MARSH   Valorie May Marsh, BELOVED BABY,   Apr 17, 1934 - Jul 20, 1934

M   MARSH   Viola A. Marsh, Wife,   1918 - 1971

S   MARTELL   Louis D. Martell, FATHER,   1874 - 1938

S   MARTELL   Valerie Martell, MOTHER,   1876 - 1931

M   MARTIN   Alfred T. Martin, FATHER,   1902 - 1958

S   MARTIN   Flora Martin, Mother,   Dec 28, 1874 - Feb 15, 1944

S   MARTIN   Hollis Martin,   1883 - 1951

M   MARTIN   Josephine V. Martin,   1906 - _____

      MARTIN   (Josephine V. Martin. Age 78. Sep 15, 1904, Roseburg, OR - Nov 29, 1984, Woodland, WA. Res: Woodland (formely of Bellingham, WA. ...... Funeral Saturday, Dec 1, at Layne's Funeral Home Chapel. Interment in Brush Prairie Cem. Obit - The Columbian)

M   MARTIN   Lewis E. Martin, In Loving Remembrance, Sep 15, 1889 - Oct 20, 1906

M   MARTIN   Martha Elizabeth Martin, Sister, Jan 13, 1893 - Jun 8, 1941

S   MARTIN   Peter G. Martin, Oregon, Pvt U 9th Spruce Sqd., June 6, 1893 - Feb 7, 1944

S   MARTIN   Tomas A. Martin, _____ - 1937

S   MARTINSON   John Martinson,   1873 - 1940

      MATSON   (Florence M. (Johnson) Matson. Age 91. Feb 5, 1891, Portland, OR. - Jan 17, 1983, Vancouver, WA. ..... Funeral Friday, Jan 21, at Vancouver Chapel. Interment at Brush Prairie Cem. VFC, Obit - The Columbian)

S   MATSON   Gladys Marion Matson, OUR BELOVED BABY, 1922 - 1924

S   MATSON   Ivan Matson, FATHER,   1898 - 1948

S   MATSON   Hilda Matson, MOTHER,   1900 - 1977

MATSON   (Rev. I. Earl Matson. Age 61. Oct 22, 1924, Kelso, WA - Dec 25, 1985, Vancouver, WA. Last lived in Stevenson, WA. Widow: Dorothy, at home. Son: Harlyn D. Matson, Rocklin, CA. Daughters: Christy Foley, Battle Ground; Kerry Moser, Soap Lake; and Heidi Gomes of Woodinville. Brother: Ralph Matson, Vancouver. Sister: Helen Newell, Ridgefield. Funeral services Dec 28, 1985. Interment at Brush Prairie, WA. Obit - The Reflector & The Columbian)

S   MATSON   Robert Allen Matson, Sgt U S Army, Korea, Apr 19, 1929 - Jun 16, 1975

M   MATTHEISIN   Ida M. Mattheisin, 1900 - 1977

N   MATTSON   Rev. Adolph Mattson, 1857 - 1935

S   MATTSON   Carl E. Mattson, Sr., Cpl U S Army, Aug 17, 1890 - Dec 4, 1974

N   MATTSON   Colleda B. Mattson, wife of   b. Dec 22, 1857, Jefferson Co., TN - d. Jan 13, 1884, Clark Co., WA. Aged 28 yrs 22 d

N   MATTSON   Edith E. Mattson, Mar 9, 1888 - Nov 1, 1888

N   MATTSON   Edla Mattson, wife of J. E., Oct 9, 1855 - Feb 23, 1908

N   MATTSON   Edwin Mattson, Jul 28, 1877 - Mar 13, 1897

N   MATTSON   Emma E. Mattson, Wife of Eric, GONE BUT NOT FORGOTTEN, Dec 11, 1851 - Apr 12, 1888

N   MATTSON   Esther O. Mattson, Mar 19, 1892 - Jan 5, 1894

N   MATTSON   Ira Mattson, Oct 9, 1866 - Sep 7, 1887

S   MATTSON   John Eng Mattson, 1841 - 1922

N   MATTSON   Rosa S. Mattson, 1861 - 1932

N   MAYER   Nadean P. Mayer, In Loving Memory, Mother & Daughter, 1924 - 1973

MEDLEY   (Robert Vinton Medley. Age 77. May 24, 1907, Vancouver, WA - Oct 13, 1984, Battle Ground, WA. Res: Vancouver, WA. Husb of Verna, at home. ..... Services Thursday, Oct 18, at Battle Ground Comm. United Methodist Church. Interment at Brush Prairie Cem. Layne's Funeral Home. Obit - The Columbian)

N   MEIER   Leo H. Meier, In Loving Memory, Looking for that blessed hope - and glorious appearing of the Lord Jesus Christ. Titus 2: 13, 1929 - 1961

N   MERRILL   Delmer L. Merrill, 1898 - 1956

M   MERRILL   Eulyssa S. Merrill, Mother, 1851 - 1940

M   MESERVEY   Philip V. Meservey, 1903 - 1957

M   MESSNER   Ella K. Messner, 1898 - 1971

N   MESSNER   Esther S. Messner, 1905 - _____

N   MESSNER   Gary P. Messner, Husband & Father, 1939 - 1970

N   MESSNER   Glenn H. Messner, 1897 - 1968

S   MESSNER   Hiram W. Messner, 1861 - 1939

S   MESSNER   Ida May Messner, 1867 - 1946

M   MESSNER   Robert W. Messner, 1944 - 1973

M   MESSNER   William F. Messner, 1882 - 1954

S   METCALF   Mary Della Metcalf, 1864 - 1946

N   MEYERS   Irene Meyers, Baby, 1919 - 1920

M   MICK   Jaan Mick, Estonian, Nov 10, 1879 - Sep 11, 1961

M   MICK   I Juri Mick, Estonian, Feb 8, 1883 - Jul 31, 1970

M   MICKEY   Evelyn Mickey, Asleep In Jesus, 1917 - 1932

M   MICKEY   Russell Mickey, Son of J. A. & Maud Mickey, Jul 19, 1912 - Mar 19, 1913

M   MILIKIN   Jacob A. Milikin, 1830 - 1914

M   MILIKIN   Sarah A. Milikin, At Rest, 1829 - 1912

M   MILLER   Adam H. Miller, 1830 - 1905

M   MILLER   Inez Pearl Miller, ASLEEP IN JESUS   ANOTHER LINK IS BROKEN, IN OUR HOUSEHOLD BAND, BUT A CHAIN IS FORMING, IN A BETTER LAND, Dec 4, 1891 - Sep 14, 1911

M   MILLER   Jack M. Miller, Husband, 1895 - 1965

S   MILLER   John Emil Miller, AT REST, 1862 - 1952

N   MILLER   Mary Miller, 1880 - 1956

S   MINKLER   Ellen Bailey Minkler, 1885 - 1957

N   MITCHAM   Clara E. Mitcham, 1904 - 1959

N   MITCHAM   Ralph A. Mitcham, 1901 - 1970

M   MITCHELL   Gillespie Jay Mitchell,   1866 - 1938

M   MOBLEY   Woodrow W. Mobley,   1913 - 1968

M   MONTGOMERY   Flora Smith Montgomery,   1888 - 1918

S   MOORE   Arthur M. Moore,   1869 - 1938

S   MOORE   Eugene J. Moore,   1877 - 1954

M   MOORE   Ferde D. Moore, In Loving Memory, In My Fathers House Are Many Mansions, 1887 - 1966

M   MOORE   Fred Moore, Washington, Horseshoer 9th Co. 20 Engrs, W W I, Nov 17, 1896 - Jun 27, 1966

S   MOORE   Herbert E. Moore, BROTHER, 1878 - 1948

S   MOORE   Mary Alice Moore,   1884 - 1967

M   MORGAN   Ada C. Morgan,   1873 - 1950

M   MORGAN   Addie Morgan, Sep 2, 1859 - Dec 22, 1930

M   MORGAN   Ann Augusta Morgan, Wife of Evan,   Oct 3, 1850 - Jun 2, 1897

M   MORGAN   Donald K. Morgan,   1916 - 1949

M   MORGAN   Dorabelle Morgan, Daughter of E and A, Aug 7, 1886 - Dec 20, 1904

M   MORGAN   Evan Morgan, IN LOVING MEMORY, July 19, 1876 - Feb 28, 1890

M   MORGAN   Even Morgan, Co F, Iowa, 29th Inf., (no dates visible)

M   MORGAN   Grant Morgan,   1868 - 1929

M   MORGAN   Irene E. Morgan, DAUGHTER, 1906 - 1928

     MORGAN   (James Evan Morgan. Age 79. Nov 16, 1907, Sunnyside, WA - Jun 20, 1987, near Nanaimo, British Columbia, Canada. Automobile accident. Res: Deerpark, WA. Husband of Sylvia Morgan of Deerpark, WA. ..... Graveside service Monday, Jun 29, at Brush Prairie Cem. Layne's Funeral Home. Obit-The Columbian)

M   MORGAN   Laura Morgan, Jan 14, 1844 - Sep 25, 1908

M   MORGAN   Leonard Morgan,   1874 - 1949

M   MORGAN   Louis Morgan, Aug 17, 1846 - Nov 22, 1915

M   MORGAN   Ruey W. Morgan, MOTHER, 1888 - 1974

M   MORGAN   Sophia Mae Morgan,   1877 - 1956

M MORGAN Susan C. Morgan, 1872 - 1895

M MORGAN W. C. "Buff" Morgan, Dec 16, 1907 - Sep 28, 1975

M MORGAN William T. Sherman, Son of E & A, IN LOVING MEMORY, Sep 5, 1871
          - Jul 7, 1882

S MORRIS Coran Morris, Aug 19, 1867 - Sep 26, 1950

S MORRIS Henry R. Morris, Mar 2, 1862 - Nov 30, 1947

S MORRIS Thos. J. Morris, 1880 - 1935

M MORRISON Nina Ward Morrison, 1914 - 1952

S MORRO Joseph J. Morro, 1866 - 1942

S MORTIMER Wesley L. Mortimer, IN LOVING MEMORY, served in U S Navy,
          1899 - 1934

M MOSHER Bernice Mosher, 1905 - 19___

M MOSHER Lloyd Mosher, IN LOVING MEMORY, 1904 - 1973

   MYERS (Florence M. Myers. Apr 7, 1901, Tallman, OR - Feb 17, 1985,
          Vancouver, WA. Age 83. ..... Funeral Thursday, Feb 21,
          at Layne's Funeral Home Chapel. Burial in Brush Prairie
          Cem. Obit - The Columbian)

M MYERS Oscar H. Myers, Brother, 1900 - 1962

M MYERS Ralph J. Myers, Washington, P F C   34 Spruce Sqad, W W I,
          May 12, 1896 - Jun 15, 1962

S McBETH Clarence McBeth, BROTHER, 1889 - 1935

S McBETH Ray McBeth, BROTHER, Jul 16, 1885 - May 14, 1943

S McBETH Roderick McBeth, MOTHER, 1854 - 1929

N McBRIDE Mark Wayne McBride, 1962 - 1962

M McBRIDE Ruby J. McBride, Mother, 1920 - 1972, IN HIS ARMS SHE RESTS

N McBRIDE Wilbur T. McBride, Father, LIFE to me, was love, 1918 - 1971

S McCALLUM Addie N. McCallum, 1875 - 1946

S McCALLUM Fenton J. McCallum, At Rest, 1910 - 1924

N McCALLUM Lulu H. McCallum, Daughter of P. W. & M. L., WEEP NOT PAPA
          AND MAMA FOR ME FOR I AM WAITING IN HEAVEN FOR THEE, Nov
          2, 1889 - Mar 9, 1895

McCOY   Patrick John McCoy, D. age 42, Bur. Sep 26, 1987, (heart attack), Wife: Linda Schmidt. (FAMILY RECORDS: b. Feb 17, 1945, Portland, Multnomah Co., OR - d. Sep 20, 1987, at home, 2217 N. E. 91st Vancouver, Clark Co., WA. Father: Patrick Earl Mc Coy, born in Spokane, WA. Mother: Margeret Heagel, born in Russia. Buried in Brush Prairie Cemetery, Little Chapel of the Chimes, Portland, OR in charge of arrangements. Survivors, wife, Linda Ann (daugh. of Edward E. Schmidt & Edna L. Radensleben) sons, Steven Roy McCoy and Saint Patrick McCoy. Step son, Steven Paul Schmidt and Step-dau, Trina Lynn Frederickson, all at home. His parents are deceased.)

Mc CREARY   (June Frances Mc Creary. Age 63. Nov 24, 1922, Vancouver - Feb 2, 1986, Vancouver, WA. Widower: Leroy A. "Mac" McCreary., at home. Son: Michael Allen McCreary, Vanc. Daughters: Launa M. Cone, Renton, WA and Nickie L. Kampmann, Heisson, WA. Brother: Lawrence "Bill" Johnson, Havre, MT. Sister: Mae Johnson Berry, Vancouver. Half-sister: Edna Blystone, Vancouver. Graveside service Wed., Feb 5, at Brush Prairie Cem. Hamilton-Mylan Funeral Home. Obit - The Columbian)

M   McKEE   Charles A. McKee, In Loving Memory, 1877 - 1953

M   McKEE   Clarissa McKee, 1888 - 1943

S   McKEE   Emaline M. McKee, 1885 - 1951

M   McKEE   Harvey McKee, 1841 - 1881

S   McKEE   Leon N. McKee, Washington Pvt. 82 Inf. TNG Bn. W W II, Aug 18, 1923 - May 21, 1961

M   McKEE   May Roller McKee, Aunt, 1878 - 1953

S   McKEE   Nelson McKee, 1875 - 1955

M   McKEE   Robert McKee, 1879 - 1882

    McKEE   Ruby Anne McKee, 1851 - 1881

    McKEE   (Willard James McKee. Age 78. Dec 5, 1907, Ridgefield, WA - Apr 29, 1986, Battle Ground, WA. Res: Ridgefield, WA. Bro: William, Ridgefield. Sisters: Ruby Osterberg, Vancouver & Leona Davis, Downey, ID. Funeral: Friday, May 2, at Vancouver Funeral Chapel. Burial: Brush Prairie CEM. Obit - The Columbian)

S   McLEAN   James Dean McLean, "Deano Cowboy", Of Such Is The Kingdom Of Heaven, Mar 21, 1972 - Aug 12, 1978

NEESE (Doris E. Neese, Age 74. Jul 24, 1911, Brush Prairie, WA - Jan 3, 1986, Rose City Nursing Home, Portland, OR. Res: Portland, OR. Sons: David Neese, Lake Oswego, OR; Gary Phillips, Portland. Daughter: Anita Sizer, Portland. Brother, Arthur Hull of Vancouver, WA. Sister: Ethel Schultz of Vancouver. Graveside service Tuesday, Jan 7, at Brush Prairie Cem. Obit - The Columbian)

M NELLIS Eld S. W. Nellis, 1856 - 1915

M NELLIS Elizabeth A. Nellis, 1856 - 1941

S NELSON 1840 - 1931

N NELSON L. Henry Nelson, 1882 - 1888

S NEILSON Carrie Neilson, 1859 - 1940

M NEWSOME Earnest E. Newsome, Born Jun 27, 1874 - Died Apr 16, 1881

M NEWSOME Frank Newsome, Born May 15, 1877 - Died Apr 25, 1884

M NEWSOME May Newsome, Born Nov 19, 1872 - Died Apr 16, 1884

N O'CONNER Elizabeth O'Conner, 1862 - 1956

N O'FLAHERTY Frank J. O'Flaherty, Son of J & H, May 25, 1874 - Jan 10, 1875

N O'FLAHERTY Olive M. O'Flaherty, May 17, 1870 - Dec 4, 1888

N O'FLAHERTY Rufus O. O'Flaherty, Aug 2, 1874 - Nov 18, 1874

N O'FLAHERTY John Q. O'Flaherty, June 10, 1880 - Jun 7, 1888

N O'FLAHERTY William E. O'Flaherty, Apr 21, 1813 - Aug 19, 1876

M OLSON Alvin F. Olson, In Loving Memory, 1900 - 1963

 OLSON (Brenda Carol Olson. Age 40. Jan 1, 1943, Miami, FL - May 29, 1983, Portland, OR. Res: Clark Co., WA. Wife of Kenneth, at home. ..... Service Thursday, Jun 2, at Meadow Glade Seventh-Day Adventist Church. Burial in Brush Prairie Cem. Layne's Funeral Home. Obit - The Columbian)

M OLSON Donald L. Olson, In Loving Memory, 1923 - 1968

N OLSOON Anders Gustaf Olsoon, Mar 22, 1843 - Nov 7, 1914, m. Nov 14, 1866 to Gustiva Louisa

N OLSOON Gustiva Louisa Olsoon, Oct 5, 1838 - Jul 3, 1899, m. Nov 14, to Anders Gustaf Olsoon

N OLSSON Minnie Matilda Olsson, Apr 21, 1875 - Jul 15, 1887

N OLSSON Emily Josefina Olsson, Jun 20, 1873 - Jun 15, 1886

M OSTERBERG Peter Osterberg, Asleep In Jesus, 1845 - 1914

   OTEY (Edwin Fay Otey. Age 63. May 25, 1923, Portland, OR - Aug 9,
         1986, Vancouver, WA. Husb of Miriam, at home. .....
         Graveside service Monday, Aug 11, at Brush Prairie Cem.
         Layne's Funeral Home. Obit - The Columbian)

S OTTERS Ray G. Otters, 1 day 1939

M OVERMAN Opel Alta Overman, OUR DARLING, 1907 - 1909

S OWENS A.D. Owens, Father, 1864 - 1936

M OWENS Altha E. Owens, 1894 - 19___ (Age 91. Mar 24, 1894, Fruitland,
         WA - Apr 9, 1985, Battle Ground, WA. Res: Battle Ground,
         WA. ..... Funeral Friday Apr 12, at Layne's Funeral Home
         Chapel. Interment at Brush Prairie Cemetery. Obit - The
         Columbian)

M OWENS Lloyd M. Owens, 1890 - 1971

M PAGH Anna M. Pagh, 1840 - 1922

M PAGH J. Alonzo Pagh, Baby, Feb 28 - Mar 2, 1921

M PAGH James K. Pagh, Jun 9, 1873 - Jan 20, 1940

M PAGH Knud K. Pagh, 1839 - 1919

N PALADINA Quinn A. Paladina, 1917 - 1959

S PALMER Richard Palmer, SON, Mar 10, 1925 - May 29, 1925

S PALMER Thomas G. Palmer, FATHER, 1886 - 1946

M PARKEY Pearl Rambo Daly Parkey, 1880 - 1975

S PARKINEN John Parkinen, FATHER, 1865 - 1926

M PAYNE Ella W. Payne, 1864 - 1943

M PAYNE John T. Payne, 1866 - 1918

M PAYSON Thelma V. Payson, 1903 - 1961

M PEA Isaac O. Pea, 1881 - 1953

M PEARSON Johanna Pearson, BLESSED ARE THE DEAD WHICH DIE IN THE LORD
         FROM HENCEFORTH SAITH THE SPIRIT THAT THEY MAY REST FROM
         THEIR LABORS: AND THEIR WORKS DO FOLLOW THEM, B. Nov 25,
         1826, Helinsborg, Sweden - D. May 14, 1895, Clark Co., WA

M PEARSON John Pearson, B. Gotheborg, Sweden, Feb 2, 1828 - Mar 20,
                1893,   Age 65 y

   PEDERSEN (Mabel Gudvor Pedersen, Age 81. Jan 4, 1903, Chicago, IL -
                Jul 22, 1984, Vancouver, WA. Res: Battle Ground, WA.
                Wife of H. Lewis Pedersen, at home. ..... Funeral Wed.,
                Jul 25, at Layne's Funeral Home Chapel. Interment, Brush
                Prairie Cem. Obit - The Columbian)

N PEDERSON Dorthea H. Pederson, MOTHER, ENDEARED TO US ALL,   1871 - 1968

S PEDERSON Lars Pederson, 1853 - 1939

M PELTO Hulda M. Pelto, Mother, 1896 - 1971

S PENDER Ada Pender, 1885 - 1972

S PENDER Albert E. Pender, FATHER, 1872 - 1927

S PENDER Arthur Pender, 1882 - 1962

N PENDER Edward Pender, Oct 22, 1838 - Apr 6, 1906

N PENDER Eliza E. Pender, Aug 30, 1843 - Mar 20, 1920

S PENDER Eunice L. Pender, 1886 - 1979

S PENDER Georgia Steckle Pender, MOTHER, 1878 - 1969

S PENDER Jesse F. Pender, 1870 - 1927

S PENDER John W. Pender, 1876 - 1951

S PENDER Kathleen L. Pender, 1880 - 1957

N PENDER Victor Pender, IN LOVING MEMORY, (No dates)

N PIERCE John Lloyd Tucker Pierce, Jan 18, 1946 - Mar 28, 1967

S PERDUE Bryan T. Perdue, FATHER, 1870 - 1942

S PERDUE Ella A. Perdue, MOTHER, 1877 - 1947

S PERSCH Afton Persch, SON, 1930 - 1936

S PERSCH Glen Persch, FATHER, 1901 - 1940

M PERRY Sarah Perry, Dec 22, 1842 - Nov 29, 1914

M PERRY Larkin Perry, In Memory Of: 1847 - 1924

M PETERSON Lena Peterson, Born Sep 4, 1848 - Died Jun 15, 1905

M PETERSON Peter Peterson, Born Feb 2, 1848 - Died Jun 24, 1907

N   PIERCE   Nancy Ellen Pierce,   Aug 23, 1959

M   PIERCE   Rosa Ann Pierce,   1867 - 1959

S   PIERSON   Flora M. Pierson,   1885 - 1936

S   PIETI   Augusta Pieti,   1872 - 1944

S   PIETI   Charles J. Pieti,   1879 - 1940

M   PISTOLESI   Rose M. Pistolesi,   1870 - 1950

     PLANTING   (Hilma Sophia Planting. Age 90. Aug 23, 1894, Houghton, Mich-
                  Sep 18, 1984, Battle Ground, WA. Res: Vancouver, WA. ...
                  Graveside service Friday, Sep 21, at Brush Prairie Cem.
                  Layne's Funeral Home. Obit - The Columbian)

M   PLUSS   Elizabeth A. Pluss,   Oct 11, 1846 - May 13, 1910

M   PLUSS   John B. Pluss,   Oct 22, 1841 - Apr 5, 1905

M   PLUSS   John E. Pluss,   Jan 2, 1876 - Aug 22, 1884

M   POTTER   Sgt. Dan'l Potter,   Co. I 2nd Iowa Cav.

M   POWELL   Errett A. Powell,   1888 - 1976

M   POWELL   Herbert Earl Powell, Washington Pfc. 861 AVN Engr. Bn. W W II,
                  Apr 16, 1918 - Mar 14, 1965

M   POWELL   Irene Powell,   1895 - 1973

S   POWERS   Martha M. Powers,   1897 - 1940

S   PREST   Charles A. Prest, FATHER,   1854 - 1939

S   PREST   Ernest H. Prest, Washington, Pvt Rcl 347th M G Bn 9,   July 6,
                  1939 - illegible

S   PREST   Ona Marie Prest, MOTHER,   1877 - 1959

M   PRESTON   Ethel R. Preston,   1904 - 1972

M   PRESTON   Herbert T. Preston,   1897 - 1937

S   PRESTON   Sarah A. Preston,   1859 - 1942

M   PRESTON   Theodore Preston,   1925 - 1929

M   PRICE   Baby Price,   1929

M   PRICE   Birdella Price, 1900 - 1945

PRITEL (Irene Clark Pritel. Age 81. Apr 20, 1904, Grants Pass, OR -
        July 17, 1985, Battle Ground, WA. Res: Vancouver, WA.
        Wife of Dr. Phillip Pritel, at home. .... Funeral Monday,
        July 22, at Vancouver Funeral Chapel. Interred in Brush
        Prairie Cem. Obit - The Columbian)

S   PROUDFIT   Cecil E. Proudfit, 1892 - 1952

N   PROUDFIT   Dale E. Proudfit, 1934 - 1976

S   PROUDFIT   Nora C. Proudfit, 1895 - 19___

S   PULFORD   Floyd Pulford, 1903 - 1929

S   PULFORD   Jane Pulford, 1878 - 1949

S   PULFORD   Ruth Pulford, 1905 - 1927

N   QUIMBY   John L. Quimby, Father, 1888 - 1957

N   QUIMBY   Mildred I. Quimby, Mother, 1889 - 19___

N   RAMBO   Harriet Rambo, 1916

N   RAMBO   James Rambo, 1896

N   RAMBO   Martha Rambo, 1871

N   RAMBO   Milton Rambo, 1879

N   RAMBO   Nye N. Rambo, 1856 - 1926

N   RAMBO   William Rambo, Died 1891

M   RAMEY   Albert J. Ramey, Kentucky Pvt. Co. D 27 Inf., Feb 20, 1878 -
        Mar 27, 1960

M   RAMEY   Betty W. Ramey, Mother, 1888 - 1976

S   RAMEY   Richard L. Ramey, 1939 - 2 yrs old

M   RAPAKKO   Olof Rapakko, 1831 - 19 ___

M   RAYBURN   Jesse Lee Rayburn, 1910 - 1951

M   REBISCH   John J. Rebisch, In Loving Memory, 1911 - 1951

M   REED   Infant Twins Reed, Children of Charles & Ruby Reed, In Memory of:
        1962

N   REED   Ronald C. Reed, Washington Sgt. U S Army Korea, Oct 7, 1922 -
        Oct 30, 1973

S   REES   Cora A. Rees, 1861 - 1950

S REES George W. Rees, 1851 - 1916

S REIS George J. Reis, Dad, 1881 - 1965

   REIS (Muriel Lucille Reis. Age 63. Nov 18, 1922, Spokane, WA - Jan 1,
         1986, Vancouver, WA. Widower: Roland H. Reis, at home.
         Son: Steven, Vancouver. Daughter: Kimberly, San Diego,
         CA. Funeral Friday, Jan 3, 1986, at Layne's Funeral Home
         Chapel. Burial in Brush Prairie Cemetery. Obit - The
         Columbian)

S REIS Oneita H. Reis, Mom, 1889 - 1944

N RENGO Josephine G. Rengo, 1880 - 1970

N RENGO Matt Emil Rengo, 1892 - 1959

N REYNOLDS Dora A. Reynolds, Daughter of J A & H, Oct 20, 1866 - Apr
         2, 1885

N REYNOLDS John H. Reynolds, Son of J A & H, Apr 24, 1864 - Aug 14,
         1877

N REYNOLDS Nancy M. Reynolds, Dau of J A & H, Sep 23, 1869 - Sep 23,
         1877

M RICHARDS Christ Richards, 1830 - 1908

S RICHTER Stella M. Richter, 1890 - 1941

S RICHTER Wesley O. Richter, 1882 - 1936

M RINEHART Charles L. Rinehart, Son of A S and E S, D. Apr 16, 1884 -
         age 1y, 2m, 12 d.

N RISHEL Grayce E. Rishel, Mother, 1897 - 1979

M ROBERTS James G. Roberts, 1952 - 1952

M ROBERTS James M. Roberts, 1876 - 1956

M ROBERTS Joseph Roberts, 1952 - 1952

N ROBINSON Almina Robinson, B. May 9, 1855 - D. Aug 3, 1910, Gone but
         not forgotten

S ROBINSON Arthur E. Robinson, 1868 - 1947

S ROBINSON Emily Robinson, 1872 - 1947

N ROBINSON Infant Sons, Same stone as Almina Robinson. No Dates

S ROGERS Ada Mae Rogers, 1885 - 1967

S ROGERS Agnes E. Rogers, 1911 - 1940

N   ROGERS   Alton D. Rogers, FATHER, 1910 - 1972

M   ROGERS   Daniel W. Rogers, illegible - 1966

      ROGERS   (John Robert Rogers. Age 87. Jan 26, 1899, Ewing, IL - Jul 12, 1986, Vancouver, WA. Res: Brush Prairie, WA. Husb. of Nellie Olson Rogers, at home...... Funeral Wednesday, Jul 16, at Vancouver Funeral Chapel. Interment in Brush Prairie Cem. Obit - The Columbian)

S   ROGERS   Lawrence E. Rogers, 1870 - 1941

N   ROGERS   Marie E. Rogers, 1906 - _____ (Age 78. Feb 18, 1906, Matoon, IL - Jul 1, 1984, at home, Vancouver, WA. Res: Hockinson, WA. .... Funeral Friday, Jul 6, at Vancouver Funeral Chapel. Interment at Brush Prairie Cem. Obit - The Columbian)

N   ROGERS   Maryellen E. Rogers, MOTHER, 1916 - _____

N   ROGERS   Roy M. Rogers, 1894 - 1980

S   ROSS   Edward M. Ross, 1955 - 1955

N   ROSIN   Caroline Rosin, 1888 - 1963

N   ROSIN   Jacob Rosin, 1890 - 1976

N   ROUSE   Bertha K. Rouse, 1890 - 1969

N   ROUSE   Guy A. Rouse, 1883 - 1957

S   ROUTH   Lewis Otterman Routh, 1851 - 1931

S   ROUTH   Margaret Ann Routh, In Loving Memory, 1861 - 1934

S   ROUTH   Sarah J. Routh, MOTHER, 1907 - 1945

S   ROUTH   Vernon C. Routh, FATHER, 1896 - 1946

M   RUGGLES   William N. Ruggles, 1859 - 1914

S   SAGE   Elbert Sage, 1871 - 1946

      SAGE   (Henry A. Sage. Age 79. Jan 18, 1908, Maywood, NB - Jan 21, 1987, Vancouver, WA. Res: Battle Ground, WA. Brother: Herbert of Gresham, OR. Graveside service Saturday, Jan 24, 1987 at Brush Prairie Cem. Layne's Funeral Home. Obit - The Columbian)

      SAGE   (Herbert E. Sage. Age 86. May 3, 1900, Maywood, NB - Mar 23, 1987, Troutdale, OR. Res: Troutdale, OR. Widow: Lillian. Sons: George, Vancouver, WA; Donald, Alaska and Michael, Troutdale, OR. Funeral Friday, Mar 27, 1987, at Woodland Church of the Nazarene. Woodland Funeral Home. Obit - The Columbian)

S   SAGE   Monora Sage,   1869 - 1947

N   SAGE   Myron E. Sage,   1897 - 1980

S   SALO   Olga H. Salo,   1901 - 1948

M   SANDS   Gregory L. Sands,   GREG WAS HERE,   Jan 25, 1952 - Nov 11, 1973

M   SAWYER   Nida V. Sawyer,   Aug 21, 1900 - Dec 21, 1934

M   SCHELL   Augusta Schell,   1893 - 1971

N   SCHIMKE   Mary Schimke,   WIFE AND MOTHER,   1891 - 1963

N   SCHIMKE   Jacob,   HUSBAND AND FATHER,   1890 - 1970

S   SCHULTZ   Daniel D. Schultz,   Pvt U S Army,   1900 - 1977

     SCHULTZ   (Ethel May Schultz. Age 77. Heart Failure. Nov 5, 1909, Brush Prairie, WA - Mar 26, 1987, Portland, OR. Res: Vancouver, WA. Preceded in death by husband, Daniel Schultz in 1977. Son: Richard T. Schultz, Gig Harbor, WA. Daughter: Marjorie Joanne Schultz, Lawndale, CA. Brother Arthur W. Hull, Vancouver, WA. Graveside service Monday, Mar 30, 1987 at Brush Prairie Cemetery. Interment Brush Prairie Cem. Vancouver Funeral Chapel. Obit - The Columbian)

M   SCHMIDT   Baby Schmidt,   Aug 1, 1965. (Daughter of Edward & Edna Schmidt)

S   SCHMIDT   Gustav Schmidt,   1876 - 1948

S   SCHMIDT   Sophia Schmidt,   1873 - 1954

S   SCOTT   Louisa Edna Scott,   Nov 28, 1902 - Apr 14, 1930

N   SCOTT   Walter B. Scott,   1889 - 1954

M   SELEY   Jess E. Seley,   1907 - 1972

S   SHANAHAN   John D. Shanahan,   Father,   1890 - 1955

     SHANAHAN   (John Douglas "Jack" Shanahan. Age 59. Sep 25, 1927, Vanc., WA. - Dec 25, 1986, Res: Vancouver. Daughter: Terry Lee Shanahan, San Diego. Sisters: June Secrest, Vancouver; Maria Testerman, Portland, OR. Funeral Monday, Dec 29, at Vancouver Funeral Chapel. Burial at Brush Prairie Cem. Obit - The Columbian)

S   SHANAHAN   Kristina,   Mother,   1891 - 1975

M   SHEPHERD   Emma Shepherd,   1881 - 1934

S   SHIELDS   Henrietta O. Shields,   1853 - 1942

BRUSH PRAIRIE CEMETERY

S	SHIELDS	Henry O. Shields, 1852 - 1927
M	SHIPP	Hiram A. Shipp, 1861 - 1930
M	SHIPP	Rose L. Shipp, 1873 - 1951
M	SHIPP	Miss Lillian Shipp, May 17, 1895 - Nov 3, 1909
S	SHOCKLEY	Burgess R. Shockley, 1904 - ____
S	SHOCKLEY	Gertha R. Shockley, 1904 - 1968
S	SHOCKLEY	William "Bill" Shockley, Our Darling, 1924 - 1943
M	SHROUP	Howard B. Shroup, Georgia Co G Ist Regt GA Infantry, Spanish American War, Dec 7, 1880 - Dec 17, 1966
M	SHROUP	Ira M. Shroup, 1890 - 1978
N	SHUSTER	Harry Shuster, 1912 - 1977
N	SILDANEN	Hilda M. Sildanen, 1873 - 1938
M	SILVO	Edna E. Silvo, 1903 - 1939
M	SIMILA	Antti Simila, Pvt U S Army, W W I, Dec 1, 1889 - Sep 27, 1955
S	SIMMS	Ernest Lee Simms, 1874 - 1942
S	SIMMS	Lottie May Simms, 1889 - 1935
M	SIMMS	Ralph F. Simms, 1928 - 1968
S	SIMONS	Amanda Simons, 1877 - 1938
S	SIMONS	Mac Simons, 1865 - 19___
S	SKINNER	Jesse W. Skinner, 1872 - 1941
S	SKINNER	Julia Skinner, 1858 - 1962
S	SKINNER	Mary Skinner, 1875 - 1967
	SMART	(Emily Rosemond Smart. Age 93. Aug 21, 1893, Waipukurau, New Zealand - Mar 21, 1987, Vallejo, CA. Preceded in death by her husbandm Matthew, and a daughter Lois Shapard. Daughters: Valma Hegstad, Angwin, CA, and Nadeen Brown, Salem. Graveside service Friday, Mar 27, 1987 at Brush Prairie Cemetery. Hamilton-Mylan Funeral Home. Obit - The Columbian)
S	SMART	Matthew S. Smart, IN LOVING MEMORY, 1890 - 1931
M	SMITH	Baby Smith, 1902

M	SMITH	Alice Smith, Wife of H. M. Smith, 1866 - 1913
N	SMITH	Benjamin F. Smith, HOW MUCH LIGHT, HOW MUCH JOY Apr 17, 1888 IS BURIED TODAY, A DARLING BOY
M	SMITH	Bertha M. Smith, 1876 - 1965
M	SMITH	Bertie A. Smith, Aug 28, 1888 - Sep 9, 1909
M	SMITH	Clara J. Smith, MOTHER, 1858 - 1931
S	SMITH	Edgar Earl Smith, 1895 - 1960
S	SMITH	Elizabeth Smith, 1852 - 1927
M	SMITH	Elwood Smith, 1886 - 1977
M	SMITH	Everett L. Smith, 1884 - 1961
N	SMITH	George O. Smith, FATHER, 1819 - 1897
S	SMITH	Gertrude E. Smith, MOTHER, 1885 - 1975
N	SMITH	Harriet Smith, MOTHER, 1825 - 1895
S	SMITH	Harry A. Smith, Father, 1846 - 1925
M	SMITH	Harvey M. Smith, 1868 - 1931
M	SMITH	Hugh M. Smith, 1856 - 1945
N	SMITH	James Smith, 1837 - 1904
M	SMITH	Jess Smith, Washington Pvt. 48 Spruce Sq. W W I, Mar 29, 1890 - Sep 10, 1964
S	SMITH	John A. Smith, BELOVED FATHER, 1859 - 1938
S	SMITH	Joseph A. Smith, FATHER, 1877 - 1939
M	SMITH	Martha C. Smith, 1868 - 1919
N	SMITH	Nancy Smith, 1844 - 1918
M	SMITH	Olive F. Smith, 1849 - 1928
M	SMITH	Roy C. Smith, 1942 - 1969
M	SMITH	Samuel S. Smith, FATHER, 1850 - 1935
S	SMITH	Sarah M. Smith, BELOVED MOTHER, 1863 - 1928
N	SNIDER	Hoyt R. Snider, Sr., Pvt U S Army, W W I, June 21, 1898 - May 18, 1975

S   SNYDER   Baby,   Apr 18, 1944   (On stone with Elgie Wimer)

S   SONGE   Martin Songe,   1877 - 1927

S   SONGE   Stu Songe,   1925 - 1957

S   SOOTER   Harold W. Sooter, "Billy",   Mar 9, 1928 - Jul 15, 1931

M   SOOTER   Mamie E. Sooter,   1888 - 19___

    SOOTER   (Mamie E. Sooter. Age 96. Jun 17, 1888, in Minnesota - Sep 18,
             1984, Loma Linda, CA. Res: Loma Linda, CA. .... Funeral
             Sat, Sep 22, at Meadow Glade Seventh-Day Adventist Church.
             Interment in Brush Prairie Cem. Layne's Funeral Home.
             Obit - The Columbian)

M   SOOTER   Thomas A. Sooter, In Thee Have I Put My Trust,   1892 - 1978

    SPENCER (Carl Harvey Spencer. Age 86. Apr 23, 1897 - Jan 19, 1984,
             Vancouver, WA. Res: Battle Ground, WA. Husb. of Hazel,
             at home. ...... Funeral Saturday, Jan 21, at Layne's
             Funeral Home Chapel. Obit - The Columbian)

M   SPIEKERMAN   Hans Spiekerman,   1900 - 1972

S   SPIRES   Ida R. Spires,   Our Mother,   1870 - 1946

S   SPURGEON   Emery S. Spurgeon, Daddy, Born May 27, 1914 - Died May 27,
             1954

S   STAHL   Louise Stahl, Mother,   1855 - 1932

S   STAHL   William Stahl, Father,   1860 - 1947

M   STALEY   Alva Staley, Washington Pfc. U S Navy, W W I,   Dec 2, 1888 -
             Sep 23, 1969

N   STALEY   Alvey Staley,   1854 - 1933

S   STALEY   Bert A. Staley,   1877 - 1944

M   STALEY   Carrie Staley, WIFE,   1890 - 1969

N   STALEY   Clarice G. Staley,   1868 - 1952

S   STALEY   Clementine D. Staley, Mother,   1886 - 1979

M   STALEY   Daniel Staley,   1840 - 1931

N   STALEY   Henry M. Staley,   1899 - 1973

M   STALEY   Lorena Staley,   1901 - 1918

M   STALEY   Mary E. Staley,   1892 - 1976

45

BRUSH PRAIRIE CEMETERY

N	STALEY	Miriam J. Staley, 1904 - ____
M	STALEY	Samuel K. Staley, 1893 - 1957
M	STALNECKER	Carl Stalnecker, DARLING, Jun 20, 1909 - Feb 8, 1911
M	STALNECKER	J. E. Stalnecker, AT REST, Apr 17, 1877 - Apr 16, 1912
S	STARR	Alice E. Starr, 1867 - 1940
S	STARR	Charles E. Starr, 1864 - 1943
S	STARR	Leola A. Starr, 1895 - 1934
S	STAINBROOK	Alpha S. Stainbrook, MOTHER, 1898 - 1976
N	STANWICK	Iver P. Stanwick, FATHER, 1873 - 1962
M	STEELMAN	Alta May Steelman, Gone But Not Forgotten, Age 2 yrs
S	STEELMAN	Heaton Steelman, In Loving Memory, 1879 - 1944
M	STEELMAN	J. L. Steelman, Born Feb 28, 1849 - Died Jul 28, 1929
M	STEELMAN	Sarah J. Steelman, Born Feb 6, 1849 - Died Jan 8, 1922
S	STEPHENS	Benjamin G. Stephens, 1885 - 1942
N	STEPHENS	James D. Stephens, 1920 - 1978
S	STEPHENS	Lena P. Stephens, 1895 - 1954
M	STRAWN	Inez N. Strawn, 1893 - 1961
M	STRAWN	James E. Strawn, 1887 - 1972
M	STRETCHER	Anna Stretcher, MOTHER, 1861 - 1941
M	STRETCHER	Charles F. Stretcher, FATHER, 1849 - 1922
M	STRETCHER	Floy F. Stretcher, Wife of William Picket, Dec 11, 188__ - Oct 15, 1908
M	STRETCHER	George H. Stretcher, GONE BUT NOT FORGOTTEN, Sep 7, 1879 - Jul 30, 1907
M	STRETCHER	Sarah J. Stretcher, 1889 - 1950
S	SUTTON	Benjamin Sutton, 1956 - 1956
M	SWEITZ	Ernest W. Sweitz, 1893 - 1972
M	SWIETZ	Lea Sweitz, 1902 - ____

BRUSH PRAIRIE CEMETERY

    SWEITZ   (Lea Sweitz. Age 82. May 5, 1902, McIntosh County, ND - Jul
              26, 1984, Gresham, OR. ..... Funeral Monday, Jul 30, at
              Meadow Glade Seventh-Day Adventist Church. Burial in
              Brush Prairie Cem. Layne's Funeral Home. Obit - The
              Columbian)

N   SYRIA   Isaac W. Syria,   1904 - _____

N   SYRIA   Ellen S. Syria,   1908 - 1974

M   TAYLOR   Dora M. Taylor, Wife,   1886 - 1936

S   TAYLOR   Layton Ward Taylor, Washington, Tech 3rd Class, W W II,   Apr
              18, 1911 - Jul 24, 1966

S   TAYLOR   Lionel F. Taylor,   1878 - 1958

S   TAYLOR   Margaret L. Taylor,   1870 - 1937

S   TAYLOR   Nancy E. Taylor,   1889 - 1927

    TECZAR   (Gregory Peter Teczar. Age 33. Nov 6, 1950, Webster, Mass.,
              Aug 2, 1984, Providence, Rhode Island. Res: Westerly,
              Rhode Island (prev. in Vancouver, WA) S/O Emil Joseph
              Teczar, Vancouver, WA; Mother: Frances Boucher, Melbourne,
              Florida. ..... Graveside service Tues, Aug 14, at Brush
              Prairie Cem. Evergreen Staples Funeral Chapel. Obit -
              The Columbian)

N   TEEL   Andi Philis Teel,   1902 - _____

M   THOGERSON   Andrew C. Thogerson,   1847 - 1929

M   THOGERSON   Rebecca Thogerson,   1858 - 1929

M   THOMAS   Alvin Thomas,   1873 - 1957

M   THOMAS   Lura Thomas,   1877 - 1957

M   THOMPSON   Arthur R. Thompson, IN LOVING MEMORY OF DAD,   1882 - 1936

M   THOMPSON   Bessie Thompson, IN LOVING MEMORY OF MOM,   1886 - 1974

M   THOMPSON   Charles Thompson,   1924 - 1980

M   THOMPSON   Ida F. Thompson, MOTHER,   1863 - 1941

S   THOMPSON   Juanita M. Thompson,   1900 - 1927

M   THOMPSON   Matthew L. Thompson,   1963 - 1963

N   THOMPSON   Wm. A. Thompson, Father,   1874 - 1954

N   THORPE   Arthur Louis Thorpe,   1930 - 1977

S   THRONSEN   Dora A. Thronsen, Mother,   1883 - 1943

S   TOMPKINS   Edith G. Tompkins, Mother,   1867 - 1959

S   TOMPKINS   John N. Tompkins, Father,   1853 - 1944

     TOMKINSON   (Lydia Lavina Tomkinson. Age 90. Heart Failure. Aug 16,
                 1896, Mason City, Iowa - Jul 17, 1987. Res: Battle Ground,
                 WA. Preceded in death by husband Frank in 1973. .....
                 Service Tuesday, Jul 21, at Layne's Funeral Home. Obit -
                 The Columbian)

S   TONJES   Henry Tonjes, Father,   1874 - 1923

M   TOWLE   Elizabeth Towle, wife of Josiah,   1830 - 1919

M   TOWLE   Josiah Towle, Maine, 1st Heavy Artillery Comm G A R,   Feb 19,
             1828 - Jul 16, 1911

S   TRACY   Addie A. Tracy,   1863 - 1938

     TRUAX   (Earl S. "Love" Truax. Age 77. Nov 16, 1907, Columbus, Neb -
             Mar 6, 1985, Vancouver, WA. Res: Vancouver area. Husband
             of Delores "Dolly" Truax, at home .... Graveside
             service Saturday, Mar 9, at Brush Prairie Cemetery.
             Layne's Funeral Home. Obit - The Columbian)

N   TUCKER   Gerald S. Tucker,   May 9, 1903 - Sep 22, 1953

N   TURNBULL   Burton W. Turnbull, Washington, A M M I U S Navy, W W II,
                Apr 6, 1919 - Feb 20, 1968

N   TURNBULL   Della Turnbull,   1909 - 1969

N   TURNBULL   George W. Turnbull,   1882 - 1966

     TURVEY   (Raymond Turvey. Age 81. Sep 2, 1903 Hanging Rock, OH - Feb 1,
              1985. Res: Battle Ground, WA. Husband of Harriet, at
              home. ...... Graveside service Sunday, Feb 3, in Brush
              Prairie Cem. Layne's Funeral Home. Obit - The Columbian)

S   URPILA   Anselim Urpila,   1885 - 1940

M   USHER   George N. Usher,   1855 - 1913

M   USHER   Irene R. Usher,   1863 - ____

M   USHER   Nelson Usher,   1808 - 1893

M   USHER   Phebe Usher,   1822 - 1896

M   UUSIMAU   Maria Uusimau,   182_ - 188_

BRUSH PRAIRIE CEMETERY

M VADNAIS Charles Vadnais, Born in Canada Apr 15, 1842 - Died in California Apr 25, 1889. A good husband and loving father
Call not back the dear departed,
Anchored safe where storms are o'er,
On the border land we left them,
Soon to meet and part no more.

S VAUGHN Minnie E. Vaughn, 1873 - 1952

S VAN ATTA Bernice V. Van Atta, OUR DARLING, 1913 - 1926

S VANATTA Danny K. Vanatta, 1951 - 1955

N VAN ATTA Eli C. Van Atta, 1847 - 1915

N VAN ATTA Elmarine J. Van Atta, 1853 - 1932

N VANATTA Gearshum Vanatta, 1813 - 1896

M VAN ATTA Matilda L. Van Atta, At Rest, Feb 3, 1860 - Mar 5, 1918

S VAN ATTA Ray Van Atta, 1890 - 1972

M VAN ATTA William Van Atta, At Rest, Sep 15, 1851 - Aug 11, 1919

M VAN MATRE Infant Girl, 1974

N VANMETER Flora Vanmeter, 19___ - 1977

S VAN WEY Charles W. Van Wey, 1856 - 1930

S VERKOUTERN John Verkoutern, 1858 - 1939

S VOLKMAR Ruby Volkmar, 1899 - 1939

S VORIS J. Lamini Voris, 1836 - 1930

M WALKER Charles Walker, 1850 - 1929

 WALKER (George Edward Walker, Age 92. Jan 12, 1892, St. Johns, OR - Jul 6, 1984, Vancouver, WA. Res: Battle Ground, WA. Husb of Olah Walker, at home...... Funeral Wed., Jul 11, at Meadow Glade Seventh-Day Adventist Church. Layne's Funeral Home. Obit - The Columbian)

S WALKER Rosella B. Walker, TOGETHER FOREVER, 1895 - 1979

S WALKER Willis E. Walker, 1894 - 1946

M WALL Emil D. Wall, Husband, 1902 - 1966

M WALL Fred Wall, BROTHER, 1901 - 1966

M WALLACE John R. Wallace, 1971 - 1971

S   WALLACE   Rebecca E. Wallace, 1957

           WALTER   (Harry E. Walter. Age 88,   Aug 22, 1897, Prescott, Wis - Oct 9, 1985. Res: Battle Ground, WA. Husb. of Ethel, at home....... Memorial service Sunday, Oct 13, at Meadow Glade Seventh-Day Adventist Church. Obit - The Columbian)

M   WARD   Abraham Ward,   FAREWELL DEAR HUSBAND
                                        A PRECIOUS ONE HAS GONE
                                        HIS PLACE WILL BE SO EMPTY
                                        WITHIN OUR HEART AND HOMES
                        Dec 2, 1831 - Jun 2, 1887

M   WARD   Chloe I. Ward, Wife, 1886 - 1965

M   WARD   Emma G. Ward, Died Oct 6, 1921, Age 60 yrs. 6 mo. 7 ds.

M   WARD   Fannie Ward, IN LOVING REMEMBRANCE OF, BORN IN OHIO, 1850 - 1920

N   WARD   J. C. Ward, 1847 - 1916

N   WARD   Louisa Ward, His Wife, (J. C. Ward), 1853 - 1931

N   WARD   Nancy Ward, Born Feb 10, 1812 - Died Sep 20, 1896

M   WARD   Perry O. Ward, Husband, 1883 - 1951

M   WARD   Richard N. Ward, Father, 1857 - 1920

M   WARD   Sarah F. Ward, Mother, 1860 - 1911

M   WARD   W. A. Ward, Died Oct 21, 1929, Age 75 yrs. 1 mo. 20 ds.

S   WATSON   Anna Faulk Watson, MOTHER, Oct 18, 1895 - Dec 28, 1965

M   WATSON   Charles G. Watson, D. Feb 2, 1919 - age 34 y.

M   WATSON   Dicie M. Watson, 1892 - _____

           WATSON   (Dicie Watson. Age 93. Jan 15, 1892, Washington - Apr 5, 1985, Vancouver, WA. Preceded in death by her husband, Robert J. Watson........Graveside services Tuesday, Apr 9, at Brush Prairie Cem. Hamilton-Mylan Funeral Home. Obit - The Columbian)

M   WATSON   Dorothy Watson, MOTHER, 1856 - 1927

S   WATSON   George Fitch, OUR DAD, Nov 6, 1881 - May 29, 1961

M   WATSON   Paul R. Watson, D. Feb 7, 1916 - age 24 yr

M   WATSON   Robert Watson, FATHER, 1848 - _____

M   WATSON   Robert I. Watson, IN LOVING MEMORY, 1887 - 1966

S	WATSON	Robert Charles Watson, May 24, 1913 - Aug 8, 1927
M	WATSON	Wilford S. Watson, BELOVED SON, 1911 - 1927
M	WEHTZE	Laurel M. Wehtze, 1915 - 1966
N	WELTON	Gertrude A. Welton, 1887 - 1961
M	WESA	Mary H. Wesa, Asleep In Jesus, 1844 - 1924
M	WESA	Matt Wesa, 1864 - 1938
M	WEST	A. A. West, GONE BUT NOT FORGOTTEN, 1850 - 1915
N	WESTERGARD	Elizabeth R. Westergard, 1897 - 1953
N	WESTERGARD	Fred D. Westergard, 1898 - 1960
S	WHALEN	Benjamin C. Whalen, 1884 - 1935
M	WHALEN	Ginda C. Whalen, MOTHER, 1854 - 1941
M	WHALEN	Thomas J. Whalen, FATHER, 1850 - 1930
M	WHEELER	Erwin D. Wheeler, 1879 - 1968
M	WHEELER	Josephine E. Wheeler, 1883 - 1964
M	WHITE	Charles N. White, "Bud", 1909 - 1974
M	WHITE	Floyd White, 1887 - 1955
S	WHITE	Harry White, 1869 - 1932
S	WIGGINS	Margaret Wiggins, 1907 - 1926
S	WIGGINS	Mattie M. Wiggins, Jul 4, 1867 - May 4, 1949
S	WIGGINS	William M. Wiggins, 1870 - 1933
N	WILEMAN	Grace Maude Wileman, 1891 - 1970
N	WILEMAN	Robert Bruce, 1887 - 1972
M	WILKINS	Lucy Ella Wilkins, 1849 - 1928
N	WILKS	George J. Wilks, 1913 - 19___
N	WILKS	Marjorie J. Wilks, 1921 - 1963
S	WILLOUGHBY	Charles H. Willoughby, 1862 - 1942
M	WILSON	Arminta M. Wilson, 1878 - 1964

N   WILSON   Jesse L. Wilson,   Tec 5 U S Army, W W II,   June 2, 1926 - Nov 1, 1978

N   WILSON   Robert N. Wilson,   DAD,   1915 - 1980

N   WILSON   Virginia H. Wilson,   MOTHER,   1919 - _____

S   WIMER   Elgie Wimer,   1890 - 1938

M   WINSTON   Claude E. Winston,   1895 - 1919

S   WINSTON   Esther F. Winston,   1897 - 1970

S   WINSTON   George A. Winston,   1899 - 1945

M   WINSTON   Lulu R. Winston,   1882 - 1939

S   WINSTON   Milton E. Winston,   Washington, 175th Infantry, 29th Div. W W II,   Jan 19, 1923 - Sep 14, 1944

S   WINTHER   Knub Winther,   1873 - 1926

S   WISDOM   Robert D. Wisdom,   Father,   1899 - 1941

N   WOLBERT   Gary W. Wolbert,   In Loving Memory,   1944 - 1962

    WOOD   (Everett E. Wood. Age 74.   Sep 24, 1911, Troutdale, OR - Jul 31, 1986.   Res: Vancouver, WA.   Preceded in death by wife, Wilma, in 1977.......Graveside service Tuesday, Aug 5, 1986 at Brush Prairie Cem.   Layne's Funeral Home.   Obit - The Columbian)   U S Navy, W W II

N   WOOD   Franklin T. Wood,   1883 - 1958

N   WOOD   Gladys C. Wood,   1886 - 1968

N   WOOD   Wilma E. Wood,   1911 - 1977

    WOODRUFF   (Elsie A. Woodruff. Age 70.   Apr 5, 1904, Centralia, WA - Feb 11, 1984, Salem, OR.   Res: Salem, OR.   Wife of Earl E. Woodruff of Vancouver,......Funeral Wed., Feb 15, at Hamilton-Mylan Funeral Home.   Interment in Brush Prairie Cem.   Obit - The Columbian)

S   WOODRUFF   Emma J. Woodruff,   Feb 29, 1940

S   WOODRUFF   Julia A. Woodruff,   In Memory Of: Asleep In Jesus,   1840 - 1939

N   WOOLDRIDGE   Myrtle Wooldridge,   1900 - 1972

N   WOOLDRIDGE   Roy Wooldridge,   1898 - 19___

WOOLDRIDGE   (Roy Pete Wooldridge. Age 87. Jan 13, 1898, Grizzly Bluff, CA - Apr 27, 1985, Portland, OR. Res: Battle Ground, WA. Husband of Lempi, at home.....Funeral Thursday, May 2, 1985. Layne's Funeral Home Chapel. Burial in Brush Prairie Cemetery. Obit - The Columbian)

M   WORDEN   Jessie E. Worden, DAUGHTER, 1914 - 1949

S   WOSTER   Edwin Woster, Father, 1860 - 1936

M   WRIGHT   George W. Wright, 1861 - 1943

M   WRIGHT   Robert C. Wright, Oregon, S Sgt U S Army, W W II, July 15, 1909 - Oct 30, 1971

M   YANDLE   Minnie Howard Yandle, Mother, Resting With The Lord, 1887 - 1956

S   ZEIGER   Phillip Zeiger, 1868 - 1939

N   ZIMMERMAN   Gabriel Zimmerman, 1840 - 1922

N   ZIMMERMAN   Jeannette Zimmerman, His Wife (Gabriel Zimmerman), 1844 - 1921

N   ZIMMERMAN   Nelson M. Zimmerman, 1869 - 1922

APPENDAGE

S	BORDON	Lewis Borden, 1852 - 1926
M	CLAUS	Angeline E. Claus, 1877 - 1965
S	VAUGHN	Carl R. Vaughn, 1902 - 1929
S	VAUGHN	William M. Vaughn, 1870 - 1947
M	WALKER	Charles Walker (other names on the same stone - no dates included) Clarence, Eldon and Dolores

Hawk (or Fairchild) Cemetery

Located just south of the Lewis River Bridge over the North Fork of the Lewis River on Interstate #5, Woodland, Wash.

HAWK (or FAIRCHILD) CEMETERY

This Cemetery is located in an area referred to as Hawks Hill by pioneers as an early settler, George Hawks and his wife, Angeline had resided there. It is one of the earliest burial places in the Lewis River valley and it is on the brow of a hill which is just south of the Lewis River bridge over the North Fork of the Lewis River on Interstate Highway #5.

Hawk (or Fairchild) Cemetery, is known by both names and is located on the Charles Fairchild Donation Land Claim which he took up in 1855. He did not remain here long and sold his claim to George Buchanan.

Since there were no roads there in early days, caskets were brought across the river by boat and carried quite a distance to the hillside, then up to the top of the brow of the hill.

Due to the widening of the highway a few years ago, the graves of Allan and Elizabeth Gillson and their sons were removed to the Gardner (also known as the Hayes) Cemetery about four miles east of Woodland, Washington.

There are other burials here unmarked. It is known that the Buchanan family owned a plot. Part of the burial ground is still enclosed with the original wire fence, but otherwise it is unkept.

HAWK (or FAIRCHILD) CEMETERY was read and recorded by GRACE DAVIS of Woodland, Washington.

HAWK (or FAIRCHILD) CEMETERY

BUCHANNAN   (_____ Buchannan, unmarked gravesite)

COPELAND   Charles William Copeland, son of J. W. & S. E. Copeland, born
                   Jan. 22, 1865 - died June 15, 1872

COPELAND   Della Copeland, dau of J. W. & S. E. Copeland, born Dec. 6, 1863
                   died June 26, 1884

COPELAND   Ludocia Copeland (dau of J. W. & S. E. Copeland - gravesite
                   unmarked)

DAVIS   E. G. Davis, died Mar. 27, 1888, aged 63 yrs 9 mos 4 da

KINDER   Nancy M., wife of G. Kinder, born Jan. 21, 1806 - died Jan. 1889
                   (second wife of Gallatin Kinder)

GILLSON   Charlie Gillson, 1853 - 1857

GILLSON   Allan Gillson, 1817 - 1870

GILLSON   Elizabeth Gillson, 1827 - 1913 (nee Johns)

GILLSON   Sumner Gillson, son of A. & E. Gillson, died Sept. 12, 1888
                   aged 24 yrs

GILLSON   Silas A. Gillson, 1855 - 1920, Our Brother

SPRINGER   U. O. Springer, died Aug. 2, 1871, aged 25 yrs 3 mos 12 da

STRATTON   Charlie Stratton, born Northfield, Mass., Oct. 4, 1819 - died
                   Woodland, Wash., Mar. 8, 1887

*****

HAWK (or FAIRCHILD) CEMETERY

"Old lady Davis died Thursday morning last - int. Fairchild Cemetery."
[from Kelso Courier, Jan. 11, 1889]

*****

"The old lady Davis lived near Pekin died on Thurs. morning last. Buried in Fairchild cemetery. She died from paralysis and general debility."
[Vancouver Independent, Jan. 18, 1889 - La Center Items]

*****

[The following obituary is from other sources and it is believed that Mr. Kulper is buried in this cemetery in an unmarked gravesite.]

Mr. Hein Kulper Sr., died at the residence of his son Mr. Henry Kulper on the sixth day of Jan. 1897, aged 84 years, 3 months and 26 days, after an illness of two months caused by old age. His death was peaceful and his death bed was surrounded by some of his children, great and grand children, who mourn his loss.

The funeral took place last sunday at 1:30 p.m. from where it was taken by the Steamer Mascot to Mr. B. S. Griffith's place where the cemetery is situated. There was quite a large attendence, but owing to the fact the people of Woodland did not know the place, they could not attend. The service at the grave was conducted by Mr. Bratton Sr., who delived quite an able sermon. Mr. Hein Culper Sr., was born near Hamburg Germany, which place he left eight years ago, after the death of his wife. He was a seafaring man for 51 years, and was mostly engaged in fishing in the Northern seas. His son Mr. Henry Kulper went to Germany to accompany his father who was then already at an advanced age, to this country.

Mr. Kulper was the father of six children, two boys and four girls, of whom only one is living, Mr. Henry Kulper.

The heartfelt sympathy of the whole community and The Press is extended to the sorrowing family.

Yacolt Cemetery

Yacolt Cemetery was established in 1915 and is located 1/2 miles south of Yacolt on County Road #16, Yacolt, Wash. and it has been compared with records at the Yacolt City Hall.

Lot No.

ALLISON, Mrs.   [no marker - no dates]   183

ALTAMA, Mr.   (buried October 1915)   [no marker]   151

ANDERSON, Peter   1872 - 1952   102

BAKER, Ellis (buried 8 May 1962)   [no marker]   17

BARRZER (?), John P. (buried 23 May 1941) [mo marker] 102

BEEBE, Thomas C. [handwritten in concrete] 1885 - 1952   54

BUTTERFIELD, Edwin A. B. (Alfred in records) 1870 - 1946 148

CAHOON, Arthur J.   S1 U.S. Navy   2 Nov. 1922 -   170
          8 Jan. 1975

CAHOON, Darrell J. J.   Our Baby and the Angles Will   170
          Watch Over Him   27 May 1971 - 19 Sept. 1974

CAHOON, Larry D.   1947 - 1980   Love Endures   170

CAMPBELL, Baby [no marker] (buried 14 June 1916)   146

CAMPBELL, John Hartman (John Harley in records)   113
          1902 - 1925

CHARLTON, Joseph H. (buried 31 Dec. 1919) [no marker] 76

CHRISTOFFER, Elsie   1917 - 1973   118

COFFEY, Annie Jane   (buried 27 Dec. 1938) [no marker] 53

COURTNEY, David   [no marker - no dates]   169

COURTNEY, Elizabeth Ann   (buried 5 Apr. 1919) [no marker 169

COX, Emma L.   16 Dec. 1890 - 11 Dec. ____   93

CURTICE, George H.   11 Mar. 1872 - 26 Nov. 1913   79

DAY, James William   24 June 1836 - 23 Aug. 1923   12
          Cpl.   Co. E.   3 Regt.   Minn. Inf.

DE JACIMO, Charles H.   1947 - 1973   Son   176

DE JACIMO, Naomi D.   16 Feb. 1978 - 8 Feb. 1980   6
          Our Daughter   [photo on the stone]

DITTMAR, Charles B.   1882 - 1941   Husband   87

EVALT, Victor E.   1937 - 1939   Our Baby   107

FERGUSON, Francis (buried 18 Apr. 1945) [no marker] 511

Lot No.

GOODNER, Elisha Dayton   24 June 1896 - 27 Dec.   144
          1977   U.S. Army   World War I

GRAHAM, William H.   1857 - 1937   Father   86

GRANSTROM, Clarence H. (buried 28 June 1918)[no marker] 92

GREENLUND, August   1881 - 1967   46

GREENLUND, Marie J.   1897 - ____   46

GREENUP, Ollie E.   1887 - 1920   14

GREGORY, Gwendolyn   (buried 18 Mar. 1925)   86
                       [no marker]

HAMILTON, Mary E.   1871 - 1943   108

HAMMOND, William H.   (buried 22 Feb. 1925)[no marker]   73

HARP, Lewis B.   (buried 16 Jan. 1922)   82
              Co. A   61 Ill. Inf.

HARP, Mary A.   (burial 30 Oct. 1915)   82
               [no marker]

HARRIMAN, Charlotte A.   1886 - 1938   In Loving   85
           Memory

HARRIMAN, Lawrence J.   (buried 7 Apr. 1939)   85
                     [no marker]

HARRIS, Baby   (buried 24 Oct. 1936) [no marker]   96

HARTELOO, Tina Marie   (buried 27 Nov. 1964)   53
              [no marker]

HARTER, George B.   1894 - 1972   In Loving Memory   175

HARTER, Lois E.   1913 - 1974   Mother   174
          In Loving Memory

HEWER, H. R.   [no marker] (burial permit 19 Oct 1915) 96

HIBBERD, Clara E.   1889 - 19__   171

HIBBERD, Grover L.   1888 - 1966   171

HICKS, M. (Margaret) Day   1903 - 1922   13

HULSHIZER, Junice C.   1910 - 1975   140

HULSHIZER, Theodore   1903 - 1980   140

HUSIE, (HUSSEY), Velma   1902 - 1913   178

YACOLT CEMETERY

JEHNSEN, Howard E.   1902 – 1974   181

JONES, Anne Minuth,   1909 – 1976   Sister   15

KA DELL, Christiper   (buried 21 June 1948)   101
          [no marker]

KALLIO, William Anthony   (buried 29 Oct. 1975)   173
          [no marker]

KLINSKI, Glenn E.   19 Oct. 1953 – 30 Aug. 1975   55
              AW 2   U.S. Navy   Vietnam

LANE, Anthony Duane   (7-4-70)   11 Aug. 1970   112

LARSON, Joseph W.   1887 – 1929   Our Beloved Brother   89
              At   Rest

LETCHER, Daniel   27 Sept. 1893 – 30 May 1971   172
          North Dakota Wt.2   USNR   World War   II

LETCHER, Ida M.   1890 – 1969   Mother   181

LINDERER, John   (record of 1924 or 1925) [no marker]   153

LOGUE, Idah C.   (buried 25 Mar. 1938)   [no marker]   45

LOZNE, Wm. A.   (buried 14 Nov. 1921)   [no marker]   45

MAGUIRE, Chas.   Co. A   1 Wis. Inf. [no dates]   81

MAGUIRE, Elizabeth   (buried 26 Mar. 1920) [no marker]   81

MANSFIELD, Chester Leroy   Died 21 Oct. 1944   106
          Aged 4 Mos. 15 Days [weathered marker]

MARSHALL, John (Jack in records) Died 1923 Aged 55   110
      years [buried 9 July 1923 – Weathered paper marker]

MAURY, Fred   (buried 8 May 1962)   [no marker]   17

MC CUTCHEN, George A.   27 Feb. 1882 – 22 Nov. 1957   76

MC CUTCHEN, J. Calvin   11 May 1887 – 12 May 1917   75

MC CUTCHEN, J. M.   23 May 1835 – 23 May 1922   75

MC CUTCHEN, Mary 31 Mar. 1854 – 18 July 1924   75

MC CUTCHEON, Donald Alson   (buried 22 Dec. 1928)   75
          [no marker]

MC DONALD, H. B.   [no marker – no dates]   16

MICHEL, Antoine   1871 – 1916   77

YACOLT   CEMETERY

Lot No.

MICHEL,   Hubertine   1871 – 1947   [1952 record book]   77

MOON,   Nora   1870 – 1911   101

MOON,   Ralph S.   1868 – 1939   101

MUNCTON,   Charlie H.   1862 – 1929   19

MUNCTON,   Elmer F.   1889 – 1975   19

MUNCTON,   George Dewey   (buried 5 July 1921) [mo marker]   19

NAUJOKS,   David   (buried 4 Oct. 1929) [no marker]   74

NAUJOKS,   Leopoldine Q. (buried 10 Sept. 1924)   74
          [no marker]

NEWMAN,   Mrs. Gus   [no marker – no dates]   143

NORD, Josephine M. [Marie]   1907 – 1927   At Rest   77

NYBACK,   Reino A.   1914 – 1972   Son and Brother   168

OATFIELD,   Betty O.   1907 – 1966   Mother   49

OATFIELD,   Thomas D.   1898 – 1973   Father

OLSON,   Martin   1873 – 1962   15

PARISH,   Pearl   1918 – 1952   52

PATTERSON,   Samuel A.   1890 – 1974   176

PAUOLA,   Fiina Nyback   1884 – 1975   Mother   168

PEARSON,   Amy   (buried 24 Sept. 1928   182
          [no marker]

PEARSON,   Ruby E.   1911 – 1978   Beloved Mother   1

PERRY,   Guy   (burial 30 Jan. 1916) [no marker]   92

PERRY,   Mary Elizabeth   (buried 20 Apr. 1918)   91
          [no marker]

PERRY,   Wilfield   [no marker – no dates]   91

PETERS,   Margaret Carrie Letcher 2 Oct. 1889 – 10 Mar   172
          1974 Loving Memories Husband Orvin, Daughter
          Betty, Son James, Grandson Jeff
          [She was listed in the records as Margaret Peterson]

PETERSON,   Edward G.   "Pete"   1906 – 1965   171

PFEIFFER,   George F.   1900 – 1974   175

Lot No.

PIKKARRAIUEN,   Victor Emanuel   (buried 9 Nov. 1939   107
                [no marker]

PLACE,   Freda R.   1903 – 1974

PLACE,   Marion A. (Initial C. in records) 1928 – 1939   108

PLACE,   Ralph C.   1901 – 1976   ?

POND,   Addiem   1902 – ____   139

POND,   Emily A.   1897 – 1976   139

PRATT,   George   (buried 4 Mar. 1927) [no marker]   182

PRATT,   Mrs. George   [no marker – no dates]   182

PULLER,   J. Elton   1906 – 1977   Father   139

PULLER.   Lelia I.   1913 – _____   Mother   139

RAST,   Alfred   1899 – 1962   48

RAST,   Mathilda   1915

RAST,   Henry H.   1903 – 1965

RODGERS,   Margaret May   Born Sept. 191? –   92
            (Buried 14 Ap. 1917   Aged ? [carved Wood]

ROMAN,   Thersa   (buried 17 May 1952) [no marker]   80

RUITER,   Mrs. Mae   (buried 28 Oct. 1963) [no marker]   53

RUITER,   Russell Scott,   1954 – 1975   Son   54
                [photo on stone]

SCHILLING,   Michael   (buried 7 July 1923) [no marker]   115

SCHILLING,   Olive   1871 – 1945   115

SCHILLINGS,   Fred   (buried 1 Feb. 1938) [no marker]   115

SCHULLER,   William V.   1889 – 1966   Father   116

SCOTT,   Douglas C.   14 Dec. 1962 – 31 Oct. 1977   112
            Our Beloved Son & Brother

SHOBE,   Cynthia Leona,   1872 – 1937   87
            Beloved Wife and Mother

SHOBE,   John   (buried 27 Dec. 1954) [no marker]   87

SIGLER,   Mr. Abe   [no marker – no dates   179

SIGLER,   Art   [no marker – no dates]   179

SIGLER,	Floyd	[no marker - no dates]	179
SMITH,	Daniel S.	(buried 17 Mar. 1950) [no marker]	102
SNIDER,	Clarence L.	1910 - 1928	84
SNIDER,	Dewey C.	1898 - 1931	84
SNIDER,	Gerald E.	1901 - 1940	109
SNIDER,	Joseph Z.	1899 - ____	
SNIDER,	Lucious	1865 - 1943	84
SNIDER,	Lucy	1874 - 1933	84
SNIVELY,	Casper R.	(buried 23 Jan. 1945) [no marker]	50
SPRINGER,	William M.	2 June 1898 - 24 May 1977	183
SPURGIN,	John E.	[no marker - no dates]	15
STASSART,	Henry D.	(buried 2 Nov. 1916) [no marker]	78
STASSART,	Joseph	(buried 10 May 1922) [no marker]	78
STASSART,	Lawbertine H.	(buried 27 Nov. 1916)	78
STILTS,	Baby	(buried 26 Oct. 1917) [no marker]	180
STILTS,	Florence	(buried 19 Nov. 1940) [no marker]	185
STILTS,	Lonnie	(buried 17 Oct. 1968) [no marker]	185
STILTS,	Mrs. M.	[no marker - no dates]	185
STRODE,	Charles Noble	12 Sept. 1859 - 12 Apr. 1946 Father	83
STRODE,	Cordelia J.	19 Mar. 1855 - 23 Sept. 1918 Mother	83
STRODE,	Lucy Noble	1896 - 19__	
TALBOT,	Minnie	(buried 5 Apr. 1917) [no marker]	179
TAUDE,	Ferdinand	(buried 25 Oct. 1927) [no marker]	142
TAUDE,	Helen H.	1883 - 1963	
TAUDE,	Otto Carl	(buried 14 Ap. 1959) [no marker]	143
TAYLOR,	Baby	(buried 19 Feb. 1939) [no marker]	91
TAYLOR,	George Dewey	1899 - 1966 Husband	49

YACOLT CEMETERY

				Lot No.
TAYLOR, James Westley	1871 – 1969	Father		80
TAYLOR, Sarah Lucinda	1877 – 1940	Mother		80
TEEL, Jacquline	(buried 7 Apr. 1946)	[no marker]		47
TODD, Shephard (Sheppard in records)	15 Nov. 1878 – 15 Sept. 1929	Beloved Brother		91
TOZIER, Orrin Waldo	21 March 1941 Oregon Mach. Mate 3 Cl. U.S. Navy			117
WELLS, Jas.	8 May 1915 Drowned [broken stone]			147
WATSY, Joe	(buried 10 Ap. 1917)	[no marker]		96
WHITTALL, Beulah	5 Apr. 1887 – 3 Jan. 1937			92
WHYBARK, Jessie D. (Baby)	– 1969			180
WILBER, Amelia	(buried 20 Nov. 1951)	[no marker]		18
WILBER, David E.	(records state 1945)	[no marker]		53
WILBER, Harry	1905 – 1978			115
WILBER, J. E. Bud	1920 – 1967			77
WILBUR, John	1948 – 1979 Sp. 4 U.S. Army Vietnam			
WILBUR, Darrell Allen	(buried 5 Aug. 1930)			18
WILBUR, Huston	(buried 1 July 1939)	[no marker]		18
WILBUR, Luscius	12 Aug. 1868 – 18 July 1913 At Rest			18
WILE, Larraine	(buried 7 May 1922)	[no marker[		20
WILKERSON, Elizabeth	1876 – 1936			52
WILKERSON, Infant	[no marker – no dates]			177
WILKERSON, Lewis (Louis in records)	1907 – 1923			52
WILKERSON, Mary	1909 – 1909			
WILKERSON, William	1875 – 1947			52
WITT, Alta M.	1891 – 1978	Mother		
WITT, Nicholas H.	1885 – 1958			187
YORK, Lillie	(buried 24 Jan. 1927)	[no marker]		111

66

Lot No.

YORK, Lloyd Marceau   (buried 6 May 1919) [no marker] 82

YORK, Morris A.   (buried 30 Oct. 1951) [no marker] 111

Page (or Red Rock) Cemetery

Located about two miles from Woodland,
Wash. on the Clark County side of the
Lewis River, on the present Harmon farm.

PAGE (or RED ROCK) CEMETERY

Page Cemetery, which is also known as Red Rock Cemetery, is located about two miles from Woodland, Washington on the Harmon farm. It is on a hillside within a wooded area. The place is overgrown with brush and ivy trails all around. There are several unmarked graves. The first burials were on a level spot which is at the left as you go into the Harmon farm. These were marked with wooden markers which weathered away long ago and names of those buried have long been forgotten. Only the older pioneers recall this burial spot.

The plot containing the grave of Rosa Beck is enclosed with an iron fence and has been kept up. An old fashioned rose bush struggles for existance in the shaded area outside the Beck plot.

PAGE (or RED ROCK) CEMETERY

PAGE   Charles H. Page, 1841 - 1920 (brother of John)

PAGE   John F. Page, April 1, 1898, aged 59 yrs (born Feb. 2, 1839 -
                       brother of Charles)

PAGE   Henry Page, born in Bucksport, Maine, Nov. 1, 1818 - died Oct.
                       21, 1867

PAGE   Mary F. Page, Born in Hope, Maine, Apr. 16, 1816 - Died June 3,
                       1893 (believed to be wife of John Page)

BECK   Rosa E. Beck, Dec. 1871 - Mar. 1945 (dau of John & Margaret
                       (Eaton) Robinson)

-- UNMARKED GRAVES --

BACKMAN   (Clara Elizabeth Backman, born May 17, 1830, Detroit, Michigan,
                       died June 23, 1910 - wife of G. J. F. Backman, Sr. - nee
                       Combs)

BACKMAN   (Emily A. Backman, born May 6, 1859, near Portland, Oregon - died
                       Nov. 23, 1886 - wife of G. J. F. Backman, Jr. who is buried
                       at Hayes Cemetery - nee Miller)

BACKMAN   (George John Fake Backman, Sr., born March 13 or 14, 1819/20 in
                       New York State - died June 14, 1902. His mother's maiden
                       name was Fake.)

BECK   (Edwin Beck, ashes here. The son of Rosa E. Beck)

GARDNER   (Floyd Gardner, born Jan. 5, 1888 - died Oct. 1, 1889, the son of
                       Daniel and Martha (Gilson) Gardner)

ROBINSON   (Margaret Ann Robinson, nee Eaton, wife of John Robinson who is
                       buried at the IOOF Cemetery)

ROBINSON   (James Robinson, Alvin Robinson and Nellie Robinson, children of
                       John and Margaret Robinson are buried in the plot with Rosa
                       Beck which is enclosed with an iron fence)

*****

WOODLAND PIONEER PASSES AWAY

    Charles Henry Page, one of the earliest pioneers of the Woodland district
passed away at his home here Thursday. Mr. Page logged the land where the town
of Woodland is now situated. He was 79 years of age and is survived by his
wife. The funeral was held from the Presbyterian Church at Woodland yesterday
P.M. April 28, 1920.

[The Twice Weekly Kelsonian]

Sunnyside Cemetery

Sunnyside Cemetery is located on S.E. Coffey Road, 5/10 of a mile from the Washougal River Road. It is on a hill overlooking the rolling hills of the Little Washougal River Valley. Land was donated by Frederick and Anna Krohn.

Sunnyside earns name

By BOB BECK
Columbian Staff Writer

The grave of Hampton and Eliza Blackwood, Sunnyside's first settlers, is in the pioneer cemetery. Mrs. Blackwood named Sunnyside.

The Little Washougal River, among Clark County's most beautiful streams, has carved a pleasant and fertile valley between two highland areas.

One side of this gorge is shrouded in the shade of Woodburn Hill. On the other side, the morning sun bathes the slopes in golden light.

That is why, in about 1874, Mrs. Hampton C. Blackwood named the area Sunnyside. It is called that today.

Sunnyside, lying about three miles north of Washougal, is still predominantly a rural area. Dairying remains a major industry, and the gentle slopes are dotted with the black and brown outlines of grazing cows.

The housing explosion that has covered much of the county with subdivisions has not yet had a major impact on Sunnyside. There are new homes, modernistic and expensive, but they are scattered along the higher elevations. The southern slopes of Sunnyside still offer a panorama of uncluttered fields.

The Hamptons and the C.H. Carletons are believed to have been the first homesteaders, building log

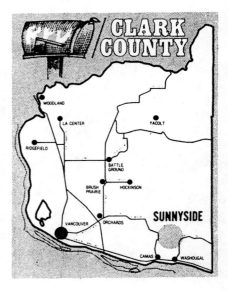

(The **COLUMBIAN**)

Friday, Nov. 24, 1978
Vancouver, Wash.

72

cabins in a dense forest in 1874. Over the years, the tall firs were felled and the stumps grubbed out or burned.

According to Mrs. Russell Morgan, who formerly covered Sunnyside as a correspondent for The Columbian, the pioneer men had wanted to call it the Valley of Jehosaphat, but the women folks talked them out of it.

The Henriksen brothers built a sawmill in 1898, according to Mrs. Morgan. This mill was sold to Ledbetter and Pittock, who had founded the paper mill in Camas.

Clarence Beatty, a Washougal mechanic now in his 80s, was born and grew up in Sunnyside. He said his father had a timber claim, but a major forest fire in 1902 wiped it out. This same fire destroyed the homes of many settlers.

The Beatty family moved south into the main Sunnyside area and cleared 40 acres of farm land.

Beatty said a flume was built from the Henriksen sawmill southwest to Camas, a distance of about eight miles, and sawn timbers were floated down to the Columbia River on it.

"I remember playing on this flume as a boy of 5, on a trestle high above the ground," Beatty said. "Later, when I was older, I was afraid to walk out on it."

Nothing remains of the sawmill or the flume. Most of the pioneer structures have long since vanished.

However, the names of the pioneer families remain memorialized in some of the roads that cross the Sunnyside area.

The pioneer cemetery sits on a knoll overlooking the valley of the Little Washougal and the gravestones, bearing such names as Hampton, Carleton, Ammeter, Sadewasser, Krohn, Johnston, Luthy and Schlegal, present a silent roll call of those who led the way.

Crumbling barn dominates scene near where first homestead in Sunnyside was settled in 1874. (Staff photos by Bob Beck)

73

			Row	Blk	Sp.
AMMETER,	Bertha Stauffer	1878 – 1947 Mother	2	40	2
AMMETER,	Esther C. Godsil	1911 – 19__	1	50	4
AMMETER,	Fred	1861 – 1937 Father	2	40	1
AMMETER,	Fritz	1902 – 1929 Father	2	40	3
AMMETER,	William	1901 – 1944	1	50	4
ANDERSON,	Baby	(no statistics, another baby in alley]	4	27	1
ANDERSON,	Clara C.	11 Mar. 1891 – 9 Sept. 1941	4	27	4
ANDERSON,	Nels C.	6 June 1864 – 10 Nov. 1949	4	27	3
ATTWELL,	Bertha Alice	1868 – 1916 [Wife]	8	15	3
ATTWELL,	James Fremont	1855 – 1947 [Husband]	8	15	4
BARBER,	Florence A. Johnston	Born 28 Sept. 1871. Died 15 June 1894. Born By Angels Hands Away, To Home Of Peace And Love." [Husband Monte Barber]	7	19	2
BARKER,	Amour Liana	1971 – 1971	9 New Section		
BEARD,	Marie Gertrude	1886 – 1914	7	19	1
BEATTY,	Alice M.	1870 – 1937 [Mother]	2	25	2
BEATTY,	Andrew	1861 – 19__ [Father]	2	25	2
BEATTY,	Carrie	[no dates]	7	3	1
BEATTY,	Francis E.	[no dates]	7	3	3
BEATTY,	Mary F.	[no dates]	7	3	2
BEGIER,	James F. Jr.	1949 – 1977 DN U.S. Navy Vietnam	11		
BERTSCHINGER,	_____	[no information available]	5	21	2
BLACKWOOD,	Eliza	1834 – 1916 "At Rest" "His Wife" [Hampton Blackwood]	8	15	2
BLACKWOOD,	Hampton G.	1831 – 1910	8	15	1
BLACKWOOD,	John F.	1859 – 1939	9	16	3

SUNNYSIDE MEMORIAL CEMETERY

Name				Row	Blk.	Space
BLACKWOOD,	Mildred	1895 – 1976		9		
BLACKWOOD,	Raymond	1895 – 1974		9	16	2
BLACKWOOD,	Ursula M.	1876 – 1917		9	16	4
BROSCHEIT,	Anna M.	1846 – 1892	Mother	5	5	2
BROSCHEIT,	Donald	2 Sept. 1920 – 4 Sept 1920		4	6	1
BROSCHEIT,	Ida M.	1878 – 1885	Daughter	5	5	3
BROSCHEIT,	George F.	1834 – 1894	Father	5	5	1
BROSCHEIT,	George W.	1914 – 1930		4	6	2
BROWN,	Alice A.	1866 – 1938		6	4	3
BROWN,	Frank	1854 – 1936		6	4	2
CAMPLING,	Mary E.	1879 – 1961		7	30	4
CARLETON,	Amelia B.	1871 – 1941		8	34	2
CARLETON,	Arthur C.	1873 – 1936	[Brother]	7	35	3
CARLETON,	Chas. "Guy"	1862 – 1927		8	34	1
CARLETON,	Cynthia Tuttle	23 Apr. 1843 – 8 Apr. 1908 Born in Illinois		7	35	2
CARLETON,	Grace A.	1889 – 1976		7	46	4
CARLETON,	G. H.	16 Feb. 1835 – 20 Jan. 1898 Born in New Hampshire		7	35	1
CARLETON,	Henry	1887 – 1955		7	46	3
CARLETON,	Lewis T.	1879 – 1944	At Rest	7	35	4
CARLETON,	Roy	1877 – 1959		9	33	2
CARLETON,	Wm. H.	Born 27, _____ 1860 – Died 2 March 1904		9	33	1
CARLETON,	Sarah	1873 – 1940 [ashes] Beloved Wife of Wm. H. Carleton		9	33	1
CARPENTER,	H. H.	28 July 1840 – 15 Jan 1920		7	46	1
CARPENTER,	Phebe R.	8 July 1864 – 22 Aug. 1921		7	46	2
CARTER,	_____	[no information available]		5	21	4
CATES,	Ison B.	1879 – 1957		6	29	2

		Row	Blk	Space
CATES, Marian A.	14 June 1901 – 29 June 1901	6	29	4
CATES, Mary E.	1880 – 1965	6	29	1
CHRISTENSEN, Christ	11 Feb. 1841 – 6 June 1881	5	28	2
CHRISTENSEN, Maren	13 Jan. 1842 – 13 Oct. 1922	5	28	4
CHRISTENSEN, Martin	19 Feb. 1879 – 19 Aug. 1879	5	28	3
COLE, Ezrah	1875 – 1931 Uncle	7	14	2
COLE, Urena	16 Sept. 1841 – 13 Nov. 1905	6	13	2
COLE, William D.	23 Aug. 1829 – 16 Sept. 1903	6	13	1
COOPER, Opal V.	1917 – 1980	12		
CROW, Mary Theresa	1909 – 1948	1	51	3
CROWDER, Jesus J.	1903 – 1977 "My Jesus Mercy"	10		
CROWSON, Andrew	[Baby – no marker]	7	30	3
CROWSON, Anna H.	27 May 1829 – 8 Jan. 1910 "No pain, no grief, no anxious fear, Can reach our loved ones here"	7	30	2
CROWSON, Emma F. [Stauffer]	1875 – 1970 "In Loving Memory"	8	31	2
CROWSON, Frances L.	1917 – 1981	10		
CROWSON, Harry J.	1910 – 1963 "In Loving Memory"	8	31	3
CROWSON, Jeremiah	14 Apr. 1822 – 13 July 1895	7	30	1
CROWSON, Jerry M.	1869 – 1927	8	31	1
DAHLGREN, Andrew	27 Jan. 1913 – 27 Aug. 1913	3	23	3
DEERY, Danny E.	1960 – 1974	10		
DODDS, Charles R.	1864 – 1943	8	34	3
DODDS, Maude [Carleton]	1881 – 1955	8	34	4
ERICKSON, Emma Barbara	26 Apr. 1926 – 3 Sept. 1926 "Safe In The Arms Of Jesus"	5	44	1
ERICKSON, Henry E.	5 May 1897 – 20 Apr. 1959 Washington F2 U.S. Navy WWI	5	44	3

SUNNYSIDE MEMORIAL CEMETERY

		Row	Blk	Space
ERICKSON, Hulda K. [Krohn] Washington		5	44	4
I Will Lift Up Mine Eyes Unto The Hills. Psalms 121				
GRIMM, Elta Elnora	1902 – 1971	1	52	2
GRIMM, Paul R.	1890 – 1966	1	51	1
GOODWIN, Ivah L.	1866 – 1925	3	10	4
GOODWIN, J. Baxter	1856 – 1927	3	10	3
HARRIS, Cameron O.	1868 – 1937	3	23	2
HARRIS, Katherine	1834 – 1919 Mother	3	26	1
JOHNSON, Pete	[no information available]	5	28	1
JOHNSTON, Alex "Sandy"	6 Jan. 1873 – 8 Dec. 1937	8	18	4
JOHNSTON, Benjamin L. Born 24 June 1843 – Died 22 June 1900		Aisle between 5 & 6, Block 12		
JOHNSTON, Benjamin F.		8	18	3
JOHNSTON, Homer V.	1891 – 1969	10 New Section		
JOHNSTON, James A.	1875 – 1967	8	18	2
JOHNSTON, Mary E.	1848 – 1916	7	19	4
JOHNSTON, W. C. Born 27 July 1840 – Died 23 July 1913 Co. I 3rd Reg't Iowa Vols.		7	19	3
JOHNSTON, William [Harry]	1885 – 1970	10 New Section		
KROHN, Anna B.	1858 – 1936	5	37	2
KROHN, Bonnie A.	1925 – 1978	6		
KROHN, Carl	1902 – 1979 Father	4		
KROHN, Charles E.	1927 – _____	6		
KROHN, Clara M. [Johnson]	1890 – 1973	4	43	4
KROHN, Donna June	1926 – 1934	6	36	4
KROHN, Emilie C. [Amos]	1884 – 1955	5	37	4
KROHN, Emilie Born 1 Sept. 1884, Died 19 Sept 1884. Daughter of Fritz & Anna B. Krohn "Safe In The Arms Of Jesus"		Aisle between row 5 & 6, Blk 36		

				Row	Blk	Space
KROHN,	Esther M.	1907 – 1979	Mother	4		
KROHN,	Fred R.	1886 – 1951		4	43	3
KROHN,	Fredrick	27 Nov. 1844 – 12 Dec. 1911		5	37	1
		At Rest				
KROHN,	Henry	Born 24 Dec. 1880 Died 19 Feb.		Aisle between		
	1881	Son of Fritz & Anna B. Krohn		rows 5 & 6, Blk 37		
KROHN,	Henry T.	[Hank] 1883 – 1944		5	37	3
KROHN,	Julius	[Joe] 1894 – 1950		6	36	3
KROHN,	Otto E.	1888 – 1954	Father	6	45	2
		Veteran of WWI				
KROHN,	Paul J.	1887 – 1958		4	38	4
KROHN,	Rose L.	[Luthy] 1892 – 1928	Mother	6	45	3
KROHN,	Rosina Kay	1958 – 1958		New part of Cemetery		
KROHN,	Shirley [Pawsey]	1924 – 1949	Mother	1	49	3
KROHN,	Theodore G.	3 Nov. 1892 – 26 Oct. 1956		4	38	1
		Washington Cpl. Btry. A 346 Arty. WWI				
KROHN,	Walter G.	1891 – 1955		6	45	4
KROHN,	Willa M.	[Templer) 1893 – 19___		4	38	___
KROHN,	William Carol	1925 – 1925		6	45	1
KLONINGER,	Anna	1869 – 1943	Mother	9	48	2
KLONINGER,	Martha Ford	188_ – 19___		9	48	1
KNAPP,	Mrs [Rachael]	[no dates]		7	14	3
		[Plot bought by Brown]				
KNAPP,	W. H.	[Military Stone, No dates]		7	14	4
		Co. E. 42 No. Ill. Inf.				
KUNZ,	Luise	[no information available]		6	4	1
LOEFFEL,	Helen	13 May 1899 – 2 Jan. 1911		4	11	1
LOEFFELL,	John	1858 – 1919	Father	4	11	3
LOEFFEL,	Marie	1864 – 1929	Mother	4	11	4
LOEFFEL,	Rose M.	1893 – 1918		4	11	2

SUNNYSIDE MEMORIAL CEMETERY

				Row	Blk	Space

LONG, Martha Born 17 Sept. 1849 – Died 27
Mar. 1883. **Aisle between 5 & 6, Blk 13**
He giveth His beloved. Psalms 127
I am the resurrection and the life.
He that believeth in Me though he were
dead yet shall live. John 11:25

Asleep in Jesus, peaceful rest, whose waking is supremely blest.
No tear or woe shall dim the hour that manifests the sources power.
Asleep in Jesus, oh for me, may such a blissful refuge be.
Securely shall my ashes be, and wait the summons from on high.

Name	Dates	Note	Row	Blk	Space
LUTHY, Martha	1863 – 1917	Mother	6	20	2
LUTHY, Fredrick	1858 – 1919	Father	6	20	1
LUTHY, John	1850 – 1910	[Brother of Rosetta Stauffer, no relation to Fredrick Luthy]	4	22	4
McINTOSH, Alexander	Died Apr 1898, age 38 yrs.		5	21	3
MANN, Nola A. [Crowson]	1901 – 1974	Mother	10	New Section	
MERTZ, Laura K. [Schlegel]	1879 – 1937		9	17	3
MERTZ, Magdalene M.	1861 – 1937	Mother	9		
NELSON, Bertha A.	1888 – 1956	Sister	4	22	3
O'CONNER, John C.	1912 – 1923	Our Darling Son of W. & E. O'Conner. Grandson of W. & M. Johnston	8	18	1
PRATT, Baby 11 Sept. 1978		God Bless Our Baby Daughter of Bob & Marvieen Pratt	10		
PRATT, Daniel E.	6 Oct. 1920 – 9 Nov. 1961	Washington Pfc. Trp. E, 12 Cavalry, WWII	10	New Section	
READ, Anna E.	1895 – 1962		3	10	2
READ, George W.	1884 – 1962		3	10	1
RENGO, Hans	1880 – 1918		9	1	1
RICKS, Minnie V. [Soderberg]	1893 – 1956		3	7	2
RICKS, V. A. George	1893 – 1960		3	7	3
SADWASSER, Lon A.	1957 – 1974	Son	2	41	3
SANDERS, Charles L.	1881 – 1953		9	1	3
SANDERS, Mary A.	1881 – 1962		9	1	2

SUNNYSIDE MEMORIAL CEMETERY

		Row	Blk	Space
SAPPINGTON, Eunice C. [Blackwood] 1855 – 1945		5	12	2
SAPPINGTON, William D. 1864 – 1938		5	12	1
SCHLEGEL, Christian 1838 – 1917 Father		9	17	1
SCHLEGEL, Christian A. 1885 – 1975 Father		9		
SCHLEGEL, Evalyn 1925 – _____ His Wife [wife of Fred T.]		11		
SCHLEGEL, Fred T. 1927 – 1979		11		
SCHLEGEL, Otillia K. 1896 – _____ Mother		9		
SCHLEGEL, Ursula 1844 – 1917 Mother		9	17	2
SODERBERG, Will [no stone]		3	7	1
STAUFFER, Adolph Born 8 Dec. 1879 – Died 15 Feb. 1908. Tho' lost to sight – To Memory Dear.		9	32	3
STAUFFER, Fredrick 1877 – 1953		9	32	4
STAUFFER, Jacob J. 1844 – 1923 Father At Rest		9	32	1
STAUFFER, Minnie C. [Nelson] 1896 – 19__		10	New Section	
STAUFFER, Rosetta [Luthy] 1845 – 1928 Mother [No relation to Fredrick Luthy]		9	32	2
STAUFFER, William 1887 – 1974 Father		10	New Section	
SUNDBERG, Emilie B. 1874 – 1940 Mother		3	39	1
SUNDBERG, Gustaphe C. 1865 – 1827 Father		3	39	1
TAYLOR, Don L. 1929 – 1963 Husband & Father		10	New Section	
THAYER, Newell L. 1855 – 1936 Always Faithful		9	New Section	
THRALL, Baby [no marker]		6	13	4
THRALL, G. W. [Baby] [no marker]		7	14	1
THRALL, Russell S. Died 17 Oct. 1889 – Age 27 Yrs. 10 Mo. 3 D. In Loving Remembrance		6	13	3
TISHAUSER, Christian 24 Jan. 1850 – 13 June 1904		5	21	1

SUNNYSIDE MEMORIAL CEMETERY

			Row	Blk	Space
VANSANT, Lucy	1893 – 1941 [Daughter of Alice M. Beatty]		2	25	3
UTEHS, Herman C.	1875 – 1931		8	47	1
WING, Anita Marie	28 Sept. 1960 – 6 Apr. 1981 "God Bless Our Loving Wife, Mother, Daughter"		11		
ZAHUMENSKY, Marie	1889 – 1974	Mother	1	49	2
ZAHUMENSKY, Peter P.	1872 – 1944	Father	1	49	1

Finn Hill Cemetery

Located at 17723 N.E. 192nd Ave., Hockinson, Washington.

****

In the year 1896 John Nelson donated land for these old settlers to form a cemetery, which is known as the "Finn Hill Cemetery." Several charter members of the Apostolic Lutheran Church became charter memberts of the "Finn Hill Cemetery Association. Times have changed. At one of the first meetings it is written how horses were used to make the roads. The plots were sold for one dollar or for working on the cemetery at a salary of $ .40 a day.

As time passed on and death came these old settlers and their children were buried in the cemetery which overlooks John Nelson Road and the Cascades to the east. One of the oldest markers in the cemetery is an old growth cedar slab which has been recently restored. It is written in the Finnish language, "Tasa Lepaa, Finland Heinakuu 24 P V 1827 Kuollu, Hockinson, Wash., Kesakuun 30 P V 1904" which means "Here lies Adolph Kankonen, born Kokkolasa, Finland on July 24th, 1827. Died at Hockinson, Wash. June 30th, 1904." This old cedar slab marks the place where Adolf Kankonen is buried. Several other tombstones are written in the Finnish language: also the old age worn cemetery map written on a large oil cloth.

Now in April, 1969, 50 years since the last meeting of the members of the Cemetery Association, a new organization has been formed and crews have been working to help restore the resting place of their loved ones.

This old cemetery has a very special place in my own heart, as on December 24, 1968 we laid our little brother to rest also among the old pioneer settlers of Hockinson community.

I got my information from a 1934 new clipping found in a scrap book of John Nelson's granddaughter, and also from "The Finn Hill Cemetery - 1896" booklet.

Tim Karlsen

Sixth Grade - 1968-69

["FROM A FOREST CLEARING" - Students Essays]

FINN HILL CEMETERY

The Finn Hill Cemetery was organized Nov. 5, 1896.
Charter members were:

John Lopakka	David Paananen
Peter Kopra	Adolph Mattson
Elias Hill	Manuel Rahaja
John Saukko	Matt Wesa
Charles Salmela	John Pietila
Eli Ahola	Jack Uusimaa
John Jauhola	John Walker
Charles Lassila	John Nelson
Abraham Lehto	Andrew Sakrison
August Johnson	Gabriel Sakrison

President: Adolph Mattson
Secretary: Charles Lassila
Treasurer: John Pietila

It was agreed that each member do his share until the land is cleared and the cemetery was fenced. Lots were divided amongst members. The rest of the lots were sold and the money used for the cemetery improvement. This land shall always be used as a cemetery and never be sold or used otherwise.

December 14, 1897, the same officers were re-elected. It was agreed lots shall be 7 feet east to west, 21 feet 3 inches, north and south. The lots are numbered starting at the east end. It was agreed lots be sold, $1.00 each, or a days work at 40 cents.

January 2, 1899, nine lots had been sold.

January 2, 1902, recommendation that a road be built.

January 2, 1905, the road was finished, land being donated by John Nelson.

Feb. 11, 1919, planned to fix road with horses.

In 1960 it is recorded that the cemetery had a major clean-up crew consisting of these persons:

Bill Nelson	Rudy Hill
George Sakrison	Bill Rapakko
Kenny Jerrow	Ben Rapakko
Ed Cook	John Pietila
David Gustafson	Eric Lucas
Fred Lucas	Zackary Sakrison
Fred Adams	

[The above information is taken from the records. In February 1987 the cemetery is well kept. There are several old stones broken with inscriptions in Finnish which are now impossible to read.]

84

FINN HILL CEMETERY

88		ANNIS	James R. Annis, 4 Feb. 1955 - 14 Nov. 1971, "Jim" (shot while hunting-carved deer on stone)
89 & 90		CARLSON	(Baby Son Carlson)
71 & 72		COOK	Elizabeth Cook, Nov. 25, 1894 - Oct. 5, 1900
53		ESTENBERG	J. P. Estenberg (no marker)
24		FORSHAUG	Cornelius Forshaug
24		FORSHAUG	Edith Pearl Forshaug, 1888 - 1975
17 & 19		GILLAS	(Baby Gillas)
		GORDON	Fred Gordon, 1901 - 1979 (double stone with Borghild)
		GORDON	Borghild Gordon, 1912 - 1984
45 & 46		GUSTAFSON	Greta Gustafson, ___ - 1906 (Kreta Lisa Gustafson, d. 31 Dec. 1906 age 63 years, Vancouver Funeral Chapel marker)
45 & 46		GUSTAFSON	Lizzie Gustafson (d. 1897, Mrs. Lizzie, died age 25 years)
45 & 46		GUSTAFSON	Joseph Gustafson (d. 18 Feb. 1905, aged 20 years)
86		HANNUS	(Baby Girl Hannus d. Nov. 1914, Vancouver Funeral Chapel Marker)
26	#2	HANSON	Terry Hanson, Oct. 20, 1955 - Feb. 5, 1980, "We Love Thee Well", Husband & Father","Our Jesus Loves Thee Best" (d. Feb. 1980, age 23 years of flu)
72		HENDRICKSON	Vaino Hendrickson
35 & 36		HILL	Anna Therisia Hill, 2 Aug. 1899 - 14 Nov. 1899
65 & 66		HILL	Eugene Peter Hill (d. 17 Oct. 1916 age 1 month)
65 & 66		HILL	John Henry Hill
1 & 2		JAUHOLA	Ero Malias Jauhola (d. 28 Sept. 1911 age 2 months)
1 & 2		JAUHOLA	Eugenia Jauhola, ___ - ___ (baby, Layne's Funeral Home)

1 & 2		JAUHOLA	Sylvester Jauhola, 1900 - 1906 (d. 29 Aug. 1906, age 6 years, Layne's Funeral Home marker)
1 & 2		JAUHOLA	Vaino Jauhola, 1902 - 1906 (d. 27 July 1906 age 4 years, Layne's Funeral Home marker)
54		JERIJARVI	Olaf Jerijarvi (b. 1840 - d. 19 June 1904, died age 63 years - marker is broken)
33 & 34		JOHNSON	August Johnson, 1846 - 1935 (d.27 July 1935 of natural death - father of Mrs. Eli Hill)
29 & 30		JOHNSON	Esther Johnson, 1896 - 1927 (d. 13 Nov. 1927 age 31 years)
33 & 34		JOHNSON	Esther Johnson (another record gives this information d. 13 Nov. 1927 age 3 years...age incorrect but lot numbers may be correct here)
33 & 34		JOHNSON	Lizzie Johnson, ____ - 1897 (d. 1897, Mrs., Vancouver Funeral Chapel marker)
33 & 34		JOHNSON	Maria S. Johnson, 1842 - 1912, Mother (Maria Susanna, new stone, old stone reads 'Tassa Hepan')
37 & 38		JUOLA	Emanuel Juola, Syntyi Maalisk, 1839 (age 72)
37 & 38		JUOLA	Mary Juola (d. 28 Dec. 1934 age 86 years)
56	#3	KAISER	Ethel Kaiser, 1916 - ____, Mother, "I Have Finished The Work Thou Gaveth Me To Do"
56	#4	KAISER	John Kaiser, 1917 - 1978, Father, "I Have Finished The Work Thou Gaveth Me To Do" (d. 4 June 1978 of cancer)
83	#2	KAISER	Kenton John Kaiser, May 27, 1966 - Aug. 11, 1977, "Jesus Loves Me", "Our Much Loved" (drowned)
45 & 46		KANKKONEN	Adolph Kankkonen, b. 24 July 1827, Kokkola, Finland d. 30 June 1904, Hockinson, Washington "Tasa Lepa, Adolf Kankkonen, Syntyny Kokkola, Finland Heinaku 24 P V 1827 Kuolli, Hockinson, Wash. Kesakuun 30 P V 1904" (This is a wooden, hand carved marker)
45 & 46		KANKKONEN	John Kankkonen, ____ - 1899 (Layne's Funeral Home marker)
45 & 46		KANKKONEN	Maria Kankkonen (d. 1891 age 14 years)

86

68   KARLSEN   Einar Karlsen, 1900 - 1979 (b. 30 Dec. 1900 - d. 4 Nov. 1980)

TETNUS VICTIM DIES OF COMPLICATIONS

An elderly Vancouver man, believed to have had the first case of tetanus in Clark County since 1961, has died from complica- of the disease, Dr. Stan Friedberg said today.

Einar Karlsen, 79, died Tuesday in St. Joseph Community Hosppital, where he had been in intensive care for about four weeks.

An autopsy was performed on Karlsen's body but the results are not yet available.

Karlsen, 8100 N. E. 162nd Ave., a retired dairy farmer and coal miner, reportedly was working on a barn at his farm in early October when he got a splinter. The deep splinter may have carried the spores of the tetanus bacteria, Friedberg said in an interview last month. Freidberg was Karlsen's physician.

Karlsen had seen the doctor complaining of stiff muscles, especially in the neck and jaws. He was admitted to St. Joseph two days later. His condition became critical during his stay and his breathing was aided by a respirator.

The incidence of tetanus is highest among persons 60 and older, but it still is contracted by only one in 1 million persons, a state health official said."

*****

KARLSEN   Elina I. Karlsen, 1905 - ____

KARLSEN   Jacob Allen Karlsen (d. 1972, stillborn)

70   KARLSEN   Joel Clayton Karlsen, Sept. 2, 1968 - Dec. 20, 1968, Our Darling (crib death)

118   #2   KARLSEN   Robert Karlsen, 7 June 1938 - 27 Sept 1969, Wash. SP 4 U.S. Army (died in highway accident)

KIVI   Jenny Kivi, 1893 - 1915 (died possible child-birth, Vancouver Funeral Chapel marker)

55   #2   KOPRA   Anna Kopra, 1866 - 1943, Mother (d. 22 Aug. 1943, Limbers 77 years, died of stroke)

55   #4   KOPRA   Emelia Kopra, (d. 11 Mar. 1896)

55   KOPRA   Emilja W. Kopra, 1895 - 1897 (Vancouver Funeral Chapel marker)

| 55 | #1 | KOPRA | Hilma K. Kopra, 1900 - 1904 (records give d. date as 1905, died in epidemic. of diptheria or smallpox?, Vancouver Funeral Chapel marker) |

| 84 | #1 | KOPRA | Nestor Kopra, 1898 - 1958 (records spelled Nester, heart attack, Evergreen Funeral Home marker) |

| 55 | #3 | KOPRA | Peter Kopra, 1864 - 1914, Father (record gives: b. 1864 - d. 21 Feb. 1951, age 64 years, Minister of the Apostolic Lutheran Church) |

| 72 | | LARSON | Fannie Larson, 1903 (d. Sept. 1903, Infant, Vancouver Funeral Chapel marker) |

| 4 | #3 | LEHTO | Andrew Lehto, 1888 - 1962 (d. 21 June 1962, Layne's Funeral Home marker, spelled Lechto) |

| 3 | #2 | LEHTO | Charles Lehto, 1886 - 1952 (d. 20 Oct. 1952, age 66 years 6 mons 2 days (killed in a tractor accident, Layne's Funeral Home marker) |

| 4 | #4 | LEHTO | Elda Maria Lehto, 1889 - 1956 (d. age 67 years, Evergreen Funeral Home marker) |

| 3 | #4 | LEHTO | Johanna Lehto, 1851 - 1928 (d. 10 Dec. 1928, age 77 years, Layne's Funeral Home marker) |

| 2 | #1 | LEHTO | John Lehto, 1884 - 1953 (d. 25 May 1953, age 69 years, died of a stroke, Layne's Funeral Home marker) |

| 3 | #4 | LEHTO | John Abraham Lehto (d. 4 Feb. 1910, age 61 years) |

| 9 | | MARSYLA | Toiva Marsyla, 23 Sept. 1908 - 24 Aug. 1910 Syntyny - Huollu, Tassa Lepaa (Here Lies) |

| 69 | #2 | MATTILA | Infant Boy Mattila, 1977 - 1977 (d. 19 July 1977 stillborn, Layne's Funeral Home marker) |

| 29 | #4 | MATTSON | Maria Mattson, Aug. - Oct. 1901 (b. 2 Aug. 1901 - d. 6 Oct. 1901, age 2 months, Layne's Funeral Home marker) |

| 65 | #4 | MOILANEN | Joseph Moilanen, d. 1928 (a single man - owned a prune orchard and dryer, Vancouver Funeral Home marker) |

| 41 | #1 | NELSON | Bernie M. Nelson, 1911 - 1919, At Rest (d. 30 Aug. 1919, burned in a sauna, Birnie Miriam Nelson) |

88

| 42 | #1 | NELSON | D. Helen Nelson, 1925 - 1933 (d. 13 Dec. 1933, age 8 years, died of Bright's Disease, Dora Helen Nelson) |

41 #3 NELSON Johanna Nelson, 1860 - 1930, Mother (Johanna Mattson Nelson, d. 15 Oct. 1930, age 69 years maiden name Johanna Kankkonen of pioneer Hockinson family. Known as an excellent midwife. Died of stroke)

41 #2 NELSON John Nelson, 1852 - 1918, Father (d. 13 Feb. 1918, born in Finland. John Nelson Road (now 174th St.) named for him. One of the pioneers who helped build the first Apostolic Lutheran Church in 1878. He married Johanna Kankkonen 1881. They had a son, Albert, born 1888. They were loggers and between times fishermen at Astoria, Oregon.)

59 #2 PIETILA Alven R. Pietila, 1910 - 1910 (child, Alvin)

59 #3 PIETILA Andrew Pietila (d. 1908, baby)

59 #2 PIETILA Antti A. Pietila, 1908 - 1908

59 #4 PIETILA Anna C. Pietila, 1911 - 1912 (age 2 years)

PIETILA Elizabeth Pietila, 1903 - 1903

PIETILA Henry Pietila, 1902 - 1902

60 #4 PIETILA John Pietila, 1861 - 1923, Father (d. 3 Oct. 1923 age 62 years)

60 #3 PIETILA Maria L. Pietila, 1869 - 1947, Mother

59 #1 PIETILA Nennie M. Pietila, 1891 - 1901 (record gives name as Nannie)

5 #2 PORKKA Hilda Porkka, ___ - ___ (daughter, Vancouver Funeral Home marker)

5 #4 PORKKA Milka S. Porkka, 1/29 1904 - 6/8 1907 (Milka Sandra Porkka, 29 Jan. 1904 - 8 June 1907)

5 #3 PORKKA Samuel Porkka, 1919 (d. 5 June 1919 age 67 years, died in a flu epidemic. He was a pioneer that homesteaded with John Nelson, Vancouver Funeral Chapel marker)

89

69	#1	PROUTY	Pearl Prouty, 1889 - 1974 (record: d. 6 Nov. 1975)
7	#3	RAHAJA	Emanuel Rahaja
19	#2	RAPAKKO	Charles Rapakko, (d. 14 June 1917 age 23 years, killed in a logging accident)
20		RAPAKKO	Hilma E. Rapakko, 1868 - 1937 (Hilma Eliza Rapakko, b. 1868 - d. 17 Aug. 1937 age 69 yrs-Vancouver Funeral Chapel marker)
19	#3	RAPAKKO	Onni August Rapakko, 1907 - 1912 (d. 5 Jan. 1912 age 4 years, Vancouver Funeral Chapel marker)
20		RAPAKKO	Peter O. Rapakko, 1870 - 1927 (Vancouver Funeral Chapel marker)
19	#4	RAPAKKO	Selina Rapakko, 1903 (record gives: d. 12 Feb. 1908 age 2 days, Vancouver Funeral Chapel marker)
76		RAUTIO	Sivert Rautio
76		RAUTIO	Gunilla Rautio
76		RAUTIO	(Daughter) Rautio
119	#4	RHOADES	Gerald Rhoades, Sept. 24, 1943 - Oct. 9, 1971, Washington SP5 U.S. Army, Vietnam (d. 14 Oct. 1971, Washington SP 5 USA, Vietnam (killed in an automobile accident)
117	#1	ROSENLUND	Helmi H. Rosenlund, 1895 - 1972, 'Auntie'
		SALMELA	Charles L. Salmela, 1889 - 1890 (Vancouver Funeral Chapel marker)
37	#2	SAKRISON	Mrs. Andrew Sakrison (d. 14 July 1915)
37	#1	SAKRISON	Andrew Sakrison (d. 14 July 1915 age 60 years)
		SAKRISON	Gabriel Sakrison, 1852 - 1917 (Vancouver Funeral Chapel marker)
39	#4	SAKRISON	Gabriel Sakrison, 1921 (d. 26 Apr. 1921 age 60 years)
39	#3	SAKRISON	Kaisa Sakrison, 1862 - 1919 (Vancouver Funeral Chapel marker)
38	#2	SAKRISON	Linea Sakrison, 1898 - 1900 (Vancouver Funeral Chapel marker)

FINN HILL CEMETERY

38	SAKRISON	Matilda Sakrison, 1889 - 1889 (b. 1888 - d. 1889 age 1 year, Vancouver Funeral Chapel marker)
38	SAKRISON	Waino Sakrison, 1897 - 1900 (Vancouver Funeral Chapel marker)
	SAUKKO	John Saukko, 11 May 1850 - 8 Mar. 1906
74	STENERSEN	Loren D. Stenersen, 1952 - 1972, "L. D. S.", "Latter Day Saint" (July 1972 electrocuted by power line accident)
	STENERSEN	Kara Meisha Stenersen, 1983 (Layne's Funeral Home marker)
	TALVITIE	Albert Talvitie, 1906 - 1906 (baby, Vancouver Funeral Chapel marker)
87	TALVITIE	Oscar A. Talvitie, 1912 - 1969 (b. 1912 - d. 26 Apr. 1969, died in a tractor accident. Was Clark Co. Road Dept. equipment operator for several years, Vancouver Funeral Chapel marker)
	TANDESKE	Donny Tandeske, 1906 - 1984, "Together Forever"
	TANDESKE	Vincent Tandeske, 1898 - 1985, "Together Forever"
51 & 52	TOMBERG	John Tomberg (died age 40 years)
	WOLF	William F. Wolf, 1900 - 1982
7 & 8	ZINK	Fanny Zink, 1884 - 1911 (d. 1912 in records, Vancouver Funeral Chapel marker)
23	UNKNOWN	(Unknown man... said to be a transient)

CEMETERY VANDALS

About 10 headstones were pushed down in the Finn Hill Cemetery in Venersborg sometime Wednesday nigh, a nieghbor reported. The person who reported the damage to the cemetery, at 17723 N.E. 192nd Ave., said that it did not look as if a vehicle was used to knock down the stones, according to a sheriff's office report.
[News item March 11, 1984]

91

Sifton Cemetery

Sifton Cemetery is located south of
76th Street and west of 128th Avenue,
at the end of a private alley. It was
established in 1863 on land donated
from the Bird Donation Land Claim.
Charles Bird was one of the areas
first settlers in 1846.

B 4	44	10	AIKEN	William Aiken, Born in Aberdeen, Scotland Jan. 1, 1848 - Died at Hockinson, Wash. Dec. 16, 1902, Aged 54 yrs 11 ms 16 ds, "In Loving Remembrance of", "I Have Anchored My Soul In A Haven Of Rest"
B 4	44	11	AIKEN	(Margaret Aiken, probably the wooden marker under a holly tree - Sept. 1987 marker is no longer there)
A 11		6	ALGAR	Rosa A. Algar, Born May 22, 1862 - Feb. 20, 1899, "None Knew Thee But To Love Thee" (stone broken)
B 14	164	8	ALLEN	Mary C. Allen, 1871 - 1945, "Mother"
B 11	128	10	AMES	Arthur A. Ames (Vancouver Funeral Home marker, unreadable)
B 18		1	ANDERSEN	John Andersen, 1866 - 1950 (s/s with Helen Andersen)
B 18	208	1	ANDERSEN	Helen Andersen, 1874 - 1918 (died Nov. 30, 1918, s/s with John Anderson)
B 14	162	6	ANDERSON	Emil J. Anderson, 1898 - 1945 (s/s with Georgia A. Anderson)
B 14		6	ANDERSON	Georgia A. Anderson, 1905 - 1978 (s/s with Emil J. Anderson)
B 18	208		ANDERSON	Charles Anderson, Died 1963 (14 Feb. 1963)
Alley of 9		14	ARMSTRONG	Leroy A. Armstrong, 1862 - 1947 (Vancouver Funeral Homer marker)
B 1	4	1	ARMSTRONG	George F. Armstrong, 1839 - 1929, G.A.R. marker
B 11		11	ARMSTRONG	Mary Armstrong, 1851 - 1939 (Stoller Funeral Home marker, not located Sept. 1987)
B 1	4	2	ARMSTRONG	Orpha C. Armstrong, 1832 - 1923, "Wife of George F. Armstrong"
B 6	64	3	ATTRIDGE	John J. Attridge, 1857 - 1912, "Father" (died 26 Aug. 1912)
B 16	192	9	BAKER	Elmer Baker, 1870 - 1950
B 7	74		BAKER	(George Baker, d. Sept. 1927, G.A.R.)

				BAKER	George Washington Baker, Cpl., Co K, 7 MO Cav, Civil War, 1834 – 1928 (same as George Baker above?)
B	7	74		BAKER	Susan Baker, 1835 – 1910, "Wife and Great Grand-mother"
A	3	4		BARNES	Cevilla J. Barnes, 1861 – 1919
B	2	24	7	BARTLES	Elsie Paynter Bartles, 1894 – 1957 (d. Nov. 1957, see also Elsie Paynter, Vancouver Funeral Chapel marker – not located Sept. 1987)
B	2	--		BARTLES	(Minnie [Day] Bartles, no information)
B	12		1	BECKET	John M. Becket, Co. A. 2 Ill. L.A. (Military stone)
B	12	133		BECKET	(J. Becket, d. Feb. 28, 1913)
B	12	133		BECKET	(Mrs. J. Becket, no further information)
				BENNETT	Elizabeth Bennett, ____ – 1911 (Mrs. Elisabeth Bennett, d. 1911, Vancouver Funeral Home marker)
B	7	76		BERTH	Florence S. Berth, 1873 – 1945 (Mrs. Florence S. Berth, d. 1945, Vancouver Funeral Chapel marker)
A	3	3		BIRD	Alice M. Bird, Born in Washington May 21, 1861, Died Apr. 3, 1866 (same mounument as Carrie J., Edgar and Edna)
A	3	3		BIRD	Carrie J. Bird, Born in Washington Dec. 25, 1872 Died Oct. 3, 1893 (same monument as Alice M., Edgar and Edna)
A	3	3		BIRD	Edgar Bird, 1880 – 1917 (E. G. Bird, same monu-ment as Alice M., Carrie J. and Edna)
A	11	15		BIRD	Edna D. Bird, Born Dec. 17, 1895 – Died Mar. 8, 1898, Daughter of Henry & Ida L. Bird, "Rest little one, A mother's tears may fall, But not for worlds would she her child recall" "At Rest"
A	3	3		BIRD	Gertrude Bird (no further info.)
A	3	3		BIRD	Henry C. Bird, 1859 – 1908 (Henry G. Bird)

A 3		3	BIRD	John Bird, Born in Manitoba Jan. 15, 1829 — Died Feb. 18, 1885
A 3		3	BIRD	Letitia M. Bird, Born in Washington Dec. 12, 1870 Died Dec. 2, 1892
A 3		3	BIRD	Mary A. Bird, 1838 — 1920
A 3		3	BIRD	Mary E. Bird, Born in Washington Dec. 12, 1870 — Died Feb. 22, 1895
B 21	252		BLOOM	(Mrs. C. Bloom, d. Apr. 18, 1903, marked "moved" in record)
A 9		5	BOLEN	F. E. Bolen, 1897 — 1908 (Evergreen Funeral Home marker)
B 19	219		BOSLEY	(P. J. Bosley, died 31 Aug. 1915)
A 3		2	BOWMAN	Madora Bowman, Died 20 May 1902, Wife of M. H. Bowman, Aged 69 yrs 4 mo 28 dys
B 2	19		BREED	Antice C. Breed, Died Oct. 9, 1911, aged 68 years (wife of John Breed, Antice E.)
B 1	7		BREED	Fred A. Breed, Died 12 June 1919, aged 49 years
B 2	19		BREED	John W. Breed, Sergt., Co. G., 8th Ill Cav.
B 17	204	2	BROWN	Ernest R. Brown, 1909 — 1933, Brother
B 9	98		BROWN	(George F. Brown Children)
B 4	48	13	BROWN	James T. Brown, 1836 — 1915, "At Rest" (d. 23 Apr. 1915, with Sophie Brown)
B 4	48		BROWN	Sophie Brown, died 1922 (Vancouver Funeral Chapel marker, with James T. Brown)
			BROWN	(Sophie Brown, died Apr. 3, 1969)
B 16	185	3	BRYAN	Hester Bryan, Born Jan. 5, 1857 — Died Oct. 23, 1917, "We Will Meet Again" (s/s James C. Bryan)
B 16	185	3	BRYAN	James C. Bryan, Dec. 23, 1853 — Dec. 20, 1931 "We Will Meet Again" (s/s Hester Bryan)

B 17	198	1		BRYAN	Robert W. Bryan, 1884 – 1969, "Daddy" "In Thee Have I Put My Trust" (died Apr. 3, 1969, Layne's Funeral Home marker)
A 8		11		BULLOCK	Marjorie A. Bullock, 1914 – 1915
B 18	210	3		BURLINGAME	Charles R. Burlingame, 1852 – 1920
B 18	209	2		BURLINGAME	George D. Burlingame, 1888 – 1929
B 16	184			BURLINGAME	(Frank Burlingame, d. Oct. 19, 1924)
B 16	184			BURLINGAME	Nellie Irene Burlingame, 1883 – 1907 (d. Sept. 10, 1917)
B 3	32	7		BURNETT	Son – 1911 Daughter – 1913, of J. Burnett (3 babies of J. Burnett)
B 5	50	1		BURNETT	Ardith Burnett, Babies, 1930 (w/Mae Burnett)
				BURNETT	(Claud Burnett, d. June 4, 1920)
B 6	71	8		BURNETT	Claude F. Burnett, 1900 – 1956
B 6	63	2		BURNETT	George F. Burnett, 1839 – 1920 (d. Apr. 4, 1920, s/s Sarah Burnett)
B 5	51	2		BURNETT	Joseph T. Burnett, 1868 – 1926 (Joe Burnett, s/s Theolinda Burnett)
B 5	50	1		BURNETT	Mae Burnett, Babies, 1916 (w/Ardith Burnett, d. Dec. 30, 1916)
B 6	71	8		BURNETT	Paul Burnett, Baby, 1931 (s/s Claude F. Burnett)
B 6	63	2		BURNETT	Sarah Burnett, 1840 – 1928, His Wife (wife of George)
B 5	51	2		BURNETT	Theolinda K. Burnett, 1876 – 1903, His Wife (Mrs. Linda Burnett, died June 24, 1903, with Joseph T. Burnett)
B 4	45	12		BURRIS	William R. M. Burris, Born Jan. 21, 1840 – Died Jan. 28, 1906 (W. R. M. Burris)
In road				BUTLER	Edward Butler (Originally in roadway – now disappeared)
B 3	14 (in alley)			CAIN	Adell Cain, Apr. 14, 1840 – Apr. 24, 1924, "Mother", "In Loving Memory"

B	3	30	12	CAIN	Bessie Cain, July 14, 1876 - Aug. 14, 1900

B 3 36 13   CAIN   E. Cain, 1836 - 1914, "At Rest",
"Call not back the dear departed
Anchored safe where storms are oe'r
On the border land we left him
Soon to meet and part no more
When we leave this world of changes
When we leave this world of care
We shall find our missing loved one
In our Father's mansion fair."

B 3 34   CAIN   William H. Cain, Co. E. III, Pa. Inf.

A 2 6   CALDER   Charles Edward son of E. & M. E. Calder, Born
Nov. 30, 1873 - Died Dec. 30, 1885
"A precious one from us is gone
A voice we love is tilled
A place is vacant in our hearts
Which never can be filled"

A 2 7   CALDER   Edward Calder, Died Jan. ___ , age 33 years 8 m's
"Farewell", "A Native of Vancouver"
(Merges & Vasper of Portland stone...stone
is broken in several pieces and 1 piece is
missing.)

A 2 5   CALDER   Flora Belle, Daughter of E. & M. E. Calder, Born
July 26, 1871 - Died Sept. 29, 1880
"Though her lifeless form lies here
Her spirit lives above
And sees with vision bright and clear
The God of life and love."
(stone is broken - Sept. 1987 stone has
disappeared)

B 11 126   CAMPBELL   (Campbell Baby)

B 6 4   CAMPBELL   Charles C. Campbell, Born July 23, 1850 - Died
July 9, 1887, "Precious in the sight of
of the Lord is death the of His saints"

B 6 5   CAMPBELL   James C. Campbell, Born Nov. 21, 1856 - Died
Sept. 30, 1891, "Blessed are the pure in
heart, For they shall see God"

B 4 3   CAMPBELL   John Campbell, Born Feb. 15, 1811 - Died
Apr. 8, 1872, "Blessed are the dead that
die in the Lord"   (John G. Campbell)

B 6   3   CAMPBELL Rollin E. Campbell, Died 26 Sept. 1884, aged 8
                     yrs 9 mo 22 days, "Gone but not forgotten"
                     "Suffer little children that come unto me"

B 11 125   CAMPBELL Sarah E. Campbell, Born june 2, 1848 – Died Apr.
                     26, 1913, "Gone but not forgotten" (Mrs.
                     William Campbell)

B 11 125   CAMPBELL William B. Campbell, Born May 12, 1841 – Died
                     Apr. 3, 1904, "Precious in the sight of the
                     Lord/Is the death of his saints"

B 13 147   CARRIER   (Nathan A. Carrier, died Jan. 29, 1916)

A 11   1   CARRIGAN Edna Carrigan, Feb. 21 – Aug. 30, 1892, "At Rest"
                     "Her Daughter" (s/s Mary E. her mother)

A 11   1   CARRIGAN Mary E. Carrigan, Wife of E. L. Carrigan, 1853 –
                     1911 (s/s Edna Carrigan)

            CHANDLER Arthur E. Chandler, Aug. 1, 1893 – Dec. 13, 1986
                     (from obit – The Columbian: Arthur Edward
                     Chandler, age 93. Born Aug. 1, 1893, Mount
                     Pleasant, died Dec. 13, 1986, Portland, Ore.
                     formerly of Vancouver. Preceded in death by
                     his wife, Grace on Dec. 3, 1986. Sons:
                     Herbert Chandler, Cascade Locks, OR; John
                     Chandler, Milwaukie, OR. Daughter: Lenora
                     Weddle, Vancouver. Sister: Vera Cox,
                     Sebastpo, CA. Funeral Tuesday, Dec. 16
                     at Vancouver Funeral Chapel. Burial Sifton
                     Cemetery.)

            CHANDLER Grace M. Chandler, Dec. 17, 1898 – Dec. 3, 1986
                     (from obit – The Columbian: Grace Mary
                     Chandler, age 87, born Dec. 17, 1898, Amery,
                     Wisc. Died Dec. 3, 1986 in Gresham, OR
                     nursing home. Res: Portland, OR. Widower:
                     Arthur, at home. Sons: Herbert, Cascade
                     Locks, OR; John of Milwaukie, OR. Daughter:
                     Lenora Weddle of Vancouver. Brother: Leon-
                     ard Smith, Vancouver. Sisters: Mabel Koyle,
                     Vancouver; Elva Radford of Brush Prairie.
                     Funeral Sat., Dec. 6, at Vancouver Funeral
                     Chapel. Burial in Sifton Cemetery.)

B 2   30   CLAVER   (Charles Claver, no further info.)

B 2   30   CLAVER   (Mrs. Charles Claver, d. Aug. 1902)

            CLAVER   Frelove T. Claver, 1833 – 1918, Mother

		CLAVER	Joshua P. Claver, 1823 – 1902, Father
B	2/3 29 4	CLAVER	Margaret Claver, 1867 – 1911, Wife of Charles Claver, "At Rest"
B	12 134 2	CLAYTOR	William W. Claytor, Co H, 92nd Ill Inf. (July 1904)
B	11 122	CLIQUE	Elizabeth J. Clique, 1846 – 1913
	11 122	CLIQUE	William E. Clique, 1837 – Mar. 10, 1910
B	11 129 11	COBIA	Marguerite M. Cobia, 1922 – 1937, Daughter
B	14/4 158 3	CRAWFORD	Florence C. Crawford, 1860 – 1938
B	14 158	CRAWFORD	Harold Berve Crawford, 1901 – 1917 (Harold Berrie)
B	14/4 159 4	CRAWFORD	Robert T. Crawford, Co. G., 4 Pa Cav.
B	10 118 9	CUMMINGS	Ota E. Cummings, 1883 – 1935, "Beloved Wife and Mother"
B	10 118 10	CUMMINGS	William E. Cummings, Apr. 7, 1871 – May 12, 1949
B	12 3	CUMMONS	Charles D. Cummons, 1861 – 1933, "Husband"
B	12 2	CUMMONS	Nancy M. Cummons, Rev., 1866 – 1946
B	12 10	CUMMONS	Wylie P. Cummons, June 19, 1894 – Oct. 23, 1962
B	12 135 3	DEAN	James H. Dean, 1830 – 1908 (Deen)
B	14 166 11	DENNIS	Amanda Rosalia Dennis, 1864 – 1957 (Mar. 20, 1957, s/s Stephen Dennis)
B	14 166 12	DENNIS	David Elmer Dennis, Born June 18, 1892 – Died Sept. 15, 1904 "Safe In The Arms Of Jesus, Safe On His Gentile Breast"...etc. (Elmer Dennis)
B	14 165 10	DENNIS	Marion Evangeline Dennis, 1895 – 1958
B	14 167 11	DENNIS	Stephen Douglas Dennis, 1861 – 1931 (s/s Amanda Dennis)
		DOPP	(see Hattie Williams)

B 15	172	3	DOWNS	Ella Downs, 1887 – 1905 (Aug. 1, 1905)
B 15	172	3	DOWNS	Baby Jack Downs, 1913
B 15	173	3	DOWNS	Laura Belle Downs, 1860 – 1932 (Oct. 1932)
B 15	173	3	DOWNS	Laura Belle Downs, 1885 – 1956 (July 1956)
B 15	172		DOWNS	Margaret Downs, 1881 – 1906 (Maggie)
B 18	217	5	DRUM	Eben H. Drum, 1872 – 1942, "Father" (s/s Nellie M. Drum)
B 18	218	6	DRUM	Mark Homer Drum, Died 1937 (0 yrs 3 mos 29 days Baby, Knapp Funeral Home marker)
			DRUM	Nellie M. Drum, 1884 – 19__ , "Mother"
			DRUM	Viola E. Drum, Feb. 11, 1924 – Mar. 18, 1986 "Beloved IV"
B 19	201		DUNKLE	(Mrs. Dunkle, d. Nov. 11, 1916)
B 11	121	1	ELLIOTT	Margaret E. Elliott, 1856 – 1916, "Wife Of Thomas W. Elliott (Margaret Ellen, d. Mar. 2, 1916)
B 11	121	1	ELLIOTT	Thomas W. Elliott, 1858 – 1939
B 20	231		EVANS	(Rostram Mark Evans, no further info.)
B 10	120	15	EWING	Cora Ellen Ewing, 1866 – 1936, "Mother"
B 11	126	7	FIKE	Mary Lavina Fike, 1879 – 1938
B 2	21		FINSTED	(George Finsted, Feb. 12, 1915)
A			FLEMING	N. A. Fleming, Born Dec. 2, 1881 – Died Jan. 2, 1889, "Beneath this sod lies this form That to us dear and lovely" (part of this stone now buried)
			FLEMING	Sarah E., Wife of Henry D. Fleming, Born Aug. 7 1852 – Died Dec. 25, 1889, "In God We Trust"
A 3		1	FREEBERG	Charles O. Freeberg, Born June 28, 1874 – Died May 3, 1901 "A precious one from us is gone A voice we loved is stilled A place is vacant in our home Which never can be filled"

A 3		1	FREEBERG	Christina Freeberg, Born in Sweden, Dec. 25, 1836 Died Mar. 13, 1899
B 19	230		FRENCH	Ida French, 1965 (Vancouver Funeral Chapel marker)
B 19	230		FRENCH	Lionel French, 1938 (Vancouver Funeral Chapel marker)
B 13	146		FRICE	(Bert Frice, 16 Feb. 1916)
B 13	146		FRICE	(John Frice, Apr. 1909)
B 10	114	6	FRITSCH	Jacob Fritsch, 1862 – 1926 (b. 1869?)
B 10	114	6	FRITSCH	Nora Fritsch, 1870 – 1922, Wife of Jacob Fritsch (d. Oct. 8, 1922)
B 16	193	10	GARRIGUS	Caroline Reynolds Garrigus, 1853 – 1931
B 9	102	8	GESSNER	Charles Gessner, 1857 – 1929
B 7		5	GILLETT	Albert G. Gillett, 1862 – 1928, "At Rest"
B 7	83	9	GLASSNER	John W. Glassner, Jan. 9, 1849 – Feb. 17, 1925
B 4	39	1	GOODWIN	Ada A. Goodwin, 1869 – 1944
B 2	28		GOODWIN	B. Goodwin's 3 Children (Baxter Goodwin, Vancouver Funeral Chapel marker)
B 4	38	2	GOODWIN	Lester Goodwin, 1853 – 1932 (Taylor Goodwin)
B 6	61		GOSSETT	Elizabeth Gossett, 1898 (died Mar. 11, 1898, Vancouver Funeral Chapel marker)
B 6	61		GOSSETT	George Gossett, 1910 (died June 16, 1910, Vancouver Funeral Chapel marker)
B 6	62		GOSSETT	W. Gossett (no further information, Vancouver Funeral Chapel marker)
B 10/11	127	8	GOULD	Andrew J. Gould, 1868 – 1952 (Vancouver Funeral Chapel marker)
B 1	7		GOULD	Anna Wood Gould, 1883 – 1962 (with Breed Family)
B 10/11	127	9	GOULD	Mary Gould, Nov. 30, 1860 – May 8, 1936, "In Loving Memory"
B 13	148		GREER	(Mary Carrier Greer, died Apr. 15, 1917)

B	19	223	3	GRIFFLES	Augusta M. Griffles, 1851 – 1925 (died Aug. 15, 1925, s/s Thomas Griffles)
B	19	223	2	GRIFFLES	Thomas Griffles, 1852 – 1924 (s/s Augusta M. Griffles)
B	12	141	10	HAAGEN	Ada May Haagen, 1870 – 1961, "In Memory Of" (s/s to John G. Haagen)
B2		142		HAAGEN	Glenn Haagen, Died 1932 (next to Ada & John Haagen)
B	12	141	11	HAAGEN	John G. Haagen, 1858 – 1935, "In Memory Of" (s/s Ada May Haagen)
B	12		12	HAAGEN	Smith V. Haagen, 1896 – 1975, Sgt., Air Service (next to John G. Haagen)
B	6	70	7	HANSEN	Donald Hansen, Mar. 1, 1920 – Jan. 17, 1921
B	2	20		HARDING	(Harding Child, died Mar. 26, 1912)
				HASKINS	Oren Haskins, 1853 – 1917, "Beloved Father and Mother" (died 19 Aug. 1917)
				HASKINS	Sadie Haskins, 1873 – 1937, "Beloved Father and Mother"
B	19		1	HASLEY	Hasley (nother further -- a wooden marker)
B	9	108	15	HENRY	Dorland W. Henry, 1865 – 1933 (s/s Susanna)
B	9	108	15	HENRY	Susanna E. Henry, 1867 – 1939 (s/s Dorland)
B	2		26	HIGDON	(Allen Higdon, Jan. 16, 1922)
B	6	62	1	HIGDON	Clara Higdon, Died July 14, 1909, "Mother Of Ray, Clyde & Grace"
B	2	15	2	HIGDON	Clyde B. Higdon, 1901 – 1969 (died June 16, 1969, Vancouver Funeral Home marker)
B	2	15	4	HIGDON	Ella M. Higdon, 1874 – 1936, "Mother" (died 20 Oct. 1936, Ella (McAllister) Higdon)
B	2	27		HIGDON	Everett S. Higdon, 1871 – 1947, "Father" (matches Ella's stone, died 1 Jan. 1947)
B	5	52	3	HIGDON	Flora E. Higdon, 1890 – 1918 (Mrs...died 15 Oct. 1918)

B	5	52	3	HIGDON	Fred G. Higdon, 1879 - 1959 (s/s Flora)
B	4	39		HIGDON	Ina May Higdon, Daughter of Mr. & Mrs. Wm. Higdon, July 27, 1907 - June 4, 1928
				HIGDON	Mary Higdon (Vancouver Funeral Home marker, no dates)
B	2	26	1	HIGDON	Sarah Frances Higdon, Died June 24, 1901 age 61 yrs 7 mo 3 days "Gone from our home, But not from our hearts", "At Rest", "Mother" (Sarah Frances (Miller) Higdon)
B	2	14	1	HIGDON	Sarah I. Higdon, 1878 - ____ (died 1963, Sarah B. Isobelle Higdon, with William Higdon, Vancouver Funeral Chapel marker)
B	2	124	5	HIGDON	William M. Higdon, 1875 - 1943
B	11	124	5	HILBERG	Anna M. Hilberg, 1855 - 1932, "Mother" (s/s Sven Hilberg)
B	11	124	5	HILBERG	Sven Hilberg, 1835 - 1908, "Father"
				HISLOP	Amanda L. Hislop, Born June 22, 1850 - Died July 1, 1893, Wife of A. Hislop, age 43 yrs 21 days, "Gone But Not Forgotten" (Sept. 1987 note: stone has recently been broken)
A	10		7	HOFF	Jacob Hoff, Born in Star Co., Ohio, Jan. 27, 1811 Died Feb. 6, 1893, "He Is At Rest In Heaven" "At Rest" (s/s Mary Hoff)
A	10		8	HOFF	Mary Hoff, Wife of Jacob Hoff, Born in Tuscarawas Co., Ohio, Jan. 9, 1809 - Died May 3, 1892, "In The Lord Have I Put My Trust", "At Rest" (s/s Jacob Hoff)
B	10	120	14	HOFFMAN	Eva May Hoffman, 1868 - 1946
B	11		7	HOLTMAN	John Holtman, Born Aug. 23, 1848 - Died Dec. 29, 1902, "At Rest", "Husband & Father", "Here Lies Our Beloved", "Born In Germany"
				HOLTMAN	John F. Holtman, 1889 - 1961
B	11		8	HOLTMAN	Minnie Holtman, Born Aug. 4, 1863 - Died Nov. 16, 1905, "In Memory of Our Darling Mother"
B	6	68	5	HONAN	Emma Honan, 1860 - 1938

B	6	68	6	HONAN	Esta Honan, 1894 – 1918 (died 21 Sept. 1918)
B	19	229	6	HONAN	Michael J. Honan, 1865 – 1948, "Father"
				HONAN	Thomas J. Honan, 1898 – 1985
B	5	55	5	HORN	Mathias Horn, Died June 10, 1906 age 72 years (in records: Martha Horn...s/s Mary Schneider)
B	12		6	HOUSER	Ethel G. Houser, 1873 – 1959, "Mother"
B	12		6	HOUSER	John H. Houser, 1869 – 1932, "Father"
B	10		9	HOUSER	Maude Houser, 1896 – 1904 (s/s May Houser)
B	10		9	HOUSER	May Houser, 1892 – 1893 (s/s Maude Houser)
B	10		5	HUFF	Jacob Huff, Born Mar. 27, 1853 – Died Sept. 24, 1901 "In Loving Remembrance Of" "A precious one from us is gone A voice we loved is stilled A place is vacant in our home Which never can be filled God in His wisdom has recalled The boon His love has given And though the body moulders here The soul is safe in heaven"
B	9	107	13	HUMFELD	Jennie Humfeld, 1865 – 1934, "Mother"
B	9	107	13	HUMFELD	John Humfeld, 1868 – 1932, "Father"
B	14	157	1	JORGENSEN	Margrethe Jorgensen, 1881 – 1917, "Mother"
B	14	157	1	JORGENSEN	Walter Jorgensen, 1871 – 1938, "Father"
B	1		5	JOHNSON	(Baby Johnson, no dates)
A	10	111	4	JOHNSON	Agnes Johnson, 1866 – 1913, "His Wife" (wife of Jefferson)
A	10	111	1	JOHNSON	Augustine Johnson, 1856 – 1919, "Father"
				JOHNSON	Jefferson Johnson, 1863 – ____
B	10	110	3	JOHNSON	Oran R. Johnson, Born Apr. 1, 1895 – Died Dec. 31, 1902 (Oran P. Johnson)
B	10	110	2	JOHNSON	Richard Johnson, Born Jan. 21, 1869 – Died Feb. 6, 1900 (June 2, 1900, Richard O.)

B 2		18	JORDAN	(A. Jordan, baby, died Aug. 27, 1911)
B 14	160		KAUFFMAN	Charlotte Louise Kauffman, 1864 - 1917 (wife of William)
B 14	160		KAUFFMAN	William Frederick Kauffman, 1861 - 1913
B 8	87	1	KAUFFMAN	Anna Wanner, 1845 - 1907, Wife of Anton Kaufman, "At Rest", "We will meet again, we trust our loss will be her gain/ And with Christ she's gone to reign."
B 8	87	2	KAUFMAN	Anton Kaufman, May 4, 1835 - Aug. 27, 1919 "At Rest", "We Meet Not To Depart Again"
B 8	88	4	KAUFMAN	Baby Kaufman, 1910
B 8	88	3	KAUFMAN	Fred Kaufman, 1872 - 1911, "In Loving Memory"
B 7	75	3	KAUFMAN	Joseph Kaufman, 1874 - 1937
B 6	72	11	KELLEY	Alwine C. Kelley, 1870 - 1955 (Alwin Kelly)
B 6	73	9	KELLEY	Heber L. Kelley, 1891 - 1950
B 6	72	10	KELLEY	John F. Kelley, 1865 - 1926 (Kelly)
			KENNEDY	Ruth O. Kennedy, 1911 - 1974 (Straub's Chapel marker)
B 8	96	7	KENOYER	John Pfrimmer Kenoyer, Feb. 17 - Nov. 10, 1932
B 17	205	3	KENWORTHY	Almeda Ann Kenworthy, 1864 - 1944
B 17	205	3	KENWORTHY	John Milton Kenworthy, 1854 - 1932
B 9	103		KING	(Charles King, no dates)
B 16	191	7	KLASSEN	Elizabeth F. Klassen, 1865 - 1954, "Mother"
B 16	191	8	KLASSEN	Henry H. Klassen, Apr. 28, 1890 - Aug. 27, 1951 Washington, Pvct. 75 Inf. 13 Div. WW I
B 8	95	5	KLASSEN	Peter A. Klassen, Feb. 13, 1898 - May 28, 1941, New York Corp, 65 Coast Artillery, W W II, Cpl.
A 9		8	LEARY	Elizabeth Leary, 1809 - 1891, "His Mother" (mother of Wilson, d. 1899?)
A 9		8	LEARY	Wilson T. Leary, 1843 - 1910

B 19		4	LINDSTROM	Clarina Cristina Lindstrom, Aug. 12, 1871 – Sept. 15, 1903, Born in Finland
A 10		2	LIVINGSTONE	John R. Livingstone, Born Dec. 21, 1883 – Died Sept 12, 1889
A 10		1	LIVINGSTONE	Olive M. Livingstone, Born Aug. 2, 1889 – Died Sept. 19, 1889
B 19	226		LUNDSTROM	(Mrs. C. Lundstrom died Aug. 18, 1907)
A 11		2	MACUMBER	Wesley Macumber, Co. K. 38 Wis. Inf.
A 7		1	MANNING	B. L. Manning, 1857 – 1912
A 7		1	MANNING	Clinton C. Manning, Apr. 4, 1887 – May 22, 1889
B 6	67		MANSETT	(Paul Mansett, no dates)
B 13	147		MARSH	John F. Marsh, Co. B. 16 Wis. Inf. (d. Jan. 25, 1916)
B 13	150	8	MARSH	Lloyd S. Marsh, 1886 – 1943, "Father"
B 13	150	8	MARSH	Margaret P. Marsh, 1886 – 1932, "Mother"
			MARSH	Marion Foe Marsh, 1912 – 1918 (Vancouver Funeral Home marker)
B 16	189		MATTHEWS	M. Matthers (Mr. Matthews, no dates, Vancouver Funeral Home marker)
A 8		10	McCAFFERTY	Adelia M. McCafferty, 1863 – 1900 (Mrs. James T. McCafferty)
A 8		10	McCAFFERTY	Clara A. McCafferty, 1884 – 1886
A 8		5	McCAFFERTY	Everett A. McCafferty, Born Aug. 20, 1867 – Died June 10, 1896, "Dearest Brother has left us/Here his loss we deeply feel"
A 8		2	McCAFFERTY	James McCafferty, Feb. 3, 1833 – Nov. 14, 1877. "Father", "Here lies at Rest"
A 8		10	McCAFFERTY	James P. McCafferty, 1881 – 1886
A 8		10	McCAFFERTY	James T. McCafferty, 1858 – 1921
A 8		1	McCAFFERTY	Mother McCafferty, 1838 – 1916 (wife of James)

A	8		6	McCAFFERTY	Samuel McCafferty, Feb. 11, 1864 – Aug. 23, 1908 (Samuel O. McCafferty, wooden board on iron stake)
B	7	73	1	McMULLEN	Jennie McMullen, 1853 – 1932
B	7	73	2	McMULLEN	John A. McMullen, 1853 – 1924 (d. Jan. 10)
B	10	116		MEAD	George Mead, 1928 (died 27 Mar. 1928, Vancouver Funeral Home marker)
B	10	116		MEAD	Linda Thomas Mead, 1930 (died 12 Nov. 1930, Vancouver Funeral Home marker)
A	2		2	MILLARD	Elizabeth A. Millard, Born in Kentucky May 10, 1817, Died Oct. 7, 1871 "Parents thou has from us flown To the regions far above We to thee erect this stone Consecrated by our love."
A	2		2	MILLARD	Gideon Millard, Born in New York June 26, 1800 – Died Jan. 21, 1869 (s/s Elizabeth)
B	3	34		MILLER	Ivia Allen Miller, 1881 – 1919 (d. May 6, 1919)
B	12	137	6	MOBLEY	J. W. Mobley, Mar. 6, 1832 – Jan. 3, 1914 (Mr. W. Mobley)
B	12	137	5	MOBLEY	Phoebe Mobley, Apr. 19, 1867 – July 7, 1907
				MOORE	(Mr. & Mrs. Moore, moved to Park Hill Cemetery)
A	9		6	MOORE	F. P. Moore, ___ – 1891 (Evergreen Funeral Home marker)
				MOORE	(George Moore, moved to Park Hill Cemetery)
B	16	183	1	MOORE	Hannah E. Moore, Mar. 18, 1837 – Dec. 29, 1915
				MOORER	Hazel Manning Moore (Vancouver Funeral Chapel marker, no dates)
B	14	161	5	MOORE	John H. Moore, Died Apr. 19, 1917, Aged 64 yrs (John Henry Moore, see Westover)
A	9		7	MOORE	Mary Ann Moore, May 24, 1857 – Oct. 7, 1905
				MOSS	Jess Moss, 1900 – 1986, "Son" (from obit: Jess Moss, age 85, born June 23, 1900, Cripple Creek, CO, died June 17, 1986, Vancouver. Widow: Lena, at home, sons: Robert J. Moss,

				MOSS (cont.)	Hayward, CA, daughter: Laura Biradel, CA. No service. Vancouver Funeral Chapel. obit. from 'The Columbian')
B	4	42	8	MOTZKUS	Ferdinand Motzkus, 1832 – 1911, "Father" (d. Apr. 7, 1911)
				MUNDY	William V. Mundy, Feb. 14, 1917 – June 6, 1979, U. S. Army
A	2		4	NERTON	Elizabeth Nerton, Died Jan. 9, 1897 Aged 64 years, "Wife of Thomas Nerton", "At Rest"
A	2		3	NERTON	John T. Nerton, 1866 – 1918 (Odd Fellows Insignia)
A	2		4	NERTON	Thomas Nerton, Died Sept. 11, 1882, Aged 62 years "In Memory Of", "At Rest"
B	17	206	4	NORD	Edith A. Nord, 1870 – 1936, "Pioneer", "In Memory Of" (Edith Adelia Nord, died May 14, 1936, aged 68 yrs 3 mos 3 das)
B	15	181	2	NORTHUP	Anna May Northup, 1893 – 1921 (with Sliderburgs)
B	15	181	11	NORTHUP	Steven E. Northup, 1882 – 1927
B	16	194		NOTESTINE	John H. Notestine, 1858 – Aug. 27, 1920, "Father"
B	16	194		NOTESTINE	Minnie Notestine, 1862 – 1920, "Mother" (wfe of John)
B	4	40	5	OHLINGER	Elizabeth Ohlinger, Feb. 25, 1842 – Jan. 15, 1916 "Heir Ruht in Gott Geboren Den 25 Feb. 1842 Gestorben Den 15 Jan. 1916" (17 Jan. 1916 burial?)
B	4	40	5	OHLINGER	Michael Ohlinger, July 7, 1838 – Aug. 8, 1910, "Heir Ruht in Gott Geboren Den 7 July 1838 Gestorben Den 8 Aug. 1910"
B	10	109	1	O'REAR	Belle Mary O'Rear, 1876 – 1937
B	10	109	1	O'REAR	Ora Adrain O'Rear, 1872 – 1919 (d. Dec. 23?)
A	11		14	OSBORN	Dorothy L. Osborn, 1910 – 1910 (Evergreen Funeral Home marker, with Hiram J. and Nancy A. Osburn)

				OSBURN	Hiram J. Osburn, Dec. 16, 1841 - Mar. 4, 1928
				OSBURN	Nancy A. Osburn, Feb. 16, 1849 - Jan. 3, 1915
B 10	115	7		PACKARD	Myron Packard, 1851 - 1926
B 1	17			PAMMO	(William Pammo, Baby, no further info.)
B 20	233			PARMITER	(A. Parmiter, d. Dec. 28, 1918)
B 15	174	5		PAYNE	George Payne, Mar. 17, 1844 - Dec. 23, 1904, "Thy Praise Would Not Annoy Nor Recall Thee From Joy"
B 16	187	5		PAYNE	Mary A. Payne, May 22, 1863 - Feb. 21, 1917, Wife of C. W. Payne
B 15	174	4		PAYNE	Mrs. Abby Payne, July 16, 1842 - Apr. 20, 1917 (Mrs. Abby Payne, dates difficult to read)
B 2	22			PAYNTER	(Billie Paynter, no further info.)
B 2	24			PAYNTER	Elsie Bartles Paynter, 1894 - 1957 (d. Nov. 1957, see Bartles)
B 2	23	6		PAYNTER	Rose E. Paynter, 1874 - 1945, "Mother"
B 2	23	5		PAYNTER	Sherman J. Paynter, 1864 - 1937, "Beloved Husband and Father", I.O.O.F. emblem
B 4	41	6		PEARCE	Richard K. Pearce, 1835 - 1913
B 4	41			PEARCE	(Mrs. Richard K. Pearce, 1913)
B 7	79	6		PENCE	Martha Pence, 1849 - 1915 (d. June 26, 1915)
A 6		1		PRESTON	Nelson H. Preston, Sept.30, 1897 - Died Aug. 8, 1946, "Father and Grandfather"
A 6		2		PRESTON	Tony Lee Preston, Apr. 9, 1966 - July 19, 1966, "Our Baby", "Bright Jewels for His Crown" (with Hazel Manning Moore and Mary Manning Preston)
B 20	237			PETERSON	Andrew Peterson, 1957 (died Nov. 23, 1957)
B 11	132			PHINNEY	Calvin Phinney (no dates)
B 12	133			PHINNEY	Delva Phinney, Died 1941 (died Apr. 9, 1941, Aged 75 yrs. 1 mo 17 ds

A 10		6	PICKETT	Jessie Huff Pickett, 1856 - 1937
B 11	123	3	PIERT	Christina Piert, 1847 - 1930, "Mother"
B 11	123	4	PIERT	Henry Piert Sr., 1846 - 1909, "Father" (18 Nov. 1909)
B 16	190	6	POLLY	Nellie A. Polly, 1881 - 1964, "Mother" (mother of Jess Moss)
B 5	58	9	POWELL	Louise Powel, May 25, 1856 - Feb. 14, 1919, "His Wife" (s/s William)
B 5	58	11	POWELL	Ferdinand Powell, 1847 - 1927 (s/s Louise Powell)
B 5	58	10	POWELL	Franz Powell, May 5, 1852 - May 24, 1923
B 5	58	11	POWELL	Louise Powell, 1845 - 1936 (s/s Ferninand Powell)
B 5	58	9	POWELL	William Powell, May 10, 1849 - Aug. 22, 1931
B 1	9	8	PRATT	Fred Cotton Pratt, 1870 - 1936
B 1	9	7	PRATT	Myra Breed Pratt, 1873 - 1943 (Vancouver Funeral Home marker)
			PRATT	Hallie Cotton Pratt, 1904 - 1986, " He Lies Not Here But Neath The Sea And Ever In Our Memory"
B 17	207		PRICE	Baby Price (no dates)
B 9	101	6	PRICE	Elizabeth G. Price, 1866 - 1950 (Mrs. Lilly Price, d. Jan. 1950, s/s Horatio N. Price)
B 9	101	6	PRICE	Horatio N. Price, 1855 - 1941 (s/s Elizabeth G. Price)
B 9	102	7	PRICE	LeBaron W. Price, 1852 - 1936, "Pioneer Timber Crusier of State of Washington"
B 9	100	4	PRICE	Robert D. Price, Apr. 21, - Dec. 5, 1918 (Baby, 7 Dec. 1918)
A 5		2	PROBESTEL	G. A. Probestel, 1862 - 1926
A 4		4	PROBESTEL	Henretta Probestel, Nov. 7, 1866 - Nov. 24, 1877 "Children of G. E. & M. A. Probestel" (with Rudolf)

110

A 5		3	PROBESTEL	Henry Oscar Probestel, 1866 - 1932, "Beloved Husband"
A 4		6	PROBESTEL	John Probestel, Born Dec. 24, 1824 - Died Dec. 11, 1882, "Father", "Though he were dead/ Yet shall He live"
A 5		1	PROBESTEL	Leota May Probestel, 1876 - 1946
A 4		4	PROBESTEL	Rudolf Probestel, Feb. 7, 1873 - Feb. 25, 1875 "Children of G. E. & M. A. Probestel" (with Henretta)
B 7	76	5	PROBESTEL	Sarah Probestel, Aug. 13, 1831 - July 6, 1898, "Mother"
A 4		5	PROBESTEL	Valentine Proestel, Died Nov. 24, 1882, Aged 67 yrs 1 mo 21 d's
B 1	8	5	RANDALL	Martha G. Randall, 1848 - 1936 (matches stone of C. Henry Wood)
B 12	144		REAGER	Ella Reager, 1862 - 1941 (home-made metal marker)
B 12	144	14	REAGER	Elmer Reager, 1852 - 1923 (home-made metal marker died Apr. 8, 1923)
B 5	57	8	REHFELT	Louise Rehfelt, Feb. 1, 1825 - May 23, 1915
B 12		8	RENNEY	Florence Renney, 1866 - 1919 (Aug. 23, 1919)
B 12	139	8	RENNEY	Joseph Renney, 1863 - 1935
B 12		8	RENNEY	Marion Renney, 1924
B 11	130	12	RENNEY	Robert J. Renney, 1886 - 1939
B 17	195		RESLER	Maud Resler, 1907 (died 16 Sept. 1907, other marker reads "M. M. Resler")
B 9	105	11	REUTER	Martha Marie Reuter, 1879 - 1930
B 20	235	2	REIM	Alta L. Riem, 1914 - 1919, "Sister" (d. Oct. 15, Reem in records)
B 20	236	2	REIM	Celina M. Riem, 1881 - 1963, "Mother" (Reem in records)
B 20	235	2	REIM	Frederick C. Riem, 1855 - 1923, "Father" (d. June 2, 1923, Reem in records)

				RICHARD	Mary Manning Richard (Vancouver Funeral Chapel Marker, no dates)
B	7	81	7	ROSS	Jane Nevin Ross, 1859 – 1920, "Mother Love Eternal, To Life Everlasting"
B	9	10612		ROSS	Jeanette Humfeldt Ross, 1900 – 1938, "Rest in peace" (see Humfeldt)
B	7	81	8	ROSS	William Ross, 1850 – 1930, "Father"
A	10		11	RUSSEL	Charlotte Russel, July 22, 1816 – Nov. 11, 1910, "Mother of Catherine (Kate) Thompson"
B	8	85	6	SALES	Baby Sales, Dec. 1926
A	12		7	SALMON	Laura B. Salmon, 1887 – 1920, "Daughter"
A	12		8	SALMON	Ralph Otis Salmon, Jan. 1883 – July 1962, "Father"
B	9	104	10	SAMPLE	Charles A. Sample, Died Dec. 28, 1951, age 70 yrs 0 mos 24 d's (79??? yrs d. NOV??, Sept. 1987 note: stone not located)
B	9	104	9	SAMPLE	Estella D. Sample, 1881 – 1945, "Wife and Mother" (d. Nov. 1945, Vancouver Funeral Home marker)
B	12	140	10	SHAUGHNESSY	Charlotte Shaughnessy, 1856, "Wife" (died 1919, Charlotte E. Shaughnessy)
B	12	140	9	SHAUGHNESSY	Thomas Shaughnessy, 1856 – 1937 (s/s Charlotte Shaughnessy)
B	18	209		SCHECKLER	James Scheckler, 1919 (died 22 Mar. 1919, Vancouver Funeral Home marker)
B	4		7	SCHEURMAN	Baby Scheurman, Died 1904
B	4	43	9	SCHEURMAN	George Scheurman, 1860 – 1941, "Father"
B	4	43	9	SCHEURMAN	Minna Scheurman, 1867 – 1944, "Mother" (Minnie, s/s George Scheurman)
B	5	15		SCHNEIDER	Mary Schneider, Died 30 Jan. 1913, Aged 75 years
B	5	56	7	SCHNEIDER	William Schneider, Died Feb. 22, 1920, Aged 83 yrs 6 mo 19 dys

A 6		4	SCHIRMER	Carl Schirmer, Born Sept. 29, 1830 - Died June 20, 1886, "Gone but not forgotten"
B 10	43		SCHOOLEY	Thelma Schooley, 1917 (died 18 Jan. 1917, Vancouver Funeral Chapel marker)
A 1		2	SLATER	Eliza Slater, Born Dec. 12, 1842 - Died Jan. 23, 1894 (b. Dec. 20?)
A 1		1	SLATER	John Slater, Born in Manitoba Apr. 1, 1827 - Died Feb. 20, 1909, "Gone but not forgotten"
A 1		1	SLATER	Clara M. Slater, Died July 22, 1878, age 6 mo 6 dys, "Children of John & Eliza" (with John S. & Thomas S.)
A 1		1	SLATER	John S. Slater, Died June 22, 1878, Age 9 yrs 2 mos, "Children of John & Eliza", (with Clara and Thomas S.)
A 1		1	SLATER	Thomas S. Slater, Died Aug. 9, 1878, age 2 yrs. 5 mo 22 dys, "Children of John & Eliza" (with Clara & John S.)
B 15	182	13	SLIDERBERG	Anna Sliderberg, 1837 - 1931
B 15	182	14	SLIDERBERG	George Sliderberg, 1836 - 1905
B 10	112		SMITH	(Alice Smith, no dates)
B 10	113		SMITH	(Harry Smith, 1932)
			SMITH	Lester B. Smith, June 1908 - Oct. 1985
B 10	112		SMITH	Sidney Alice Smith (no dates, Vancouver Funeral Chapel marker)
B 15	169	1	SPIRES	C. W. Spires, 1870 - 1915, Spanish American War Veteran
B 15	177	8	SPIRES	Edith Spires, 1888 - 1950
B 9		2	SPIRES	Elizabeth Spires, Born Oct. 16, 1842 - Died Sept. 19, 1890, "Wife of J. L. Spires"
B 9		3	SPIRES	James K. Spires, 1846 - 1936
B 15	177	9	SPIRES	James O. Spires, Sept. 27, 1882 - Apr. 6, 1967, Oregon, Spanish American War Vet., Cox. U.S. Navy

B 9		1	SPIRES	John L. Spires, Born June 2, 1833 - Died June 1, 1898
B 15	178	10	SPIRES	John Orville Spires, 1906 - 1970 (d. 17 Nov. 1970)
B 15	170	2	SPIRES	Maud Parks Spires, 1886 - 1907, Wife of J. O. Spires
			SPIRES	Marcella Sprire, May 21, 1900 - July 20, 1900 (Sept. 1987 note: this appears to be a new stone)
B 9		3	SPIRES	Nancy J. Spires, 1852 - 1928
B 13	156		SPIRES	(Nina Spires, baby, July 1900)
B 6	65	4	STALNAKER	Alba J. Stalnaker, 5 Nov. 1871 - Jan. 12, 1911 (baby buried with her)
B 6	65	4	STALNAKER	(Baby Stalnaker, with Alba, mother)
B 6	66		STALNAKER	E. Stalnaker, 1913 (died 16 June 1913, Vancouver Funeral Chapel marker)
B 6	66		STALNAKER	Mrs. E. Stalnaker (no dates, Vancouver Funeral Chapel marker)
B 7	84	11	STARR	Emmett F. Starr, 1889 - 1957, "Nothing between my soul and the Saviour", "Son"
			STARR	(from obit. - The Columbian: Ethel B. Starr, age 99, born Mar. 17, 1886 in Rockford, Wash., died July 4, 1985, Vancouver, Wash. Funeral Tuesday, July 9, at Vancouver Funeral Chapel. Interment in Sifton Cemetery.
B 7	84	10	STARR	Samuel F. Starr, 1858 - 1934, "Father", "We have a building of God"
B 8	85		STEWART	D. H. Stewart, 1903 (13 July 1903, Vancouver Funeral Chapel marker)
B 9	99	3	STOJEUA	Helen A. Stojeua, 1907 - 1910 (Stojewa? baby)
B 18		4	STONER	Nellie Drum Stoner, 1910 - 1972, "In Memory Of" (Nellie C. Stoner d. 18 Sept. 1972, Evergreen Funeral Home marker)
B 10	119	11	STOUP	James A. Stoup, 1858 - 1935

SIFTON CEMETERY

A	7		3	STREETER	Arthur D. Streeter, 1860 - 1942, "Brothers" (s/s Henry M., Odd Fellows Emblem on stone)
A	7		3	STREETER	Henry M. Streeter, 1852 - 1933, "Brothers" (s/s Arthur)
A	6		2	STREETER	Mildred I. Streeter, 1901 - 1921 (s/s Nellie E.)
A	6		2	STREETER	Nellie E. Streeter, 1871 - 1929 (s/s Mildred I.)
A	6		6	STREETER	Rueben Streeter, 1823 - 1889, "Father" (s/s Sarah M.)
A	6		6	STREETER	Sarah M. Streeter, "Mother", 1829 - 1909 (s/s Rueben)
				STURGEON	Blanche C. Sturgeon, Jan. 4, 1907 - Nov. 16, 1982 "They Graced Their Family With Acts Of Loving Kindness"
				STURGEON	Jewel E. Sturgeon, Sept. 25, 1898, "They Graced Their Family With Acts Of Loving Kindness"
B	13	151	7	TAFT	Anna Jane Taft, 1871 - 1941
B	13	151	6	TAFT	George L. Taft, 1861 - 1913 (d. 22 Aug. 1913, gravestone matches Marshall Terrel)
B	13	155	1	TALBOT	Alfred Talbot, 1904 - 1906 (Vancouver Funeral Home marker)
B	13	153	3	TALBOT	Charles Talbot, 1899 - 1927 (Vancouver Funeral Home marker)
B	13	154	3	TALBOT	Ellen Talbot, 1893 - 1909 (1898? with Baby, Vancouver Funeral Home marker)
B	13	153		TALBOT	(Mary Talbot, no further info.)
B	14	163		TAYLOR	(Allen Taylor, d. Sept. 10, 1904)
B	14	163	7	TAYLOR	Allen J. Taylor, 1851 - 1937 (Masonic Emblem on stone)
B	14	163	7	TAYLOR	Civilla M. Taylor, 1869 - 1944
B	15		6	TAYLOR	Daisy Ethel Taylor, 1890 - 19__
B	15	175	6	TAYLOR	Guy Allen Taylor, 1889 - 1946
B	13	152	5	TERRELL	Marcus H. Terrell, Born in Deposit, Broome Co. NY, Aug. 16, 1859 - Died July 27, 1906, "In Memory Of Our Dear Brother"

115

B 13	152	5	TERRELL	Marshall D. Terrell, 1854 – 1938
			TERRILL	Marcus H. Terrill, 1859 – 1906 (separate stone for Marcus Terrell, above)
B 10	117	8	THERIEN	Alfred N. Therien, 1884 – 1967
B 10	117		THERIEN	Leana P. Therien, 1885 – 1940 (Hamilton Funeral Home marker, Linda Therrien)
A 10		10	THOMPSON	Catherine "Kate" Thompson, 1857 – 1949 (with mother Charlotte Russell and L. Z. Thompson)
B 9	97	2	THOMPSON	Francis A. Thompson, Dec. 21, 1915, Aged 85 yrs 3 mo 13 dys, "Rest in peace"
A 4		8	THOMPSON	Jane E. Thompson, 1829 – 1912, "Mother", " His Wife" (wife of Silas)
A 4		7	THOMPSON	L. Z. Thompson, Crpl., Co. D, 44th Ind. Inf.
B 9	96	1	THOMPSON	Mary E. Thompson, Died Oct. 2, 1926, Aged 85 yrs 10 mo 13 dys
A 10		10	THOMPSON	Monson W. Thompson, 1849 – 1924, "Father"
A 4		8	THOMPSON	Silas Thompson, 1823 – 1902
			TOWLE	(Albert W. Towle, from obit. – The Columbian – Age 85, born Oct. 1, 1897, Orchards, Wash., died June 12, 1983, Portland, Ore. Res: Vancouver, Wash. wife: Josephine Towle, at home. Funeral Wednesday, June 15, at First Evangelical Church of North America. Interment in Sifton Cemetery.)
B 5	54	4	TOWLE	Alice M. Towle, 1869 – 1925 (May 1925)
B 5	54	4	TOWLE	Esma E. Towle, 1901 – 1919 (Apr. 9, 1910)
B 5	54	4	TOWLE	Herbert Towle, 1890 – 1897
			TOWLE	(Josephine M. Towle, from obit. – The Columbian: Age 85 of a stroke. Born Dec. 26, 1901 in Orchards, Wash. Died Apr. 29, 1987 in Vancouver, Wash. Preceded in death by her husband, Albert, in 1983. Son: Robert, Vancouver. Daughters: Bernice Thompson, Letha Thompson & Margaret Dean, all of Vancouver. Funeral Monday, May 4, 1987, at First Evangelical Church of North America.

TOWLE (cont.) Burial in Sifton Cemetery. Vancouver
Funeral Chapel in charge of arrangements)

B 5	54	4	TOWLE	Josiah Towle, 1856 - 1930 (June 1930)
B 10	119	13	TRIBE	Phyllis Tribe, 1931 - 1939, "Our Baby Darling"
B 10	119	12	TRIBE	Baby Tribe, June 1947
			TRITSCH	Jacob Tritsch, 1862 - 1926
			TRITSCH	Nora Tritsch, 1870 - 1922, "His Wife" (wife of Jacob)
B 3	33	8	TYLER	Clare E. Tyler, Born Mar. 11, 1880 - Died Nov. 24, 1900, "Sweet flower transplanted to a clime, Where never comes the blight of time."
B 3	33	8	TYLER	Dewitt C. Tyler, Born Mar. 6, 1856 - Died 21 June 1903, "Where immortal spirits reign, There we shall meet again."
B 12	136	4	TYSON	George W. Tyson, Co. G. 1st Minn. H.A.
B 12	136		TYSON	(J. W. Tyson, Oct. 12, 1912)
A 11		12	UELTSCHI	Peter Ueltschi, Born Aug. 1841 - Died May 4, 1908, Aged 63 yrs 9 mo, "Them Also Which Sleep In Jesus Will God Bring With Him"
A 4		1	VANNAUSDSLE	Charles E. Vannausdle, Feb. 11, 1864 - July 1, 1864, "His son"
A 4		1	VANNAUSDLE	Jerome B. Vannausdle, Born Dec. 1841 - Died 4 Dec. 1864, "Blessed are the dead that died in the Lord"
B 18	211		VILES	William Viles, 1927 (died Aug. 10, 1927, Vancouver Funeral Chapel marker)
			WEDDLE	Frank J. Weddle, Aug. 20, 1922 - June 19, 1983, Pvt., U. S. Army (from obit. - The Columbian: Frank J. Weddle, age 60, born Aug. 20, 1922, Portland, Ore. - died June 19, 1983. Wife: Lenora Weddle, at home. Graveside service Wed., June 22 at Sifton Cemetery.)
B 3	35	11	WEHRUM	Allen Wehrum, July 4, 1911 - Mar 4, 1914, Son of A. E. & Gladys Wehrum (5 Mar. 1914)

B 5	49		WELCH	(Lester Welch, June 10, 1901)
B 13	145	10	WENDLICK	John A. Wendlick, June 26, 1842 – Jan. 12, 1916
B 13	145	10	WENDLICK	Rosa Wendlick, Feb. 27, 1845 – June 3, 1918, His wife, (wife of John A., d. June 4?)
B 9	99		WENGAR	(Gaby Wengar, no info.)
			WEST	George F. West, 1871 – 1917
B 20	234	1	WESTOVER	Emma A. Westover, Dec. 26, 1924, Age 79 yrs, "His wife" (wife of John Henry Moore)
B 14		9	WHEELER	Ruth Olive Wheeler, Oct. 2, 1911 – May 24, 1974 (Little Chapel of the Chimes Funeral Direct. Knapp Funeral Home marker)
A 4		1	WILEY	A. A. Wiley, Oct. 19, 1834 – Nov. 7, 1904, "Father" (H. A. Wiley)
A 4		1	WILEY	S. J. Wiley, July 12, 1841 – Jan 13, 1912, "Mother"
B 17	197		WILLIAMS	(Hattie [Dopp] Williams, no further info.)
B 17	197		WILLIAMS	(Lester Williams, no further info.)
B 20	232		WILLIAMS	(John Williams, Dec. 10, 1916
B 17	196		WILLIAMS	(Ruth Williams, no further info.)
			WILSON	(A. Wilson, no further info.)
B 15	176	7	WILSON	Paul J. Wilson, 1909 – 1921
A 10		3	WITMYER	Son of L. V. & S. Z. Witmyer, Died Feb. 5, 1874, age 35 days, "Our Darling Son", "Sleep On Sweet Babe"
A 1	8		WOOD	(Charles Wood, Nov. 8, 1922)
			WOOD	C. Henry Wood, 1869 – 1922 (matches Martha G. Randall's gravestone)
			WOOD	(Baby Wood, no further info.)
B 12	138	7	YOUNG	Anton C. Young, Dec. 22, 1872 – Feb. 27, 1937, "Gone Home To Rest"

B 12	138	7	YOUNG	Melitta 1. H. Young, Jan. 4, 1879 – Oct. 19, 1947 "Gone Home to Rest"
B 19	228	5	YOUNG	Frances M. Young, Jan. 2, 1962, "Home To Her Saviour" (home made stone)
			YOUNG	Rebecca Lee Young, Nov. 29, 1940, age 1 day, "Home to her Saviour" (home made stone, broken stone)

*****

STONES NO LONGER READABLE:

"Rest In Peace, 1875" (a home-made stone)

Funeral Home marker: "1897 – 1908" next to wooden marker

The bottom of stone reads: "Sept. 29, 1860 (or 1880) "Though Her Lifeless..." nothing of name remains of this stone

Fern Prairie Cemetery

The Fern Prairie Cemetery was originally the Van Fleet burial grounds. The family donated the land for a community cemetery with the agreement that the Fern Prairie Cemetery as a community group maintain the Van Fleet burial sites along with the rest. Many of the pioneers of the area are buried here. The earliest burial found was in 1855.

Apparently some of the earliest records were destroyed by fire many years ago and that information was reconstructed from the tombstones and family records. Accurate records have been kept since 1918.

The cemetery is located on Highway 500, about two miles north of Camas at the intersection of N. E. 267th Avenue and N. E. Robinson Road. Row one runs parallel to N. E. 267th Avenue. The triangular section bordering on N. E. Robinson Road is known as the "new addition."

ABBOTT, Webster   1821 - 1878   Row No.
      One of Clark Co. early settlers died at his home on Mill   13
      Plain Dec. 31, 1878. b Lawrence Co. NY. Widow Mary L.
      Coffey Abbott, and three childrn. Consumption cause of death.
      Obit. Vancouver Independent, Jan. 9, 1879.

ABBOTT, Mary Louise Coffey   1833 - 1922   13
      Died August 19, age 89. born near Booneville, MO. Aug. 9
      1833. Her husband, her brothers, Mac & Alexander Coffey
      and her brother-in-law were vital forces in early Legislative
      assemblies of the territory. Two children, Henrietta M.
      Abbot of Portland and Webster Abbot of Mill Plain survive.
      Obit.

ABBOTT, Alice Ella   1856 - Nov. 21, 1863
      Daughter of W. & M.L. Abbott Aged 7 yrs. 10 mo's. 19 d's.

ABBOTT, Lucetta Caroline   1859 - Nov. 19, 1863   13
      Daughter of W. & M.L. Abbott Aged 4 yrs 6mo's, 4 d's

ABBOTT, Flora May   1861 - Nov. 18, 1863   13
      Aged 2 yrs, 2 m's, 17 d's

ABBOTT, Mary Alabama   1864 - 1880   (22 July)

ABBOTT, Robert Edward   1867 - 1868

ABBOTT, Webster G.   1871 - 1942

ALBERT, Cecil Ernest [Aged 78. b aug. 5, 1907 Salem, IL - d   10
      July 8, 1986 Camas, WA - Widow Charlotte at home. Son
      Richard of Camas, Daughter Rebecca Huss of Camas. Graveside
      Service Friday July 11. Brown's FH. Obit. "The Columbian"]

ALBERT, Emma C.   1874 - 1958   10

ALBERT, Lewis A.   1871 - 1953   10

ANDERSON, Alma C. born April 25, 1870 - died Aug. 15, 1897   5
      Daughter of J.A. & C.H. Clausen   Born in Sweden

ANDERSON, Baby   Born and Died Apr. 9, 1896   5

ANDERSON, Elmer   Born Apr. 9, 1896 - Died April 14, 1897   5
      Children of N.P. & A.C. Anderson [see Christina Clausen plot]

ANDERSON, Alvira C. M. Born Mar. 29, 1892 - Died Oct. 10   5
      1894 - Dau. of N.P. & A.C. Anderson [see J.P. Emil Clausen]

ANDERSON, Hannah   1868 - 1951   4

ANDERSON, Charlene Donahe [Age 65. b Feb. 26, 1921, Webster City
      IA - d Feb. 8, 1987, Auburn. Widower; Charles "Lucky" And-
      erson, at home. Son; Frank Donahe of Camas, Daughters Carol
      Azure, Zortman, MT; Betty Peschand & Carla Donahe both of
      Camas & Donna Spurgeon, Portland. Brothers and Sisters.
      Stoller FH. Obit. "The Columbian"]

				Row	No.
ANDERSON,	Nels P.	1862 – 1927			4
ANHOLT,	A Loretta	1893 – 1972			13
ARMSTRONG,	Daniel	Born & Died July 28, 1910			6
ARMSTRONG,	David	Born & Died July 28, 1910			6
		My Babies			
ARMSTRONG,	Margaret E.	1855 – 1905			4
ARMSTRONG,	Thomas S.	1847 – 1920			4
ARMSTRONG,	Ruth E.	1911 – 1932			10
ATKINS,	Anna Lois	Mar. 24, 1856 – Mar. 16, 1923			4
ATKINS,	William E.	Feb. 2, 1855 – June 13, 1928			4
ATKINS,	Bertie A.	1877 – 1957			5
ATKINS,	Mollie S.	1889 – 1962	Our Mother		3
ATKINS,	Evangeline M.	1901 – 1901			3
ATKINS,	John Everett	1912 – 1974			3
ATKINS,	Lois Alberta	1907 – 1929			4
ATKINS,	Mabel	1877 – 1932			5
ATKINS,	Marian M.	1913 – 1934			5
AUSTIN,	Willard W.	1904 – 1964			9

BAILIE, Roy K. [Age 74, Jan. 16, 1912, Brooks, OR – Oct. 9, 1986. Camas, WA Wife Latrell at home... Graveside services Sat. Oct. 11. Brown's FH Obit. "The Columbian"] .

				Row	No.
BAINTER,	Baby Randall	1956			7
BALCOM,	Harry A.	1877 – 1969			10
BALCOM,	Rena Mae	1885 – 1969			10
BALL,	Lena M.	1879 – 1938			7
BANCROFT,	Baby	[unmarked grave]			11
BARNETT,	Alice A.	1890 – 1945	Mother		9
BARNETT,	Robert L.	1888 – 19	Father		9
BARNETT,	Anna e.	1893 – 1912			6
BARNETT,	George W.	1864 – 1939			10

FERN PRAIRIE CEMETERY

			Row No.
BARNETT, Harriet N.	1855 – 1937		10
BARNETT, Martha A.	1868 – 1917		6

BARNETT, Nadene Louise born 7 July 1930 – died Jan. 23, 1981
[The Tribune; Feb. 1981-- died Friday, Jan. 23, 15 age 50.
born July 7, 1930 in Vancouver, WA and a resident all her life.
Enjoyed flowers, oil painting and china painting. survived by
husband Dean Barnett, Vancouver; mother; Mrs. Ester Messner,
Battle Ground, daughter; Mrs. Marlene Traver, Springfield,OR,
Miss Charlene Barnett, Vacnouver, Two brothers.

BARTLEY, Ramona A.	1960 – 1977		13
BARTON, Bertha May	1872 – 1931	Mother	10
BARTON, Zachariah	1872 – 1955	Father	10
BARTON, Claude E.	Born Nov. 15, 1892 – Died Dec. 20, 1964		12
BARTOW, Charles E.	1846 – 1906	Father	4
BASSETT, George M.	1860 – 1935	Father	11
BASSETT, Sarah Ruth	1862 – 1935	Mother	11
BATES, Dossie M.	1912 – 1977	Father	7

Married Jan. 12, 1942

BATES, Edgar H. [Age 40. Murdered. b Oct. 19, 1945 in
Durant, OK – d Sept. 19, 1987. Resided Washougal, WA.
Wife, Sylvia at home, Services Thurday, Sept. 24, 15
Evergreen Staples FC. Obit. "The Columbian"]

BATES, Edith I. 1917 – Mother 7
[Age 68. b Sept 20, 1917 in Bokshito, OK – d NOv. 13, 1985
Vancouver, WA. Resided Washougal, WA. Services Nov. 15,
at Bethel Community Church, Washougal. Brown's FH.
Obit. "The Columbian"]

BEACOCK, Arthur C.	1882 – 1962	Father	8
BEACOCK, Charles T.	1851 – 1947		9
BEACOCK, Clyde E.	1858		9

BEACOCK, Eugene [Age 57. b May 25, 1927, Ypsilenti, MO – d Jan.
5, 1985, Tacoma, WA. Graveside services Tuesday Jan. 7.
Memorial Gardens FC . Obit. "The Columbian"]

BEAGLE, Almon E.	1851 – 1921		2
BEAGLE, Ruth A.	1858 – 1934		2
BEAGLE, Myron A.	1887 – 1934		2

BEAGLE, Baby Vean   2

BEESON, Charles W. [Age 83. b Apr. 17, 1904, SD – d Aug. 23,
     1987 – Resided Vancouver, WA. Son of Dorothy Beeson of
     Geddes, SD. Graveside services Thursday, Aug. 27,
     Brown's FH.   Obit. "The Columbian"]

BENNETT, Ivan Earl   Born Feb. 7, 1912 – Died Dec. 16, 1951   6
     Wash. TEC 3   U.S. Army   W.W. II

BERGGREN, Carin   1837 – 1922   Mother   1

BERGGREN, Peter   1839 – 1927   Father   1

BERGGREN, Robert   1866 – 1934   1

BERGMAN, A. F. "Tiny"   1905 – 1966   Husband   13

BERGMAN, Clara R. (Rose) 1902 – 1973   Wife   13

BERGMAN, Elda E.   1906 – 1944   13

BERGMANN, Frank F.   1859 – 1935   3

BERGMANN, Mary A.   1869 – 1947   3

BEVARD, Dennis L.   1945 – 1964   Son   10

BEVARD, Ellen [b May 25, 1913, Linder, – d Feb. 10, 1987,
     Portland, OR. Resided Camas, WA. Widower Bert at home,
     Son; James Rodgers of Glendora, CA; stepson; Jim of Camas
     and Michael and Gary, both of Vancouver. Daughters; Katherin
     Willer of Long Beach, CA and Donna Knutson of Lake Oswego, OR.
     Sister; Dollie Gilbertson of Portland. Services Straub's FH.
     Feb. 14, 1987.   Obit. "The Columbian"]

BEVARD, Virginia May   1940 – 1945   9

BLAIR, Arthur E.   Mar. 22, 1888 – Aug. 6, 1902   3

BLAIR, Jasper M.   1840 – 1930   2

BLAIR, Sarah P.   1843 – 1919   His Wife   2

BLAIR, Herron E.   1870 – 1887   Their Son   2

BLAIR, Rufus   1848 – 1917   8

BLAIR, Louise   1846 – 1916   His Wife   8

BLAIR, Infant children of Rufus and Louise Blair   8

BLAIR, Sally   Jan. 24, 1818 – Jan. 11, 1898   3

BRADFORD, Anna M. [Age 88. b Apr. 30, 1896 in MO – d Sept. 2
     1984, Vancouver, WA. Resided Clark Co. WA. Graveside

BRADFORD, Anna M.   Cont'd   Row No.
    services Thursday, Sept. 6.   Straub's FH. Obit"The Columbian"]

BRASKET, Margie Ellen   [Age 63.   b May 29, 1921, Fern Prairie
    WA. She the wife of Harold P. at home. Funeral Monday, Mar.
    25, at Straub's FH.   Obit. "The Columbian"]

BRIDGEFARMER, Evelyn Katherine   1912 - 1936   Mother   5

BRINK,   Infant girls   1965 - 1965   5

BROWN,   Cecil b.   1910 - 1945   8

BROWN,   Dorothy   1943 - 1962   12

BROWN,   James M.   Sept. 18, 1899 - July 11, 1969   11

BROWN,   Thomas E.   1876 - 1916   7

BROWNING, Mary L.   1892 - 1932   10
    ["Post Record" 28 Oct. 1932. Mrs. Mary L. Browning, 40
    of Island Paradise, died suddenly Wed. morning. Services
    Swank FC with Rev. earl baker officiating. Children, Bernice
    20, Charles 16, Mary 15, and Hazel 13. Six Brothers including
    Fred McKinney of Proebstol, two sisters and her mother, Mrs.
    I. E. McKinney of Roseville, CA. Mrs. Browning was the Island
    Paradise correspondent for the Post Record.]

BROWNING, Walter L.   1890 - 1962   10

BROWNLEE, Viola M.   1923 - 1946   Sister   8

BRUNNER, August W.   1891 - 1974   11

BRUNNER, Florence E.   1900 - 1977   11

BRUNNER, Charles R.   1893 - 1977   9
           PFC   U.S.   Army   W.W.   I

BRUNNER, Evelyn May   1917 - 1934   11

BRUNNER, John   1859 - 1933   Father   9

BRUNNER, Katharina   1855 - 1929   Mother   9

BURRES, Mabel E.   1889 - 1977   Mother   10

BUSCH,   Johanna   1896 - 1969   10

BUSH,   George G.   1885 - 1955   10

CALLAWAY, Nora M.   1876 - 1969   Ma   12

CANADA, Faye   1887 - 1935   7

CARR, Luu M.   1887 - 1975   8

CAVITT, Albert   1953 - 1899   4

CAVITT, Lydia   1848 - 1955   4
[Post Record, Fri. May 21, 1955--..Early settler in this
part of the county died at her home in Paradise. Born July
7, 1818, in Cooley Co. IL. Crossed the plains with her
parents at the age of 5 years, to CA. Forty years ago she
came to this county and resided here ever since. Eleven
children, six of whom are alive, were born to the deceased.
Those who survive are; Mrs. Hulda Wilson, Mrs. Hazel Odoms,
J. H., Arthur, Ben and Richard Cavitt.

CAVITT, Arthur   1881 - 1948   4

CAVITT, Benjamin F.   1884 - 1966   4
[Post Record, Mar. 1966-- Age 81. A lifelong resident of
this area whose profession was gardening, died Wed. Mar.
23, at his home. Services Sat Mar. 26, at Stoller Roselight Chapel in Washougal with Rev. George Jefferson Officiating. Born in the Burton District of Clark Co. on Sept.
12, 1884 and is survived by wife, Susan, one brother, Richard
of Brush Prairie and one brother Richard of Brush Prairie and
one sister, Mrs. Hazel Odoms of Oakland, CA.

CAVITT, Baby Donald

CAVITT, James H.   1879 - 1956   7
[Post Record May 1956 --James Hiram Cavitt, a resident of
Clark Co. and Washougal all of his life, died May 19, in
Vernonia, OR, aged 76. Born Dec. 18, 1879 in Vancouver and
moved to Washougal. A retired lumberman and sawmill operator.
Survived by wife Maggie, at home; two brothers and one sister.
Services May 22 at Stoller Roselight Chapel with Rev. E.R.
Kaemmer officiating.

CAVITT, Glen Bud   Jan. 17, 1920 - May 9, 1920   7
                   Son of J. H. & G. Cavitt

CAVITT, Richard H.   1892 - 1969   Dad   7
[Post-Record Feb. 1969--Retired Crown Zellerbach employee,
age 77, died Fri. Jan. 31 in a Portland Hospital. Services
at Stoller Memorial Chapel, Pastor Duane Corwin officiating.
Born in the Ireland District Jan. 21, 1892, he lived his
entire life in the Camas-Washougal area. Survivors, wife
Edna Cavitt; four daughters, Mrs. Wilma Haskins, Camas, Mrs.
Pauline Young and Mrs. Lauretta Johnson both of Portland and
Mrs. Agnes Heiser of Vancouver, and the mother of the four
daughters Mrs. Reta Cavitt of Vancouver; Stepson Ralph Chubb,
Milwaukie, OR, stepdaughter Ruby Chubb at home. A sister of
Oakland, CA.

CAVITT, Rita   1900 - 1979
[Post Record, Jan. 24, 1979. Former Camas resident, Rita Mae
Cavitt, 78, died Jan. 2, in Vancouver Hospital. Born March
12, 1900, in Porbstel, she had lived her life in the Camas-
Vancouver area. Survivors, 3 daughters, Loretta Johnson, and

CAVITT, Rita Cont'd   Row No.
     Pauline Young, both of Portland and Agnes Hieser of Vancouver
     A sister, Gertrude Stone of Vancouver and an aunt Golda
     Campbell of Washougal. Hamilton Mylan FH.

CLAPP, Richard L.   1938 - 1940   3

CLAUSEN, Christina   Born Sept. 8, 1839 in Sweden   5
                  [see Anderson, Alma C.]

CLAUSEN, J. P. Emil   June 15, 1877 - Mar. 30, 1895   5
        son of J.A. & C.H. Clauson   [see Anderson, Alvira C.M.]

COBURN, Sheldon R.   June 19, 1918 - Apr. 19, 1974   8
        Minn. PFC   W.W. II

COCHRAN, J. (James) V.   1873 - 1939   9

COCHRAN, Johanna R.   1907 - 1941   Mother

COFFEY, Alexander L.   Mar. 15, 1831 - Aug. 8, 1913
              [On Van Vleet Plot]

COFFEY, Joel   June 15, 1789 - Dec. 10, 1855 [On Van Vleet Plot]

CONNER, Helen Irene (Todd)   1894 - 1943   11

CONNER, Steve W.   Mar. 21, 1956 - July 24, 1974   5

CONNOLLY, E. Vona   1908 - 1968   [See also Gates]   1

CONNOLLY, John Henry   1896 - 1978   1
                          Husband and Father

COOK, Lauretta   Feb. 20, 1852 - Dec. 7, 1917   Mother   3

CRAIG, Ella Florence   1907 - 1961   5

CRAIG, Ethel C.   1888 - 1965   6

CRAIG, George A.   1876 - 1956   6

CRAIG, Boyd   1906 - 1910   Son   6

CROMBIE, Lary A. [Age 48. b Aug. 24, 1934, Long Lake Wis.
     d May 28, 1983, Camas, WA. Residence Camas. Wife, Delores
     Crombie, at home. Straub's FH. Obit. "The Columbian"]

DAVIS, Merle U.   1907 - 1975   Dad   13

DAVIS, Opal Dean   1909   Mother   13

DAVIS, George Franklin [Age 72. b Feb. 15, 1911, Lemmon, SD
     d. June 24, 1983, Vancouver, WA. Resided Camas, wA.
     Wife, Florence Davis at home. Brown Stoller Memorial
     Chapel. Obit. "The Columbian']
                          127

FERN PRAIRIE CEMETERY

DAVIS, Sadie	1859 - 1946		8
DAY, C. Arthur	1873 - 1944	Brother	10
DAY, Charles	1842 - 1927	Father	7
DAY, Delbert	1875 - 1965		10
DE TEMPLE, Emma	1886 - 19	Mother	10
DE TEMPLE, Frank	1883 - 1956	Father	10

DICKSON, Arthur R. [Age 83. b Jan. 28, 1901, Stuart, Iowa –
d June 18, 1984, Vancouver, WA. Resided Fern Prairie
area. Wife Laura E. at home. Services United Methodist
Church. Brown Stoller Mem. Chapel. Obit. "The Columbian"]

DICKERSON, Avery O.	1911 - 1970		5
DICKERSON, Dorothy E.	1919 - 1975	Father	9
DONAHE, Frank L.	1916 - 1974	Father	9
DONAHE, L. Charlene	1921 -	Mother	9
DORMAN, Clara A.	Feb. 6, 1867 - Sept. 29, 1883		7
DORMAN, Lester M.	Aug. 27, 1871 - Sept. 22, 1876		7

son and Daughter of Thomas & S.E. Dorman

DORMAN, Sarah Ellen	1845 - 1915		7
DORMAN, Thos. Co. A	12 IA Inf.		7
DUNN, Frank M.	1892 - 1976	father	7
DUNN, John M.	Aug. 15, 1856 - June 21, 1926		7
DUNN, Julia	1850 - 1933		7
DUNN, Patrick	1846 - 1924		7
DUNN, Peter H.	Feb. 3, 1891 - Nov. 22, 1973		7

EBY, Arloene M. [Age 65. b Jan. 28, 1919, Peck, Idaho – d Nov.
7, 1984, Vancouver, WA. Resided Camas, WA. Husband Jack
at home. Brown Stoller Memorial Chapel. Obit."The Columbian"]

EDWARDS, Baby	July 1940	[unmarked]
ERICKSON, John	1867 - 1947	6

ETHIER, Roberta [Age 72. b May 14, 1912 IL – d May 24, 1984
Richland, WA. Formerly of Camas, WA. Brown Stoller Memorial Chapel. Obit. "The Columbian"]

Row No.

EVERETT, Charles F. [Age 81. b Aug. 29, 1902, Coldridge, Neb.-
 d June 2, 1984, Portland, OR. Wife Laura at home. Services
 Straub's FH.   Obit. "The Columbian"]

FAIR, Mildred L. [Age 87. b Apr. 2, 1919, Sedalia, MO - d May
 13, 1986, Portland, OR. Widower C.T. "Tom" Fair at home.
 Sons; Don Fair, Washougal and Larry Fair, Tenino. Sister;
 Mae Magines, Salem, OR.   Brown"s FH Obit. "The Columbian"]

FAY, Lary   1915 - 1916

FEREE, George A.   1876 - 1947   11

FERRIN, Herbert J.   Aug. 3, 1874 - June 30, 1913   2

FERRIN, Delia   Mar. 9, 1908 - Oct. 1, 1910   2

FERRIN, Jacob R.   June 17, 1829 - Nov. 3, 1900   2
                        Born Buffalo, NY

FIDELLE, William J.   1882 - 1946   1

FINCK, Larry L.   U.S. Marine Corps   [Age 44. Heart
 attack b July 20, 1941, Kenoaha, WI - d Mar. 11, 1986,
 Camas, WA. Daughter; Danae Finck, Vancouver. Parents, Leo
 and Mary Finck, Camas WA. Brothers, Robert & Randy, both
 of Camas; Dennis, Kelso, WA; Roger of Washougal, WA. Sisters, Patricia Lougheed, Camas, and Margie Shoemaker, Washougal. Straub's FH.   Obit. "The Columbian"]

FLETCHER, Clifford   1880 - 1952   Brother   1

FLETCHER, Dorothy O. Born Nov. 26, 1916 - Died Oct. 25, 1968 10

FLETCHER, Emma G.   1895 - 1949   Mother   10

FLETCHER, Omar L.   1884 - 1952   Father   10

FLETCHER, Ephraim J.   Died 1948 [unmk. grave next to Omar] 10

FLETCHER, Irvin R.   1871 - 1954   1

FLETCHER, Julia Ann   1851 - 1941   Mother   1

FLETCHER, Robert J.   Died Sept. 8, 1902 - Aged 56 yrs   1

FLYNN, John E.   1852 - 1921   8

FLYNN, Rose E.   1863 - 1946

FORNER, Elwood   1921 - 1941   12

FRANKLIN, Twin Boys   1978 - 1978   5

FREEMAN, Stella Van Vleet   Van Vleet Plot
          Dec. 22, 1867 - Apr. 27, 1948
                    129

Row No.

FREEMAN, Stella Van Vleet Cont'd

[Post Record--Fern Prairie, Friends here were saddened by the death of old time resident of this place, Mrs. William M. Freeman (Stella Van Fleet) who passed away at her home, 202 N.E. Graham St. Portland, OR Tuesday morning July 27. Age 80yrs 7mo and 5 dys. Teacher for many years in the Portland schools and began her profession in the schools of Clark County, having taught at Fern Prairie, Mill Plain and other schools here. She was also a Music Instrctor. Survived by her husband, William M., a step son, William Jr. and one brother Lewis Van Fleet of Portland, numerous nephews and nieces. Services on Thur. July 29, at 1 p.m. in the Pearson Funeral church in Porltand with graveside services in the Fern Prairie Cem. at 3 p.m. at the Van Fleet family polt, a section of the cemetery which was donated by her parents for a public burying ground many years ago.

FRYBERGER,	Blanche T.	1904 –	Mother	7
FRYBERGER,	Deemar S.	1904 – 1969	Father	7
FRYBERGER,	Mary A.	1959 – 1977 [Sarah R. Woods--same st.]	Wife	6
FRYBERGER,	Samuel H. PVT	1930 – 1977 U.S. Army	Korea	7
GARLAND,	Gilbert	1890 – 1944		13
GATES,	Charles E.	1909 –		1

GATES, Elfriede K. [Age 57. b Nov 16, 1929 Winkels, Germany – d Nov. 17, 1986 Portland, OR. Resided Camas, WA. Survivors husband Charles at home. Son: Daniel, Camas. Brother: Richard Schmidt, Oberrod, West Germany. Sisters: Hildegard Kreis and Rosel Bell of Offenbach, West Germany. Funeral Sat. Nov. 22, at Brown's FH, Camas. Obit. "The Columbian"]

GATES,	Effie V.	1882 – 1977	1
GATES,	Lewis W.	1882 – 1960	
GATES,	Elma V.	1926 – 1974	1
GATES,	Margaret F.	1906 – 1933 [One stone with E. Vona Connolly]	1
GATES,	Sarah Frances	1848 – 1943	1
GAY,	Cheryl Sue	Oct. 20, 1954 – Feb. 22, 1956	8

GENTRY, Gerald E. [Age 70. b Feb. 3, 1914, Ohio. d June 2, 1984, Vancouver, WA. Resided in Camas-Washougal and Fern Prairie area. Graveside services June 8, 1984. Brown's Stoller Memorial Chapel. Obit. "The Post Record"]

FERN PRAIRIE CEMETERY

GILMAN, Loyd A.   U.S. Army   W.W. II   Row No.
[Age 61. b Feb. 24, 1926, Stroud, Okla. - d Oct. 1, 1987,
at home, Camas, WA. Leaves a wife, Betty Gilman of Washougal.
Services Monday, Oct. 5, at Straub's FH, Camas.
Obit - "The Columbian"]

GODSIL, Kate L.   1873 - 1950   7

GODSIL, Maurice S.   1872 - 1951

GOLDSMITH, Stephen L.   [Age 27.   See Keegan]

GOODWIN, Elin A.   1908 - 1961   Wife   6

GOULD, Bella R.   [Age 86. b July 13, 1898 - d Oct. 1, 1984,
Bloomington, MN, previous resident in Washougal. Last 2 yrs
in Minn. Services at Jehovah Witness Kingdom Hall in Minn.
Ashes were interred in Fern Prairie Cem. Oct. 21st.
Obit. "Post Record"]

GURNSEY, Eunice A.   1903 - 1970   13

GURNSEY, Lewis E.   1889 - 1964   13

GUSTAFSON, Harold S.   U.S. Navy   W.W. II
[Age 61. Cancer.   b Apr. 29, 1926, Carney, Mich. -
d July 6, 1987 at home, Camas, WA. Wife, Ruth at home.
Services Thurs. July 9, at Brown's FH. Obit. "The Columbian"]

HACKMAN, Hugo Henry   1887 - 1949   8

HALL, Eva A.   1852 - 1924   8

HALL, Nellie   1891 - 1918   Mother   3

HALL, William E.   1876 - 1939   Father

HALL, W. S.   1842 - 1919   GAR   1

HALL, Alice M.   1852 - 1935   His Wife

HALL, Minnie J.   1868 - 1894

HALL, Cora M.   1872 - 1894

HALL, Emogene   1889 - 1889

HANCOCK, Clayton E.   1913 - 1948   9

HARGIS, Mary   Aug. 6, 1846 - Aug. 28, 1930   Mother   9

HASKELL, Christine S.   1856 - 1939   8

HASKELL, Herbert M.   1853 - 1932   8

HAYNES, Ardella M.   [Age 67. b Sept. 25, 1915, Huntington,
    W. VA – d Feb 18, 1983, Portland, OR. Resided Camas WA.
    Services Brown's Stoller Memorial Chapel, Wed. Feb. 23.
    Obit. "The Columbian"]

HEISER, Agnes. B. [Age 58. b May 17, 1927, Silver Creek. (?)
    d May 13, 1986. Resided Vancouver, WA. Surivors, Wife
    Cleo Heiser at home. Sons: Ralph Heiser Vancouver and C.
    Wayne Tikka, Pasco, WA. Daughters: Wanda Schlecht, Bellingham
    Bettie Vainikka, Vancouver. Sisters: Lauretta Johnson and
    Pauline Young, both Portland.   Services Sat. May 17,
    Evergreen Staples FC.   Obit. "The Columbian"]

HENDRYX,	Clair S.	Oct. 13, 1936			11
	IA	Pharmacist's Mate	2CL	U.S. Navy	
HENLEY,	Bessie May	1888 – 1974			8
HENLEY,	William A.	1882 – 1948			8
HOBBS,	Thomas M. "Little Tom"	Oct. 10, 1943 –Oct. 1, 1976			13
HOLMES,	Frank M.	1884 – 1964		Father	
HOLMES,	John R.	1881 – 1951		Father	11
HOLMES,	Gertie Marks	1893 – 19		Mother	
HOLMES,	Lester J.	1914 – 1954		Son	
HOLMES,	Vance D.	1936 – 1975		Son	11
HOOD,	Flora E.	1909 – 1967		Mother	13
HOOD,	Walter F.	1904 –		Father	
HOPKINS,	Robert W.	1868 – 1942		Father	10
HOSMER,	Mr.			Van Fleet Plot	
HOWARD,	Barbara O.	1904 – 1963			7
HOWARD,	Frank J.	1864 – 1949			6
HUNTER,	Bill (Ernest William)	1917 – 1971		Father	11
HUNTER,	Robert A. (Allen)	1950 – 1967		Brother	12

HUNTER, Malcolm H.   [Age 48. b Nov. 19, 1935, Omaha, Neb. –
    d Jan. 30, 1984, Vancouver, WA. Resided Camas, WA. Wife
    Donna H. at home. Memorial services Thurs. Feb. 2, at
    Straub's FH.   Obit.   "The Columbian"]

ISRAEL,	Floyd H.	1901 – 1969		Father	9

FERN   PRAIRIE   CEMETERY

Row No.

JEFFERSON, Allen A.   1908 -   [see Gates & Connolly]   1

JEFFERSON, Lila F.   1917 - 1976

JESTER, Harry George   1877 - 1952   9

JESTER, Infant   1950   8

JOHNSON, Axel W.   July 18, 1896 - Sept. 10, 1970   11
          Wash.   Pvt.   Coast Artillery   W.W.   I

JOHNSON, Clyde E.   1898 - 1969   2

JOHNSON, Lelia A.   1898 - 1967

JOHNSON, George W.   1901 - 1962   11

JOHNSON, John A.   1867 - 1936   4

JOHNSON, Pauline E.   1879 - 1964   Mother   4

JOHNSON, Alice F.   1877 - 1958   Mother   5

JOHNSON, Edward L.   1873 - 1921   Father

JOHNSON, George Edward   1902 - 1959   Father   7

JOHNSON, Mabel G. [Age 79. b Aug 22, 1903, Franklin Minn.-
     d Feb 17, 1983, Camas, WA where he resided. Services
     Wed. Feb. 23, at Straub's FH.   Obit. "The Columbian"]

JOHNSON, Roy L.   U.S. Navy   W.W.   II
     [b Apr 20, 1926 in WA - d Nov. 18, 1985, Camas, WA. Resided
     in Camas, WA. Services Thurs. NOv. 21, 15 Brown's FH.
     Cremation.   Obit. "The Columbian"]

JOHNSON, Thula Mae [Age 82. b Mar. 31, 1900 MO. - d Mar. 24, 1983
     Vancouver, WA. Resided in Camas, WA.   Services Mon. Mar. 28,
     at Brown's Stoller Memorial Chapel. Obit. "The Columbian"]

JOHNSTON, Ruth Ellen   1907 - 1957   Mother

JONAH, Sarah   Indian Grave   11

JONES, Charles F.   1868 - 1943   3

JONES, Harriett   born Mar. _7, 18   died Jan. 11, 1917   3

JONES, J. K. P.   born Jan. 5, 1835   died June 11, 1917
                    [Numbers missing]

KAUFMAN, George   1851 - 1925   9

KAUFMAN, Lide   1853 - 1930

133

Row No.

KAYS, William James   Apr. 29, 1880 – Sept. 12, 1964   3
    Wash. Pvt   Co. G   1 Reg.   Wash Inf. Spanish Amer. War

KAYS, Laura Pearl   1885 – 1964   3

KEEGAN, Stephen Goldsmith   [See Stephen L. Goldsmith – Age 27.
    Auto Accident, b 30 Dec. 1956, Louisville, KY – d Oct. 26,
    1984, Vancouver, WA. Resided Vancouver, WA. Survived by
    Wife Cheri, at home. Mother & Step-father, Elizabeth and
    Robert Keegan, Vancouver. Graveside services Wed. Oct. 31,
    with Brown's Stoller Mem. Chapel in charge.
    Obit. "The Columbian"]

KERRON, Walter Scott   [unmarked]   9

KIRBY, Letta Giles   1878 – 1967   7

KIRBY, William   1888 – 1941   7

KIRSCHNER, Aldo A.   1916 – 1973   11

KIRSCHNER, Faye P.   1927 –

KISTER, Karen Annette   1960 – 1976   10

KRAMER, Bert S.   1874 – 1952   9

KRAMER, Minnie S.   1873 – 1956

KRAMER, Carl   1916 – 1922   6

KRAMER, Fred   1915 – 1919

KREHSLER, John W.   1874 – 1967   7

KREHSLER, Merilla M.   1875 – 1970   7

LA BRANCH, Nellie   1910 – 1972   12

LA FRANCE, Lawrence E.   1892 – 1968   2

LA FRANCE, Phillip Earl [Age 63. b July 22, 1920, Oregon, MO –
    d Oct. 13, 1983 Vancouver, WA Resided Camas, WA. Wife,
    Inez A. at home. Funeral Saturday Oct. 15, at Brown's
    Stoller Mem. Chapel. Obit. "The Columbian"]

LA FRANCE, Viva L.   1895 – 1964

LAKE, Daniel A.   1887 – 1904   2

LAKE, David S.   1847 – 1925   2

LAKE, Olive U.   1872 – 1902   2

LAKE, Stanley D.   1896 – 1946   2

FERN PRAIRIE CEMETERY

LANCASTER, Gordon E. [Age 61. Heart Attack. b May 9, 1926,
     Camas, WA – d Oct. 13, 1987, Vancouver, WA. Leaves Wife
     Marie at Home. Graveside service Sat. Oct. 17.
     Obit. "The Columbian"]

LANGFORD, Harleigh F.	1892 – 1928	10
LANGFORD, Oliver L.	1860 – 1943	10
LANGFORD, Susana L.	1856 – 1943	10
LAWS, Carrie	1859 – 1908	5
LAWS, Isaac	1860 – 1935	
LAWS, Preston		
LAWS, Catherine		
LAWS, Mumford		
LEE, Leander M.	1869 – 1947	9
LIENESCH, Henry H.	1858 – 1946	8
LINDER, Jacob	Aug. 29, 1866 – Oct. 21, 1913	9
LINDER, Jacob F.	1892 – 1952 Son	11
LINDER, Margaret	1869 – 1929 Mother	11
LINDER, William A.	1898 – 1970	8
LITTLETON, Clifford D.	Oct. 3, 1944 – July 18, 1956	11
LIVINGSTONE, Arty M.	Apr. 26, 1834 – Dec. 10, 1886	4
LYNCH, Anna F.	May 11, 1853 – June 30, 1912 Mother	5
LYNCH, John C.	1856 – 1932 Father	
LYNN, Jim	died 1940 [unmarked grave]	12
MAC ALEVY, Sandi V.	1948 – 1974 [see Gates Plot]	1
MAKI, Sam	]unmarked]	8
MANOR, Alfred E.	1892 – 1966 Father	8
MANOR, Harriet C.	1893 – 1977 Mother	8
MANECKE, Jarrod Paul	1968 – 1974	12

MARKS, Gertie F.   [Age 93. b Sept. 27, 1893, Cabool, MO –
     d July 24, 1987 Resided Camas, WA. Preceded in death
     by her husb. Paul in 1986. Service Mon. July 27 at
     Brown's F H. Obit. "The Columbian"]

FERN PRAIRIE CEMETERY

MARTELL, Jeneanne Craig   1939 - 1973   6
                In Memory of my Mother

MARTIN, Jacob T.   1899 - 1970   Father   9

MARTIN, Lillian O.   1905 - 1987   Mother
          [Age 82. Heart Attack. b June 28, 1905 Winnipeg, Manitoba -
          d July 9, 1987, Camas, WA. Brown's Stoller FH.
          Obit. "The Columbian"]

MARTIN, Victor L.   Oct. 10, 1921 - Feb. 22, 1962   11
          Wash.   Sgt.   U.S. Army   W.W. II

MAXWELL, John   1879 - 1924   Brother   7

MAXWELL, William R.   1848 - 1972   Father   7

MC ALLISTER, George   1876 - 1906   4

MC ALLISTER, Joseph B.   1898 - 1964   4

MC ALLISTER, Lois B.   1902 - 1978

MC ALLISTER, Joseph S.   1849 - 1938   Father   4

MC ALLISTER, Rebecca Ann   1857 - 1913   Mother   4

MC CRORY, Mary Grace   1939 - 1971   5

MC QUEEN, Clara A.   1904 - 1965   6

MC QUEEN, John B.   1900 -

MC QUEEN, John Robert   Feb. 7, 1925 - July 30, 1936   6
                In Loving Memory of Our Son

MC QUEEN, John P.   1879 - 1946   Father   7

MC QUEEN, Julia Etta   1879 - 1972   Mother

MELTON, Jimmy   July 11, 1961 - Oct. 18, 1971   Son   10

MELTON, Samuel W.   Jan. 25, 1930 - Dec. 8, 1969   Father   10

MENHENNETT, Alice A.   1914 - 1952   12

MENHENNETT, Everett M.   1910 -   Masonic Emblem

MERRILL, Ernest G.   1883 - 1955   13

MERRILL, Ida M.   1883 - 1974

MICHAEL, Egbert D.   Sept. 23, 1913 - Sept. 15, 1970   8
          Missouri CPL   Army Air Forces   W.W. II   Husband

MICHAEL, Lorene A.   1919 -   Wife
                136

			Row No.
MITCHELL, Esther	1843 - 1925		2
MITCHELL, Geo.	1840 - 1930		2
MITCHELL, Children (4)	[unmarked- no names]		2
MORGAN, Bernice G.	1896 - 1978	U.S. Army	12
MORRIS, Arnold Oren PFC	Dec. 8, 1924 - Dec. 14, 1975 U.S. Army W.W. II		9
MOUSER, Lloyd G.	1904 - 1968		9
MYERS, Frank	1902 - 1963		6
NEAL, Olive Lois	1888 - 1931	Mother	4
NEAL, Wm. H.	1887 - 1948	Father	
NEBLOCK, Howard A. Wash. SA	May 11, 1934 - Nov. 5, 1967 U.S.N.		9
NELSON, Carl O.	Apr. 10, 1883 - July 21, 1923 Odd Fellows		4
NEVITT, Joseph Abe	1903 - 1972		10
NICHOLS, Anna V.	1905 - 1947		9
NICHOLS, Mabel L.	1911 -	Mother	5
NICHOLS, Mike J.	1901 - 1969	Father	5
NICHOLS, Baby Thomas	1961 - 1961		12
NIEBUHR, Amelia B.	1890 - 1976	Mother	11
NITSCHELM, Arthur F.	1890 - 1912		7
ORNDUFF, Clara L. Hall	1875 - 1941	Mother	5
ORNDUFF, Joseph	1871 - 1916		
OSTENSON, Clarence S.	1908 - 1976		8
OSTENSON, Karen		Mother	8
OSTENSON, Severt		Father	
OSTENSON, Baby	1937		10
OTTERSON, Nellie B.	1891 - 1934	Mother	10
PETRAIN, Etna	1877 - 1932	Mother	5
PEURA, Aroe	1907 - 1918		9
PEURA, Eric	1878 - 1948		4

FERN   PRAIRIE   CEMETERY

Row   No.

PEURA,   Hanna   1873 – 1947   4

PFEIFER,   Alvina   L.   1883 – 1955   8

PFEIFER,   Otto A.   1884 – 1977

PLATT,   Frank B.   Mar. 18, 1896 – Dec. 19, 1967   6
                                        Husband & Father

PLACE, Bruce Allen   [Age 21.   Auto Accident – b. Sep 29, 1964,
      Vancouver, WA – D Mar. 29, 1986, Camas, WA. Daughter:
      Tasha Nicole Place, Camas. Parents; Burton & Karen Place,
      Camas. Gr-Parents Ron & Laverne Craig, Camas. Funeral Wed.
      Apr. 2, Brown's FH   Obit. "The Columbian"]

PLUMM, Linda Sue   [Age 35.   Auto Accident. b Apr. 8, 1948
      Vancouver, WA. – d Jan. 28, 1984 Vancouver, WA. Wife of
      Walt L. Plumm, Vancouver. Graveside services Thursday Feb.
      2.   Staples FC.   Obit "The Columbian"]

POWELL,   John Lee   1876 – 1939   1

PRIETZEL,   Thomas Leroy   Died 1945   [unmarked]   11

PRIETZEL,   Baby   Died 1936   [unmarked]   10

PRINCE,   David   1852 – 1934   Father   11

PRITZEL,   Baby   [unmarked]   11

PRUETT,   Charles L.   Mar. 15, 1916 – Sept. 6, 1972   11

RAETZ, Frederick A.   [Age 68.   b Feb. 27, 1917 on high prairie of
      Alberta, Canada – d May 5, 1985, Portland, OR.   Resided
      Camas, WA. Leaves Wife Annetta at home. Service Wed. May 8
      at Zion Lutheran Church, Camas. Straub's FH. Obit. "The
      Columbian"]

RANKIN,   Mary Alice   1931 – 1932   11

RASMUSSEN,   Anne M.   1857 – 1918   6

RASMUSSEN,   C.   1857 – 1931   6

RASMUSSEN,   Chris   Apr. 2, 1896 – Aug. 27, 1967   Father   6

RASMUSSEN,   David Lee   [Age 36.   Massive coronary attack.
      b Jan. 19, 1951, Vancouver, WA. – d Mar 9, 1986, Vanacouver
      WA. Widow Judith Rasmussen, at home. Sons: Derek L.
      Elledge, Stevenson, WA and Christopher A. Rasmussen, at
      home. Parents; Glenn & Grace Beacock, Orchards, WA. Bro.
      Wayne Rassmussen, Seattle, WA. Step-brothers & step-
      sister. Services Mar 12.   Memorial Gardens FC in charge.
      Obit. "The Columbian"]

RASMUSSEN,   Esther F.   1900 – 1932   Mother   6
                                        138

FERN PRAIRIE CEMETERY

Row No.

RASMUSSEN, ERBA V.	1907 – 1970		7
RASMUSSEN, Soren H.	1884 – 1956		8
REBENSDORFF, Carl H.	[unmarked]		10

REINEL, Nicholas   June 15, 1838 – June 22, 1892   2
           Pvt   9 Wis. Inf.   Civil War

RICE, Eunice E.   1897 – 19   Wife   12
[Age 85.   b Dec. 19, 187, Wilsonville, Neb. – d Sept 2,
1983, Camas. WA.   Resided Camas.   Services Wed. Sept. 7,
   at Straub's FH.   Obit. "The Columbian"]

RICE, Louis A.   1895 – 1975
           Pvt   US Army   W.W. I

RICHARDS, Jefferson T.   June 21, 1894 – Jan. 22, 1960   13
    Wash.   Sgt.   U.S. Army   W.W. I

RICHI, John   Died Apr. 1, 1907   Aged 21 years   2

RICHI, Susan   1861 – 1931   Mother   2

RINEHART, Dora Lee	1917 –	13
RINEHART, Edgar	1915 – 1976	13
ROBINSON, Charles P.	1911 – 1957	2
ROBINSON, Etta Mae	1905 – 1974	3
ROBINSON, Sarah Bertha	1881 – 1963	
ROBINSON, Thomas Watt	1880 – 1926	
ROBINSON, Lewis W.	1903 – 1958	13
ROBINSON, Verna M.	1907 –	

ROBINSON, W. W. "Bud"   [Age 78.   Dec. 20, 1906 Fern Prairie area.
   d Oct. 7, 1985 Gresham, OR.   Resided Camas, WA.   Wife, at
home.   Graveside service Thurs. Oct. 10.   Straub's FH.
   Obit.   "The Columbian"

ROBISON, Ernest	1885 – 1960	6
ROBISON, Lula	1887 – 1971	

RODGERS, Anna Leona   [Age 81.   b Jan 27, 1905, Irenton, OH – d
   Oct 15, 1986, Vancouver, WA.   Graveside services Sat. Oct.
   18.   Brown's FH   Obit. "The Columbian"]

RODGERS, Walter A.   1902 – 1966   13

ROESER, Steven David   Oct. 17, 1933 – Sept. 12, 1962   13

139

				Row No.
RUNYAN, Lillie	1870 – 1938	Mother		9
RUNYAN, Samuel C.	1859 – 1937	Father		
SADEWASSER, Florence E.	1896 – 1976			13
SADEWASSER, Henry	1894 – 19			
SCOTT, Edith	1909 – 1975	Mother		12
SCOTT, William M.	1909 –	Father		
SCOTT, Forest A.	1906			6
SHERRELL, Addison W.	1877 – 1957			11
SHERRELL, Cleo G.	1911 – 1934			11
SHERRELL, Mary M.	1846 – 1933			11

SHERRELL, Lemuel D. [Age 100. b Aug 30, 1882, Salem, MO. – d
    Feb. 17, 1983, Vancouver, WA. Wife Olive E. Sherrell at
    home. Services Mon. Feb 21, at Vancouver FC.
    Obit. "The Columbian"]

SHERRELL, Mary M.	1846 – 1933			11
SHERRELL, Olive V.	1886 – 1963			11
SHERRELL, Nora Bell	1881 – 1961	Mother		13
SMITH, Dorothy Ann	1926 – 1966			5
SPELLMAN, Mary J.	1862 – 1947	Mother		4
STANTON, Lorenzo J.	1882 – 1971			9
STANTON, Mary Andrew	1869 – 1956			9
STEBBENS, Albert W.	1881 – 1978			8
STEBBENS, Bertha Louise	1912 – 1917			8
STEBBENS, Clara P.	1861 – 1925			9
STEBBINS, Orville D.	1855 – 1943			
STEBBINS, Dwight H.	1887 – 1979			9
SNYDER, William	[unmarked grave]			1
STEELE, Delphia	1867 – 1938			8
STEELE, George (W)	1869 – 1934			8
STEPHENSON, Deborah S.	1854 – 1930	Mother		9

				Row No.
STEPHENSON,	Lorenzo C.	1857 – 1928	Father	
STEPHENSON,	John P.	1860 – 1944	Father	10
STEPHENSON,	Langley T.	1889 – 1962		10
STEPHENSON,	Stanley G.	1891 – 1961		10
STEPHENSON,	W. S.	[unmarked]		
STEUER,	Anna Ruth	1895 – 1971	[See Fitzgerald, Maxine]	4
STEUER,	William C.	1895 – 1976		
STEVESON,	Fred S.	1881 – 1942		10
STOFER,	Baby Phil	1917 – 1917		7
STONE,	Vay Edward	1901 – 1971		10
STRANGE,	Harry A.	1877 – 1949		9
STRANGE,	Sarah J.	1874 – 1953		
STRUNK,	Anna M.	1883 – 1951		12
STRUNK,	Edwin M.	1885 – 1961		12
STRUNK,	Rose K.	1904 – 1970	Wife and Mother	12
STUMPFF,	Georgia M.	1896 – 1972		6
STUMPFF,	Richard S.	1892 – 1974		
SUND,	Carrie	1858 – 1932		8

TATE, Mack   [Age 76. b June 22, 1908 Pine Bluff, Ark. –
     d Dec. 12, 1984 Camas, WA. Service Fri. Dec. 14, at Brown's
     Stoller Mem. Chapel   Obit. "The Post Record"]

TAYLOR,	Arthur Early	Dec. 28, 1888 – Nov. 7, 1956		1
	Wash Pvt 143 Co. Trans Corp	W.W. I		
TAYLOR,	Ethel W.	1900 – 1974		1
TAYLOR,	Senella	1922 – 1935	Daughter and Sister	1
TEMPLER,	Cecil B. (Bryan)	Oct. 6, 1901 – June 26, 1966		9
	Wash. MMSI	USNR	W.W. II	
TEMPLER,	Dewey I.	1898 – 1971	Father	13

TEMPLER, Earl A. [Age 76. b Jun. 21, 1909, Haynes, ND –
     d Jan. 5, 1986, at home in Washougal, WA. Wife Alyce, at
     home. Sons: Errol, Washougal, & Dennis, Goldendale, WA.
     Daughter: Dianna Kennison of Greenleaf, ID. Sisters.
     Obit. "The Columbian" Straub's FH]

Row No.

TEMPLER, Ernest Roy   Sept. 23, 1926 – June 1, 1934   9

TEMPLER, Louise M.   1871 – 1943   Mother   10

TEMPLER, Milo E.   1862 – 1915   Dad   5

TEUTSCH, Richard G. [Age 45. b Oct. 20, 1938, Newton Falls,
     Ohio – d May 16, 1984, at his job in Camas, wA. Wife,
     Elsie, Camas. Services Fri. May 18. Straub's FH.
     Obit. "The Columbian"]

TIFFANY, Baby Boy   1854 – 1954   12

TIFFANY, E. Rena CRAIG   [Age 79. Cancer. b Aug. 18, 1907 –
     d Aug. 11, 1987, Spokane, WA. Last resided in Hope, Idaho.
     Wife of Harold Tiffany, at home. Service Thurs. at Fern
     Prairie United Methodist Church, Camas. Obit. "The Columbian"]

TOWNSEND, Tabitha   1978 – 1978   10

TRANGMAR, Benita   Dec. 20, 1887 – Nov. 13, 1967   Mother   11

TROXEL, Frank L. [Age 88. b Nov. 5, 1887, Hoskins, OR. – d
     Feb. 1, 1986. Survived by Son: Sidney Troxel, Vancouver, WA
     Daughter: Esther Marsengill, Camas, WA. Funeral Tues. Feb.
     4, at Brown's FH. Obit. "The Columbian"]

TROXEL, Leona   [Age 82. b Dec. 25, 1900 Medford, OR – d July 2,
     1983, Camas, WA. Wife of Frank, at home. Funeral Wed. July
     6, at Brown's Stoller Mem. Chapel. Obit. "The Columbian"]

TUMM, Julis (J.J.)   1881 – 1936   10

TURNER, James Welcome   1874 – 1934   1

TWEEDT, Karol Ivaloo   1913 – 1930   10

VAIL, James W.   1872 – 1956   Father   4

VAN FLEET, Alfred C.   May 3, 1904 – Oct. 31, 1929   12
     Burial services of Alfred C. Van Vleet of Seattle. .....
     Killed in an airoplane accident at Bremerton. The young mans
     grandparents Mr. and Mrs. Lewis Van Vleet, Sr...earliest
     settlers and donated land for the cemetery and all deceased
     members of the family have been laid to rest here.
     Obit. Camas Post-Record Nov. 8, 1929]

VAN VLEET, Bertha   May 19, 1879 – Aug. 25, 1944 Van Vleet Plot

VAN VLEET, Edith   Mar. 14, 1865 – Aug. 7, 1912   Van Vleet Plot

VAN VLEET, Elizabeth Angeline   May 8, 1836 –   Van Vleet Plot
                Apr. 12, 1905

VAN VLEET, Felix F.   Jan. 11, 1878 – Nov. 25, 1919
Van Vleet Plot

Row No.

VAN VLEET, Harriet Lewis   Nov. 7, 1858 - Nov. 16, 1863

Van Vleet Plot

VAN VLEET, Lewis   Oct. 21, 1826 - Apr. 15, 1910   Van Vleet Plot

VAN VLEET, Lewis   May 18, 1875 - Aug. 27, 1957   12
                    Masons   Father

VAN VLEET, Lewis   Feb. 20, 1906 - Aug. 30, 1936   12

VAN VLEET, Lois   Dec. 25, 1856 - May 13, 1857 VanVleet Plot

VAN VLEET, Olive   July 30, 1880 - Mar. 20, 1941   Mother   12

WAKEFIELD, Mary F.   1853 - 1924   Mother   6

WARREN, Deroyn W.   [Age 64. b Aug 6, 1920, Eminence, MO. -
   d June 24, 1985, Vancouver, WA. Resided camas, WA. Wife,
   Betty at home. Funeral Mond. July 1, at Straub's FH.
   Obit. "The Columbian"]

WALKER, Arch E.   1894 - 1968   9

WALKER, Virginia M.   1897 - 1967

WALKER, Hal Gene   Jan. 13, 1926 - Jan. 6, 1959   10
      Wash.   Pvt   386 Infantry   W.W. II

WARING, Robert C.   1863 - 1967   13

WATSON, Harriette L.   1872 - 1959   Mother   9

WATZIG, Gertrude M.   1894 - 1952   8

WEBBERLEY, Clarence F.   1874 - 1960   Father   13

WEBBERLEY, Edgar   [Age 79. b Mar 12, 1905 Ironton, OH - d
   May 21, 1984 at home, Camas, WA. Wife, Edith at home.
   Funeral Sunday May 27, at Reorganized Church of Jesus Christ
   of Latter Day Saints. Brown's Stoller Memorial Chapel.
   Obit. "The Columbian"]

WEBBERLEY, Martha E.   1877 - 1959   Mother

WEBBERLEY, Neal C.   [Age 81. b May 8, 1903, Ironton, OH -
   d Oct. 6, 1984, Camas WA. (Bro. of Walter Webberley buried
   in Evergreen) Services Tuesday Oct. 9, at the Latter Day
   Saints. Brown's Stoller Memorial Chapel. Obit. Post Record]

WEBBERLEY, Dan Ray   1948 - 1948   11

WEBBERLEY, Louis Robert   1912 - 1949   13

WEBBERLEY, William   1907 - 1961   13

WEBBERLEY, William   1853 - 1937   12

FERN PRAIRIE CEMETERY

				Row No.
WEBBERLY, Theodochia Ernest	1873 – 1943			
WEEKS, Arleigh J.	1907 –	Father		13
	Married July 3, 1929			
WEEKS, Faye Opal	1910 – 1964	Mother		
WELCH, Frank	1862 – 1930	Father		8
WELCH, Hannah	1859 – 1916	Mother		8
WELCH, Katie	1857 – 1909	Mother		8
WENGER, Janette M. (Michele)	1948 – 1948 9June 6)			
WETHERED, Pearl Ann	1845 – 1950			10
WHITROCK	[unmarked]			1
WILSON, Arthur	1875 – 1956			9
WILSON, James	1849 – 1919			9
WILSON, Mary A.	1854 – 1947			

WILSON, Mary E. [Age 90. b Jan. 12, 1894, Wilhoite, OR – d
    Apr. 25, 1984, at home, Camas, WA. Graveside service Sat.
    Apr. 28.   Brown's Stoller Memorial Chapel. Obit. " The
    Columbian"]

WILSON, Nathan	1881 – 1970			10
WILSON, Steven	1950 – 1950			2
WILSON, Will X.	1878 – 1958			9
WINTER, Bette M.	1921 – 1972			7
WINTER, Lawrence R.	1915			
WINTER, Kenneth E.	1909 – 1969			8
WOLFE, Amanda	1853 – 1932	Mother		10
WOLFE, Meeker	1851 – 1926	Father		
WOODS, Sarah R.	Apr. 3, 1977 – Aug. 12, 1977	Niece		6
WRIGHT, Louisa Van Vleet M.D.	Oct. 30, 1862 –			
	May 30, 1913		Van Vleet Plot	
WYLIE, Charles A.	1856 – 1926	Father		8
WYLIE, Rosetta	1859 – 1923	Mother		
WYLIE, Charles E.	1893 – 1955			11

FERN PRAIRIE CEMETERY

YOUNG, Baby Melvin

St. John's Catholic Cemetery

St. John's Catholic Cemetery is located on N. E. 109th Street and Maitland Road, two blocks west of St. John's Road. The area now called the Barberton District, was earlier called St. John's. The property was originally owned by Gratien LeBlanc and was donated to the Sisters of Charity of Providence by his daughter Cleophine and her husband Thomas J. Thornton. The first person buried in St. John's was Anna Cora Lee, who was born in 1864 and died in 1868.

ANFIN, Blanche   1884 - 1966   Mother

ANFIN, L. Ole   1881 - 1967   Father

APRIMIS, Minerva   1903 - 1964

AUGER, Albert W.   1885 - 1953

AUGER, Anna Fox   1883 - 1971

BARNETT, Eva L. (A'Hearn)   1895 - 1960

BARNETT, George S.   1891 - 1986
    [Hamilton-Mylan F H. Obit. Columbian]

BARNETT, Margaret Sharp   Born1896 - Died 1979
    Wife of Vernon Barnett

BARNETT, Mary V. (Thornton)   1862 - 1938   Mother

BARNETT, Seth E.   1852 - 1936   Father

BARNTETT, Virginia   Feb. 29, 1918 - July 13, 1920
    Daughter of of George and Eva Barnett

BEESON, Ray Edw.   1903 - 1975

BEESON, Minerva (Caldwell)   1899 - _____

BALANGER, Flevia   Apr. ___ 1836 - Oct. 5, 1907
    Age 71 yrs.

BELANGER, John   Jan. 16, 1867 - Oct. 15, 1909

BELANGER, Moses   Mar. ___ 1831 - June 6, 1908   Age 77 yrs.
    Born in Three Rivers Canada   Father

BELISLE, Alex O.   1831 -. 1970

BELISLE, Luda M.   1908 - _____

BELONGIA, Andrew   1862 - 1938   Father

BIRCHMAN, Fred E.   July 4, 1917 - Sept. 26, 1964
    Wash. S. Sgt.   3502 Base Unit   A.A.F.   WW II
    [Husband of Florine]

BIRRER, Ann J.   1908 - ____   [Wife of John]

BIRRER, John   1901 - 1960   [son of Joseph & Mary Birrer]

BIRRER, John   May 10, 1844 - May 7, 1918   [Bro. of Joseph]

BIRRER, Joseph F.   1857 - 1950

BIRRER, Mary E. (Golden)   1865 - 1945

BOYER, Veronica "Ronnie" M.   [Age 71. Sept. 30, 1915. Thief River Falls, MN - Nov. 3, 1966. Resided Vancouver, WA. Wife of F. "Pat" Patrick Boyer, Hamilton-Mylan FH. Obit. Columbian.

BRENNEN, James   1839 - 1919

BRENNEN, Johanna   1833 - 1910

BRENNEN, Patrick   Born at Dundalk Co., South Ireland
                 Died May 14, 1900   Age 70 yrs.

BROSIUS, [Edward H.   Age 63.   Sept. 1, 1920 Oakwood, ND - July 16, 1984 at home in Vancouver, WA. Husband of Olive Brosius at home. Mass at St. John's Catholic Church. Obit: The Columbian]

BUMP, [George C.   Age 76.   Sept. 23, 1909, Grant Co. MN - Nov. 24, 1985, Vancouver, WA.   Husband of NOra R. Bump, at home. Hamilton Mylan F H   Obit: The Columbian]

CALDWELL, Anne Louise   1888 - 1969
                 [Mother of John Richard Caldwell]

CALDWELL, Boyd   1900 - 1933   Lost at Sea
              [Son of Harriet & Edward Caldwell]

CALDWELL, Daniel K.   Died Oct. 4, 1915   Age 3 yrs.
              [Son of Harriet & Edward Caldwell]

CALDWELL, Dickie   1928 - 1937   [Drowned in the Columbia
     River   Son of Leslie & Cecilia Caldwell]

CALDWELL, Edward   1869 - 1936   Father
                 [Husband of Harriet]

CALDWELL, Georgie H.   Died Oct. 5, 1915   Age 5 yrs.
                 [Son of Harriet & Edward]

CALDWELL, Harriet R.   1878 - 1957   Mother
                 [Wife of Edward]

CALDWELL, [Helen Blanche   Age 80 of Pneumonia.   July 11, 1906, Grand Forks, ND - (no date-Obit printed in Wed. May 13, 1987 Columbian) Died at Glisan Care Center, Portland, OR. Two Bro. and Three sisters. Corinthian Group Funeral Services of Portland in charge of arrangements. Obit - The Columbian]

CAREY, John Reuben   1884 - 1951
                 [Husband of Mary Luring]

CARROLL, Daniel, Sr.   1889 - 1979
                 [Husband of Mary Irene]

CARROLL, [Mary I.   Age 88.   Oct. 4, 1894, St. John, WA. - Mar. 1, 1983, at home in Brush Prairie, WA.   MGM Obit. Columbian]

CAULEY, James   B. Mar. 26, 1871 - D. Age 5 yrs.
                 [Son of Pat & Margaret]

CAWLEY, Pat'k   Co. B   15th Inf.   N.Y.   [No dates =
      next to Cauley Plot -   Husband of Margaret]

CAULEY, Margaret   [no dates]

CAULEY, Thomas   B. Oct. 25, 1868 - D. Age 12 yrs.
                [Son of Pat & Margaret]

CHANDLER, Fred S.   1907 - 1962   [Husband of Margaret]

CHANDLER, Margaret   1913 - 1979   [Ashes]

CHANEY, Wm.   [No dates - First husband of Annie
                Thornton Stephens]

CLEARY, Edward   1859 - 1936 [Born in N.Y. - Husband of Mary
                Son of Patrick & Ellen Cleary]

CLEARY, Ellen   Born in Limerick, Ireland 1822
            Died Nov. 5, 1901   Age 79 yrs. [Wife of Patrick]

CLEARY, John   1850 - 1923   [Born in N.Y., son of
                Patrick & Ellen]

CLEARY, Mary   1856 - 1919   [Wife of Edward]

CLEARY, Patrick   Born in Limerick, Ireland 1824 - Died Dec. 18,
       1896   Age 79 yrs.   Civil War Veteran [Hus. of Ellen]

CLIFTON, John Dewey   1898 - 1961   [Husband of Sarah]

CLIFTON, Sarah (Dupuis)   1901 - _____

CODY, Allan A.   1889 - 1975   Father
                [husband of Emma]

CODY, Anna   1869 - 1918 [2nd wife of James Cody]

CODY, Ellen   1846 - 1911 [1st wife of James Cody]   Mother

CODY, Emma L.   1899 - 1971   [Wife of Allan]   Mother

CODY, James   1838 - 1930   Father

CODY, Rodney Allan   Died Dec. 27, 1965
                [Twin, son of Donald Cody]

COFFEY, Flossy   Sept. 12, 1896 - Oct. 13, 1897

CONDON, Anthony John   1946 - 1979

CONNOLLY, Annie F.   1881 - 1966   Mother

CONNOLLY, Charles H.   1879 - 1960   Father

CONNOLLY, JOhn Clair   1911 - 1979

149

CONNOR, Kevin Casey   Apr. 19, 1974 - June 5, 1978
            [Nephew of Mathew Connor]

CONNOR, Matthew T.   1952 - 1963   Beloved Son

COSSETTE, [Judy Ann   Age 33.   Sept. 20, 1949, in Fargo, ND -
      June 6, 1983, Vancouver, WA. Daughter of Robert and Eileen
         Cossette, Castle Rock, WA. Hamilton-Mylan FH Obit: Columbian

COSTELLO, Wm.   Died Jan. 9, 1912   Age 56 yrs.

COURT, Louise M. (Fox)   1894 - 1969   Mother

COURTIAN, Antoniette   1851 - 1905   Mother

COURTIAN, Peter   1828 - 1920   Father

CRUZ, David   Jan. 30, 1944 - May 6, 1972   Husband and Father

CURTIN, Abbie E. (Sullivan)   1875 - 1937

CURTIN, Abbott M.   1869 - 1936   [Son of Wm. & Margaret]

CURTIN, Flora J. "Babe"   1913 - 1970   Wife of John Curtin
                [Vancouver Funeral Home]

CURTIN, John T.   Nov. 9, 1908 - Dec. 1, 1973
            Wash.   Pfc.   U.S. Army   W W II

CURTIN, Margaret   Born County Cork, Ireland   Died Apr. 5, 1908
            Age 80 yrs.   [Wife of William Curtin]

CURTIN, Mary   Infant   [Grandaughter of Wm. & Margaret]

CURTIN, William   Born County Limerick, Ireland   Died Feb. 24,
      1903   Age 74 yrs.   [Husband of Margaret]

DAY, Johanna   June 3, 1862 - June 16, 1898
         Wife of Joseph Day   [Daughter of Wm. & Margaret Curtin]

de LAGASSE, Lena M.   1905 - 1974   Mother

de LAGASSE, Leslie H.   1906 - 1965   Father
      [Brother to Rouque M. de Lagasse, Son of George H. de Lagasse
            and Tillie Ann Quesnell]

DIETZ, Marla Jo   1956 - 1958

DONOVAN, Jerry   [no dates]

DONOVAN, Annie   [no dates]

DONOVAN, Jack   [no dates]

DONOVAN, Julia   [no dates]

DONOVAN, Mother (Joanna)   [no dates]

DONOVAN, Father   (John)   [no dates]

DONOVAN, Margaret   [no dates]

DUPUIS, Adler L.   Died 30 Sept. 1942   [Son of Philip & Nancy]
      Washington Pvt. 17th Co.   Coast Arty

DUPUIS, Alfred Philip   5 Aug. 100 - 11 May 1938
      [Son of Philip and Nancy]

DUPUIS, Frank   [no information - Father of Philip]

DUPUIS, John T.   7 Jan. 1904 - 29 Sept. 1960
                  [Son of Philip and Nancy]

DUPUIS, Mary E.   [no information - Mther of Philip]

DUPUIS, Nancy   1868 - 1947   Mother

DUPUIS, Philip   1863 - 1943   Father

ELLIS, David Byron   13 Dec. 1960 - 10 Jan. 1962

ERNST, Charles   [unmarked]

ERNST, Eva R.   Died 11-18-1898

ERNST, George   [unmarked]

ERNST, Harry   [unmarked]

ERNST, Mary   [unmarked]

ERNST, Wm. L.   [unmarked]

FISHER, Francis L.   Died 11-18-1973
            [Son of Frank and Margaret]

FISHER, Margaret   1897 - 1951   Mother

FISHER, Jonas   11 Oct. 1832 - 11 Feb. 1871
            Age 38 Yrs 9 Days 4 Mos.

FISHER, Phoebe   13 Mar. 1828 - 8 Oct. 1900
            Age 72 Yrs. 6 Mos. 26 Days

FOLEY, Timothy M.   1852 - 1928

FOLTZ, Jeffrey Paul   6 Oct. 1965 - 7 oct. 1965

FOX, [John L.   Age 87.   June 5, 1887, Chicago, IL - Feb. 9, 1985,
      Vancouver, WA. Husband of Mary M. Fox. Died at home. Mass at
      St. John's Catholic Church. Hamilton-Mylan FH. Obit. Columbian.

FOX, Joseph J. Sr.   1857 - 1956   Father

FOX, Kathryn   1858 - 1928   Mother

FOX, Joseph H. Jr.   1887 - 1931

FOX, Alice L.   8 Dec. 1885 - 26 Nov. 1981
                       [Wife of Joseph Fox Jr.]

FRACKIEWICZ, [Victor Cash   Age 45.   Aug. 27, 1938, Warsaw,
        Poland - Mar. 18, 1985, Vancouver, WA.   Husband of Judy Frac-
        kiewicz, at home.   Evergreen Staples FC.   Obit: Columbian.]

GARANT, Roseanne   1884 - 1969   Mother
            [Mother of Mrs. Theodore Jagelski (Genevieve)]

GOGGIN, Christopher   1976 - 1976   Vancouver Funeral Home

GOLDEN, John   1837 - 1900   [Husband of Rose Agnes]

GOLDEN, Rose Agnes   1844 - 1915

GOLDEN, Thomas F.   9 aug. 1870 - 3 July 1936
                       [son of John and Rose]

GOLDEN, John J.   1872 - 1943   [Son of John and Rose]

GRIFFITH, [Jeremie Michael   Age 2 Mos. Nov. 4, 1982, Portland
        OR - Jan. 7, 1983, Vancouver, WA.   Mother is Adele Lelonde
        Griffith, at home.   Hamilton-Mylan FH.   Obit. The Columbian]

HASS, Oscar   20 Feb. 1918 - 14 June 1972
        Kansas   Pfc   U.S.   Marine   Corp.

HAGAN, _____   [No information]

HALL, Infant   1961 - 1961   [Child of Kenneth & Majorie Hall]

HANEY, Mary Ann (Cleary) [B. 1849 N.Y. - D. 1883 Calif.
                       Wife of James Haney]

HANRATTY, Patrick   [no stone or information]

HANRATTY, Peter   [no stone or information]

HARRISON, Delia   1881 - 1937

HEGARITY, Dan   Born in Sligo, Ireland 28 Sept. 1868 - Died
            12 Apr. 1903

HEARN, James A. (also listed as A'Hern) Died 26 Apr. 1922
            Illinois   14th Inf.
            [Father of Eva Barnett - In Barnett plot]

HEBERT, Alfred   [no marker or information - Father of
            Nancy Dupuis - Husband of Sara Hebert]

HEBERT, Sara   [no marker or information]

ST. JOHN'S CATHOLIC CEMETERY

HINCHEY, Dorothy I.   25 June 1923 - 27 Feb. 1974   Sister
        [Sister of Vincent Meyer]

HOGAN, Neil   [unmarked]

HUETTL, Clifford J.   1909 - 1969

HUETTL, Sophia S. (Jagelski)   1914 - _____

JAGELSKI, David J.   1947 - 1971   [Son of Theodore & Genieve]

JAGELSKI, Theodore K.   1911 - 1972

JAGELSKI, Mark   1959   [infant]

JAGELSKI, Gary   1960   [infant]

JAGELSKI, Kenneth   1961   [infant]

JAGELSKI, Ronald   1964   [Infant

JASKER, Robt. A.   1904 - 1970

JASKER, Frances H.   1907 - 1977   [Daughter of Philip and
                          Nancy Dupuis]

JENKINS, Albert F.   1906 - 1977   Father

JENKINS, Gerald   [no information]

JENKINS, Harriet E.   1912 - _____   Mother

JENKINS, Bruce L.   1934 - 1974   Father

JOHNSON, Rolland L.   1905 - 1964

JONES, Harvey Britton IV   Born 1978 - Died 28 Aug. 1980
        [Drowned - Son of Harvey & Anna Jones]

KAUFMAN, Barbara   8 Nov. 1860 - 4 July 1909   Mother

KAUFMAN, Henry   15 May 1891 - 5 May 1907   Father
        [Husband of Barbara]

KAUFMAN, Joseph F.   1880 - 1957

KAUFMAN, Joseph   4 Jan. 1849 - 16 Nov. 1935

KELLY, John S.   1895 - 1971   Father

KELLY, Marie E. (Fox)   1892 - 1963   Mother

KELLY, Mary Catherine   Infant   [Stillborn]
        14 May 1981   [Parents] John & Carol Kelly]

KEMP, Clement A.   1914 - 1973   Father
                153

ST. JOHN'S CATHOLIC CEMETERY

KEMP, Florence E. (Jagelski) 1919 - 1968   Mother

La LONDE, Clarence   1885 - 1967

La LONDE, Kate G. (Curtin)   1887 - 1972

La LONDE, Yvonne   Died 6 Dec. 1958   Our Baby
        [Daughter of Clarence and Helen LaLonde]

LaLONDE, Pamela M.   Age 4 MOs.   1958
        [Daughter of Clarence and Helen LaLonde]

LeBLANC, Gratian   1806 - 1880

LeBLANCE, Victoria   1809 - 1871

LEE, Anna Cora   1864 - 1868
        [First person buried in this cemetery]

LEE, James J.   1871 - 1903

LEE, John   1827 - 1908   Father

LEE, May   1870 - 1880

LEE, Philomena (LeBlanc)   1838 - 1905   Mother

LEE, Philip   1877 - 1880

LEE, Robert   Infant Son   1925

LILLARD, Joyce Ann   1937 - 1981

LUCKMAN, Eric Harvey 1 July 1962 - 28 Aug. 1963   Baby Son

LUCKMAN, Mark Allen   1947 - 1961

LUCKMAN, Verna L.   1915 - 1954

LUGO, Ygnacio   1 Feb. 1917 - 10 Oct. 1977
        Tec. 3   U. S. Army   W W II

LYNCH, Joyce Jolene   1932 - 1971

LYNCH, Stephen Douglas   Died 1969

McCARTHY, Margaret   Born in Creigh, Westriding near Ballimore,
    Cork Co., Ireland   15 Mar. 1824 - Died 22 Feb. 1891

McCARTHY, T. J.   Born in London, England   30 Nov. 1853 -
        Died 5 Apr. 1892

McCARTHY, Mary   [unmarked]

McCARTHY, Robert   Died 3 Nov. 1904   Age 60 Yrs.

McGUIRE   [unmarked] 154

McKAY, Infant   [Child of George McKay]

MERSMAN, Victor   1882 - 1965   Father

MERSMAN, Bernadina   1880 - 1960   Mother

MERTON, Henry   [unmarked]   Father

MERTON, Mrs. Henry   [unmarked]

MERTON, Henry   [unmarked]   Son

MERTON, Lewis   [unmarked]

MEYER, [Vincent L.   Age 67 of Cancer.   Feb. 29, 1920, New York
    City - July 7, 1987, at home, Vancouver, WA. Wife Amelia
    At home.   Memorial Gardens Mortuary Obit. The Columbian]

MICHELS, [Frances M.   Age 81. Oct. 2, 1905, Detroit Lakes, Mich.
    June 10, 1976, Vancovuer, WA. 2 sons, 2 daughters, named.
    and 4 sisters. Graveside Services. Hamilton-Mylan FH.
    Obit; The Columbian.]

MORROW, Daniel F.   1861 - 1928   Father

MORROW, Margaret A.   1871 - 1914   Mother

MORROW, Dannie   Died 12 Jan. 1889   Age 4 Yrs.

MUNIZICH, Richard   1939 - 1980

O'CONNELL, Anna G.   1907 - 1971   [Wife of Thomas]
*
O'CONNELL, Thomas F.   1909 - 1960

O'CONNELL, Edward J.   1884 - 1945   [Husband of Marie]

O'CONNELL, Marie I. (Dahl)   1892 - 1955   [Wife of edward J.]

O'CONNELL, Isabell (Cleary)   1875 - 1915   Mother
                [Mother of Edward]

*NEHLER, [Neal Edmund   Age 64. Dec. 9, 1919, Greeley County, NB -
    Mar. 16, 1985, Vancouver, WA. Husband of Leona K. Nehler,
    Vancouver. Evergreen Staples FC.   Obit: The Columbian]

PARSENS, Mildred Anne   1926 - 1962   Mother

PARTHENAY, Eugene F.   1889 - 1977   Father

PARTHENAY, Matilda C. (Jagelski)   1906 - 1980   Mother

PATNOE, Joe   [no information]

PEABODY, Peter   b. 1858 - d. _____   [umarked]

ST. JOHN'S CATHOLIC CEMETERY

POWELL, Cathey   1958 - 1980   Ashes
        [Grandaughter of Fred & Margaret Chandler]

PRAGER, James   1962 - 1981
        [Son of Veronica & Kenneth Prager]

PRAGER, Veronica T.   1927 - 1979   [Wife of Kenneth]

QUIGG, [Mabel M. 'Pat' Age 73.   Mar. 18, 1913, American Falls, ID
        - Sept. 17, 1986, Vancouver, WA. Hamilton-Mylan FH.
        Obit: The Columbian.

QUIGG, Thomas James   1909 - 1969   [Husband of Patricia]

QUITUGUA, [Enrique T. "Rick" born MAR. 12, 1911, Guam - died
        17 Jan. 1984, Brush Prairie, WA. Resided Vancouver, WA.
        Evergreen Staples FC.   Obit. The Columbian]

REESE, Dennis   1973 - 1979

SEIFERT, Catharina   Geb. 14 Nov. 1863 - Gest, 15 Mai 1903
        Was Ter Ted Getrennt Vereinigt Die Ewigheit
        [Unmarked - Stone stolen 1980]

SIEMIENCZUK, Stanley Frank   1920 - 1982   [Husband of Margaret]

STEPHENS, Robert   4 June 1867 - 8 June 1927
        [Second husband of Annie Thornton White Stephens]

STEPHENS, Annie Thornton-White   22 Mar. 1866 - 21 May 1954
        [Twin of Josephine Thornton]

STRINGFELLOW, Donna May   1926   Infant Daughter

STRINGFELLOW, Child   [Unmarked]

SUTTER, Louis P.   1889 - 1965   Father

SUTTER, Mary J.   1900 - 1970   Mother

SWERINGEN, Mrs.   [no dates - umarked]

THIBADEAU, Joseph   [unmarked]

THIBADEAU, Fred   [unmarked]

THOMAS, Margaret   1874 - 1946   [Wife of Joseph]

THOMAS, Joseph   1872 - 1918

THOMAS, Frank   1880 - 1957   [Husband of Goldie]

THOMAS, Goldie M. (Barnett)   1885 - 1973
        [Daughter of Seth and Mary Barnett]

THOMAS, Katherine   22 Oct. 1842 - 6 Dec. 1905   [Wife of Paul]

THOMAS, Katherine   1914   Infant Daughter   [of Frank & Goldie]

THOMAS, Paul   22 May 1838 - 12 May 1912
          [Husband of Katherine]

THOMAS, Phillip A.   Born 10 Dec. 1870, Kansas - Died 24 Oct.
          1898 , Portland, OR.   [Son of Paul and Katherine]

THOMPSON, James   [unmarked]

THORNTON, Children   [unmarked - Children of Alfred Thornton]

THORNTON,   [3 children - of Silas and Mary Thornton- unmarked]

THORNTON, Philip   1858 - 1926   [Unmarked in Thornton Plot-
          Son of Thomas and Cleophine]

THORNTON, Thomas J.   Born in Spotsylvania, VA. 24 Jan. 1822 -
          Died 17 Sept. 1877 in Portland, Oregon   Age 35 Yrs. 2 mos.
          25 Dys.

THORNTON, Cleophine (LeBlanc)   Beloved Wife of Thomas Thornton
          Born in LaFourche, Lou. 10 Apr. 1828 - Died 19 Jan. 1887
                    Age 58 Yrs. 9 Mos. 8 Dys.

THORNTON, Josephine   Youngest daughter of Thomas & Cleophine
          Born in St. Johns, W.T.   22 Mar. 1866 - Died 29 Nov. 1877
                    Age 11 Yrs. 8 Mos.   8 Dys.

THULIN, [Arthur Henry   Age 73. July 31, 1914, Turkey Ford OK.
          Sept 16, 1987 at home, Vancouver, WA. Husband of Mary Agnes.
          Vancouuver FC   Obit: The Columbian.]

THULIN, Brenda Ann   1978 - 1978   [Niece of Don Thulin]

THULIN, Donald   21 Oct. 1946 - 4 Apr. 1967
          Washington   Pfc   Co. B   7 Cav. 1st Cav. Div.
               Vietnam PH   [Son of Arthur and Agnes]

THULIN, Ernest E.   1941 - 1970   [Son of Arthur and Agnes]

TRAMBLAY, Alfred   [unmarked]

TRAMBLAY, Ernst   [unmarked]

TRAMBLAY, HOmer   [unmarked]

TRANT, Ellen A.   Died 14 Dec. 1878   [9 mos. Old]

TRANT, Cathrine   Died 1 Oct. 1879   Wife of William H. Trant

TRANT, T. G.   23 Nov. 1893 = 15 Sept. 1894

TRANT, Wm.   [unmarked]

TRANT, W. T.   [unmarked]

USIETO, Asuncion 1910 - 1980
[Mother of Mrs. Dan Carroll Jr.]

VALENCIA, [Rodrigo Elisea Age 31. Shot. Mar. 3, 1956, Aguililla, Michoacan, Mexico - Oct. 3, 1987, Aloha, OR. Son of Maria Valencia Ochoa, Aguililla, Michoacan, Mexico. Hamilton-Mylan FH. Obit. The Columbian.

WEIMER, Jesse A. 1878 - 1954

WEIMER, Carrie E. 1884 - 1952

WEIMER, Mary Adabel 1913 - 1944 [Daughter of Jesse & Carrie]

WERNER, Bernered 1910 - _____

WEST, Baby [no dates - Hamilton-Mylan FH]

WOLF, [Pauline G. Age 58. June 25, 1927, Berwick, ND - Aug. 8, 1985, Vancovuer, WA. Wife of Mathias Wolf at home. Hamilton-Mylan FH. Obit: The Columbian]

WOODS, John [Unmarked]

WOODS, Lela [Unmarked]

WOODSON, Tarleton 1910 - 1982

ZERR, Barbara M. 1928 - 1953 Mother
[Daughter of Clarence and Kathleen Thomas Falk]

Crawford Cemetery

Crawford Cemetery is located on N. E. Allworth
Road, also known as N. E. 244th Street. originally known as Kent's Cemetery, after Stephen Kent
who had a homestead there. Mr. Kent planned for
a church and cemetery on the site, but the church
was never built. In later years the cemetery became
known as Crawford after the settlement of that
name. The cemetery was established approximately
in 1885, and has about 125 burials.

CRAWFORD CEMETERY

ALLWORTH, Alfred A. (Sr.)   1855 – 1949
        [Husband of Fannie A.]

ALLWORTH, Fannie A.   1859 – 1935
        [Wife of Alfred A.]

ALLWORTH, Alfred (Jr.)   1885 – 1972

BAKER, Orval   1892 – 1904   [Son of Geo. Baker]

BOHLING, Anna   1884 – 1957   Mother

BOHLING, Frederick   1870 – 1935   [son of Fritz]

BOHLING, Fritz   1835 – 1889

BURNETT, Pearl   1885 – 1975
        [mother of Mrs. A. Allworth Jr.]

BUSWELL, Infant   [no marker]

BUSWELL, Infant   [no marker]

BUSWELL, Infant   [no marker]

CALDWELL, Bruce   Died Sept. 21, 1920
                Age 6 years 7 mos. 17 days

CALDWELL, Marjorie   [Can't read marker]

COLLINS, Nora [Thom]   1916 – 1971

COLLINS, Robert E. L.   1914 – _____

CRONIN, Arthur E.   1879 – 1963
        [on stone with Emma M.]

CRONIN, Emma M.   1887 – 1937

CRONIN, Mary   1842 – 1937   Mother

DEMAREST, Julia C.   1870 – 1943   Mother
        [mother of Paul and Richard Linn]

DEMAREST, Laura P.   Sept. 20, 1859 – Aug. 12, 1916

DEMAREST, Robert   Dates not known

DUVALL, Donald   1923 – 1974
        [son of R. and M. Duvall]

DUVALL, Robert   1879 – 1948   [Sp. War Veteran]

DUVALL, Mary   1887 – 1976   [Mary McCollum Duvall]

DUVALL, Infant   [child of Mr. and Mrs. Roy Duvall]
                162.

CRAWFORD CEMETERY

DUVALL, Infant   [child of Mr. and Mrs. Roy Duvall]

FIALA, Frank   Died FEb., 1918
                                  [Father of James Fiala]

FIALA, James   1914 - 1974   Husband

FIALA, Ida White   1909 - 1976   Wife and Mother

FREUDENTHAL, Henry F.   1886 - 1978
             Pvt.   U.S. Army   W. W. I

GRAHAM, A. G.   Died May 9, 1917   Aged 63 years

HALVORSON, Gladys L.   1902 - 1960   Mother

HALVORSON, Henry J.   1898 - _____
             [on stone with A. G. Halverson]

HANSEN, Andrew   1881 - 1952   Father

HANSEN, Minnie   1893 - _____   Mother
             [on stone with Andrew Hansen]

HANSEN, Hans Able   April 5, 1887 - Nov. 17, 1948
             [Brother of Andrew Hansen]

HARRIS, Ida May   Aug. 3, 1855 - Apr. 18, 1947
             [Sister of G. Whitney]

HEISEN, A. C.   1824 - 1912

HEISEN, Mary   1835 - _____
             [on stone with A. C. Heisen]

HEISEN, Avery C.   Sept. 14, 1896 - Oct. 29, 1968
        Washington   Pfc   U.S. Army   W. W. I

HEISEN, Elda Isabel   Born Feb. 1, 1904 - Died Nov. 26, 1904

HEISEN, Henry R.   1866 - 1942

HEISEN, Ida L.   1876 - 1943   [shares stone with
             [On stone with Henry R.]

HEISEN, Sidney C.   1911 - 1962

HILDEBRAND, Abraham   Died Feb. 19, 1943   Age 84 years 3mos. 22days

HILDEBRAND, Eunice   [Marker from Hendry-Gardner Mortuary
             in Stevenson, Wash. is unreadable]

HILDEBRAND, Bertha   [marker unreadable]

HILDEBRAND, Jesse   [marker unreadable - Mortuary Records show
        Jesse Samuel Hildebrand - Husband of Bertha Jane -
        Date of Death 24 May 1935 - date of birth 23 Jan. 1886
        died in Skamaia County-Bonneville - Son of Abraham.]
163

CRAWFORD CEMETERY

JOHNSON, Charles   [Died circa 1922]   [Son of Frank Johnson]

JOHNSON, Frank   Died May 29, 1903 - Age 78 years 8 mos.

JOHNSON, Jane   Died Dec. 12, 1906 - Age 67 years. 6 mos.
                        [Wife of Frank Johnson]

JOHNSON, Infant   1898

JOHNSON, _____   [no marker]

KIDDER,   [There is three infant graves with no markers,
        They were born circa 1920's and children of Mr. & Mrs.
        Davis Kidder.]

LINN, Paul. L.   Aug. 24, 1899 - May 28, 1974
                Pvt.   U.S. Marine Corps

LINN, Richard W.   1903 - 1961   Father

LINN, Lillian J.   1906 - _____   Mother

LINZ, Anna M.   1849 - 1896   At Rest
                Wife of Frederick L. Linz.

LINZ, Frederick L.   [no marker]

LINZ, George   [illegible]

MAURY, Vic (Victor?)   [no marker]

McCOLLUM, Earl Dwight   1902 - 1906   [Son of Mary & Perry]

McCOLLUM, George A.   Dec. 23, 1895 - Sept. 21, 1919   W.W. I
          "Liberty"   "America"

McCOLLUM, Sarah   1864 - 1941   [mother of George & Walter]

McCOLLUM, Walter P.   Born Sept. 7, 1900 - Died Feb. 7, 1906

McCOLLUM, Mary Jones   1866 - 1951   [Wife of Perry]

McCOLLUM, Perry W.   1857 - 1938
        [Althought the name is spelled the same, the Perry McCollum
        and Sarah McCollum families are not of the same family]

MILLER, Hutha   1880 - 1956   [Wife of James F.]

MILLER, James F.   1875 - 1937

MIKSCH, Iva   [Mrs. Henry Miksch]

NELSON, Clyde W.   1912 - 1955

NELSON, Roger   June 1942 - May 1944

164.

CRAWFORD CEMETERY

NORTHRUP, B. A.	1875 – 1930	
NORTHRUP, Louise	1879 – 1930	[Wife of B.A. Northrup]
O'JAY, _____?	[no marker]	
OST, Albert	1879 – 1918	[Husband of Meta Ost]
OST, Meta	1882 – 1961	
OST, Paul	1906 – 1970	[Son of Albert and Meta]
OWINGS, Audry L.	1924 – 1971	

PANCOSKA, Joseph Sr.   1873 – 1948   Father
          [Husband of Josephine]

PANCOSKA, Josephine   1882 – 1962   Mother

PANCOSKA, Joe J. Jr.   May 3, 1921 – April 8, 1945
          Washington   Pfc.   128 Inf.   W.W. II (K.I.A.)

PATTIS, Herman   1898 – 1976   [Husband of Lydia]

PATTIS, Lydia   1904 – _____

PRICE, Nancy   1812 – 1879   Mother

ROBERTSON, Fred W.   Dec. 17, 1880 – March 27, 1963
                              Brother and Uncle

SCHUMACHER, Amalie   Feb. 22, 1835 – Dec. 15, 1905
                         [Wife of William Schumacher]

SCHUMACHER, William   Born Oct. 5, 1834

SCHUMACHER, Anna L.   1871 – 1956   [Wife of Ferd C.]

SCHUMACHER, Ferd C.   1867 – 1956   [Husband of Anna L.]

SCHUMACHER, Wm.   1902 – 1971   Father

SCHUMACHER, Leona M.   1918 – _____   [Wife of Wm.]

SEGER, Mary   1847 – 1935

THOM, Carl G.   1856 – 1927

THOM, Charles F.   1905 – 1928   [Son of Charles L. Thom]

THOM, Charles L.   1880 – 1953   [Wife of Tillie J.]

THOM, Tillie J.   1884 – 1978

UNDERHILL, Infant   1974

WEBB, Geo. Leonard   1909 – 1953   Son   Husband

CRAWFORD CEMETERY

WEBB, Geo. W.	1869 – 1938	[Brother of Sam. M.]
WEBB, Mary E.	1846 – 1930	[Wife of Sam M.]
WEBB, Sam M.	1835 – 1934	
WEBB, Nores E.	1892 – 1972	[Mother of Geo. Leonard]
WEBB, Sam B.	1878 – 1953	Father
WILLIAMS, Frank	1854 – 1927	Husband
WILLIAMS, Marian	[no dates]	Wife
WINSTON, Charlotte E. "Chuck"	1927 – 1976 In Loving Memory	
WINSTON, Joseph Roy	1935 – 1952	
WILLE, Nellie	[no marker]	
WHITNEY, Florence E.	1873 – 1934	Mother
WHITNEY, Grant B.	1869 – 1934	Father

Gravel Point Cemetery

Gravel Point Cemetery is located approximately one-half mile east of the intersection of Risto Road and Ward Road, near a private drive indicating Risto Heights. It was established in December of 1893.

GRAVEL POINT CEMETERY

ALESHEIMED, Geo.   d.   1 - 10 - 1894

AXFORD, Forrest L.   1897 - 1976

AXFORD, Pearl   1901 - 19_____

BAKER, Florence   died 3 - 14- 1901 [Vancourver Independent]

BARTHOLOMEU, Meritt   d. 7 - 23 - 1905

BLYSTONE, Eliza J.   d. 12 - 11 - 1909   [51 years]

BLYSTONE, Henry L.   d. 7 - 9 - 1918   Co. C   150   Ill. Inf.

BLYSTONE, John W.   1884 - 1968

BLYSTONE, Margaret J.   1891 - 19_____

BODIN, Fred W.   1889 - 1953

BODIN, Ollie M.   1888 - 1970

BODIN, Peter Willim   1865 - 1934

BODIN, Marta Helena   1865 - 1940

BOLICH, Alpha E.   1892 - 1963

BOLICH, Mary K.   no dates

BURWELL, R.   d. 2 - 5 - 1894

CHALKE, Twins   1974 - 1974

CURTIS, Jesse Arthur   3-10-1898 "Jesse Arthur dearly beloved
                          son of Daniel and Jennie Curtis died Mar.
                          10, 1898 age 8 yrs. 4 ms. Farewell dear,
                          but not forever there will be a glorious
                          dawn, we shall meet to part no never on
                          the Resurrection morn."

DALY, Ransom   1826 - 1911

DALEY, Matilda   2-14-1903 "Matilda wife of R. Daly died Feb.
                      14, 1903, aged 73 ys 10 ms. 10ds."

DALEY, W.   12-4-1893

DALEY, W. E.   d. 6-7-12   [6-7-1912 ?]

ENGVALL, Carl A.   1835 - 1914

ENGVALL, Carl J.   1894 - 1918

ENGVALL, Oliva   1891 - 1916

ESKELI, Esther V.   1905 - 1978

GRAVEL POINT CEMETERY

ESKELI, William M.   1896 - 1975

FOREMAN, Cacelia   1865 - 1825

FOREMAN, August   1854 - 1935

GUSTAFSON, Baby   11-17-1944

HALE, Greta Johanna 1892 - 1924 [same as Johanna Pura Hale]
    "Greta Johanna Hale died 9 April 1924, 55 yrs 5 mos 17dys"

HALE, Johanna Pura

HARVEY, Michael A.   Baby   1966 - 1966
                  [buried with the Chalke Twins]

HEISEN, Alemmak   10-2-1870 - 10-22-1893

HEISEN, R. H.   1-5-1894

HILL, Hilja K.   1886 - 1959

HILL, Peter   1884 - 1963 ["Jan. 5, 1922 - May 29, 1956"]

HILL, Rebecca Louise   1954 - 1968

HILL, David Michael   2-20-1952 - 5-20-1954

HILL, Rudolf   5-4-1922

HILL, Martha C.   1909 - 1922   "11-3-1922"

HILL, Roy R.   1921 - 1922

KENNINGTON, John   1876 - 1951

KENNINGTON, Emelia K.   1882 - 19_____

KIVISTO, Richard   12-11-37
            [Ashes in Jacob Nikkola lot, Son-in-law]

KORHONEN, Onnie W. 1908 - 1956   Father
        [d July 7, 1956 - aged 47yrs 8mos 16days]

KORHONEN, David G.   1945 - 1965

KULLA, Janet Rose   3-25-1967   -   9-10-1974
            [daughter of Carl]

KULLA, Pauline Joy   1957 - 1960

LAITINEN, Kalle   1882 - 1965

LAITINEN, Matilda   1877 - 1931

LEHTO, August   1864 - 1944   Father

169

GRAVEL POINT CEMETERY

LEHTO,	Augusta	1868 - 1920	Mother
LEHTO,	Hulda C.	1868 - 1938	Wife
LUKAS,	Ida Selina	1904 - 1924	Daughter
LUKAS,	John August	1865 - 1945	Father
LUKAS,	Jemina	1877 - 1947	Mother
LUKAS,	August	_____	

MARTENSON, C. J. "Ed"   1893 - 1950

MARTENSON, Mary M.   9-6-50

MATSON, Albert H.   1893 - 1970   Father

MATSON, H. Vivian   1898 - 1968   Mother

MATSON, Kathryn V. (baby)   1960 - 1960

MATILLA, Nels Jalmer   3-0-1897 - 8-18-1964
     Washington Pvt Btry F. 27 Arty Cac   W W I
          March 1, 1897 - Aug. 18, 1964

MAUKE, Reinhardt E.   1868 - 1960

MAUKE, Mary C.   6-8-1882   8-5-1914   Mother
          Wife of Reinhard Mauke   June 7, 1882 - Aug. 5, 1914

MAUKE, Reuben E.   Mar. 28, 1908 - Aug. 29, 1937

Mc ALAVY, Allen   6-30-1903

Mc ALAVY, Mary E. Harkin   Mother
     Mary E. Harkin McAlavy born July 27, 1845 - died July 27, 1903

Mc ALAVY, James   born Jan 16, 1820 - died June 10, 1903 At Rest

Mc ALAVY, Earl   1882 - 1958

Mc DANIELS, J.   10-14-1895

MORGAN, B.   9-12-1896

MORGAN, L.   10-13-1896

MORTENSON, John   1868 - 1952   [d. March 1952]   Father

MORTENSON, Elna   1872 - 1951   [d. Sept. 1, 1951]   Mother

NIKKOLA, Jacob   1869 - 1927   [2 Feb. 1927]

NIKKOLA, Maria   1871 - 1936

NIKKOLA, Hugo H.   1910 - 1937   Son

170

NISKANEN,	Dennis	3-24-1948		Our Baby
NISKANEN,	Arnold	1909 - 5-1-50		
NISKANEN,	Gertrude	1913 - 1975		His Wife
		[Wife of Arnold]		
OPPERMANN,	Phillip	1829 - 1904		
OPPERMANN,	Margarethe	1853 - 1930		
OTT,	John J.	12-4-1893		
PURA,	Henry	1853 - 1920		
PURA,	Anna	1851 - 1934		His Wife
PURA,	Jennie E.	1892 - 1977		
PURA,	Frank O.	1890 - 1965		
RAWSON,	Albert	[Removed]		
RISTO,	Oscar Wilho	1873 - 1938		Father
RISTO,	Anne Marie	10-29-46	6-21-69	Daughter
RHOADES,	Norma May	[baby] 1967		
ROPPOLA,	John	1856 - 1923 (July 13, 1923)		Father
ROPPOLA,	Lisa	1864 - 1939		
RUZICKA,	G.	8-22-04 (1904)		
RUZICKA,	Frederick	5-15-18 (1918)		
RUZICKA,	Olamph	(age 73)		
RUZICKA,	V.	(63 or 65)		
SARKELA,	Gary D.	5-7-1946 - 1-7-1968		
	Oregon L Cpl	U. S. Marine Corps		
SHERBLOOM,	Ernest A.	1874 - 1956		Husband and Daddy
STURGESS,	Josie	1884 - 1970		
STURGESS,	N. Park	1887 - 1977		
THOGERSON,	Doug W.	1949 - 1968		Son
UELTSCHI,	David	1834 - 1914		
WALLWAY,	Fred George	1879 - 1961		
WALLWAY,	Emma Sophia	1886 - 1969		

GRAVEL POINT CEMETERY

WARD, Frank A.	2-12-1896 - 9-24-1898
WARD, Alonzo	9-2-1849 - 1-31-1908
WARD, Amanda	1-23-1864 - 1-2-1957
WEST, Burdette W.	1905 - 1978
WHITE, Wallace	1862 - 1927
WHITE, Walter	1907 - 1908

No Name   [Male killed in Portland and buried in 1976 without service
           and buried next to Chalke Twins.]

DATE LOTS PURCHASED

Alesheimer, Geo.	1-10-1894	
Baker, Geo.	3-16-1901	
Bartholemeu, Meritt	7-23-1905	
Bodin, Fred W.	8- 9-1934	
Bleiston, H. (Blystone)	12-26-1898	
Burwell, R.	2- 5-1894	
Curtis, Daniel	11- 9-1896	
Daly, Ransom	12- 7-1903	
Engwald, Mrs. L.	6- 7-1912	
Forman, K.J.	5-29-1925	
Gustafson, Fred	4- 1949	
Heison, R. H.	1- 5-1894	
Hill, Peter	5-29-1951	1 lot
Hill, Peter	1- 5-1922	
Kennington, Emelia	6-12-1951	
Korhonen, Jennie	7-20-1956	1 lot
Laitanen, Carl T.	1931	
Lehto, August	6- 7-1912	
Lukas, August	8-30-1924	
Martenson, Mary H.	9- 6-1950	
Matson, Harold W.	5- 6-1961	4 spaces
Mauke, Reinhardt E.	9-11-1914	
McAllavy, Allan (McAlavy)	6-30-1903	
McDaniels, J.	10-14-1805	
Morgan, B.	9-12-1896	
Morgan, L.	10-13-1896	
Nikola, Jacob	2- 2-1927	
Niskanen, Arnold	5- 1-1950	
Oppermann, Margarethe	4-18-1904	
Pura, H.	10-22-1920	
Rawson, Albert	2-27-1901	removed
Rawson,	9- 8-1917	
Rhoades, Richard R.	1967	
Risto Estate	3- 1938	
Roppola, Mrs. John	7-13-1923	
Ruzicka, F.	8-22-1894	
Shobloom, Ernest	9-12-1896	
Speeler, M.	10-16-1895	

Stoddard, Eliz.	1- 5-1894	cancelled 4-10-1896
Ueltschi, David, Sr.	9-11-1914	
Ward, Alonzo	9-25-1898	
Ward, R.N.	11-10-1895	Richard N. 1857-1920 buried in Brush Prairie Cemetery
White, W.	8-15-1916	

Wilson Bridge Cemetery

Wilson Bride Cemetery is located on
N. E. 144th Street, four miles south
of Dollar's Corner, adjacent to
Memory Memorial Cemetery.

ALBINSON, John W.   9 Oct. 1889 – 20 April 1950
        Washington   Pfc   166 Depot Brigade   W.W. I

ALEXANDER, Alice   1861 – 31 August 1950
                        [Wife of James Kansas]

ALEXANDER, Ann E.   1826 – 1903
                        [Wife of Rev. J.H. Alexander]

ALEXANDER, Charles E.   1865 – 1929   Father
                [husband of Emma]

ALEXANDER, Emma   1872 – 1963   Mother

ALEXANDER, Howard J.   15 Dec. 1893 – 27 March 1962
            Washington   Pfc.   Co. K   101 Inf.   W.W. I

ALEXANDER, J. Howard   1894 – 1969   [Husband of Kate E.]

ALEXANDER, J. Howard, Rev.   (James)   died 3 Nov. 1893
        Age 71 yrs. 7 mos.   17 days   [Husband of Ann E.]
            In Loving Remembrance of Rev. J.H. Alexander

ALEXANDER, James Kansas   1855 – 1936

ALEXANDER, Kate E.   1895 – 1940   [wife of J. Howard]

ALEXANDER, Mary E. (Bartlett-Cross)   1861 – 1956
            [born 3 Feb. 1861 Iowa – died 31 Aug. 1956]
        [Came via covered wagon 1862 – Member of Salmon Creek
    Methodist Church – Teacher 1902 – 1932]

ALEXANDER, Robert W.   28 Aug. 1907 – 3 Dec. 1944
        Washington   Pvt.   330 Inf.   W. W. II

ALEXANDER, W. H. (William)   1852 – 1936
            [buried next to Mary E. Alexander]

ALLEN, Edwin R.   1880 – 1948   [Husband of Ora A.]

ALLEN, Mary F.   1851 – 1913   [grave beside Oliver Allen]

ALLEN, Oliver   Co. B   1 Bn   Dakota Cav.

ALLEN, Ora A.   1886 – 1944   [wife of Edwin R.]

ALSTAD, Dagny L.   1894 – 1936

ANDERSON, A.   1841 – 1941   At Rest

ANDERSON, Anna L.   1870 – 1934   Mother
            [Wife of John L.]

ANDERSON, Arthur E.   1916 – 1967   [Husband of Ferna A.]

ANDERSON, Arthur G.   18 Feb. 1928
            Washington   Landsman   U.S. Navy

MANOR WILSON BRIDGE CEMETERY

ANDERSON, Baby   Died 25 Mar. 1878

ANDERSON, Christina   Died 30 Nov. 1887   Age 2 yrs.
            Daughter of A & C Anderson

ANDERSON, Fern A.   1914 - 19____   [wife of Arthur E.]

ANDERSON, Forny   1886 - 1968   [wife of Martin]

ANDERSON, John L.   1866 - 1951   Father
            [Husband of Anna L.]

ANDERSON, John S. Dec._____   Age 95 yrs. 9mos
            [Vancouver Funeral Chapel marker in poor shape]

ANDERSON, Lydia J.   1881 - 1950

ANDERSON, Marie   1918 - 1923

ANDERSON, Martin   1882 - 1973   [husband of Forny]

ANDERSON, Mary J.   Died 5 Dec. 1887   Age 7 Mos.
            Daughter of A. & C. Anderson

ANDERSON, Phillip   1921 - 1921

ANDERSON, Ramus H.   1869 - 1943   Father

ANDERSON, Thomas   1880 - 1913   I.A.B. & S.I.W.

ARMSTRONG, Baby   Died 15 Aug. 1924

ARMSTRONG, George W.   1894 - 1961

AUGEE, Charles H.   1864 - 1961

AUGEE, Charles Joe   [no dates - grave next to Charles H.]

AUGEE, Charles H.   1864 - 1961

AUGEE, Lilly Blanch   [no dates]   [near Charles H. Augee]

AUGEE, Millard   [no dates]   [near Charles H. Augee]

_____, Joseph   Died 7 Dec. 1922   Aged 63 yrs.

BADE, Annie M.   1907 - 19____   [wife of Lindsay E.]

BADE, Lindsay E.   1904 - 1976

BAILEY, Julia (Walker)   26 June 1876 - 19____
            Daughter of W.C. & Satestia Walker- Member of Christin
                Church. [name on same stone as Satestia Walker
                    and Eli]

BAILEY, Mardell M.   1913 - 19____   [wife of Ovid B.]
                                176

BAILEY, Ovid B.   1910 - 1965   [husband of Mardell M.]

BALSIGER, Arnold W.   1870 - 1933

BALSIGER, Hattie M.   1874 - 1963

BARLOW, John C.
      Washington   Co. G   1 Inf.   Spanish American War

BATES, Terry Lee   31 Jan. 1943 - 13 Aug. 1944
    "Gone with Jesus to where the Pretty Flowers Grow"

BECKER, John   1817 - 1888   [husband of Marie]

BECKER, Marie   1818 - 1899

BEEBE, Fredrica H.   1899 - 1976

BEEBE, Frederick Kenneth   3 June 1919 - 29 Oct. 1977
    A.O.M..3   U. S. Navy   W.W. II

BEEBE, Leroy D.   1915 - 1974

BEER, Anna   1846 - 1920   [wife of Hans Ulrich]

BEER, Daniel   1874 - 1945

BEER, Hans Ulrich   1827 - 1907   [husband of Anna]

BEER, Jacob   1890 - 1941

BEER, Samuel   1886 - 1966

BEERS, Paul E. Jr. "Sunny"   3 July 1946 - 1 Sept. 1965

BEESON, Anna E.   1838 - 1921   Mother

BELONGIA, John A.   1898 - 1973

BENJAMIN, Louisa M.   1879 - 1974   [wife of Wesley T.]

BENJAMIN, Wesley T.   1873 - 1940

BENNETT, Nettie   Weaver   18 Jan. 1862 - 24 May 1919

BENNETT, Nora L.   1897 - 1940   Mother

BENNETT, William   1838 - 1920   In Loving Remembrance

BERRY, Albert L.   1863 - 1914   In Loving Memory of Albert

BERRY, Jane Fair   1869 - 1952

BERRY, Jasper E.   1892 - 1978   [husband of Urith L.]

BERRY, Myrtle   5 July 1896 - 14 Jan. 1931

BERRY, Urith L.   1896 – 19   [wife of Jasper E.]

BERTLETT, John W.   1835 – 1902   At Rest

BETHJE, Carl W.   1889 – 19____   [husband of Elsie M.]

BETHJE, Elsie M.   1895 – 1975

BETTS, Alvin S.   1847 – 1926   [husband of Lucinda]

BETTS, Charles   1875 – 1975

BETTS, Lucinda   1851 – 19___   [wife of Alvin S.]

BETTS, Olive   1866 – 1935   [wife of Thomas C.]

BETTS, Thomas C.   1853 – 1909

BILLS, Catherine T.   1878 – 1960   Father

BILLS, Francis M.   1868 – 1951   Husband & Father
                              [husband of Catherine T.]

BILLS, Lucious   1915 – 1936

BLAKE, Catherine G.   8 May 1876 – 15 May 1972
                              [wife of Rennie L.]

BLAKE, Rennie L.   2 July 1898 – 27 May 1979   [husband of Catherine]

BLOMQUIST, John   5 July 1894 – 22 July 1906
                "Sheltered and safe from sorrow"
               Son of Hokan and Ingrid Blomquist

BLOMQUIST, Maria   10 June 1892 – 25 Feb. 1905
              Daughter of Hokan and Ingrid Blomquist

BLOOM, Estella C.   1907 – 1944
              [shares stone with Frank Christensen]

BLOOM, Frank Christensen   1915 – 19____

BOLEN, A. Mason   19 March 1885 – 3 May 1903

BOLEN, Clara Jane (Hursh)   1893 – 1921

BOLEN, J. H.   27 April 1846 – 14 Feb. 1927   Father
                  [husband of Malinda R.]

BOLEN, Malinda R.   1858 – 1942
                  [wife of J. H. Bolen]   Mother

BOLEN, William E.   20 April 1880 – 25 July 1904

BRADER, Alvin H.   17 Jan. 1918 – 17 Jan. 1928

BRADER, Frieda   4 April 1920 – 14 April 1920

MANOR   WILSON   BRIDGE   CEMETERY

BRADSHAW, Roxie Ann   1869 - 1936   Mother

BRADY,   Alice C. Coleman, Leachman   26 Aug. 1857   Illinois
         31 March 1939 Vancouver, Wash.   Survived by a son,
         Walter Leachman, who was also son of Samuel Leachman.
                  [no marker for this grave]

BRAMHALL, Sadie A.   1870 - 1936   [wife of William]

BRAMHALL, William I.   1868 - 1961

BREMMERMAN, Henry   1857 - 1941   [husband of Nellie]

BREMMERMAN, Nellie   1882 - 19_____

BREWSTER, Albert P.   1819 - 1902   [husband of Malinda J.]

BREWSTER, Anna C.   1879 - 1963   [wife of George]

BREWSTER, Charles S.   1890 - 1908
              [son of Albert and Malinda J.]

BREWSTER, Donald E.   1930 - 1958   [son of Dora E.]

BREWSTER, Dora E.   1898 - 1961   [mother of Donald]

BREWSTER, George   1879 - 1960   [husband of Anna C.]

BREWSTER, Jessie L.   1881 - 1969

BREWSTER, Kate M.   1883 - 1973

BREWSTER, Malinda J.   1857 - 1946

BREWSTER, William   1888 - 1955

BRIDGER, Baby   30 April 1940

BRIGNER, Baby Girl   10 Oct. 1949

BROWN, Mike   1866 - 1933   [grave beside Ina Brown Morelock]

BRYANT, Ethel M.   1930 - 1948   [Vancouver F. H. marker]

BULLARD, Hamilton   1 April 1854 - 21 July 1912

BULLARD, Lima H.   2 Dec. 1857 - 13 Dec. 1918

BUNTING, George   1863 - 1935   [husband of Marjorie E.]

BUNTING, Grover L.   4 Dec. 1892 - 10 July 1975
              Pvt.   Air Force   W.W. I

BUNTING, Marjorie E.   1861 - 1948

BUNTING, Ruby A.   1896 - 1959   [Layne's F. H. marker]
                         179

BURNETT, Bedford L.   30 April 1895 – 4 Jan. 1932
          Pvt   102 Engineer   27 Div.   W.W. I

BURNETT, Gladys Jean   1935 – 1939   At Rest
                      Little Sweetheart

BURNETT, Rose E.   21 June 1906 – 19 April 1974
                Our Loving Mother

BURNETT, Vernon W.   21 Aug. 1899 – 14 July 1913

BURNETT, Violet W.   1878 – 1947   Mother

BURNETT, Virginia L.   20 Aug..1931

BURNETT, William Melvin   10 Dec. 1896 – 30 March 1920

BURNETT, William F.   1872 – 1943   Father
                [husband of Violet W.]

BURTON, Russell J.   1895 – 1937
          "Truth is known by its deeds"

CAIN, Arminta J.   1866 – 1945

CAIN, Arthur A.   1894 – 1925   B.P.O.E. 823

CAIN, Clinton   1887 – 1904

CAIN, Newton F.   1852 – 1924

CAMPBELL, Dora – Dollar   1908 – 1932

CAMPBELL, Emma   1869 – 1960   [wife of Jacob R.]

CAMPBELL, Jacob R.   1857 – 1932

CAMPBELL, Russell V.   1891 – 1941   W. W. Veteran

CANON, Joe F.   1883 – 1954

CANON, Nellie A.   1883 – 1968   [wife of Joe F.]

CARNER, Frances A.   7 Jan. 1931 – 5 Feb. 1965   Mother

CARSON, Infant Girl   16 July 1908
          Infant daughter of M.E. and A.L. Carson

CARSON, Infant Girl   30 Oct. 1930
          Daughter of Clare and Anita Carson

CARSON, Caroline W.   1864 – 1937   At Rest

CARSON, Earl Eugene   1879 – 1945   [husband of Mattie]

CARSON, George C.   1868 – 1934   [son of Samuel & Mary A.]

MANOR WILSON BRIDGE CEMETERY

CARSON, Helen M.   1880 - 1970   At Rest

CARSON, John C.   1867 - 1919   [son of Samuel & Mary A.]

CARSON, John M.   10 Jan. 1885 - 13 Sept. 1901
        Aged 46 yrs. 7 mo. 3 days "A Loved One at Rest"

CARSON, Lezetta A.   4 April 1884 - 10 Jan. 1963
        [grave next to Samuel L. Carson[

CARSON, Mary A.   1846 - 1909   [wife of Samuel F.]

CARSON, Mattie   1880 - 1965   [wife of Earl Eugene]

CARSON, Muriel F.   29 Aug. 1912 - 31 Aug. 1912

CARSON, Ralph W.   1887 - 1948   Father   "At Rest"

CARSON, Samuel F.   1845 - 1913   [Husband of Mary A.]

CARSON, Samuel L.   30 Sept. 1872 - 20 Aug. 1945
        [next to Lezetta A. Carson]

CARSON, William S.   1871 - 1944   At Rest

CASE, Ralph J.   1904 - 1977   [husband of Ruth E.]

CASE, Ruth E.   1904 - 19____   [wife of Ralph J.]

CASSELS, Vioma   1910 - 1968

CAWLEY, John P.   1897 - 1941   Father

CHAPMAN, Tena   1873 - 1963   [wife of W. Chapman]

CHAPMAN, W.   16 Aug. 1865 - 27 June 1931

CHRISTENSEN, Maybelle E.   1900 - 1939

CHRISTENSEN, Sophie N.   1878 - 1937   In Loving Memory

CHRISTENSEN, Walter Dewey   1899 - 1941   In Loving Memory

CHRISTIAN, Anna Marie   1907 - 1973   [wife of Paul]

CHRISTIAN, Paul   1906 - 1964

CHITTESTER, Margaret C.   1873 - 1933   [wife of Edward]

CLAPP, Alexander   1865 - 1943   [husband of Fannie]

CLAPP, Fannie   1873 - 1938

CLAPP, Maude Avis   1895 - 19____   [wife of Orie Oliver]
        Married 22 March 1913

CLAPP, Orie Oliver   1893 - 1964
                181

COCHRAN, Eliza M.   1880 - 1969   [wife of Norton H.]

COCHRAN, Norton H.   1874 - 1972

COFFEY, Carrie   1890 - 1935   [wife of Ira]

COFFEY, Ira   1892 - 1959

COLE, Charles H.   1871 - 1961   [husband of Lulu D.]

COLE, Elsie E.   1878 - 1958   [wife of Louis M.]

COLE, Lillian Pauline   1919 - 1942   Daughter

COLE, Louis M.   1868 - 1943

COLE, Iline L.   1903 - 1912

COLE, Lulu D.   1882 - 1951   [wife of Charles H.]

COLYAR, Elsie and Baby   [no dates - in Lindsay plot]

COOK, Annis E.   1859 - 1931   Mother
          [wife of Isam D. Cook]

COOK, Isam D.   1870 - 1953   Father

COMEAU, Danny Joe   11 Aug. 1945 - 27 Oct. 1948   Our Baby

CONVERSE, Davis G.   1864 - 1929

CONVERSE, Lloyd   1897 - 1916

CONVERSE, Nancy E.   1864 - 1957

CONVERSE, Mary   [no dates-only the name on stone]

COOPER, Emma Mulkey   1852 - 1925

COOPER, Lester E.   13 May 1906 - 24 Sept. 1975

COOPER, Norman L.   1901 - 1977

COOPER, William K.   1908 - 1973

COX, L. Mabel   1903 - 19____

COX, Rupert E.   1904 - 1971   [husband of L. Mabel]

CRAIG, Fremont C.   1862 - 1944

CRAMER, Baby Girl   died 4 March 1902 - Daughter of J.E. & Isabel
          Cramer

CRAMER, Isaac   died 20 July 1891 - Aged 59 yrs

CRAMER, James J.   died 17 Feb. 1900 - Aged 1 yr.   6 mos.
          Son of J.E. & Isabel Cramer

CRAMER, J. E.   3 Dec. 1865 - 9 Dec. 1901   At Rest

CRAMER, John   died 7 Nov. 1903 - Aged 73 yrs.   At Rest
    "A loved one has gone to rest.
    His place can never be filled,
    His footsteps and voice is never heard,
    He lies beneath the silent sod;
    A waiting and waiting for the coming of our God."

CRAMER, Roxie   1831 - 1910   Wife of John Cramer

CRATHY, Rueben F.   U. S.   18   Inf.

CRESAP, Edward E.   1876 - 1959   Father

CRESAP, Lucy M.   1880 - 1945   Mother

CROSS, Sarah Hannah   Age 72 yrs. 11 mo. 20 days [no marker-
    Crossed plains with parents -taken from record of Early Clark
        County people]

CULP, Charles   1865 - 1938   Father

CULP, Rachel   1869 - 1938   Mother

CULVER, Jessie   1859 - 1953   [Vancouver F.H. marker]

CULBERTSON, Andrew   1857 - 1927   Father   At Rest

CURLEW, Aaron   died 30 Nov. 1928   [year questionable]

CURLEW, May   1859 - 1896   [Funeral Home marker in bad shape]

DALY, Charles   1858 - 1917   [husband of Mary H.]

DALY, Jean F. (Baby)   March 1923

DALY, Mary H.   1863 - 1900

DAVENPORT, W. B.   1874 - 1937   Father

DAVIS, Harry E.   1914 - 1979

DAVIS, Luther E.   1905 - 1957

DAVIS, Richard E.   1953 - 1973   Son

DAY,   [nothing else-small concrete stone]

De HART, James H.   1932 - 1945   Grandson

De HART, Joseph H.   1936 - 1964   Grandson

De HAVEN, Shirley Ann   31 July 1923 - 31 July 1923

DEVINE, Charles J.   1843 - 1930

DEVINE,   Frank   S.   1867 - 1929

DEVINE,   Indianna   Whilelsey   1850 - 1930

DICKENSON,   W.   S.   1867 - 1937

DIETDERICH,   Bessie   N.   1899 - 1973
        [buried near Edmond and Emma Dietderich

DIETDERICH,   Edmond   M.   1873 - 1947   [husband of Emma May]

DIETDERICH,   Emma   May   1874 - 1944

DIETDERICH,   Ruth   [no dates]
        [daughter of Mr. and Mrs. F.M. Dietderich]

DIMICK,   Charles   1874 - 1942

DIMICK,   Walter   1880 - 1920   Father

DIXON,   Anne   Elizabeth   1906 - 1973

DIXON,   Archie   Hiram   1893 - 1957   [Vancouver Chapel marker]

DIXON,   Sarah   7 April 1804 - 3 Feb. 1871   Resting in Peace

DIXON,   Walter   Archie   3 Oct. 1925 - 21 June 1946
        Wash. (Sic)   U. S.   Navy

DOLLAR,   Edgar   Dana   27 April 1900 - 30 July 1960
        Washington   EM3   U. S. N. R.   W. W. II

DOLLAR,   Fred   J.   1911 - 1941
        [son of S.L. and Ruth Dollar]

DOLLAR,   Mary   E.   1878 - 1955   [wife of William C.]   Mother

DOLLAR,   Ruth   E.   1884 - 1961   [wife of S.L. Dollar]

DOLLAR,   S. L.   1880 - 1953

DOLLAR,   Vaughn   W.   1949 - 1966   [son of Virgil & Verna]

DOLLAR,   Verna   L.   1921 - 19____

DOLLAR,   Virgil   W.   1917 - 19____

DOLLAR,   William   C.   1874 - 1937   Father

DRISKELL,   Emery   Ely   1864 - 1942

DRISKELL,   Josephine   I.   1864 - 1936   [wife of Emery Ely]

DUNLAP,   Ernest   E.   31 Dec. 1897 - 7 March 1976

DUNLAP,   Harry   L.   1870 - 1945   [husband of Rebecca E.]

MANOR WILSON BRIDGE CEMETERY

DUNLAP, Rebecca E.   1879 - 1955   Mother

EDNER, Gertrude   1891 - 1904

EDWARDS, A. J.   28 Aug. 1831 - 21 April 1886
                              [grave next ot Electa]

EDWARDS, Electa   1842 - 1930   Mother

EDWARDS, Etta C.   1867 - 1950   [wife of Sherman F.]

EDWARDS, Fred Day   1877 - 1966   [next to Electa & A.J.]

EDWARDS, Sherman F.   1865 - 1931

EDWARDS, William T.   1851 - 1934

ELLIS, Matilda   1868 - 1938   Mother

ELLISON, Bert   1890 - 1969   [husband of Anna E.]

ENGELBART, John E.   1894 - 1931

ENGELKING, August   1872 - 1957   [father of Martha]

ENGELKING, Ida   1885 - 1919   [wife of August]

ENGELKING, Martha L.   1937 - 1959   [daughter of August & Ida]

ETEN, Lewis J.   10 July 1898 - 17 June 1973
        Washington   Cox   U.S. Navy   W.W. I

ETTING, Kathryn G.   1898 - 1942   [wife of Walter G.]

ETTING, Walter G.   18___ - 19____

EVES, Martha L.   1866 - 1943

EVES, Thomas J.   1871 - 1943   Father

EWING, Eva E.   1879 - 1968   Mother
        Our heritage, Love, Faith, Courage

FAIR, Elizabeth   23 March 1840 - 19 October 1897
        "Kind Angels watch the sleeping dust
        Till Jesus comes to raise the just
        And may she wake in sweet surprise
        And to her Savior's image rise."

FAIR, John P.   1871 - 1933

FALK, Casper R.   1899 - 1951   [husband of Jennie J.]

FALK, Charles A.   1866 - 1939   At Rest

FALK, Jennie J.   1895 - 1962
                              185

FALK, Karina   1862 – 1951   At Rest

FELT, Emma J.   2 Jan. 1891 – 18 March 1916
          [wife of Charles C. – in the Lindsay plot]

FENIMORE, Levi   6 Sept. 1870 – 21 Jan. 1946

FENIMORE, Milton   6 Aug. 1868 – 27 Aug. 1946

FENIMORE, Nancy   3 Jan. 1849 – 25 Feb. 1932   Mother

FLOHAUG, Antone J.   1901 – 1963

FLOHAUG, Melkior S.   14 Jan. 1868 – 14 Aug. 1940
                    Born in Norway

FLOHAUG, Oline   1882 – 1966

FORBES, Sarah A.   1 Jan. 1838 – 31 March 1903

FULMER, Charles W.   1856 – 1936   [husband of Lucy A.]
               B.P.O.E.   Lodge 823

FULMER, Lucy A.   1856 – 1942

GARDNER, Lewis   1883

GARDNER, Lydia   1886

GATES, Goldie F.   15 April 1890 – 18 March 1938
                    In Loving Memory

GARLAND, Leveta Fay   1913 – 1941   Wife

GARRETT, James L.   1861 – 1931
          [father of Vivian – husband of Mary Florenah E.]

GARRETT, Mary Florenah E.   1866 – 1944

GARRETT, Vivian   1893 – 1911

GARRISON, Mary   1874 – 1915   Mother

GARRISON, Russell W.   6 Dec. 1896 – 11 June 1974
                    Pvt.   U. S. Army

GATTO, Alexander   3 July 1834 – 11 Feb. 1905

GAYTON, Edna Joy   1905 – 1951
          [on same stone with Orpha Jane Joy]

GENTIS, Bill   [small aluminum marker next to Mantha
               and Mary – no dates]

GENTIS, Mantha   [small aluminum marker next to Bill & Mary]

GENTIS, Mary   [no dates]

186

GESLER, Mary   1900 - 1969   Born in Chicago, Ill.
          [next to John Gesler - Vancouver F. H. marker]

GESLER, John   1882 - 1954   Born in Lithuania

GERVAIS, Clara Garner   1878 - 1971

GILMORE, Winfield S.   1891 - 1977   [husband of Goldie L.]

GILMORE, Goldie L.   1904 - 1949

GOFF, Maggie C.   1868 - 1934
          [wife of Rolin A. - mother of Riley A.]

GOFF, Riley A.   1903 - 1953

GOFF, Rolin A.   1863 - 1926

GORDON, George Stub   1907 - 1979

GOODWIN, Carrie D.   11 April 1908 - 16 April 1908
          Aged 5 days - Infant daughter os S.R. and Cora Goodwin

GRAHAM, Clara E.   1901 - 1947   Dedicated by brother Paul
          Engelking and friend Rudy Lobey.

GRANT, Ethel   1881 - 1946   Mother

GRANT, William G.   1879 - 1953   [next to Ethel Grant]

GRATREAK, Connie Eileen   13 June 1943 - 15 June 1943
          Our Baby

GREEN, Andrew J.   1877 - 1960   Dad

GROSS, Infant Girl   d. 15 March 1865
          [daughter of William N. & Sarah H.]

GROSS, Sarah H.   23 March 1843 - 13 March 1916

GROSS, William N.   6 Jan. 1840 - 20 Sept. 1914   Rest from Labor
          [husband of Sarah H.]

GRUBER, Carolyn Lou   1945 - 1947   At Rest
               Our Darling Baby

GRUBER, Clarence Alfred   1907 - 1975

GRUBER, Henry   1870 - 1943   Father
          [husband of Lillian M.]

GRUBER, Karen Luanne (baby)   25 July 1949

GRUBER, Lillian M.   1878 - 1968   Mother
          [wife of Henry]

GUSEY, John E.   23 Sept. 1894 - 22 Jan. 1942

HAINES, Anna F.   5 Nov. 1888 – 27 Jan. 1972   [wife of Joseph]
        Married 15 Oct. 1907 [in DeHart plot]

HAINES, Joseph   10 Oct. 1886 – 18 April 1962

HAINES, Paul J.   1930 – 1946   Son
        [in Haines–DeHart plot]

HALL, Anna C.   1899 – 1975   [wife of Charles L. Sr.]

HALL, Charles L. Jr.   1922 – 1938
        [son of Charles L. Sr. & Anna C. Hall]

HALL, Charles L. Sr.   1895 – 1967

HANEY, Amanda Jane   1850 – 1933

HANEY, Dora A.   1896 – 1972

HANEY, Ernest E.   1914 – 1947

HANEY, Ernest H.   1890 – 1935

HANSEN, Lena Cramer   1890 – 1949   In Memory Of

HANSON, Flora L. Hollenbeck   1889 – 1912   Sister
        [buried in Hollenbeck plot]

HARLAND, Bertha   1896 – 1977   [husband of Bert T.]

HARLAND, Bert T.   1889 – 1956

HARLAND, Frances   1925 – 19___

HARLAND, Margaret   1926 – 19___

HARPER, Baby   6 Nov. 1904   [next to Katie & Charles]

HARPER, Charles   1881 – 1962

HARPER, Katie L.   1884 – 1968   [wife of Charles]

HARPER, Louisa Jane   1855 – 1906   In Loving Remembrance
        [wife of William R.

HARPER, William R.   1835 – 1893   In Loving Remembrance

HARRIS, Alvin R.   1915 – 1928
        [son of Edward & Olive E.]

HARRIS, Asa A.   1873 – 1950

HARRIS, Benjamin A.   1876 – 1961   Father
        [husband of Naomi]

HARRIS, Edward J.   1876 – 1968   [husband of Olive E.]

HARRIS,   Effie   A.   24 June 1863 - 3 April 1877
            "Suffer   little children to come unto me"
            [shares stone with Albert P. Stabard]

HARRIS,   Emry   1838 - 1912   [husband of Jane]

HARRIS,   Jane   1842 - 1934

HARRIS,   Naomi   1882 - 1939   Mother

HARRIS,   Olive   E.   1891 - 1977

HARRIS,   Orville   Ira   [no   dates]

HASELHORST,   Henry   1859 - 1935

HAWKIN,   Aura   Belle   1871 - 1938   Mother

HAYNES,   Jacob   W.   1852 - 1950

HAYNES,   Katie   1857 - 1941

HAZELWOOD,   Dora   1887 - 1941   At   Rest
            [wife of Will]

HAZELWOOD,   Will   1879 - 1962   At   Rest

HEFTY,   Fred   28 Jan. 1876 - 16 Dec. 1903   At   Rest
      "To live in the hearts we leave behind, is not to die."

HEFTY,   John   9 Sept. 1877 - 16 Oct. 1906
      "Gone in his young years, Afar from his lifes cares."

HEFTY,   Katharina   26 dec. 1852 - 10 July 1887

HENRY,   Cora   5 March 1870 - 14 April 1908

HENRY,   George   16 Dec. 1900 - 2 Sept. 1902

HENRY,   Thomas   J.   2 March 1867 - 31 Jan. 1893

HIGDON,   Albert   G..   1900 - 1912
         [share Higdon plot with Aley S., Mary, Lloyd E. & Robert
               R. SHARP]

HIDGDON,   Aley   S.   (Albert)   1873 - 1920

HIGDON,   Eliza   A.   16 Sept. 1838 - 17 June 1917
            "Call not back the dear departed
             Anchored safe where storms are o'er."
      [stone has names Joseph, Josephine & Elizabeth on it]

HIGDON,   Elizabeth E.   2 Oct. 1858 - 12 April 1876
            daughter of j.B. & E.A. Higdon
            "The pains of death are past
             Labor and sorrow ceased
             and lifes short warfare slosed at
             Her soul is found in peace at last"

HIGDON, Eva   2 Dec. 1889 - 14 May 1909
        [in Higdon plot-shared with (?)Albert, Inez, Frankie, Fannie]

HIGDON, Fannie   14 Mar. 1895 - 7 Oct. 1895
                Daughter of John B. and Nettie E. Higdon

HIGDON, Frankie   31 July 1893 - 25 Nov. 1895
                Son of John B. and Nettie E. Higdon

HIGDON, Inez   25 Jan. 1899 - 14 Feb. 1899

HIGDON, Joseph B.   18 April 1837 - 31 Dec. 1907   [husband
        of Eliza A.]
                "Asleep in Jesus, Blessed sleep
                From which none ever wake to weep"

HIGDON, Josephine   15 April 1875 - 28 April 1876
                [daughter of J.B. & E.A. Higdon[

HIGDON, Lloyd E.   1808 - 1898

HIGDON, Mary Elizabeth   1879 - 1964

HINRICH, Anna H.   1870 - 1952   [wife of William H.]

HINRICH, William H.   1868 - 1954

HOAK, John   1846 - 1930   [husband of Sophia]

HOAK, Ruth Mary   1898 - 1931   [daughter of Sophia & John]

HOAK, Sophia   1854 - 1919   [husband of John]

HOFFMAN, Eva   1868 - 1938   [wife of Nick]
                Beloved Mother and Father

HOFFMAN, Nick   1860 - 1916   Beloved Mother and Father

HOGUE, Louisa   1881 - 1932   Mama

HOLLAND, Beverly June   1926 - 1939
        [daughter of James W. and Jessie (Welp) Holland]

HOLLAND, Gertrude   1881 - 1965   [wife of James]

HOLLAND, James   1863 - 1935   [husband of Gertrude]

HOLLAND, James Farley   1933 - 1935
        [son of James W. and Jessie (Welp) Holland

HOLLAND, James W.   1900 - 1950 [husband of Jessie Welp
        father of James Farley and Beverly June]

HOLLAND, Jessie Welp   1907 - 1971   [wife of James W. and
        mother of James Farley and Beverly June]

MANOR WILSON BRIDGE CEMETERY

HOLLENBECK, Mary   1859 - 1925   [wife of Willard F.]
       Died 24 Aug. 1925 - Age 65 yrs. 15 days

HOLLENBECK, Willard F.   1856 - 1934

HOLSTINE, Fred   1888 - 1949

HOLSTINE, Jane   1851 - 1890

HOMAR, Nellie   1887 - 1967   [wife of George]

HOMAR, George A.   1880 - 1971

HOMAR, Gustavis   1851 - 1931   [husband of Ruthie A.]

HOMAR, Harry N.   14 March 1890 - 13 Nov. 1891

HOMAR, James G.   1882 - 1952

HOMAR, John G.   1878 - 1936

HOMAR, Ruthie A.   1860 - 1943

HOOKER, Ella   1884 - 1971   [wife of Thomas A.]

HOOKER, Thomas A.   1876 - 1949

HORNE, Robert W.   1877 - 1941

HORNOR, Charles W.   1868 - 1949

HORNOR, Emma B.   1870 - 1932   [wife of Charles W.]

HOWELL, Simon Peter   1844 - 1922

HUGHES, Alida   1856 - 1941   Mother

HUGHSON, Alexander   died 22 Sept. 1891   Aged 34 yrs 11mos
       "Kind hearted and always trusted in Providence."

HULETT, James   2 Nov. 1835 - 25 Sept. 1903

HULETT, E. L.

HULETT, Sarah Ann   1853 - 1915

HULETT, W. P.

HUNT, Charles A.   1878 - 1940

HUTTO, Ida   1886 - 1947   [wife of Charles H.]

HUTTO, Charles H.   1888 - 1948

HURSH, George E.   1881 - 1956

HURSH, George W.   [no dates]
191

HURSH, James M.   1860 - 1930

HURSH, Marie   [no dates]

HURSH, Sophrinia   1862 - 1956   [wife of James M.]

HYKE, Floyd F.   1889 - 1965   Father

JACOBS, Dorothy E.   1896 - 1965

JANSSEN, John F.   1870 - 1932

JANSSEN, Kate G.   1878 - 1956   [wife of John F.]

JENSEN, Larry Rueben   21 Nov. 1947 - 18 Jan. 1948   Our Baby

JOHNSON, Carl J.   1864 - 1943

JOHNSON, Ernest L.   1884 - 1937   Father

JOHNSON, John   17 April 1871 - 24 June 1948

JOHNSON, Marie   1848 - 1931   [wife of Ole]

JOHNSON, Ole   1833 - 1922

JOHNSON, Sarah E.   28 Dec. 1876 - 14 Jan. 1964   [wife of John]

JORGENSON, Jackie Lee (baby)   b. & d. 20 April 1937
                    [Vancouver F.H. marker]

JOY, Evelyn Grace   Baby   1907

JOY, Gordon   1912 - 1972

JOY, Henry Waldon   [baby]   1908

JOY, James   14 Jan. 1842 - 10 July 1916   G A R
                Co. I   1st. Regt.   Heavy Art.   Ohio Vol.

JOY, Johnny H.   1896 - 1921

JOY, Lewis Henry   1898 - 1898

JOY, Loren H.   Corp. 4   U.S. Cavalry   Spanish American War

JOY, Nancy J.   13 Sept. 1848 - 17 June 1924   [wife of James]

JOY, Orpha Jane   1907 -   [shares stone with Edna J. Gaton]

JOY, Ruth Belle   25 March 1892 - 6 April 1963
                        [wife of Sidney E.]

JOY, Sidney E.   26 April 1888 - 26 August 1957

JUNIOR, Catherine Margaret   19 May 1899 - 26 Oct. 1899

JUNIOR, Mary M.   1871 - 1941   [wife of Hugh]

KENISON, Grace E.   1898 - 1942

KIELMAN, Herman   1882 - 1963   [husband of Florence] Father

KIELMAN, Florence   1884 - 1958   Mother

KING, Addie   1868 - 1950

KING, Ben   1854 - 1937

KNIFFIN, Carl W.   8 Dec. 1912 - 31 May 1978   In Loving Memory

KNIFFIN, Effie A.   1873 - 1969

KNIFFIN, Robert J.   1902 - 1917

KNIFFIN, Robert W.   1864 - 1936

KNIGHT, Rebecca   1865 - 1946   Mother

KNIGHTON, Loretta   1875 - 1949

KNIGHTON, William A.   1868 - 1964

LARSON, Lucille M.   1916 - 1963   Mother
[wife of Norris Larson]

LARSON, Norris   1904 - 1966   Father

LASATER, Mina Nye   1944 - 1975

LEEPER, Andrew   3 Dec. 1830 - 26 April 1929

LEEPER, Sarah J.   17 Oct. 1838 - 4 Sept. 1915   [wife of Andrew]
"The Lord is my shepherd, I shall not want,
He maketh me lie down in green pastures,
He leadeth me beside still waters."

LEEPER, William W.   1858 - 1929   Father

LEMMONS, Loran W.   1886 - 1953   [Evergreen F.H. marker]

LINDSAY, Infant Son   died 30 Aug. 1895
Son of Mr. and Mrs. W.S. Lindsay

LINDSAY, Albert   [no dates]   [son of George & Bertha]

LINDSAY, Alexander Gustavis   18 May 1879 - 1944
[son of John & Mary E. Lindsay]

LINDSAY, Andrea and Lavern (twins)   1960 - 1960
[daughters of James E. and Donna Lindsay]

LINDSAY, Andrew J.   28 Jan. 1884 - 3 Jan. 1966

MANOR WILSON BRIDGE CEMETERY

LINDSAY, Bertha A.   1868 - 1975   [wife of George W.]

LINDSAY, Cordellia   1878 - 1940   Mother
                    [wife of William S.]

LINDSAY, George W.   1859 [9 May 1857] - 1928
                    [husband of Bertha A.]

LINDSAY, John Ambrose   26 dec. 1896 - 10 May 1982
                    [son of George and Bertha Lindsay]

LINDSAY, J. H.   4 Dec. 1866 - 22 March 1892
          [Joseph Harvey]   Aged 26 yrs. 4 mos.
            "Call not the dear departed
            Anchored sure where storms occur
            On the borderland
            Welcome them soon to meet and part no more."

LINDSAY, John B.   25 Dec. 1820 - 6 March 1907

LINDSAY, Oliver Francis   15 Dec. 1881 - 1974
                [son of John D. and Mary E. Lindsay]

LINDSAY, S. Dewey   19 Oct. 1898 - 1967
                    [son of George and Bertha]

LINDSAY, William S. (Samuel)   (6 May 1872) 1873 - 1949 Father
                    [husband of Cordellia]

LITTLE, Alice J.   1869 - 1947   [wife of Roy A.]

LITTLE, Roy A.   1862 - 1939

LORD, John W.   1854 - 1936   [husband of Sarah]

LORD, Sarah F.   1859 - 1946

LUCAS, F. Mae   1918 - 19___

LUCAS, Ivan O.   1915 - 1977   [husband of F. Mae]

LUCAS, Lewis A.   1940 - 1971   [son of Ivan and F. Mae]

MACKIE, George   1868 - 1937   [husband of Margaret]

MACKIE, Margaret   1860 - 1945

MALLORY, Eva B.   1898 - 19___   [wife of Henry E.]

MALLORY, Henry E.   1890 - 1947

MALONE, David T.   1895 - 1967

MANLEY, Anna   died 27 Feb. 1904 - Aged 82 yrs.

MANLEY, Andrew   died 21 Jan. 1901 - Aged 79 yrs.
                    194

MANLEY, August   1843 – 1909   [husband of Nora]

MANLEY, Gustave   1880 – 1958
                                "Taint"
              "Taint what we have, but what we give,
               Taint where we are, but how we live,
               Taint what we do, but how we do it,
               That make this life worth going through it."

MANLEY, Nora   1850 – 1922

MANWELL, Phebe V.   died 1 March 1902 – Aged 49 yrs 7mos 14days
                         Beloved wife of John

MANWELL, Mary Jane   22 Jan. 1856 – 17 Jan. 1938
                             Grandmother

MARTIN, Baby   1 Sept. 1949

MARTIN, Charles C.   1896 – 1926

MARTIN, John H.   1858 – 1937   [husband of Lillie H.]

MARTIN, Lawrence J.   4 May 1898 – 24 Nov. 1978
                        U. S.   Army   W. W.   II

MARTIN, Owen J.   1890 – 1892

MESSAGE, Ada Prutzman   1895 – 1935

MASTERS, Mary   1852 – 1894   [wife of Walter]

MASTERS, Walter   1853 – 1928

MATHISEN, Gretchen   1893 – 1950   [wife of Jack C.]

MATHISEN, Jack C.   1885 – 1971   [husband of Gretchen]

MATTOX, Allie "Ike"   1899 – 1956

MATTOX, Alfred A.   1856 – 1933

MATTOX, Anna E.   1866 – 1943   [wife of Alfred]

MATTOX, John E.   1892 – 1972

MATTOX, Joseph L.   1889 – 1914

MATTOX, Michael L.   1944 – 1946

MEISNER, Gustaf   1896 – 1950   [husband of Myrtle R.]

MEISNER, Myrtle R.   1885 – 1968

MEYER, Ida   1 Dec. 1894 – 2 Dec. 1977   [wife of Otto W.]

MANOR   WILSON   BRIDGE   CEMETERY

MEYER,   Margaretha   1856 – 1939   [wife of William]

MEYER,   Otto G.   1923 – 1959   [son of Otto W. & Ida]

MEYER,   Otto W.   4 April 1889 – 17 Nov. 1948

MEYER,   Rudolf   1859 – 1939   Father

MEYER,   William   1858 – 1889

MICHAELIS,   Byrle H.   1899 – 1973   Father
                          [husband of Dora]

MICHAELIS,   Dora   1907 – 19___   Mother

MICHAELS,   Bertha   1876 – 1942   Mother
                        [wife of William]

MICHAELS,   William   1869 – 1947   Father

MILLER,   Anton E.   5 Feb. 1911   Pvt.   11 Regt.   U.S.M.C.

MILLER,   Baby   1915

MILLER,   C. A. W.   1898 – 1950

MILLER,   Ellen   1852 – 1896   Mother

MILLER,   Elvin   [no dates – in Lindsay plot]

MILLER,   Emily O. McCafferty   1869 – 1895

MILLER,   Herman R.   1907 – 1977   U.S. Army   W.W. II

MILLER,   John C.   28 Jan. 1847 – 7 Oct. 1902

MILLER,   John Ben   1876 – 1939

MILLER,   Mary and Baby   [no dates – in Lindsay Lot]

MILLER,   Sarah J.   1846 – 1883

MILLER,   Stella J.   1884 – 1976

MINKLER,   C. V.   1891 – 1940   Father

MITCHELL,   George Elmer   1908 – 1937

MORCROFT,   Herbert W.   1884 – 1932

MOOREHEAD,   Baby   2 July 1907 – 16 July 1907

MOOREHEAD,   Mary A.   24 April 1877 – 4 July 1907

MORECROFT,   Emma   1860 – 1913   [wife of John]

MORECROFT,   John   1855 – 1933
                          196

MORELOCK, Ina Brown   1882 – 1967   [grave next to Mike]

MORGAN, Alonzo W.   died 15 Aug. 1884
          Aged 31 years. 2 mo. 7 days [8 June 1853]   Farewell

MORGAN, Edna   died 10 Jan. 1884   Aged 1 mo. 2 days
          daughter of A.W. & M.B. Morgan

MORGAN, Martha B.   29 Jan. 1863 – 15 Oct. 1888   Gone Home

MUNTZ, Eva   1887 – 19___   [wife of Fred]

MUNTZ, Fred   1898 – 1969

MUNTZ, Fritz   1923 – 1946

MURPHY, Edith R.   1881 – 1942   [wife of Joseph]

MURPHY, Joseph   1877 – 1952

McCAFFERTY, Everett   1889 – 1892

McCAFFERTY, Jessie M.   1893 – 1899

McCARTHY, Alice V.   1862 – 1945   Mother

McCOLLUM, Alice H.   1887 – 1972   [wife of Oliver]

McCOLLUM, Margaret J.   1848 – 1924   [wife of Robert T.]

McCOLLUM, Oliver   1875 – 1921

McCOLLUM, Robert T.   1849 – 1926

McCOY, Emma D.   1898 – 1942

McCOY, James E.   1862 – 1939   Father

McCOY, Mary C.   1865 – 1942   [wife of James E.] Mother

McDANIELS, Clara E.   16 Aug. 1857 – 29 Jan. 1894
          [wife of Daniel N. McDaniels]

McDANIELS, Daniel N.   Co. B.   1 Dak.   Cav.

McDANIELS, John   1878 – 1936

McKAY, Doris R.   1904 – 19___   [wife of George F.]

McKAY, Edith J.   1873 – 1950   [wife of Fred W.]

McKAY, Fred W.   1859 – 1942

McKAY, George F.   1899 – 1976

McKAY, Harriet A.   23 June 1878 – 14 May 1968

MANOR WILSON BRIDGE CEMETERY

McKAY, Maud Ethel	10 April 1895 – 8 Oct. 1909	
McKAY, Owen	1915 – 1937	
McLEOD, James H.	1879 – 1937	
McCLURE, Elizabeth Murray	1874 – 1948	
McClure, William Henry	1911 – 1920	
McRAE, Robert	1845 – 1923	
NEAL, Walter	1892 – 1951	
NEMCHICK, Archie Lee	1885 – 1936	
NEMCHICK, Lester V.	16 July 1914 – 29 July 1944	
Washington Pfc.	5 Field Art.	W.W. II
NEMCHICK, Mattie Alice	1889 – 1978	
NEUBAUER, John	1877 – 1951	
NEWTON, Grace E.	1881 – 1961	[wife of Oliver P.]
NEWTON, Oliver P.	1867 – 1943	
NOBLE, Anna B.	1866 – 1938	
NOBLE, Frank O.	1870 – 1952	
NOBLE, William A.	1840 – 1915	G A R [Emblem]
NUGENT, George L.	1882 – 1957	
NUGENT, Gladys L.	1894 – 1976	[wife of George L.]
NUTBROWN, Carrie	1849 – 1892	
OLSON, Roy P.	1884 – 1968	
PARKER, Claire Alvin	1919 – 1948	
PARKER, Ina Jane	1915 – 1975	[wife of Oren]
PARKER, Jennie A.	1889 – 1972	Mother
PARKER, Jesse I.	1883 – 1947	
PARKER, Josie A.	1887 – 1974	[wife of Jesse I.]
PARKER, Oren	1911 – 19___	
PERDUE, Rebecca O.	1852 – 1899	[wife of James]
PERDUE, Josephine	1906 – 1936	[wife of William

Perdue, daughter of Melkion & Oline Flohaug]

MANOR WILSON BRIDGE CEMETERY

PERSON, Magnus   1884 – 1972

PETERSON, Clifford B.   8 May 1916 – 28 Oct. 1973
    Washington   Lieutenant   U.S. Navy   W.W. II

PIEPER, Augusta   17 Feb. 1827 in Saly Delfurth
    died 2 Aug. 1887   Gone but not forgotten

PLUID, Cecil Holmes   1891 – 1945

POGRO, Thomas   1843 – 1930

PORTER, Russell V.   1905 – 1967   Dad   Husband

POWELL, Daisy B.   1882 – 1972   [wife of Edgar C.]

POWELL, Edgar C.   1880 – 19___   [husband of Daisy B.]

PRUTZMAN, Ella M.   6 Dec. 1880 – 11 Jan. 1886

PRUTZMAN, Flora G.   1877 – 1971   [wife of William H.]

PRUTZMAN, Infant Son   24 Dec. 1885 – Died 24 Dec. 1885

PRUTZMAN, Mary A.   21 May 1869 – 26 March 1886

PRUTZMAN, William H.   1874 – 1939

RADFORD, Elmer V.   1893 – 1971   [husband of Myrtle I.]

RADFORD, Myrtle I.   1902 – 19___

RATLIFF, Eli P.   1860 – 1942   Father

READ, Ann E.   1826 – 1894

REEVES, Amanda J.   1851 – 1935   Mother
     [wife of John F.]

REEVES, John F.   1856 – 1948   Mother

RESBURG, Asa C.   died 14 May 1879   Age 3 yrs. 9mos. 2 days

RESBURG, Charles S.   1878 – 1936

RESBURG, Mary J.   15 April 1840 – 1 March 1910

RESBURG, William   Co. C.   24 Illinois Inf.

REYNOLDS, Mary L.   1884 – 1949   [next to Robert H.]

REYNOLDS, Robert H.   1877 – 1932

RICKETTS, Amanda M.   22 March 1838 – 16 Aug. 1922

RICKETTS, E. J.   24 June 1833 – 19 April 1917   Father

RICKETTS, Herbert A.   6 July 1863 – 28 Feb. 1879
            Son of E.J. & A.M. Ricketts

RICKETTS, Ira P.   3 March 1861 – 24 Feb. 1879
            Son of E.J. & A.M. Ricketts

RICKETTS, Iva A.   1 June 1869 – 5 March 1879
            Daughter of E.J. & A.M. Ricketts
        "We have laid thee in the grave little Iva,
         And our home was made lonely by our loss,
         But we know we will meet thee little Iva,
         When the dark river we have crossed."

RITTER, Laura   1883 – 1956   Mother

ROBERTS, Fanny A.   1880 – 1955   [wife of William]

ROBERTS, William M.   1868 – 1946

ROBINSON, W. H.   1858 – 1942   Father

RUNYON, John P.   1879 – 1926

RUST, Arthur   1887 – 1973

RUST, Clarence A.   11 Aug. 1918 – 25 Oct. 1973
            Washington   AMMI   U.S. Navy   W.W. II

RUST, Fanny M.   1887 – 1969   [wife of Arthur]

RUST, Ida Marie   1887 – 1926   Mother

SCHEEL, August F.   1892 – 1973

SCHEEL, Hans Christ   1858 – 1924   [husband of Barbara M.]

SCHEEL, Margaretha   1863 – 1942   Mother
            [wife of Hans Christ]

SCHULTZ, August   died 4 April 1925   Aged 70 yrs.
            [husband of Martha Loretta]

SCHULTZ, Ed R.   1885 – 1950

SCHULTZ, Ed W.   1864 – 1947

SCHULTZ, Martha Loretta   died 10 August 1910   Aged 36 yrs.

SCOGGINS, Justina Leone   4 July 1949 – 19 July 1949

SCOLOS, August   1871 – 1931

SCOLOS, Benjamin   1872 – 1956

SECREST, Mary   3 July 1819 – 28 Sept. 1910   [wife of Michael]

MANOR WILSON BRIDGE CEMETERY

SECREST, Michael   20 Feb. 1813 - 20 Nov. 1894

SEIG, Edna I.   1888 - 1977   Mother

SELBY, Charles J.   1860 - 1940
    [plot shared with John, Phoebe, John M. and Clara]

SELBY, Clara   (2 May 1872) died 13 Aug. 1895
              Aged 23 yrs. 3 Mos. 11 days

SELBY, Effie A.   1885 - 1918   Our Darling
    [near Mark T. Selby grave]

SELBY, John M.   1868 - 1923

SELBY, John M. Sr. (May 1832) died 3 Jan. 1877
              Aged 44 yrs. 7 mos.

SELBY, Mark T.   1879 - 1968

SELBY, Phoebe M.   1841 - 1920

SHARP, Robert R.   10 Jan. 1889 - 12 July 1965
        Washington   Sgt.   322 Co. MTC   W.W. I

SHAW, Sarah   1 May 1879 - 2 April 1914   [wife of Wm. B.]

SHERWOOD, Roy W.   25 Aug. 1897 - 26 Jan. 1978

SHERWOOD, Zolo   27 Nov. 1904 -   [wife of Roy W.]

SHOEMAKER, _____   1931 - 1946

SHORES, Orin E.   1904 - 19____   [wife of Jessie]

SHORE, Orine E.   1904 - 1974   Husband

SHORE, Frank R.   1908 - 1967

SHORES, Harold A.   1912 - 1930
    [Son of Lourena and Richard G. Shores]

SHORES, Jessie E.   1907 - 1964   [wife of Orin]

SHORES, Lourena M.   1872 - 1948

SHORES, Richard C.   1871 - 1915

SIMPSON, Alice R.   1909 - 1954

SMITH, Catherine   1908 - 19___   [wife of Clyde]

SMITH, Clyde   1904 - 1967

SMITH, Ellen G.   1900 - 1974   [wife of Vernon B.]

SMITH, Helen   10 March 1935 - 17 Feb. 1936
          The Angels watch over her.
                201

MANOR WILSON BRIDGE CEMETERY

SMITH, Vernon B.   1900 – 1946   Father

SMITH, Wilhelmina K.   1892 – 1966

SMELTZ, Howard   – 1941
              Ohio   Pvt.   11 U.S. Vol. Cav.

SMITHLINE, Charles A.   1881 – 1926

SMITHLINE, Pearl O.   1886 – 1958   [wife of Charles]

SNYDER, Mary L.   1856 – 1930

SOMMERS, Florence E.   1922 – 1968

SOPER, Cathrine   1918 – 1950

SPENCER, Candice   14 Mar 1952 – 1978   [no marker]
              [daughter of LeMar and Marjorie Spencer]

SPROUL, Charles Ivan   19 March 1917 – 8 April 1917

SPROUL, Eliza Eleanor   1868 – 1972   Mother

SPROUL, George A.   1861 – 1941   At Rest

SPROUL, George A.   13 April 1825 – 10 July 1903
              "Asleep in Jesus! Blessed sleep,
              From which none ever wake to weep."

SPROUL, Manley A.   8 March 1891 – 24 July 1944
              [son of George & Sarah Ann]

SPROUL, Sarah Ann   4 Aug. 1823 – 5 Dec. 1904
              [wife of George]

STABARD, Albert P.   23 Sept. 1861 – 1 Sept. 1861
              [shares stone with Effie A. Harris]

STEELE, N. Elizabeth   1872 – 1939

STEIN, P. Homer   1906 – 1974   Father

STENGER, John H.   23 March 1839 – 15 March 1913
              Aged 73 yrs   11 mos.   23 days
              "He died as he lived, a pure upright man."

STENGER, Mamie   12 Nov. 1883 – 3 April 1887
              Gone but not forgotten

STENGER, Elisha A.   1862 – 1929   Father

STENGER, Emma J.   1871 – 1945   Mother
              [wife of Elisha A.]

STENGER, Lola   1903 – 1929

MANOR WILSON BRIDGE CEMETERY

STENGER, Ray A.   1890 - 1968

STEPHENSON, Alma   1858 - 1912   Beloved Mother

STEVENS, John M.   17 Oct. 1916 - 1 July 1972
         Minnesota   Pfc. 20 Inf. 6 Inf. Div.   W.W. II

STEVENS, Brian A.   - died 1968

STEVENS, George F.   1872 - 1947

STEVENS, Susan H.   1882 - 19____   [wife of George F]

STILL, Mary Ann   1856 - 1916   Mother
                          [wife of William]

STILL, William   1853 - 1912   Father

STODDARD, Donald   1934 - 1945

STUDER,   1835 - 1910   Father

STUDER, Frank   30 Aug. 1886 - 23 Feb. 1947
        Washington   Pvt.   Engineers   W.W. I

STUDER, Joseph   1878 - 1915

STUDER,   1844 - 1905   Mother

STURGES, Annie   24 Oct. 1871 - 17 July 1903
                    Wife of A. R. Sturges

SWEET, Charles E.   1862 - 1940   In Loving Memory

SWEET, Dicy   1866 - 1938   In Loving Memory

SYPNESKI, Daisy   1902 -   6 mos. of age
              [daughter of Veona Sypneski]

SYPNESKI, Verona   1868 - 1902   [mother of Daisy]

TAPPAN, Lena   1847 - 1936   Mother

TAYLOR, Cynthia   1862 - 1932

TAYLOR, Hollis   1849 - 1916

TAYLOR, Richard Floyd   1878 - 19____
              [husband of Myra Jeanette]

TEAL, Nina Edna   1883 - 1929   Mother

THEIL, Lola G.   1902 - 1945

TILTON, Frank E.   1887 - 1947

TILTON, J. D.   17 Aug. 1862 - 14 July 1925
                          203

TILTON,   Sarah B.   1863 – 1937   [wife of J. D.]

TIMMEL,   Doris   1915 – 1936   Our Beloved Daughter

TOOLEY,   Emma E.   1875 – 1947   In Memory Of
                                    [wife of William W.]

TOOLEY,   William W.   1865 – 1935   In Memory Of

TUCKER,   Dexter N.   1875 – 1949

TUCKER,   Maud L.   1887 – 1955   [wife of Dexter N]

TUETH,   Donald   11 June 1938 – 8 July 1938
                    [son of Ray & Elizabeth Waggoner (Gellipeau) Tueth]

TURNBULL,   Cornealus H.   15 Mar. 1870 – 17 Oct. 1890

TURNBULL,   D. F.   23 July 1867 – 13 March 1896

TURNBULL,   Flora   20 Aug. 1880 – 27 Aug. 1880

TURNBULL,   Lizzie   b. 19 Nov. 1887 – 19___

UELTSCHI,   J. Augusta   1871 – 1949   Mother
                          [wife of David]

UELTSCHI,   David C.   1903 – 1970

UELTSCHI,   Gottfried   1871 – 1958

WALKER,   Amelia C.   9 Feb. 1889 – 22 Aug. 1977   Mother
                          [wife of William W.]

WALKER,   Eli   b. 21 Aug. 1867   Son of W.C. & Stestia Walker
            [name on same stone as Satestia Walker and Julia Bailey]

WALKER,   Satestia   2 May 1847 – 22 Jan. 1901
            Killed by dynamite explosion. Member of Baptist Church.

WALKER,   William C.   1841 – 1927

WALKER,   William W.   8 March 1883 – 19 April 1947   Father

WALLACE,   William W.   24 Feb. 1873 – 7 Feb. 1907
                "Farewell dear, but not forever,
                 There will be a glorious dawn,
                 We shall meet to part, no never,
                 On the resurrection morn."

WALTHER,   Adolph L.   20 Feb. 1909 – 14 Aug. 1969
            Washington   Pvt.   Inf.   W.W. II

WALTHER,   Ernest E.   1902 – 1931
                                                            Son

WALTHER,   Emile   1867 – 1917
                                                            Wife

WALTHER, Frederic Wm.   1901 - 1947   Son

WALTHER, Rosa   1876 - 1945   Mother
                       [wife of Emile]

WARD, Dale I.   16 March 1931 - 21 August 1931

WARD, Hiram S.   1895 - 1955

WARD, Wadie B.   1898 - 1969   [wife of Hiram S.]

WARNER, Curtis D.   1882 - 19___

WARNER, Loretta E.   1885 - 1951   [wife of Curtis D]

WARREN, Rachel A.   1874 - 1930   Mother
                    [grave on Lindsay plot]

WATSON, Hazel M.   1906 - 1970

WATSON, Robert R.   1873 - 1945   Father

WEAVER, Lucy Dee   31 Jan. 1900 - 3 July 1907

WEBB, Maud   1883 - 1943

WEBBER, William Silas   Age 6yrs 3 days
                       Son of George and M.T. Webber

WELP, Jessie W.   1907 - 1971

WESTERGARD, Anna M.   1867 - 1927   [wife of Mads]

WESTERGARD, Mads   1861 - 1946

WHITE, Arthur H.   1882 - 1931   Father

WHITE, Daniel H.   1879 - 1949

WHITE, Emma J.   1859 - 1925   Mother

WHITE, Jane I.   1881 - 1949   [wife of Daniel H.]

WHITE, Perry A.   1849 - 1905

WHITNEY, Frank B.   1875 - 1945   Father

WHITNEY, Iva M.   1877 - 1953   Mother
                    [wife of Frank B.]

WIEBOLD, Ernest H.   1872 - 1947

WIEBOLD, Henrietta W.   1872 - 1954   [wife of Ernest H]

WIEBOLD, Harry G.   1897 - 1952

MANOR WILSON BRIDGE CEMETERY

WILEY, James F.   28 June 1880 – 20 Sept. 1904
        In Memory Of
        "Greater love hath no man than for his friend."

WILKER, Bertha   1876 – 1959   Mother

WILKER, Henry W.   1873 – 1957   Father

WILLIAMS, Alfred N.   29 Nov. 1884 – 13 Feb. 1927

WILLIAMS, Baby   died 1911   [Laynes F. H. marker]

WILLIAMS, Anita A.   1901 – 19   [wife of Jay L.]

WILLIAMS, Elsie J.   died 1972   [Laynes F.H. marker]

WILLIAMS, Emma O.   14 April 1882 – 26 Msy 1977
                        [wife of Joseph T.]

WILLIAMS, Harold   1909 – 1972

WILLIAMS, Jay L.   1882 – 1968

WILLIAMS, Joseph L.   4 Feb. 1848 – 19 Aug. 1928   Father

WILLIAMS, Joseph T.   9 July 1879 – 28 Nov. 1952

WILLIAMS, Judah C.   23 July 1843 – 20 May 1907
                Prepare to meet me in Heaven.

WILLIAMS, Oliver S.   1873 – 1959

WILLIAMS, Patricia J.   1935 – 1936   [Laynes F.H. marker]

WILLIAMS, Theodore Richard   8 Nov. 1904 – 26 May 1952

WILLIAMS, Virgil E.   1872 – 1958

WILLIAMS, William C.   31 March 1871 – 20 Aug. 1937   Father

WILSON, Angeline M.   1878 – 1940   [wife of Thomas S.]

WILSON, Douglas E.   1888 – 1971

WILSON, Floyd   1886 – 1937   Son

WILSON, Hubert C.   1890 – 1950   [husband of Vera]

WILSON, Lillian L.   1903 – 1941   [wife of Douglas E.]

WILSON, Sarah J.   1850 – 1929   [wife of William E.]

WILSON, Thomas S.   1871 – 1928

WILSON, Vera   1897 – 19___   [wife of Hubert C.]

WILSON, William E.   1852 – 19___

WOOD,   Arthur   1905 - 1920

WOOD,   Chester   1888 - 1889
                    [near W. Scott and Mellissa Wood]

WOOD,   Edgar   E.   1907 - 1969

WOOD,   James   R.   1836 - 1905   [husband of Rebecca J.]

WOOD,   Julia   Ann   1880 - 1962

WOOD,   Lloyd   1892 - 1895

WOOD,   Mellissa   J.   1865 - 1931   [wife of W. Scott]

WOOD,   Merle   1905 - 1918   [next to Ole Wood]

WOOD,   Ole   1881 - 1913

WOOD,   Rebecca   J.   1844 - 1910

WOOD,   W. Scott   1861 - 1931

WORTHEN,   Augusta   M.   1863 - 1929

YANKEE,   Infant babies
               [children of Mr. & Mrs. Pete Yankee]

YANKEE,   Peter   M.   1908 - 1970

YOUNG,   Mary   1882 - 1937   Mother
                      [wife of William]

YOUNG,   Nancy   1839 - 1895

YOUNG,   William   1876 - 1942   Father

ZUMWALT,   Joanne   8 April 1939

ZIMMERMAN,   Edward   G.   1866 - 1939   [husband of Martha H]

ZIMMERMAN,   Gordon   (baby)   1896

ZIMMERMAN,   Harry   (baby)   1891

ZIMMERMAN,   Martha   H.   1871 - 1959   [wife of Edward G.]
                    [mother of Harry & Gordon]

Northwood Park Cemetery

Northwood Park Cemetery is located
at 16407 N. E. Union Road, Vancouver,
one half mile southeast of the Clark
County Fair Graounds at 179th Street
and I-5 exit. There are approximately
175 burials.

NORTHWOOD PARK CEMETERY

ABLEIDINGER   Robert T., L. Cdr., U. S. Navy, WWII   1916 - 1979

ACKLEY   Richard W., U. S. Navy, 1923-1979

AHLBOM   Axel W., "2 Cor. 5:8"   1905 - 1978

ALEXANDER   Herman A. "Father"   1918 - ____

ALEXANDER   Violet M. "Mother"   1915 - 1979

ALLEN   Albert Frank. (Age 70. b. 11 Aug 1913, LaCenter, WA - d. 9 May 1984, Vancouver, WA. Husband of Mary B. Allen, at home. Graveside service Friday, May 11, at Northwood Park Cemetery. VFC. Obit - The Columbian)

ALLEN   Albert M. (Age 78. b. 1 May 1907, Trail, OK - d. 10 Feb 1986, Vancouver, WA. Sons: Kenneth of Fort Walton Beach, FL; Raymond of Lancaster, CA; Roy of Emigrant Gap, CA. Daughter: Patricia Sherer of Vancouver. Brothers: James and Vernon of Council Bluffs, IA. Sister: Leola Luttrell of California. Burial in Northwood Park Cemetery. VFC. Obit - The Columbian)

ANDERSON   David Charles. (Age 54. b. 14 Dec 1928, Vilona, AR - d. 17 Apr 1983, Portland, OR. Res: Vancouver, WA. Husband of Fern Anderson, at home. Graveside service Tuesday, April 19, at Northwood Park Cemetery. VFC. Obit - The Columbian)

ASHFORD   Helen I. 1903 - 1980

BAKER   Andrew ("Andy"). (Age 85. Pneumonia. b. 8 Feb 1902, Anoka MN - d. 8 June 1987, Res: Vancouver, WA. Widow: Bernice, at home. Daughters: Ellen Ringnalda, Vancouver, and Sandra Burgett, Portland, OR. Sister: Florence Storrs, Minnesota. Graveside service Friday, June 12, at Northwood Park Cemetery. VFC. Obit - The Columbian)

BAKER   Grace E. 1888 - 1981

BARGER   Ronald J. (Age 48. b. 14 Oct 1934, Arcadia, NE - d. 13 Mar 1983, Ilwaco, WA. Husband of Marilyn Y. Barger, Vancouver, WA. Funeral Thursday, March 17, at Ridge Dell Seventh Day Adventist Church. Interment at Northwood Park Cem. VFC. Obit - The Columbian)

BARHITTE   Henry Vere. (Age 73. b. 2 Jul 1911, Harrietta, MI – d. 21 Feb 1985, Vancouver, WA. Res: Ridgefield, WA. Husband of Marian G. Barhitte of Ridgefield, WA. Funeral Monday, Feb. 25, at Evergreen Staples Funeral Chapel. Interment in Northwood Park Cem. EFC/EFH. Obit - The Columbian)

BATES   LeRoy Eugene. U.S. Marine Corps/WWII (Age 55. b. 23 Dec. 1928, Guymon, OK – d. 16 Apr 1984, Vancouver, WA. Memorial service Saturday, April 21, at VFC. Inurnment at Northwood Park Cem. Obit - The Columbian)

BEVARD   Alice. Mom. 1894 - 1979

BEVARD   Paul E. Dad. "Together Forever" 1889 - 1957

BIRKLAND   Virginia K. (Age 64. b. 5 Aug 1921, Brush Prairie WA – d. 22 Mar 1986, Vancouver, WA. Res: Ridgefield, WA. Wife of Norman R. Birkland, at home. Services Tuesday, March 25, at Ridgefield Reorganized Church of Jesus Christ of Latter Day Saints. Interment in Northwood Park Cem. VFC. Obit - The Columbian)

BISENIUS   Robert M. ("Bob"). (U. S. Army. Age 69. Cancer. b. 21 Sep 1917, Cascade, IA – d. 8 Apr 1987, at home, Vancouver, WA. Res: Vancouver. Widow: Marjorie (("Marge")), at home. Son: Michael John Bisenius, Vancouver. Daughters: Susan Marie Tomer, Stanwood, WA; Barbara Ann Bisenius, Vancouver; Wendy Louise Dent, Riverton, WY. Brothers: John L., Matt and James, of Portland, OR; Richard, of Lake Oswego, OR, and Allen, Eagle Creek, OR. Mass of Christian Burial Saturday, April 11, at St. James Catholic Church, Interment: Northwood Park Cem. VFC. Obit - The Columbian)

BLACK   Kristopher Ryan. (Age 13-1/2 months. b. 22 Sep 1985 – d. 14 Nov 1986, Portland, OR. Res: Vancouver, WA. Parents: Sue and Rick Black, of Hazel Dell. Grandparents: Ralph and Marilyn Brown, Vancouver; Ron and Terry Black, Wishram, WA. Great-Grandparents: Dick and Faye Black, Vancouver; Al and Hazel Taylor, Portland; Mildred Roys and Margaret Brown, both of Seattle. Great-great-grandmothers: Lucy White, Portland and Mildred DeFoer, Washougal. Godparents: Jay and Rachel Settles of Vancouver. Service Monday, Nov. 17, at Hazel Dell Church of Christ. Burial in Northwood Park Cem. VFC. Obit - The Columbian)

BLAIR   Allen Ashton. (Age 57. Ruptured aneurysm. b. 3 Mar 1938, Omaha, NE – d. 24 Apr 1985, Portland, OR. Husband of Betty Jean, at home. Funeral Tuesday,

April 30, at St. Luke's Episcopal Church. Graveside service Wed., May 1, at Northwood Memorial Park. VFC. Obit - The Columbian)

BLOOM   J. Herbert. "In God's Care" 1906 - 1979

BLOOM   Montie Ree. (Age 75. b. 13 Jun 1907, Knowles, MN - d. 12 Jun 1983, Vancouver, WA. Res: LaCenter, WA. Funeral Wednesday, June 15, at Layne's Funeral Home Chapel. Burial at Hearthwood Park Cem. LFC. Obit - The Columbian)

BOUCHARD   Jami Lee. "Our Darling" Jan 15 - Mar 13, 1981.

BOYER   Wanda Lucinda. (Age 85. b. 3 Oct 1897, Enderlin, ND - d. 4 Sep 1983, Portland, OR Res: Vancouver, WA. Funeral Thursday, September 8, at Vancouver Funeral Chapel. Interment at Northwood Park Cem. VFC Obit - The Columbian)

BRINDLE   Jason K. "In God's Care" 1973 - 1979.

BROWNING   Catherine Diane. (Age 26, b. 12 Jun 1957, Ft. Worth, TX - d. 23 Sept. 1983, Portland, OR. Res: Battle Ground, MAR Daughter of Mr. and Mrs. Howard Browning, at home. Services Tues., Sep 27, at the Faith Church of the Nazarene. Interment in Northwood Park Cemetery)

BUMP   Benjamin P. 1905 - 1979

BUMP   Dorothy M. 1906 - _____

BURNETT   Leanne Brooks. (Stillborn 26 Aug 1986, Vancouver, WA Daughter of Ken and Kimberlee Burnett. Res. Vancouver. Graveside services and interment Wednesday, August 27, at Northwoods Park Cem. VFC. Obit - The Columbian)

CALSTOY   Mary F. (Age 40. Auto Accident. b. 14 Nov 1942, Vancouver, WA - d. 12 Aug 1983, Vancouver, WA. Daughter of ((Mother and stepfather)) Margaret and Walter Hageman, Vancouver; ((Father and stepmother)) Thomas J. and Eunice Macchione, Vancouver. Funeral Wed. 17 Aug at Hamilton Mylan Funeral Home. Interment in Northwood Park Cem. HMFH. Obit - The Columbian)

CAMERON   Alta. 1899 - 1973

CAMERON   Harvey. 1887 - 1947

CARR   Roger Wayne. (Age 39. b. 28 Jun 1945, Yakima, WA. - d. 11 Jul 1984, Vancouver, WA. Husband of Susan K. Carr, at Home. Funeral Friday, 13 Jul at Vancouver

Funeral Chapel. Interment in Northwood Park Cem. VFC. Obit - The Columbian)

CARROLL   Andrew Michael. (Age 4. b. 15 Mar 1981, Korea - d. 9 Nov 1985, Vancouver, WA. Son of Rev. Richard and Launda Carroll, Vancouver. Funeral Wednesday, 13 Nov. at Twenty-first Avenue Baptist Church. Interment: Northwood Park Cem. VFC. Obit - The Columbian)

CLARK   Ismena I. (Age 63. b. 25 Oct 1922, Martinex, CA - d. 9 Jan 1986, Portland, OR. Res: Vancouver, WA. Sons: Ricke, Vancouver; Gregory, San Bernardino, CA. Brother: Harry Meret, Van Nuys, CA. Sisters: Theresa Breen, Norwalk, CA; Helen Mosier, Torrance, CA. Funeral Sat. 11 Jan at Vancouver Funeral Chapel. Burial in Northwood Park. Obit - The Columbian)

CLARK   Laurine Annette "Wood". (Age 39. b. 27 Feb 1946, Vancouver, WA - d. 6 Dec. 1985, Vancouver, WA. Dau of Mr. and Mrs. Roy Wood, Vancouver. Service Wed., 11 Dec. at First Evangelical Free Church. Interment in Northwood Park Cem. VFC. Obit - The Columbian)

CLOSSON   David S. 1945 - 1980 "To Everything There Is A Season And A Time For Every Purpose Under Heaven"

CLOSSON   Pamela S. 1948 - 1980 "To Everything There Is A Season And A Time for Every Purpose Under Heaven"

COLE   George E. U. S. Army. (Age 66. b. 6 Oct 1920, Hoquiam, WA - d. 29 Aug 1987, at home, Vancouver, WA. Graveside service Thursday, 3 Sep, at Northwood Park Cem. VFC. Obit - The Columbian)

CONLEY   Linda Sue. (Age 37. b. 24 Feb 1949, Champaign, IL. - d. 17 Sep 1986, Portland, OR. Res: Vancouver, WA. Graveside services Fri., 19 Sep at Vancouver Funeral Chapel's Northwood Park Cem. VFC. Obit - The Columbian)

CONNER   Floyd M. (Age 25. Auto Accident. b. 31 Dec 1958, Big Springs, TX - d. 7 Oct 1984, Nephi, Utah. Res: Vancouver, WA. Son of Robert and Lillian Conner, Vancouver. Graveside services Wed., 10 Oct, at Northwood Park Cem. MGM. Obit - The Columbian)

COOK   Shelly Rae. (Age 19. b. 13 Mar 1964, Wenatchee, WA. - d. 14 Apr 1983, Vancouver, WA. Res: Vancouver, 3 yrs., previously Albuquerque, NM. Daughter of Edward and Gayle Cook, at home. Services Monday, 18 Apr, at Vancouver Funeral Chapel. Interment in Northwood Park Cem. VFC. Obit - The Columbian)

COOKSEY   Russell W. 17 Sep 1974

COWAN   Donald E. (Age 57. b. 28 Jul 1927, Henry Co, MO - d. 19 Aug 1984, Vancouver, WA. Husband of Orva J. Cowan, at home. Funeral Wed., 22 Aug, at Vancouver Funeral Chapel. Interment at Northwood Park Cemetery. VFC. Obit - The Columbian)

CRANE   Clara Fern. (Age 62. b. 15 Mar 1925, Lake City, IA - d. 20 Aug 1987, Portland, OR. Res: Vancouver, WA. Dau of Clyde Logan, Jefferson, Iowa. Memoral service Tues., 25 Aug, at Manor Evangelical Church, Battle Ground, WA. Burial in Northwood Park Cem. Portland Funeral Alternatives in charge. Obit - The Columbian)

CRONE   Albert A. U. S. Navy/WWII. (Age 57. b. 10 Jun 1926, Everett, WA - d. 20 Jun 1983, Portland, OR. Res: Ridgefield, WA. Husband of Wilma Crone, at home. Graveside service Thurs., Jun 23, at Northwood Park Cem. VFC. Obit - The Columbian)

CURTIS   Linda L. Age 40. (b. 8 May 1947, Denver, CO - d. 6 Aug 1987. Res: Vancouver, WA. Daughter of Kenneth and Janice Curtis, Vancouver. Graveside service Monday, 10 Aug, at Northwood Park Cem. VFC. Obit - The Columbian)

CVETICH   John. "Together Forever" 1892 - 1980

CVETICH   Lillian Flora. Age 62. (b. 21 Feb 1923, Olympia - d. 24 Sep 1985, Vancouver, WA. Auto Accident. Wife of John Cvetich, at home. Funeral Saturday, 28 Sep, at Vancouver Funeral Chapel. Interment in Northwood Park Cem. VFC. Obit - The Columbian)

CVETICH   Mary. 1903 - ____

DAVIS   Gordon Leroy. (Age 6 days. b. 25 Apr 1984, Portland, OR - d. 1 May 1984, Portland, OR. Res: Vancouver, WA. Son of Mr. and Mrs. Charles Davis, Jr., at home. Funeral Fri., 4 May, at Vancouver Funeral Chapel. Interment in Northwood Park Cem. VFC. Obit - The Columbian)

DE BUHR   Elizabeth B. "Mother" 1907 - 1981

DE BUHR   Harry A. "Father" 1904 - ____

DELANEY   Marcella Carolan. (Age 72. b. 24 Mar 1912, Fremont, IA - d. 11 Dec 1984, Portland, OR. Res: Vancouver, WA. Wife of Thomas E. Delaney, at home. Mass of Christian Burial Monday, 17 Dec, at St. Joseph's Catholic Church. Interment at Northwood Park Cem. VFC. Obit - The Columbian)

DELANEY

Thomas E. (Age 74. b. 9 May 1911, Friday Harbor, WA - d. 1 Nov 1985, Queenstown, New Zealand. Mass of Christian Burial Thurs., 14 Nov, at St. Joseph's Catholic Church. Interment at Northwood Park Cem. VFC. Obit - The Columbian)

DE SLOOVER

Annie Hopgood. (Age 88. b. 9 Sep 1897, Fort Saskatchewan, Canada - d. 9 Apr 1986, Vancouver, WA. Res: Ridgefield, WA. Wife of August, at home. Graveside service Sat., 12 Apr, at Northwood Park Cem VFC. Obit - The Columbian)

DIXON

Paul A. U.S. Air Corps/WWII (Age 67. b. 2 May 1917, Dayton, WA - D. 21 Aug 1984, at home, Ridgefield, WA. Vancouver, WA. Husband of Fay Dixon, at home. Memorial service Fri., 24 Aug., at VFC. Obit - The Columbian)

DORSCH

Robert H. (Age 57. b. 15 Sep 1925, Muskegon, MI - d. 9 Aug 1983, Milwaukie, OR Res: Vancouver, WA. Husband of Patricia A. Dorsch, at home. Funeral Sat., 13 Aug, at Vancouver Funeral Chapel. Interment in Northwood Park Cem. Obit - The Columbian)

EBERHARDT

Willard L. (Age 72. b. 16 Sep 1913, Perrysville, OH - d. 16 Sep 1985, Portland, OR. Res: Vancouver, WA. Widow: Tharza L. Eberhardt. Funeral Friday, 20 Sep, at ESFC. Interment in NPC. Obit - The Columbian)

EKEBERG

John David. "Son" 1956 - 1978

ELLINGSON

Belva M. (Lien). (Age 60. b. 24 May 1925, Portland, OR - d. 1 Jul 1985, Portland, OR. Res: Vancouver, WA. Wife of Ardon P. Ellingson. Funeral Monday, 8 Jul, Vancouver Funeral Chapel. Interment at Northwood Park Cem. Obit - The Columbian)

ERCEG

Daniel. 1979 - 1979

EVENSON

Euphemia B. "In Loving Memory" 1902 - 1978
Footstone: First Interment in Northwood Park Feb. 14, 1978.

EWART

Rowland. 1917 - 1980

FARRAR

Marny Esther. (Age 30. b. 6 Sep 1955, Austin, TX - d. 20 Jan 1986, Vancouver, WA. Widower: Chris J. Farrar. Daughter: Marilyn Joalene Farrar, Vancouver. Parents: Mr. and Mrs. Hal Haynes, Vancouver. Brothers: Bill Haynes, Johnson City, TX, and Hal Haynes, Kingsport, TN. Graveside service Thurs., 23 Jan., in NPC. ESFC. Obit - The Columbian)

FISCH   Sterling Jackson. 18 Jun 1981 - 18 Jun 1981

FOSTER   Charles Brooks. U. S. Army/WWI. b. 20 Nov 1889 - d. 17 Jan 1980

FOX   Laurence K. "Larry". (Age 48. b. 9 Mar 1939, Coos Bay, OR - d. 16 Oct 1987, Vancouver, WA. Husband of Sherri, at home. Son of Marion Fox, Vancouver, WA. Service Wed., 21 Oct, at Vancouver Funeral Chapel. Burial in Northwood Park Cem. Obit - The Columbian)

FRANCIS   Deborah. "Beloved Daughter" (Stone has picture of Deborah on it) 1962 - 1978

FROST   Wilbert Eugene "Bill". (Age 57. b. 1 May 1926, Portland, OR - d. 21 Nov 1983, Vancouver, WA. Res: Ridgefield, WA. Husband of Grace V. Frost, at home. Funeral Friday, 25 Nov, at Vancouver Funeral Chapel. Interment at Northwood Park Cem. Obit - The Columbian)

GAIN   James Stewart. (Age 42. ((State Trooper)) b. 3 Aug 1944, Vancouver, WA - d. 2 Mar 1987, Vancouver, WA. Res: Battle Ground, WA. Widow: Rosemary, at home. Sons: Nicholas and Todd, both of Cincinnati, OH. Daughter: Danielle Marie Gain, at home. Father: Stewart Gain, Jr., Vancouver. Brother: John F. Gain, Vancouver. Funeral Service Friday, 6 Mar, at St. Joseph Catholic Church. Interment Vancouver Funeral Chapel's Northwood Park Cem. Obit - The Columbian)

GARDNER   Casey E. 1911 - 1978

GERMAN   Thomas Dale. (Age 20. b. 12 Aug 1963, Vancouver, WA - d. 18 Sep 1983, St. Ignatius, MT. Res: Vancouver, Wa. Parents: Arden and Shirley German, Vancouver. Funeral Thurs., 22 Sep, at Vancouver Funeral Chapel. Interment at Northwood Park Cem. Obit - The Columbian)

GERVAIS   Annie Sylvia. (Age 73. b. 29 Nov 1910, Yorkton, Saskatchewan - d. 5 Jul 1984, Vancouver, WA. Wife of Clarence F. Gervais, at home. Memorial Service Monday, 9 Jul, at Vancouver Funeral Chapel. Interment in Northwood Park Cem.

GIDDINGS   Sarah Ellen. 1865 - 1932

GIOVANNONE   Domenic. "Love Lives On" 1905 - 1980

GIOVANNONE   Emma M. (Age 74. b. 20 Jun 1910, Brockville, Ontario - d. 18 Jun 1984, Vancouver, WA. Mass of Christian Burial Thurs., 21 Jun, at St. James Catholic Church.

Burial in Northwood Park Cem. VFC. Obit - The Columbian)

GOBEL-WIRTH | Janae. (b. 21 Nov 1962, Reno, NV - d. 31 Aug 1983, Vancouver, WA. ((double murder victim with her mother, Shirley Ann Wirth)). Daughter of Shirley Ann Wirth, Vancouver, and Mickey Wirth, Vancouver. Graveside service Thurs., 4 Aug., at Northwood Park Cem. VFC. Obit - The Columbian)

GOODPASTER | Margaret Louise. "Daughter" 10 Dec. 1947 - 11 May 1980

GOINGS | Reginald A. 15 Nov 1914 - 9 Jun 1978

GOWINSKI | Leo. 1893 - 1978

GRIMM | Edward B. (b. 22 Sep 1904, Southbend, IN - d. 19 Dec 1986, Vancouver, WA. Widow: Helen, at home. Sons: Edward, Roseburg, OR; Jack and Patrick, both of Vancouver; Richard Taylor, Issaquah. Sister: Helene Hafron, San Francisco. Funeral 23 Dec at Northwood Park Cem. Hamilton-Mylan Funeral Home. Obit - The Columbian)

GROVES | Ferne L. "Wife" 1910 - 1981

HAISCH | Jocob R. 1908 - 1979

HALL | Bobby Ray. U. S. Air Force/Korea. (Age 54. b. 24 Jun 1930, Shawnee, OK - d. 25 Nov 1984, Vancouver, WA. Husband of Carolyn Jean Hall, at home. Funeral Wed., 28 Nov, at Vancouver Funeral Chapel. Interment at Northwood Park Cem. Obit - The Columbian)

HALL | E. Ruth. 21 Apr 1917 - 1 Mar 1980

HARCOURT | Roy L. (Age 57. b. 26 Feb 1926, Hagerstown, IN - d. 16 Jul 1983, Vancouver, WA. Res: Battle Ground, WA. Husband of Dolly Harcourt, at home. Funeral Thurs., 21 Jul, at Vancouver Funeral Chapel. Interment at Northwood Park Cem. Obit - The Columbian)

HARVEY | Franklin H., Jr. "Butch" b. 15 Oct 1960 - d. 20 Jul 1978

HATHAWAY | Michael R. 1981 - 1981 (Vancouver Funeral Home marker)

HAYNES | Doris M. "Mother. Psalm 23" 1909 - ____ (w/Laurence)

HAYNES | Laurence B. "Father. Psalm 23" 1907 - 1980 (w/Doris M.)

216

HEBNER	Amelia F. "Mom" 1919 - ____
HEBNER	Lee W. "Dad" 1914 - 1979
HENRY	John P. "Loving Memories Last Forever" 1954 - 1978
HILL	George A. "Husband" 1918 - 1981
HOGAN	Juanita M. "Beloved Daughter" 10 Sep 1949 - 24 May 1978 (in corners also reads "Don" and "Bill")
HOGAN	Ralph Leo. (Age 57. b. 24 Feb 1928, Conesville, IA - d. 13 May 1985, Vancouver, WA. Graveside services at Northwood Memorial Park Thurs., 16 May. VFC. Obit - The Columbian)
HOWELL	Eugene O. (Age 71. b. 12 Jun 1914, Havre, MT - d. 10 Dec 1985, Vancouver, WA. Husband of Vivian E., at home. Funeral Fri., 13 Dec, at Vancouver Funeral Chapel. Interment in Northwood Park Cem. Obit - The Columbian)
HUMES	Helen Jane. (Age 61. b. 9 Oct 1924, Lewiston, ID - d. 4 Jan 1986, Vancouver, WA. Widower: Leon, at home. Son: Patrick Black, Easton, TX. Daughters: Marie Black and Karen Black, both of Vancouver. Sister: Marie Birtholf, Priest River, ID. Funeral Tues., 7 Jan, at Vancouver Free Methodist Church. Burial in Northwood Park Cem. VFC. Obit - The Columbian)
HUNT	Norma Ann. (Age 46. b. 14 Dec 1938, Hutchinson, MN - d. 15 Dec 1984, Portland, OR. Res: Vancouver, WA. Funeral Wed., 19 Dec, at Crossroads Community Church. Interment at Northwood Park Cem. VFC. Obit - The Columbian)
IMUS	James Robert. (Age 36. b. 20 Aug 1947, Portland, OR - d. 15 May 1984. Res: Vancouver, WA. Husband of Sondra, at home. Funeral Friday, 18 May, at Vancouver Funeral Chapel. Burial in Northwood Park Cem. Obit - The Columbian)
JOHNS	Thomas Russell. U. S. Navy/Vietnam. b. 8 Dec 1946 - d. 3 Jun 1979
JOHNSON	Beulah A. (Age 77. Heart attack. b. 23 Jul 1909, Riley County, KS - d. 17 Jun 1987, Ridgefield, WA. Res: Ridgefield. Wife of Marvin, at home. Graveside service Sat., 20 Jun, at Northwood Park Cem. VFC. Obit - The Columbian)
JOHNSON	Hazel R. (Age 83. b. 19 Apr 1903, Winlock, WA - d. 24 Nov 1986, Vancouver, WA. Widower: Ned, at home.

Son: Perry Johnson, Canby, OR. Graveside services and interment Friday, 28 Nov, at Northwood Park Cem. VFC. Obit - The Columbian)

JOHNSON   Ned. "In God's Care" 1899 - ____

JOHNSTON   Adele J. 1920 - ____

JOHNSTON   Merle C. 1918 - 1978

JONES   Hazel F. 1909 - 1979

JONES   Ralph Waldo. U. S. Army/WWI. b. 21 Feb 1892 - d. 18 Jan 1980

JORDON   Kaylid E., Sr. 1908 - 1981 (Vancouver Funeral Home marker)

JUDSON   Harry T. 1903 - 1980

JUNKER   Albert. (Age 72. Cancer. b. 2 May 1911, North Dakota - d. 23 Sep 1983. Res: Battle Ground, WA. Funeral Tues., 27 Sep, at Layne's Funeral Home Chapel. Burial in Northwood Park Cem. Obit - The Columbian)

KADOW   Audrey. (Age 72. Cancer. b. 4 Nov 1914, Ridgefield, WA - d. 28 May, 1987, Portland, OR. Widower: Richard, at home. Son: Maj. David R. Godfrey (USAF). Daughter: Donna Ramirez, Woodlake, CA. Stepdaughter: Judith Zimmerly, Ridgefield. Stepsons: Mike Kadow, Yorba Linda, CA, and Richard L. Kadow, Astoria, OR. Sister: Louise Strother, Portland. Funeral Tues., 2 Jun, at St. John's Funeral Home, Portland. Interment: Northwood Park Cem. Hustad Funeral Home, Portland, OR. Obit - The Columbian)

KANEEN   Klea B. "Beloved Mother" 1924 - ____

KANEEN   Ralph H. "Beloved Father" 1922 - 1980

KEITH   Mabel D. "Beloved Mother" b. 27 Jun 1916 - d. 22 Aug 1978

KNOWLING   Robert Wayne. (Age 45. b. 8 Feb 1939, Iowa City, IA - d. 14 Dec 1984, Vancouver, WA. Husband of Mary Knowling, at home. Funeral Sat., 15 Dec, at Vancouver Funeral Chapel. Interment at Northwood Park Cem. Obit - The Columbian)

KOCH   August E. (Age 68. b. 9 Mar 1915, Akron, IA - d. 7 Mar 1984, Vancouver, WA. Husband of Wilma Koch, at home. Funeral Fri., 9 Mar, at Vancouver Funeral Chapel. Interment at Northwood Park Cem. Obit - The Columbian)

KOCH   Benjamin Hastings.   "God Bless Our Son"   b. 10 Jan 1980 - d. 13 Jan 1980

KOCH   Wilma E.   1916 - _____

KOEPKE   Helen F.   (Age 83.   Heart failure.   b. 31 Mar 1904, Stuart, MT - d. 10 Apr 1987, Vancouver, WA.   Res: Vancouver.   Preceded in death by husband, Harry Koepke in 1972.   Daughters: LaRae McCarrel, Medford, OR; Joyce Ackley, Vancouver, WA.   Brother: Carl Petersen, Modesto, CA.   Sister: Thelma Shupe, Ogden, UT. Services Mon., 13 Apr, at Memorial Lutheran Church. Burial Northwood Park Cem.   VFC.   Obit - The Columbian)

KRIEGER   Kathleen M. "Tyke".   (Age 56.   b. 25 Feb 1928, Seattle, WA - d. 17 Nov 1984, Vancouver, WA.   Wife of Dan C. Krieger, at home.   Memorial services Tues., 19 Nov, at the First Presbyterian Church.   Interment in Northwood Park Cem.   VFC.   Obit - The Columbian)

KUHLMANN   Daisy Josephine.   "Wife.   My Beloved Husband Rest In Peace In The Arms Of The Lord For In A Little While We Will Be Together Again With The Lord"   1925 - _____

KUHLMANN   Harold.   "Husband.   My Beloved Husband Rest In Peace In The Arms Of The Lord For In A Little While We Will Be Together Again With The Lord"   1918 - 1978

LAMB   James Earnest   1980 - 1980

LANDERS   Jason Michael.   "In Loving Memory Of"   b. 7 Feb 1979 - d. 16 May 1979

LAVENDER   Allan P.   1916 - 1980

LAVENDER   Edwardeen   1917 - _____

LEEDY   Janet M.   (Age 62.   b. 13 Mar 1920, Portland OR - d. 1 Mar 1983, Vancouver, WA.   Wife of Russell H. Leedy, at home.   Funeral Friday, 4 Mar, at Vancouver Funeral Chapel.   Interment in Northwood Park Cem.   Obit - The Columbian)

LEWIS   Horace J. "Tiny", Jr.   (Age 43.   b. 10 Apr 1942, Chrisfield, MD - d. 7 May 1985, Vancouver, WA.   Res: Vancouver.   Husband of LaVella D. Lewis, at home. Memorial Service Friday, 10 May, at First Church of God.   Interment at Northwood Park Cem.   VFC.   Obit - The Columbian)

LINDQUIST   Carl.   1896 - 1974

LINDQUIST   Stanny.   1902 - 1979

LINK   Mark C.   1932 - 1981

LOEWEN   Marie Ellertson. (Age 82. b. 8 Apr 1904, Vancouver,
                WA - d. 25 Nov 1986, at home, Vancouver, WA. Preceded
                in death by her husband, John Loewen, April 1974.
                Sons: Ken Ellertson and Rev. Rod Ellertson, both of
                Vancouver; Don Ellertson, Battle Ground, WA.
                Daughter: Mrs. Lawrence (Kathleen) Molyneux,
                Vancouver. John Loewen's children: Curt Loewen and
                Mrs. Ken (Donna) Ellertson, Vancouver; Mrs. Jane
                (Marilyn) Lasater, Bella Vista, AR. Sister: Mrs. Les
                "Tootie" Spangler, Vancouver. Funeral service Fri.,
                28 Nov, at Trinity Lutheran Church. Interment:
                Northwood Park Cem. VFC. Obit - The Columbian)

LUEBBERT   Rose E. Luebbert. (Age 65. b. 25 May 1920, Brooklyn,
                NY - d. 5 Feb 1986, Vancouver, WA. Widower: Edward
                H., at home. Daughters: Rosemary Gain and Cindy
                Marschel, both of Vancouver; Marianne, Reno, NV.
                Sisters: Barbara Kaufman, Vancouver, and Ann
                Antonelli, Bronx, NY. Graveside services: Tues., 11
                Feb, at Northwood Park Cem. VFC. Obit - The
                Columbian)

MALONEY   Ann M.   1920 - 1980

MALONEY   Avery J. (Age 55. b. 8 Jan 1928, Wisconsin - d. 17
                Apr 1983, Tacoma, WA. Res: Vancouver, WA. Graveside
                service Wed., 20 Apr, at Northwood Park Cem.
                Hamilton-Mylan Funeral Home. Obit - The Columbian)

MARKEGARD   Warren V. "In Thee I Have Put My Trust"   17 Nov
                1929 - 11 Jan 1980

MARSHALL   Gale E.   1908 - 1979   "Parents of Pat, Mike and
                Casey"

MARSHALL   Lawrence H.   1939 - 1980

MASSISON   E. O. "Mort"   "Dad"   1924 - ____

MASSISON   Lora M.   "Mom"   1923 - ____

MARTINSON   John Roy. (Age 74. b. 21 Dec 1909, Anacortes, WA -
                d. 24 Jan 1984, Vancouver, WA. Graveside services
                Friday, 27 Jan, at Northwood Park Cem. VFC. Obit -
                The Columbian)

MAST   Pamela K. (Age 29. Complications following surgery.
                b. 25 Sep 1955, San Benito, TX - d. 30 May 1985,
                Portland, OR. Res: Vancouver, WA. Wife of Tim I.
                Mast, at home. Service Monday, 3 June, at the Family
                of Christ Lutheran Church. Interment Northwood
                Memorial Park. VFC. Obit - The Columbian)

MATHER   Marjorie Lillian. (Age 68. b. 27 Sep 1915, Nashville, TN - d. 16 Dec 1983, Vancouver, WA. Wife of Norman Mather. Graveside rites Tues., 20 Dec, at Northwood Park Cem. Evergreen Staples Funeral Chapel. Obit - The Columbian)

MC KNIGHT   Jesse A. (Age 55. b. 15 Apr 1931, Iowa - d. 17 Dec 1986. Widow: Millie, at home. Funeral Tues., 23 Dec, at Vancouver Funeral Chapel. Interment in Northwood Park Cem. Obit - The Columbian)

MC MAHON   Nellie O. "Mother" 1892 - 1980

MC NEIL   Ronald A. (Age 71. b. 23 Mar 1915, Midland, MI - d. 29 Sep 1986, Portland, OR. Res: Vancouver, WA. Husband of Irene, at home. Graveside service Wed., 1 Oct, at Northwood Park Cem. EFC/EFH. Obit - The Columbian)

MERITT   Raymond. "Dad" 1914 - 1980

MESERVE   Richard William. U. S. Army/WWII. (Age 72. b. 12 Feb 1911, Astoria, OR - d. 3 Jan 1984, Vancouver, WA. Husband of Rosamond Meserve, at home. Funeral Sat., 7 Jan, at Vancouver Funeral Chapel. Interment in Northwood Park Cem. Obit - The Columbian)

METCALF   Norma K. (Age 57. b. 15 Feb 1927, Detroit, MI - d. 6 Sep 1984, Vancouver, WA. Graveside service Tues., 11 Sep, at Northwood Park Cem. MGM. Obit - The Columbian)

MILLER   Raymond P. (Age 69. b. 25 Dec 1905, Vancouver, WA - d. 2 May 1985, Vancouver. Husband of Vivian E. Miller, at home. Graveside services Monday, 6 May, at Northwood Memorial Park. VFC. Obit - The Columbian)

MITCHELL   Edgar A. "This God Shall Be Our God Forever Ps:48" (No date)

MITCHELL   Eva M. "This God Shall Be Our God Forever Ps:48" 1904 - _____

MOLYNEUX   John R. "Jack". (Age 82. b. 24 Jun 1900, Grace City, ND - d. 18 Jun 1983, Vancouver, WA. Husband of Minnie Molyneux, at home. Funeral Wed., 22 Jun, at Vancouver Funeral Chapel. Interment at Northwood Park Cem. Obit - The Columbian)

MOON   Joyce Ann. (Age 50. b. 3 Mar 1935, Tyler, TX - d. 27 Sep 1985, Portland, OR. Res: Vancouver, WA. Wife of Kenneth G. Moon, at home. Services Tues., 1 Oct, at Hamilton-Mylan Funeral Home. Interment Northwood Park Cem. Obit - The Columbian)

MOORE   Christopher Lee. (Age 2 days. SIDS. b. 14 Dec 1985, Portland, OR - d. 16 Dec 1985. Res: Vancouver, WA. Son of Tracy and Carrie Moore. Graveside service Sat., 21 Dec, at Northwood Park Cem. Layne's Funeral Home. Obit - The Columbian)

MOORE   M. Fred. (Age 75. b. 29 Nov 1909, Vancouver, WA - d. 11 Dec 1984, at home, Vancouver, WA. Husband of Florence A. Moore, at home. Memorial services Fri., 14 Dec, at First United Methodist Church. Inurnment at Northwood Park Cem. VFC. Obit - The Columbian)

MUELLER   Michelle S. (Age 2 Mos. b. 8 Aug 1986, Vancouver, WA - d. 24 Oct 1986 at home, Vancouver. Daughter of Keith and Song Mueller. Memorial service Tuesday, 28 Oct, at Vancouver Funeral Chapel. Graveside service Monday, 27 Oct, at Northwood Park Cem. Obit - The Columbian)

MUMPER   Wylie H. (Age 58. b. 30 Dec, 1927, Wheeling, WV - d. 19 Feb 1986, Vancouver, WA. Widow: Mary Jane, at home. Mother: Laura Mumper, Folsom, CA. Daughters: Donna Armstrong, Yucaipa, CA; Janice Olsen, Arroyo Grande, CA; Sheryl Schaaf, Forks, WA; Laura Ziebart, Springfield, OR and Mary Jane Bennett, Vancouver. Brothers: Richard, of Russell, OH and Robert, San Jose, CA. Sisters: Alyce Setnik and Laura Booth, both of Shingle Springs, CA; Shirley Carpenter, Downey, CA. Mass of Christian Burial Monday, 24 Feb, at St. Joseph Catholic Church. Burial in Northwood Park Cem. Obit - The Columbian)

NELSON   Jolynn. (Age 38. b. 21 Apr 1947, Portland, OR - d. 12 Mar 1986, Battle Ground, WA. Res: Battle Ground. Parents: Don and Joanne, of Vancouver. Brothers: Gregory, Vancouver, and Steven, Walla Walla, WA. Sister: Annette Thomas, Gresham, OR. Grandfather: Hubert Nelson, Sacramento, KY. Graveside service Monday, 17 Mar, at Northwood Park Cem. VFC. Obit - The Columbian)

NEWBOLD   Gertrude E. b. 20 Apr 1896 - d. 15 Aug 1980

NICHOLS   Betty Jean. (Age 58. b. 13 Mar 1925, Hood River, OR - d. 19 Aug 1983, Vancouver, WA. Services Monday, 22 Aug, at Vancouver Funeral Chapel. Interment at Northwood Park Cem. Obit - The Columbian)

NOCE   Alfonso. (Age 84. Heart failure. b. 26 Aug 1903, Miscufio, Italy - d. 8 Oct 1987. Res: Vancouver, WA. Preceded in death by his wife, Alma Hawkins, in 1986. Graveside service Monday, 12 Oct, at Northwood Park Cem. VFC. Obit - The Columbian)

NOCE	James Joseph. b. 29 Oct 1905 - d. 8 May 1978
NOCE	Peter J. U. S. Army. b. 3 Aug 1916 - d. 29 Mar 1980
NORRIS	Orin J. 1916 - 1981
NORRIS	Ruby A. 1918 - ____
OFFICER	Susan Rae. "Daughter - Sister" "In Thee I Have Put My Trust" 26 Nov 1954 - 24 Feb 1979
OLSON	Arlid Thoralf "Jack". (Age 82. b. 16 Dec 1902, Tromso, Norway - d. 4 Jun 1985, Portland, OR. Res: Portland, OR. Husband of Esther Olson, at home. Graveside service Friday, 7 Jun, at Northwood Memorial Park. VFC. Obit - The Columbian)
OLSON	Edmund Stanley. 1903 - 1978
OSBORN	Amos W. 1897 - 1979
OSBORN	Claribel 1894 - 1981
PARKER	Mary M. "Mother" 1900 - 1980
PETERSEN	Sonia T. (Age 21. Stab wounds. b. 29 Jun 1965, Stuttgart, Germany - 10 Apr 1987, Vancouver, WA. Res: Vancouver. Father, Norman Petersen, Vancouver. Mother and stepfather, Linda and Gary Gerschweiler, Sherwood, OR. Son: Joshua. Brother: Jay Petersen, Vancouver. Sister: Melanie Petersen, Vancouver. Grandmother: Esther Farr, Omak, WA. Great-grandmother: Florence Breshears, Omak. Funeral Tuesday, 14 Apr, at Vancouver Funeral Chapel. Burial in Northwood Park Cem. Obit - The Columbian)
PHAM	Vien. (Age 78. b. 1 Jan 1907, Oui Nhon, Vietnam - d. 5 Sep 1985, Camas, WA. Res: Vancouver, WA. Graveside service Friday, 6 Sep, at Northwood Park Cem. VFC. Obit - The Columbian)
PHILLIPS	Aubrey James. (Age 58. Heart failure. b. 7 Jul 1927, in West Virginia - d. 7 Jul 1985, at home, Battle Ground, WA. Funeral Wed., 10 Jul, at Layne's Funeral Home. Burial at Northwood Park Cem. Obit - The Columbian)
PHILLIPS	Betty Lorraine. (Age 51. Cancer. b. 12 Feb 1934, Beardsfork, WV - d. 13 Apr 1985, Battle Ground, WA. Res: Battle Ground. Wife of Aubrey, at home. Funeral Tuesday, 16 Apr, at Layne's Funeral Home Chapel. Burial in Northwood Park Cem. Obit - The Columbian)

NORTHWOOD PARK CEMETERY

PIERSON — Irving L. U. S. Marine Corps/WWII. b. 3 Mar 1919 – d. 13 Feb 1980

POLLOCK — Walter E., Jr. (Age 77. b. 30 Jun 1908, Orlando, FL – d. 31 Jan 1986, Vancouver, WA. Widow: Grace L. Pollock, Vancouver. Sons: Walter E. Pollock, III, of Portland, OR; Warren W. Pollock, Seattle, WA; Weston J. Pollock, Burke, VA. Brother: Martin Pollock, Los Angeles, CA. Sister: Mary Pollock, Sun City, CA. Graveside service and interment Tuesday, 4 Feb, at Northwood Park Cem. Evergreen Staples Funeral Chapel. Obit – The Columbian)

POWERS — Joel Jay. "Our Baby" October 17, 1980

PREW — Arthur "Herb" Herbert. (Age 65. b. 23 Jun 1919, Vancouver, WA – d. 18 Jan 1985, Battle Ground, WA. Husband of Betty Prew, at home. Graveside service Tuesday, 22 Jan, at Northwood Park Cem. Layne's Funeral Home. Obit – The Columbian)

PRICE — Robert Jeremy. "Our Son" Oct 18 – Oct 28, 1978.

PUCKETT — Ruth F. (Age 69. b. 7 Feb 1916, Spokane, WA – d. 23 Jan 1986, Vancouver, WA. Daughter: Linda Durrell, Vancouver. Grand-daughters: Laurie Duyck, Forest Grove, OR; Suzanne Alapal, Vancouver. Mother: Hilda Flaig, Vancouver. Memorial services Saturday, 25 Jan, at Vancouver Funeral Chapel. Interment in Northwood Park Cem. Obit – The Columbian)

REDEIF — Pearl O. "In Thee Have I Put My Trust" 1886 – 1978

REED — Annie Laura. (Age 14 Days. b. 25 Jul 1983, Vancouver, WA – d. 9 Aug 1983, Vancouver. Daughter of Mr. and Mrs. Robert C. Reed, Vancouver. Graveside Service Sat., 13 Aug, at Northwood Park Cem. VFC. Obit – The Columbian)

RESCORLA — George Clark. (Age 60. b. 18 Jun 1925, Gunnison, CO – d. 26 Aug 1985, Sacramento, CA. Res: Camas, WA. Graveside services Friday, 30 Aug, in Northwood Park Cem. VFC. Obit – The Columbian)

REUDINK — Leonard Norman. U. S. Navy/WWII. (Age 66. b. 18 Sep 1918, Wisner, NE – d. 26 Dec 1984, Portland, OR. Res: Vancouver, WA. Husband of Goldie Reudink, at home. Funeral Friday, 28 Dec. at Vancouver Funeral Chapel. Interment at Northwood Park Cem. Obit – The Columbian)

REYNOLDS — Ronald. (Graveside service Tuesday, 26 Aug 1986 at Northwood Park Cem. Vancouver Funeral Chapel Funeral Services. Obit – The Columbian)

RICHARDS	Ralph T. 1942 - 1980
RICKS	Jason Whiting. (Photo in stone) b. 28 Mar 1968 - d. 30 July 1980
RINTA	Elsie ____ - ____
RINTA	Jaako 1903 - 1980
ROARK	Billie Gene. U. S. Marines/Korea. (Age 53. b. 16 Sep 1930, New Haven, IL - d. 26 May 1984, Portland, OR. Res: Vancouver, WA. Husband of Mary Roark, at home. Service Wed., 30 May, at Vancouver Funeral Chapel. Interment in Northwood Park Cem. Obit - The Columbian)
ROBERTSON	Leon Wynn. (Age 81. b. 2 Sep 1905, Osage, IA - d. 20 Dec 1986, Portland, OR. Res: Oregon. Son: Lee, of Vancouver, WA. Daughter: Judie Loveall, Vancouver. Brothers: Kenton, Spooner, WI; Wayne, Beaverton, OR; Wallace of Wamic, OR. Sister: Zelda Livingston, of Anoka, MN. Service Saturday, 27 Dec, at Vancouver Funeral Chapel. Burial in Northwood Park Cem. Obit - The Columbian)
ROBERTSON	Virginia E. "Mother" 1911 - 1981
ROMEO	Francis. World War II. (Age 77. b. 11 Apr 1909, Cambra, WY - d. 28 Nov 1986, Vancouver, WA. Widow: Margaret S., at home. Son: Charles A., Vancouver. Sister: Mary Ellis, Ottumwa, IA. Memorial service Wed., 3 Dec, at First United Methodist Church. Inurnment at Northwood Park Cem. Obit - The Columbian)
ROOT	Glenna L. "Mother" 1928 - 1978
SADLER	Cloyd H. 1908 - 1978
SADLER	Gladys L. 1912 - ____
SCHAEFER	Heidi Ann. (Age 21. Lung Disease. b. 9 May 1965, Vancouver, WA. - d. 11 Mar 1987 Seattle, WA. Res: Seattle, WA. Parents: Don and Shirley Schaefer, Ridgefield. Brother: Robert, at home. Sister: Shanna Schaefer, at home. Grandparents: Katherine Smith, of San Bernadino, CA, and Agnes and Charles Schaefer, of Ridgefield. Graveside Service Sat., 14 Mar, at Northwood Park Cem. Vancouver Funeral Chapel. Obit - The Columbian)
SCHLENKER	Arnold H. (Age 66. Stroke. b. 3 Apr 1918, Leola, SD - d. 21 Jan 1985, Vancouver, WA. Funeral Sat., 26

Jan, at Vancouver Funeral Chapel. Interment in Northwood Park Cem. Obit - The Columbian)

SCHLIEF   Beverly Jean. (Age 45. b. 18 May 1939, Los Angeles, CA - d. 26 Apr 1985, at home in Vancouver, WA. Wife of Jerry, at home. Graveside service Saturday, 27 Apr, at Northwood Memorial Park. VFC. Obit - The Columbian)

SCHLOSSER   Jeremy Keith. "God's Little Angel" b. 18 Aug 1978 - d. 29 May 1980

SCHLOSSER   Mike. (Age 86. b. 12 Apr 1900, Strasburg, Ukraine, South Russia - d. 7 Sep 1986, Battle Ground, WA. Res: Ridgefield, WA. Husband of Anna M., at home. Funeral Wed., 10 Sep, at Vancouver Funeral Chapel. Interment in Northwood Park Cem. Obit - The Columbian)

SEETH   Bertha M. 1914 - 1981

SEETH   Darl E. 1921 - 1978

SELEY   Stephen C. Seley (Herlin). (Age 21. b. 26 Jun 1964, Astoria, OR - d. 29 Jul 1985, Portland, OR. Knife wound. Res: Vancouver, WA. Son of Lois Herlin, of Vancouver. Graveside service Wed., 30 Jul, at Northwood Memorial Park. VFC. Obit - The Columbian)

SETON   Eva R. "Mother" 1897 - 1979

SHETLER   Charlotte Ruth. (Age 71. b. 31 Mar 1915, San Gabriel, CA - d. 9 Apr 1986, Vancouver WA, at home. Wife of Daniel, at home. Funeral Monday, 14 Apr, at Hillcrest Church of the Nazarene. Burial in Northwood Park Cem. Layne's Funeral Home. Obit - The Columbian)

SIEK   Henry. 1901 - 1978

SIMS   Florence E. 1918 - ____

SIMS   Vernon O. 1918 - 1978

SMITH   Bryan D. "Son" 1960 - 1980

SMITH   Christopher Paul. (Age 3 Mos. SIDS. b. 14 Sep 1986, Vancouver, WA. - d. 8 Dec 1986, Vancouver. Parents: Donald and Michele Smith. Sister: Emily, at home. Grandparents: Lloyd and Stella Harris, Seattle; Laura Smith, Vancouver. Graveside service Thur., 11 Dec, at Northwood Park Cem. Vancouver Funeral Chapel. Obit - The Columbian)

SMITH   Harold Kenneth. (Age 83. b. 26 Jul 1903, Wendell, MN - d. 24 Mar 1987, Vancouver, WA. Res: Vancouver. Widow: Margaret, at home. Daughter: Helen L. Schwartz, Alpine, OR. Sister: Helen M. Bousman, Spokane. Grandsons: Dan Schwartz, Oakland, CA and David Schwartz, Albany, OR. Memorial Service Friday, 27 Mar, at Vancouver Funeral Chapel. Burial Northwood Park Cem. Obit - The Columbian)

SMITH   Lloyd C. "Smitty". (Age 63. b. 2 Apr 1922, Tacoma, WA - d. 20 Oct 1985, Vancouver, WA. Husband of Mona M. "Mickie", at home. Funeral Wed., 23 Oct, at Messiah Lutheran Church. Interment in Northwood Park Cem. VFC. Obit - The Columbian)

SMITH   William R. 1905 - 1980 (Vancouver Funeral Home marker)

SONNEY   Buron L. (Age 83. b. 26 Apr 1899, Vale, TN - d. 22 Apr 1983, Vancouver, WA. Preceded in death by wife, Mabel E. Sonney. Services Monday, 25 Apr, at Vancouver Funeral Chapel. Interment in Northwood Park Cem. Obit - The Columbian)

SPARKS   William E. 7 May 1902 - 22 Aug 1979

STEPHENS   Willard H. "Bill". U. S. Marines/WWII. (Age 65. Cancer. b. 25 Sep 1921, Park Rapids, MN - d. 26 Jun 1987, Portland, OR. Res: Vancouver, WA. Husband of Alma Stephens, at home. Memorial service Tuesday, 30 Jun, at the Crossroads Community Church. Burial Northwood Park Cemetery. VFC. Obit - The Columbian.

STEVENS   Hattie R. (Age 74. b. 27 Dec 1908, Neva, TN - d. 22 Dec 1983, Vancouver, WA. Wife of J. Earl Stevens, at home. Services Tuesday,. 27 Dec, at VFC. Interment at Northwood Park Cem. Obit - The Columbian)

STEVENS   Ida M. (Age 91. b. 22 Jul 1895, Redland, OR - d. 2 Jan 1987, Vancouver, WA. Res: Brush Prairie, WA. Son-in-Law: Don Zumstein, Vancouver. Daughter: Joanne Zumstein, Vancouver. Funeral Tuesday, 6 Jan, VFC. Interment NPC. Obit - The Columbian)

STRICKLAND   L. Lee. U.S. Navy. (Age 40. Hardening of arteries. b. 15 Dec 1946, Colfax, WA - d. 1 Apr 1987, at home, Edmonds, WA. Prior resident of Vancouver, res. Edmonds since May 1986. Widow: Cindy Strickland, at home. Daughter: Kim Strickland, Vancouver. Mother: Helen Strickland, Ridgefield, WA. Brothers: Scott Strickland, Winslow, WA; Jon Strickland, with U. S. Navy; Mike Strickland, Vancouver; and Kurt Strickland,

Woodland WA. Sister: Mrs. Kathy Stallings, Ridgefield, WA. Funeral services Wed., 8 Apr, at Family of Christ Lutheran Church. Interment Vancouver Funeral Chapel's Northwood Park Cem. VFC. Obit - The Columbian)

STRUCK   Joan. (Age 72. Heart attack. b. 7 Jul 1915, Garfield, WA - d. 8 Sep 1987. Res: Vancouver, WA. Graveside service Friday, 11 Sep, at Vancouver Funeral Chapel's Northwood Park Cem. VFC. Obit - The Columbian)

SUESS   Gertrude P.   1900 - 1980

SUESS   Otto P.   1896 - 1980

SULLIVAN   Blanche. (Age 94. b. 21 Jul 1890, Paulding, OH - d. 4 Sep 1984, Vancouver, WA. Graveside service Wed., 5 Sep, at Northwood Park Cem. VFC. Obit - The Columbian)

SUTTON   Christine Lindberg. (Age 56. b. 4 Jun 1927, Cook County, IL - d. 25 Dec 1983, Vancouver, WA. Memorial service Wed., 28 Dec, at Vancouver Funeral Chapel. Interment at Northwood Park Cemetery. Obit - The Columbian)

SWANSON   Ramona Elsie. (Age 68. b. 23 Feb 1915, Los Angeles, CA - d. 24 Oct 1983, Vancouver, WA. Wife of James J. Swanson, at home. Funeral Wed., 26 Oct, at Vancouver Funeral Chapel. Interment at Northwood Park Cem. Obit - The Columbian)

THOMAS   Howard S. "Howdy". (Age 62. Renal Failure. b. 13 Aug 1924, Colfax, WA - d. 26 Apr 1987, Vancouver, WA. Res: Ridgefield, WA. Widow: Dorthea, at home. Sons: Gayle, Northport, WA, and Russell, of Ridgefield. Step-daughters: Marion G. Erath, San Diego, CA; and Lorna Ann Mallonee, Upland, CA. Brother: Clarence, of Ridgefield. Sisters: Esther Holmes, Spokane and Eleanor Pemberton, Ridgefield. Funeral Wed., 29 Apr, at Layne's Funeral Home Chapel. Burial Northwood Park Cem. Obit - The Columbian)

THOMPSON   Van "Nicky" N. (Age 27. b. 25 Dec 1959, Vancouver, WA. - d. 23 Jan 1987, LaCenter, WA. Res: Clark County, WA. Father: Albert, Issaquah, WA. Brothers: Vince and Vic Thompson, both of Vancouver. Cremation. Graveside service Tuesday, 27 Jan, at Northwood Park Cem. Layne's Funeral Home, Battle Ground. Obit - The Columbian)

THORKILDSON   Torger.   1907 - 1981

THROOP	Barbara Ann. (Age 33. Cancer. b. 20 Jun 1951, Vancouver, WA - d. 18 Jun 1985, Vancouver. Wife of George Throop. Funeral Friday, 21 Jun, at Pleasant View Church of the Nazarene. Interment at Northwood Memorial Park. VFC. Obit - The Columbian)
THROOP	Jamie Lynn. "Our Baby" 25 Feb - 2 Mar 1980
THROOP	Jerry. "The Lord is My Shepherd" 1961 - 1979
TINGLEY	Danielle Macey. "Our Baby Angel" 14 Jan - 12 May 1981
TOIVONEN	Jennifer L. 1980 (Vancouver Funeral Home marker)
VAN HOVEL	John C. (Age 81. b. 17 Dec 1902, Paterson, NJ - d. 17 Aug 1984, Vancouver, WA. Husband of Emma C. Van Hovel, at home. Graveside service Monday, 20 Aug, at Northwood Park Cem. VFC. Obit - The Columbian)
VON ESSEN	Herbert J. "Love Lives On" 1908 - 1980
WALLS	Shirley Jean "Betty". (Age 54. b. 14 Dec 1932, in Missouri - d. 23 Sep 1987, Vancouver, WA. Service Monday, 28 Sep, at Vancouver Funeral Chapel. Burial in Northwood Park Cemetery. Obit - The Columbian)
WARMAN	Ella Viola. (Age 85. b. 6 Apr 1900, in Elk City, OK - d. 24 Jan 1986, Vancouver, WA. Sons: C. Dale Warman, Portland, OR; Clinton Warman, Springfield, CO. Her late husband was Rev. W. T. Warman. Funeral Tuesday, 28 Jan, at First Church of God. Interment: Northwood Park Cem. Vancouver Funeral Chapel. Obit - The Columbian)
WARMAN	Rev. W. T. (Age 85. b. 3 Oct 1898, Charleston, IL - d. 21 Aug 1984, Vancouver, WA. Husband of Ella V. Warman, at home. Funeral Thursday, 23 Aug, at First Church of God. Interment in Northwood Park Cem. VFC. Obit - The Columbian)
WARNER	Jessica Rosalie. (Age 2 Mos. b. 26 May 1983, Seoul, South Korea - d. 24 Aug 1983, Vancouver, WA. Res: Vancouver, WA. Daughter of Phillip and Linda Warner, at home. Graveside service Friday, 26 Aug, at Northwood Park Cemetery VFC. Obit - The Columbian)
WHEELER	G. Grant, Jr. "Son" b. 12 Oct. 1961 - d. 17 Dec 1980
WHITE	Joseph C., Sr. "Dad" 1907 - 1978
WHITNEY	Glen R. U. S. Navy. b. 24 Feb 1918 - d. 29 Sep 1978

WHITTEY	Patrick J. "P.J." (Age 2. b. 30 Oct 1980, Vancouver, WA. - d. 30 Jan 1983, Vancouver, WA. Son of Charles and Sheila Whittey, at home. Graveside service Wed., 2 Feb, at Northwood Park Cem. VFC. Obit - The Columbian)
WILLARD	Katherine L. "Mother" 1912 - 1980
WILLIAMS	Nicole Marie. "Little Angel" b. 12 Mar 1976 - d. 13 Nov 1978
WILLIAMS	Nora Lee. (Age 56. b. 7 Jul 1927, Yellow Springs, OH - d. 16 Nov 1983, Vancouver, WA. Wife of Charles E. Williams, at home. Funeral Friday, 18 Nov, at Vancouver Funeral Chapel. Interment at Northwood Park Cemetery. VFC. Obit - The Columbian)
WILLIAMSON	Clinton J. 1887 - 1980
WINSTON	Margaret "Peggy" M. (Age 47. b. 1 Mar 1938, New York - d. 19 May 1985, Vancouver, WA. Res: Battle Ground, WA. Wife of Ted Winston. Mass of Christian Burial Thursday, 23 May, at Sacred Heart Catholic Church of Battle Ground. Interment in Northwood Park Cemetery. Layne's Funeral Home. Obit - The Columbian)
WINTER	Charles H. (Age 71. Cancer. b. 18 Dec 1915, Twin Falls, ID - d. 14 May 1987, Vancouver, WA. Res: In Campers Hideaway on the Lewis River, north of Amboy, WA. Widow: E. Greta Winter, at home. Son: Charles, Vancouver. Daughters: Vernie Mahoney and Jo Olesen, both of Vancouver. Brother: Al, of Cypress, CA. Service Tuesday, 19 May, at Vancouver Funeral Chapel. Burial in Northwood Park Cem. Obit - The Columbian)
WIRTH	Shirley Ann. (Age 47. Murdered. b. 2 Jun 1936, Centralia, WA - d. 31 Aug 1983. Wife of Mickey Wirth, of Vancouver, WA. (Refer to Janae Gobel-Wirth) Graveside service Thursday, 4 Aug, at Northwood Park Cem. Vancouver Funeral Chapel. Obit - The Columbian)
WISER	Joseph A. U. S. Navy/WWII. 1922 - 1978
WOOD	Doris Laurine. (Age 69. b. 6 Jul 1917, Lucas, IA - d. 30 Dec 1986, Vancouver, WA. Widower: Roy Wood, at home. Daughter: Mrs. Duane ((Christine)) Goochey, Vancouver. Brother: Leroy Hancuff, Battle Ground, WA. Sister: Anna M. White, Sutter Creek, CA. Mother-in-law: Aeneid Wood, Vancouver. Funeral Friday, 2 Jan, at First Evangelical Free Church. Interment: Northwood Park Cem. Vancouver Funeral Chapel. Obit - The Columbian)

NORTHWOOD PARK CEMETERY

WOODWARD   Ellis E.   b. 27 Sep 1908 - d. 5 Sep 1979 (semi-truck carved on stone)

WORDEN   Juanita M.   1930 - ____

WORDEN   Stanley G.   "In Thee Have I Put My Trust"   1929 - 1978

YORK   Miles Joseph. Stillborn 1 Oct 1986, Vancouver, WA. Son of Daniel and Lori York, Vancouver. Funeral Monday, 6 Oct, at Northwood Park Cem. VFC. Obit - The Columbian)

YOUNG   Melisa D. "Our Darling"   5 Mar - 23 Sep 1980

ZINDELL   Barbara H.   "Beloved Mother"   1916 - 1980

ZUBER   Zachary J.   1973 - 1978

# # # # #

Memory Memorial Park Cemetery

Memory Memorial Cemetery is
located at 6906 N. E. 144th
Street, four miles south of
Dollar's Corner, adjacent to
Manor Wilson Bridge Cemetery

ACHEN   Louis L. Age 57. "Together Forever" b.1907 -
                 d.2Nov1964. Wife: Mrs. Lynn Achen, of Vancouver, WA
                 Layne's Funeral Home, Battle Ground, WA. Interred
                 5Nov1964, Christus Gardens, Lot S-71-5.

ACHEN   Lynn M.   Age 65.   b.19Nov1914 - d.28Nov1979.
                 Daughter: Mrs. Lance (Linda) Burton, of Vancouver,
                 WA. Layne's Funeral Home, Battle Ground, WA. Interred
                 30Nov1979. Lot S-71-4.

ACKLEY   Melvin K. Age 43.   b.1Jan1930 - d.25Jul1973. Wife:
                 Doris Ackley. Sons: Stephen and Bryan Ackley.
                 Daughter: Mrs. Gary Smith. Layne's Funeral Home,
                 Battle Ground, WA. Interred 31Jul1973, Garden of
                 Chimes, N-18-8.

ADAMS   G. Juanita. "Mother" 1921 - ____

ADAMS   Gladys E. Age 66. b.19Sep1912 - d.20Dec1978
                 Husband: Martin O. Adams, Battle Ground, WA. Layne's
                 Funeral Home, Battle Ground. Interred 27Dec1978.
                 Lot N-84-5.

ADAMS   Homer A. Age 65. "Father" b.30Jul1910 -
                 d.27Dec1975. Wife: Gertrude, Lot B-9. Layne's
                 Funeral Home, Battle Ground, WA. Interred 30Dec1975.
                 Lot S-178-4.

ADAMS   Martin O. Age 73. (b.26Jun1909 Spokane, WA -
                 d.16Mar1983, Battle Ground, WA. Daughter: Vallene
                 Kelley, Libby, MT. Funeral Sat., 19Mar1983., at
                 Layne's Funeral Home Chapel. Interment at Memory
                 Memorial Park Cem. Obit - The Columbian) Lot N-84-4.
                 No marker.

ALEXANDER   Carl J. Age 83. b.25May1899 - d.4Jan1983. Wife:
                 Elma Alexander, Vancouver, WA. Interred 7Jan1983.
                 Lot S-74-8. No marker.

ALEXANDER   Elma G. (Age 83. b.28Jun1902, Aetna Twp., MI -
                 d.17Nov1985, Portland, OR. Res: Vancouver, WA.
                 Funeral Wed., 20 Nov. at Memorial Garden Funeral
                 Chapel. Interment in Memory Memorial Park. MGM.
                 Obit - The Columbian)

ALRED   Mildred Odessa.   1918 - ____. (W/Paul)

ALRED   Paul. Age 61. b.1912 - d.20Jan1973. Wife: Mildred,
                 of Vancouver, WA. Funeral Director: Little Chapel of
                 Chimes, Portland, OR. Int. Memory Memorial, Lot
                 N-13-1.

ANDERSEN   Carroll G. Age 69. b.18Mar1905 - d.8Apr1974. Wife:
                 Dorothy, of Vancouver, WA. Brother: Hardy C.

Andersen, Vancouver. Garden of Christus, Int. #159, Lot S-16-5

ANDERSEN   Dorothy Ann. Age 68. b.1904 - d.27Nov1972. Husband: Carroll. Interred 29Nov1972. Int. #128, Christus Gardens, Lot S-16-2.

ANDERSEN   Hardy C. (Age 79. b.1Jan1907, Lake Park, MN - d.13Jan1986, Portland, OR. Res: Vancouver, WA. Widow: Clara, at home. Brother: Donald W. Andersen, Battle Ground, WA. Funeral Friday, 17Jan1986, at Vancouver Funeral Chapel. Interment in Memory Memorial Park Cem. Obit - The Columbian)

ANDERSON   Blanche Mildred. (Age 76. b.19Oct1907, South Dakota - d.17Mar1984, Vancouver, WA. Res: Battle Ground, WA. Wife of Alton, at home. Funeral Wed., 21Mar1984, at Meadow Glade Seventh Day Adventist Church. Burial in Memory Memorial Park, Lot N-36-8. Layne's Funeral Home. Obit - The Columbian)

ANDERSON   Myrtle Ming. b.1920 - d.7Dec1969. Husband: Cecil F. Anderson, Vancouver, WA. VFC. Int. #70, Memory Memorial, Lot S-68-8.

ANDERSON   Natalie L. Age 35. b.5Apr1946 - d.1Feb1982. Brother: Rodney Bidwell, Vancouver, WA. Vancouver Funeral Chapel. Int. 6Feb1982, Lot S-191-4. No marker.

ANDERSON   Rosalie (Gertz). Age 77. b.18Mar1899 - d.7Jul1976. Interred 10Jul1976, Christus Lot S-197-5.

ANDERSON   Rosalie Irene. Age 55. b. 17Jan1926 - d.27Aug1981. Son: Rodney Bidwell, Vancouver, WA. F.D.: Hamilton. Ashes Int. 14Oct1981, Lot S-197-4. No marker.

ARRABEE   Elsie E. ___ - ___ (w/Sidney)

ARRABEE   Sidney A. "Together Forever" 1911 - 1976 (w/Elsie)

ATKINS   Clyde A. Age 79. b.1891 - d.15May1971. Relative: Myrtle V. Atkins, of Vancouver, WA. Int. 18May1971, Christus Space 9-8.

ATKINS   Myrtle V. Age 96. b.1896 - d.22Sep1982. Funeral Dir. Macey & Sons, McMinnville, OR. Int. 27Sep1982, Lot 5-9.

ATTEBERRY   Gladys E. Age 69. b.4Oct1903 - d.15Aug1973. Husband: William B. Atteberry. VFC. Int. 17Aug1973, Garden of Devotion, S-92-1.

ATTEBERRY   William B. The Salvation Army. (Age 84. b.17Jan1900, Moline, KS - d.11Mar1984, Vancouver, WA. Graveside service Thurs., 15 Mar., at Memory Memorial

Park. VFC. Obit - The Columbian) Garden of Devotion, Lot S-92-2.

AUMILLER   Geraldine J. Age 60. "In God's Care". b.21Nov1919 - d.24Nov1979. Husband: Virgil G. Aumiller, Sr., of Vancouver, WA. Interred 28Nov1979, Lot N-275-2, Chimes. (W/Virgil)

AUMILLER   Virgil G. "In God's Care". 1918 - ____ (w/Geraldine)

AUMILLER   Virgil Gordon. (Age 43. b.27Apr1943, Lockport, IL - d.7Jan1987. Res: Vancouver, WA. Widow: Margaret. Father: Virgil, Grand Junction, CO. Sons: Danny, Ernie and David, Vancouver. Daughter: Tina, Vancouver. Brothers: Danny, Vancouver; Cecil, Albuquerque, NM. Sister: Janice Hawkins, Blanding, UT. Burial Memory Memorial Park. Evergreen Staples Funeral Chapel. Obit - The Columbian)

BAKER   Ida Anne. (Age 79. b.29Aug1904, Odessa, WA. - d.15Mar1984, Vancouver, WA. Preceded in death by her husband, Elmer Baker. Nephews: Leslie and Dewey Oltman, of Ridgefield, WA. Service Mon., 19 Mar., at Hamilton-Mylan Funeral Home. Interment MMP. Obit - The Columbian) Lot N-65-3

BAKER   Millard O. "Winkie". Age 59. b.25Aug1912 - d.3Mar1972. Int. 7Mar1972, Garden of Devotion, Lot S-99-8, w/Lee Baker. VFC.

BAKER   Opal Lee. "Together Forever" 1914 - ____

BARE   Della I. 1910 - ____

BARE   Elmer L. 1904 - ____

BARNES   Bryan Gene. FA U. S. Navy. Age 29. b.11Oct1947 - d.7Sep1977. Father: Tracy Barnes, Vancouver, WA. Brother: Walter (Bud) Sears, Vancouver. Christus Court, S-135-4. EFC.

BAUER   Oscar R. Age 58. b.28May1925 - d.8Aug1983. Wife: June B. Bauer. Interred 11Aug1983. Gateway Chapel of Chimes. Lot N-76-2. No marker.

BECHTOLD   Emil "Dutch". (Age 73. Heart attack. b.29Aug1910, Naper, NE - d.10Feb1984, Portland, OR. Res: Battle Ground, WA. Husband of Mildred, at home. Funeral Monday, 13Feb1984, at Battle Ground Comm. United Methodist Church. Layne's Funeral Home. Interment in MMP Mausoleum. Obit - The Columbian) G.S. Maus. Tier 3 Crypt 10 W.

BEHERNS   Geneviev M. (spelling is correct) 1907 - ____ (w/Ivan)

BEHERNS   Ivan L.   Age 73.   b.29Jan1906 - d.7Dec1979.   Widow: Geneviev Beherns.   Interred 10Dec1979, Garden of Devotion, S-103-2

BELCHER   Glenna A.   Age 58.   "In Loving Memory"   b.27Feb1918 - d.19Feb1977.   Daughter: Glenda Coats, of Vancouver, WA.   Layne's Funeral Chapel, Battle Ground, WA. S-111-5.

BELONGIA   Charles Orville.   Age 73.   "Together Forever" b.25Aug1900 - d.30Nov1973.   Widow: Cora M. Belongia, Vancouver, WA.   VFC.   Space S-112-6.

BELONGIA   Cora M.   Age 75.   b.14Apr1907 - d.29June1982.   Int. 20July1982, Garden of Devotion, Space S-112-5.

BENEDICT   Earl T.   "Together Forever"   1905 - ____   (w/Winifred)

BENEDICT   Ercell A.   Age 79.   b.12Mar1901 - d.15Feb1981   Int. 20Feb1981, Space N-22-8, Chimes.   (w/Lula)

BENEDICT   Glen M.   b.19Feb.1898 - d.4Mar1965.   LBGFH.   Int. 9Mar1965, Space N82-1.   Owner: Nellie Benedict, Ridgefield, WA.

BENEDICT   Lula.   1917 - ____   (w/Ercell A.)

BENEDICT   Nellie M.   (Also PUNKO).   Age 73.   b.27May1903 - d.6May1977.   LBGFH.   Husband: John Punko, Vancouver, WA.   First husband: Glen Benedict.   Lot N-82-2.

BENEDICT   Perry L.   Age 47.   "Home is the Hunter Home From the Hills"   b.8Dec1923 - d.30May1971.   Mother: Winifred M., Richfield, WA.   Int. 30May1971.   EFC, Vancouver, WA.   Space N-86-2.   (w/Winifred and Earl)

BENEDICT   Winifred M.   Age 76.   "Together Forever"   b.16Sep1903 - d.25Apr1980.   Coleman Mortuary, Hoquiam, WA.   Space N-86-3 Chimes.   (w/Earl)   Owner: Pearl T. Benedict, of Copalis, WA.

BERGER   Iris B.   Age 56.   b.30Sep1925 - d.12Dec1981.   Husband: William Berger, Vancouver, WA.   Staples Funeral Home. Int. 22Jan1982, Lot Tier 10-N-11.

BERGER   Joseph G.   Age 81.   b.23Dec1898 - d.2Aug1980.   ESFC. Tier 10, niche 10, in Good Shepherd Mausoleum.   Owner: Ida C. Berger, of Vancouver, WA.

BERGERON   Violet M.   Age 60.   b.12Nov1920 - d.4Jan1981. Evergreen Staples Funeral Home Marker.   Interred 6Jan1981, Lot N-183-8, Chimes.   Owner: husband, Arthur Bergeron, of Amboy, Washington.

BERRY   John W. 1952 - 1967. Father: Emerald Berry, of Brush Prairie, WA. Lot N-197-5.

BETTGER   Rachel A. (Age 69. b.16May1917, McClusky, ND - d.2Jan1987, Portland, OR. Res: Vancouver, WA. Widower: Ray A. Bettger. Sons: Ken Bettger, Suisun City, CA; Bob Bettger, Vancouver. Daughter: Carol Bales, Vancouver. Brothers: John Bender, Bismark, ND; Reuben Bender, Hibbing, MN; Henry Bender, Lemon, SD, Adopted Brother: Herb Bender, Lisbon, ND. Sisters: Marie Loewens and Esther Wahl, both of Puyallup, WA. Funeral Tues., 6Jan1987, Battle Ground Baptist Church. Interment MMP. Vancouver Funeral Chapel. Obit - The Columbian)

BILES   LeRoy A. "Husband" 1906 - 1968. Int.20Jul1972, S-145-7. Owner: Wife, Ruth M. Biles, of Wenatchee, WA.

BILES   Ruth M. "Wife" 1914 - _____

BILLS   William O. Age 85. b.6Aug1876 - 26Jul1961. LBGFH. N-193-3.

BILYEU   Mae B. Age 54. b.20Jan1925 - d.17Sep1980. Husband: Frank E. Bilyeu, Kalama, WA. F.D.: Detleusen Moor, Kelso, WA. Lot N-91-5. (Note: Mrs. Bilyeu was first buried at "Wilson Bridge Cemetery" and transferred 25Mar1983.)

BLANKENBAKER   Robert M. Age 69. "Beloved Husband & Father" b.12Dec1908 - d.20Jun1978. Wife: Frances Blankenbaker. S-135-7.

BOEHM   Elizabeth J. 1915 - _____. (w/Jack D.)

BOEHM   Jack D. Age 63. b.31Mar1914 - d.7Sep1977. Wife: Elizabeth J., of Vancouver. Int. 10 Hamilton F.H. Space 1-S-16, Garden of Christus.

BOMER   Denny A. Age 15. "Our Son" b.31Oct1959 - d.17Jul1975. Parents: Mr. and Mrs. Allen Bomer, of Vancouver, WA. VFC. Interred 21Jul1975, S-52-5, Garden of Devotion.

BORCHERDING   Stanley H. Age 55. b.19Aug1917 - d.22Jan1972. Wife: Helen Borcherding, of Vancouver, WA. Int. N-131-1.

BORCHERS   Walter H. Age 70. Pvt. U.S. Army. b.20Jun1908 - d.8Oct1978. Wife: Merian Borchers, of Vancouver, WA. LBGFH. Int.11Oct1978, N-72-7.

BRANDT   Harold John. Age 24. "In Loving Memory". b.22Jan1934 - d.24Nov1976. Wife: Elizabeth Brandt, of Portland, OR. Dempsey Funeral Home, Portland, OR. Int. 3Dec1976, S-158-1.

BROCK — Mary Rose. (Age 57. b.9Sep1926, St. Helens, OR. - d.11Jan1985. Res: Vancouver, WA. Wife of Carl, at home. Funeral Tuesday, 15Jan1985, at Evergreen Staples Funeral Chapel. Burial in MMP. Obit - The Columbian)

BROOKS — Ernest J. Age 72. "Together Forever". b.23Aug1904 - d.27Oct1976. Wife: Frances, of Vancouver, WA. VFC. Int. 1Nov1976, Space N-154-6 Chimes.

BROOKS — Frances D. ____ - ____ "Together Forever" (w/Ernest)

BROOKSHIRE — Ann E. Age 73. "Together Forever". b.12Aug1907 - d.19Jun1981. Husband, Otis F. Brookshire. LBGFH. Int. 23Jun1981, Garden of Devotion, S-113-2. (w/Otis F.)

BROOKSHIRE — Otis F. "Together Forever" 1902 - ____. (w/Ann E.)

BROUHARD — Leslie. (Age 66. b.24Mar1917, Beaver Creek, NE - d. 1May1983, Portland, OR. Res: Vancouver, WA. Husband of Hester Brouhard, at home. Funeral Wed., 4May1983, at Evergreen Staples Funeral Chapel. Interment in MMP, Lot N-202-4. Obit - The Columbian) No marker.

BROUHARD — William E. (Craven). Age 20. "Son". b.17Mar1955 - d.26Jun1975. Parents: Mr. and Mrs. Leslie Brouhard, of Vancouver, WA. FDH. Int. 1Jul1975, MMP, Space N-202-3

BROWN — Ethel E. Age 60. b.28Dec1921 - d.22Jul1982. Husband: Lonie G. Brown, Ridgefield, WA. VFC. Lot N-6-32.

BROWN — Gerald N. Age 47. b.25Dec1934 - d.30Oct1982. VFC. Int. 6Oct1982, Lot N-164-8, Vet.

BROWN — Harry N. Age 71. b.24Dec1907 - d.9Feb1978. Wife: Zoza M. Sons: Jack, Gerald, Robert, and Larry. Daughters: Patricia Bare, of Vancouver, WA., and Norma Tutar, of Portland, OR. VFC. Int. 13Feb1978, N-224-1 (w/Zoza M. Brown)

BROWN — Lucille N. (Age 81. b.4Dec1904, Wichita Falls, TX. - d.30Sep1986. Res: Clark Co., WA. Preceded in death by her husband, William, in 1974. Funeral Sat., 4Oct1986, at MMP. LBGFH. Obit - The Columbian)

BROWN — Raymond O. U. S. Army/WWII. Age 66. b.3Jan1911 -- d.14Sep1977. Wife: Violet Brown, of Camas, WA. Int.

20Sep1977, Space 234-4, Garden of Devotion. Stewart Swank.

BROWN William C. "Poppop". Age 77. b25Oct1896 - d.28Jul1974. Wife: Lucille, of Vancouver, WA. LBGFH. Int. Space S-226-4.

BROWN Zora Mae. Age 55. b.19Mar1914 - d.21Apr1969. Husband: Harry Brown, Vancouver, WA. Daughter: Patricia Bare, Vancouver. Int. 21Apr1969, Space N-224-2.

BRUBAKER Donald W. Age 64. b.4Feb1918 - d.8Nov1982. Wife: Toni Brubaker, Washougal, WA. Int. 10Nov1982, Lot S-118-2. Browns, Camas. No marker.

BRYANT Mollie Frances. Age 73. Holy Rosary b.28Jul1901 - d.28Dec1974. Husband: Fred Bryant, Ridgefield, WA. LBGFH. Int. #180 N-65-5.

BUIS John W. Age 66. b. 20Mar1912 - d.10Mar1978. Wife: Rita Buis, of Vancouver, WA. Int. 13Mar1978, Space Tier 1-13, Good Shepherd Mausoleum. EFC.

BUNTING Clarence R. b.1899 - d.16Feb1961. Wife: Hattie Bunting, of Ridgefield, WA. Interred Space N-192-4.

BUNTING Hattie H. 1908 - ____

BURNS Lynette. Age 22. "In Loving Memory" b.26Jun1949 - d.30Oct1971. Husband: Roger Burns, of Vancouver, WA. Int. N-23-8. FD: Hamilton.

BUSWELL Peggy C. Age 65. b.16May1909 - d.21Jan1975. Son: Roger Perkins, Vancouver, WA. Lot: 2-N-210. VFC.

BUSWELL William L. Washington SF3 USNR/WWII. Age 62. b.21Dec1910 - d.23Jun1973. Wife: Peggie, of Orchards. VFC. Int. N-210-1.

CANFIELD Robert Earston. (Age 82. b.1Jul1904, Kansas City, KS. - d.7Oct1986. Res: Battle Ground, WA. Husband of LaVern, at home. Funeral Saturday, 11Oct1986, at Layne's Funeral Home. Burial in MMP Cem. LFC. Obit - The Columbian.)

CARLSON Casper A. Age 86. b.22Feb1888 - d.22Apr1974. Brother: Tonnes C. Carlson, Vancouver, WA. LBGFH. Lot S-154-3. No marker.

CARLSON Tonnes C. Age 86. b.21Sep1896 - d.18Apr1983. Wife: Ruth Carlson. LBGFH. Int. 21Apr1983, Lot S-154-2. No marker.

CARMAN Milvin E. Age 60. b.14Apr1919 - d.7Sep1974. Wife: Velmer Carman. VFC. Lot 1-S-195. No marker.

MEMORY MEMORIAL PARK

CARNEY	Dorothy P. Age 63. b.15Apr1914 - d.14Jan1978. Sister: Ruth Nathan, of Phoenix, AZ. Int. 18Jan1978, S-157-1. EFH.
CARR	Emmett T. Age 76. "Together Forever". b.24Mar1905 - d.4Apr1981. Daughter: Jackie Johnson. Int. 7Apr1981, Space N-139-1, Chimes. VFC. (w/Florene)
CARR	Florene. "Together Forever". b.24Sep1904 - d.25Jul1977. Husband: Emmett Carr, of Vancouver, WA. Int. 28Jul1977, Space N-139-2, Chimes. LBGFH.
CARSON	Dale L. Age 49. "Together Forever" b.9Oct1929 - d.9Sep1979. Wife: Judith Carson, Aberdeen, WA. Interred 13Sep1979, Space S-155-6, Devotion. MGM.
CARSON	Judith D. 1941 - ____
CARTER	Almond A. (Age 69. b.3Mar1915, Vancouver, WA. - d.18Jan1985, Portland, OR. Res: Ridgefield, WA. Husband of LaVerne Carter, Ridgefield. Son: Vern Hulett Carter, of Ridgefield. Graveside services Monday, 21Jan1985, at MMP. EFC/EFH. Obit - The Columbian) N-29-4
CARTER	Audery E. Age 57. b.25Aug1925 - d.16Apr1983. Husband: Richard A. Carter, Yacolt, WA. Ashes placed Lot: Tier 2-10, Good Shepherd.
CASPER	Mabel A. Age 87. b.6Feb1886 - d.16Aug1973. Husband: William Casper, Portland, OR. Daughter: Zella M. Young, Portland. Space N-266-2, Chimes.
CASPER	William. Age 101. b.6May1878 - d.6Jul1979. Granddaughter: Alice Shinn, Salem, OR. Int. 6Jul1979, Space N-266-1, Chimes. FD: Rose, Portland. OR.
CAYCE	Howard M. "Together Forever". Age 63. b.22Nov1912 - d.13May1976. Wife Lois E. Son: Robert Cayce, Vancouver, WA. Ashes Int. 27May1976, Sp. N-80-8, Chimes, with wife, Lois. VFC.
CAYCE	Lois E. "Together Forever". Age 53. b.18Dec1917 - d.9Apr1970. Husband: Howard Cayce, Vancouver, WA. Portland Crematorium, Portland, OR. Int. 20Apr1970, Space N-80-8, Chimes.
CHILDRESS	Barry E. "Light Of Our Lives". Age 21. b.10Apr1957 - d.17Dec1978. Parents: Mr. and Mrs. Albert Childress, Vancouver, WA. Int. 20Dec1978, Sp. S-60-6, Devotion. VFC.
CHRISTENSEN	Jacob M. b. 1874 - d.Nov1961. Son: Elmer Christensen, Vancouver. VFC. Space 1-N-126.

CHRISTENSEN   Elmer C. Age 73. b.30Oct1903 - d.23Mar1977. Wife:
Elsie Christenson, Washougal, WA. Int. 26Mar1977,
Space S-150-8, Devotion. FD: Straub, Camas, WA.

CHRISTENSEN   Elsie G. Age 71. b.5Oct1907 - d.4Jan1979. Son:
Fred Latta, Hagerstown, MD. Int. 8Jan1979, Space
S-150-7, Christus. FD: Straub, Camas, WA.

CHRISTLER   Dennis A.   Washington Bul 3 U. S. Navy.   Age 22.
b30Jun1946 - d.18Nov1968. Wife: Diana Christler
Wick.   Interred MMP, 21Nov1968 - Space N-186-1.
VFC.

CHRISTLER   Franklin. Age 52. b.11Jun1914 - d.13May1966. Wife:
Barbara Christler, Vancouver, WA. Lot: 5-N-126.
EFH. No marker.

CICCO   Marie E. "Mother"   Age 91. b.18Jul1892, Italy -
d.17Feb1984, Vancouver, WA. Service Monday,
20Feb1984, at Vancouver Funeral Chapel. Interment at
MMP. Obit - The Columbian)

CLAPP   Anna Bertha. Age 76. b.2Dec1906, Donalda, Alberta,
Canada - d.13Aug1983, Astoria, OR. Res: Warrenton,
OR. Son: Alvin Clapp, of Vancouver, WA. Preceded in
death by husband, Lynn M. Clapp. Services Tues.,
16Aug1983, at Vancouver Funeral Chapel. Interment in
MMP. Obit - The Columbian) Lot N-115-8 Vets

CLAPP   Genevieve S. Age 50. b.15Apr1914 - d.20Dec1964.
Husband: Harry Clapp. Space N-66-5. VFC.

CLAPP   Lynn Martin. Oregon Lt. JG U.S. Coast Guard
Ret./WWII, Korea. Age 65. b.8Aug1906 - d.17Jan1972.
Wife: Anna B. Clapp, Warrenton, OR. Int. 21Jan1972,
Space N-175-1 Vets. VFC.

CLAPP   Maynard E. (Age 69. b.12Jun1913, Kalama,, WA. -
d.21Apr1983, Vancouver, WA. Husband of Betty L.
Clapp, at home. Funeral Monday, 25Apr1983, at
Vancouver Funeral Chapel. Obit - The Columbian)
Interment at MMP, Lot N-115-6 Vet.

CLARK   George W. Age 87. b.28Nov1892 - d.5Dec1979. Son:
George W. Clark, Jr., Ephrata, WA. Int. 7Dec1979,
Space S-164-6, Devotion. LBGFH.

CLARK   Jeffery Allen. "Our Darling". Age 1 Day. b.3Jun1974
- d.3Jun1974. Parents: Mr. and Mrs. Ray D. Clark,
Sr., Vancouver, WA. MMP Space S-79-1. FD: Hamilton.

CLARK   Nora L. Age 76. b.1895 - d.23Nov1971. Husband:
George W. Clark, Woodland, WA. Space S-164-3,
Devotion. LBGFH.

CLEMENTS   Wayne L. SF2, U.S. Navy. b.29Apr1910 - d.26Oct1974. Wife: Lauretta Clements, Vancouver, WA. Space N-111-7. VFC.

CLOUD   Robert Earl. (Age 58. b.28Dec1927, Portland,OR. - d.13Aug1986, Vancouver, WA. Husband of Joyce, at home. Nicheside services and entombment Sat., 16Aug1986 at MMP Columbarium. VFC. Obit - The Columbian)

COCHRAN   Samuel Burney. "Our Dad" Age 69. b.22Jan1904 - d.27Dec1974. Son: Samuel I. Cochran, Vancouver. Space S-51-5. VFC.

COFFIELD   James Anderson. Age 47. b.27Dec1931 - d.22Jun1979. Int. #313, Space N-38-4. Evergreen Staples Funeral Chapel.

COFFIELD   John B. Age 68. b.6Sep1906 - d.19Jun1975. Frances G. Coffield, Vancouver, WA. Interred 21Jun1975, Space N-38-1, Chimes. FD: EFC, Vancouver.

COFFIELD   Thomas C. SP5 U.S. Army/Vietnam. Age 21. b.7May1955 - d.2Aug1976. Frances G. Coffield. Int. 4Aug1976, Lot 3-N-38. No marker. EFH.

COGDILL   Earl Ray. Age 52. "Dad" "Rise and Shine" b.16Jan1928 - d.2Apr1980. Wife: Gladys Cogdill, Vancouver, WA. Int. 7Apr1980, Space N-159-7, Chimes. LBGFH.

COGDILL   Gladys Mae. "Mom" b.10Mar1929 - ____

COLBY   Ed R. Age 81. b.22Nov1900 - d.26Jul1982. Wife: Velda L. Colby, Vancouver, WA. Lot: 1-N-39. VFC.

CONNELL   Yulah May. Age 71. b.1898 - d.16May1970. Son: Patrick Lafferty, Sr., Ridgefield, WA. Int. 20May1970, Lot 2-N-172, Vet. LBGFH.

COOK   James H. Age 56. b.11Feb1925 - d.29Aug1981. Wife: June Cook, Vancouver, WA. Int. 1Sep1981, Lot S-74-4. Hamilton-Mylan. No marker.

COOPER   Frederick H. Age 69. Iowa S2 U.S. Navy/WWI. b.14Oct1897 - d.13May1967. Wife: Ruth Cooper, Battle Ground. Son: Charles F. Cooper, Ellensburg, WA. Space N-6-1. (w/Ruth J.) LBGFH.

COOPER   Ruth J. Age 61. b.12Apr1913 - d.7Oct1974. Son: Charles F. Cooper, Ellensburg, WA. Space N-6-2. (w/Frederick) LBGFH.

DAVIS   Edith O. ae. 70-b.Dec.8,1915,Vancouver,Wa.d.Dec.21,1985

Wife of Leroy Davis, at home. Graveside service
Tues., 24Dec1985, at MMP. VFC. Obit - The Columbian)

DAVIS   Edna M. (Age 84. b.22Jan1901, in Oklahoma -
             d.14Nov1985, Sonora, CA. Res: Fowler, CA. Service
             Monday, 18Nov1985, at Vancouver Funeral Chapel.
             Interment MMP. Obit - The Columbian)

DAVIS   Elizabeth. Age 83. b.2Aug1893 - d.31Aug1976.
             Husband: Fred J. Davis, of Vancouver, WA. Int.
             3Sep1976, Space N-117-6, vet. VFC.

DAVIS   Frederick J. U.S. Army/WWI. Age 85. b.22Sep1893 -
             d.23Feb1979. Stepson: Calvin Pearson. Interred
             27Feb1979, Space N-117-5. VFC.

DECKER   Pauline B. Age 66. b.25May1916 - d.24May1983.
             Husband: Robert C. Decker, of Sandy, OR. Int.
             27May1983, Space N-31-8. FD: Sandy Funeral Home.

DECKER   Robert Clark. (Age 72. b.23Feb1913, Pocatello, ID. -
             d.9Sep1985, Brush Prairie, WA. Res: Sandy, OR.
             Funeral Sat., 14Sep1985, at Hamilton-Mylan Funeral
             Home. Interment in MMP. Obit - The Columbian)

DE HART   Margaret Mae. Age 79. b.17Nov1898 - d.1977. Son:
             Ellis O. DeHart, of Vancouver, WA. Interred
             28Aug1977, Space N-24-4. On stone: "Husband/Ora Ray"
             "Married Dec. 19, 1914" VFC.

DE HART   Ora Ray. Age 80. b17May1893 - d.27Mar1975. Wife:
             Margaret Mae DeHart. Son: Ellis DeHart. Space
             N-24-3. On stone: "Married Dec. 19, 1914". Fern
             Hill Funeral Home, Aberdeen, WA.

DE MARCO   Mofried. Age 64. b.26Oct1906 - d.28Oct1970. No next
             of kin. Space 293-4 Vet.

DERRICOTT   Kenneth G. Age 18. b. 10May1962 - d.14Aug1980.
             Aunt: Ernestine Hershey, of Vancouver, WA. Interred
             16Aug1980, Space N-37-6.

DICKINSON   Chester R. "Together Forever" 1916 - ____ (w/Elsie)

DICKINSON   Elsie J. "Together Forever" Age 61. b.3Feb1915 -
             d.31Jul1976. Husband: Chester R., of Vancouver, WA.
             Int. 5Aug1976, Space N-25-8.

DIETEL   Clarence H. Age 68. b.26Mar1911 - d.8Mar1980. Wife:
             Ora L. Dietel, of Vancouver, WA. Mausoleum G.S.
             W.Tier 2, Crypt 12. LBGFH.

DOBAK   Glee Nola. (Age 79. b.10Nov1905, Brumley, MO -
             d.17Jan1985, Grayland, WA. Cancer. Res: Vancouver,
             WA. Wife of Boyd Dobak, at home. Funeral Tuesday,

22Jan1985, at LBGFH. Obit - The Columbian) Interred MMP Space N-208-8.

DONNELLY   Juanita G. "Wife". Age 53. b.29Aug1921 - d.17Jun1975. Husband: Robert D. Donnelly, of Battle Ground, WA. Int. 21Jun1975, Space S-34-6. VFC.

DONNELLY   Robert Dudley. (Age 66. b.27Aug1916, Holyoke, CO. - d.13Jan1983, Vancouver, WA. Funeral Monday, 17Jan1983, at Vancouver Funeral Chapel. Interment at Memory Memorial Park. Obit - The Columbian) Sons: Terry and V. L. Donnelly, of Vancouver, WA. Int. Space S-34-7.

DOUGLAS   Mary Esta. Age 82. b.26Jul1892 - d.16Oct1974. Brother: Jesse Goodrich, of Vancouver, WA. Int. Space N-78-6. VFC

DOWNHAM   Esther. Age 76. b.29Feb1896 - d.4Mar1972. Husband: Raymond Downham, of Vancouver, WA. Space S-54-7. EFH.

DOWNHAM   Raymond E. "Father" 1896 - 19__. Wife: Esther.

DUCK   Murel J. Oct. 4, 1902 - _____

DUCK   Shirley S. Cpl. U.S. Army/WWI. b.17Aug1895 - d.29Sep1980. Husband: Murel Duck, of Vancouver, WA. Staples Evergreen, Int. 2Oct1980, Space N-114-4 Vet.

DUERR   Beat John. (Age 88. Heart attack. b.24Dec1894, Gamms, Switzerland - d.19Mar1983, Battle Ground, WA. Husband of Ida, at home. Mass of Christian Burial Tuesday, 22Mar1983, at Sacred Heart Catholic Church. Interment at MMP Cem. Obit - The Columbian) Space S-141-2. LBGFH.

DUERR   Ida F. (Age 80. b.17Jun1906, Portland, OR - d.23Jan1987, Vancouver, WA. Preceded in death by husband, Beat, in 1983. Res: Battle Ground and Amboy areas. Sons: Ray Waser and Al Waser, both of Amboy, WA.; Ed Waser, of Ridgefield; and John Waser and Robert Duerr, both of Vancouver, WA. Daughters: Dorothy Fry, LaCenter; Jane Wilson and June McKee, both of Amboy. Brothers: Joe Kiser and Ed Kiser, both of Portland, OR.; Robert Kiser, Kelso, WA.; Jack Kiser, Orchards, WA.; Fred Kiser, Beaver, OR. and Wally Kiser, Bend, OR. Sister: Helen Baumgartner, Longview, WA. Int. at Memory Memorial Park Cem. Funeral Tues., 27Jan1987. Layne's Battle Ground Funeral Home. Obit - The Columbian)

DYE   Frances C. 1910 - ____

DYE
William A. "Together Forever" Age 72. b.28Dec1904 - d.7Dec1977. Wife: Frances Dye, of Vancouver, WA. Int. 10Dec1977, Spece N-116-3. VFC.

EDWARDS
Joseph B. b.1911 - d.12Feb1969. Wife: Dolly Edwards, of Portland, OR. Space N-149-1.

EMINETH
Leo. Age 58. b.29May1921 - d.6Jul1979. Wife: Margaret Emineth, of Battle Ground, WA. Interred 9Jul1979, Maus. G.S. Tier 3, Crypt 13. LBGFH.

EMINETH
Margaret M. Age 60. b.27Jan1922 - d.8Aug1982. No survivors. Interred 12Aug1982, G.S. Maus. Tier 3, Crypt 12. LBGFH.

ETEN
Ethel M. (Mrs. Forrest Crawford) Age 80. b.18Dec1895 - d.7Dec1976. Son: Richard Eten, of Vancouver, WA. Sister: Ellen Clark, of Gold Beach, OR. Interred 12Dec.1976, Space 200-5. VFC.

FALK
Richard G. (Age 53. Cancer. b.23Aug1930, Portland, OR. - d.6Feb1984, Portland, OR. Res: Battle Ground, WA. Husband of Shirley, at home. Funeral Wed., 8Feb1984, at Layne's Battle Ground Funeral Home. Burial in MMP. Obit - The Columbian) Int. Space N-238-1 Vet.

FAUST
Helen P. "Wife". Age 75. b.1889 - d.1Mar1965. Husband: Roy C. Faust, of Vancouver, WA. Int. 4Mar1965, Space N-123-5. LBGFH. (w/Roy C.)

FAUST
Roy C. "In Thee I Have Put My Trust" Age 79. b.2Feb1897 - d.4Aug1976. Space N-123-4. LBGFH. (w/Helen)

FEEZOR
Hallie J. Age 65. b.8May1919 - d.30Dec1984. Husband: William W. Feezor, of Vancouver, WA. Int. 2Jan1985, Space N-103-2. VFC. No marker.

FEMLING
Frank L. "Together Forever" ____ - ____
(w/Louise and Fredrick)

FEMLING
Fredrick W., Jr. Age 76. b.16Jan1902 - d.25Jan1978. Wife: Grace Femling, of Vancouver, WA. Int. 26Jan1978, Space S-94-7. VFC. (w/Frank and Louise)

FEMLING
Louise Rose. "Together Forever" Age 67. b.3Feb1905 - d.6Feb1978. Husband: Frank L. Femling, of Vancouver, WA. Int. Space S-94-5. Hamilton-Mylan. (w/Frank and Fredrick)

FINCH
LeRoy L. "Together Forever" b.29Sep1931 - d.1Jul1980. Wife: Vionne E. M. Int. 5Jul1980, Space S-87-8. ESFH. (w/Vionne E.M.)

FINCH   Vionne E. M.   "Together Forever"   1937 - ____
                  (w/LeRoy)

FISHEL   George A.   Age 87.   b.22Jun1892 - d. 27Jan1980.   Wife:
                  Minnie Fishel, of Battle Ground, WA.   Interred
                  31Jan1980, Space N-92-4.   LBGFH.

FISHEL   Minnie.   1898 - ____

FITZGERALD   Mervin W.   (Age 59.   b.5Sep1924, Ness, KS. -
                  d.14Jan1984, Portland, OR.   Res: Vancouver, WA.
                  Husband of Wilmah Fitzgerald, at home.   No Service.
                  MGM.   Obit - The Columbian)   Interment 21Jan1984, G.S.
                  Mausoleum Tier 17, Niche 10.

FLEMING   Claude E.   Age 69.   b.1903 - d.27Jan1973.   Wife:
                  Thelma Anna Fleming, of Ridgefield, WA.   Interred
                  30Jan1973, Space S-160-2.   VFC.   (w/Thelma)

FLEMING   David E.   U.S. Army/Korea.   b.26Feb1929 - d.10May1975.
                  Son: David Fleming, of Longview, WA.   Mother: Thelma
                  Fleming, of Ridgefield, WA.   Space S-100-6.

FLEMING   Thelma A.   Age 76.   b.14Dec1904 - d.18Aug1981.
                  Daughter: Barbara Stewart, of Lebanon, OR.   Interred
                  21Aug1981, Space 160-1.   VHC.   (w/Claude)

FLETCHER   Robert E.   (Age 68.   b.23Apr1917, Berkeley, CA. -
                  d.31May1985, Vancouver, WA.   Husband of Mary R.
                  Fletcher, at home.   Funeral Tuesday, 4Jun1985, at
                  Evergreen Staples Funeral Chapel.   Interment at MMP.
                  Obit - The Columbian)

FLOHAUG   George M.   U.S. Army/WWII.   Age 60.   b.5Nov1917 -
                  d.17Apr1978.   Wife: Lorraine A. Flohaug.   Int.
                  20Apr1978, Space S-112-2.   VFC.

FLOHAUG   Howard Raymond.   (Age 40.   b.15Aug1946, Vancouver, WA.
                  - d.18Dec1986, Vancouver.   Widow: Bonnie L. Flohaug,
                  at home.   Daughters: Wendy and Christine Flohaug,
                  Vancouver.   Mother: Lurraine Flohaug, Vancouver.
                  Brother: Dean Flohaug, Vancouver.   Funeral Monday,
                  22Dec1986, at Vancouver Funeral Chapel.   Interment in
                  MMP.   Obit - The Columbian.)

FLOOD   James.   Age 85.   b.13Apr1877 - d.24Nov1962.   Son:
                  Gelford R. Flood, of Vancouver, WA`.   Interred Space
                  N-199-1.   Evergreen Funeral Home.   (w/Jessie)

FLOOD   Jessie.   Age 62.   b12Sep1889 - d.7Jul1961.   Husband:
                  James Flood, of Battle Ground, WA.   Int. Space
                  N-199-2.   Evergreen F.H.   (w/James)

FORSYTHE   Casper Lyle.   Pvt. U.S. Army/WWI.   Age 85.
                  b.25Feb1893 - d.9Jan1979.   Sister-in-law: Leona

Forsythe, of Ridgefield, WA. Int. 13Jan1979, Space S-205-2. Evergreen F.H.

FORSYTHE   Leona L. 1907 - ____

FORSYTHE   Ronald H. Age 78. b.1897 - d.1975. Int. 12Jun1975, Space 205-3.

FOSSAND   Kenneth Kolbin. Age 20. b.10Jun1958 - d.21Feb1979. Parents: Mr. and Mrs. Cardiff A. Fossand, of Battle Ground, WA. Interred 26Feb1979, Beautiful Memories Mausoleum, Tier 6, Crypt 14. Layne's Battle Ground Funeral Home.

FOSTER   Albert. Age 82. b.23Oct1898 - d.18Jan1981. Wife: Vera Foster, of Vancouver, WA. Int. 21Jan1981, Space N-269-1. Evergreen F.H.

FOSTER   Ernest "Ernie". (Age 65. b.12Oct1919, in Washington State - d.14Oct1984, Vancouver, WA. Res: Ridgefield, WA. Husband of Ileen Foster, at home. Cryptside services Tues., 16Oct1984, at Memory Memorial Park Cem. Layne's Battle Ground Funeral Home. Obit - The Columbian) Interred 15Oct1984, G.S.M. Tier 6, Crypt 1. No marker.

FOSTER   Hattie L. "Mother". b.1875 - d.Dec1961. Mrs. S. H. Purdy, of Vancouver, WA. Int. 9Dec1961, Space N-127-5. VFC.

FOULKE   Wennifred A. Age 64. b.26Aug1914 - d.11Jul1979. Leonard Foulke, of Vancouver, WA. Interred 13Jul1979, Space S-100-7. VFC.

FRAHM   Virginia H. Age 57. b.3Nov1920 - d.20Jan1978. Husband: John Frahm, of Vancouver, WA. Interred 23Jan1978, G.S.M., Tier 3E, Crypt 12.

FRANKE   Bertha E. Age 88. b.10Oct1890 - d.20Aug1979. Nephew: Harold Cox, of Vancouver, WA. Interred 10Aug1979, Mausoleum G.S., Tier 6, Crypt 7. Staples Evergreen F.H.

FRASER   Anna R. Age 71. b.1893 - d.7Sep1964. Sister: Rose Reny, of Vancouver, WA. Interred 9Sep1964, Space N-71-3. VFC.

FRAZIER   George L. PFC U.S. Army/WWII. Age 59. b.21Dec1917 - d.23Nov1977. Wife: Margret Frazier, of Vancouver, WA. Int. 28Nov1977, Space N-84-2. LBGFH.

FREEMAN   Edna E. Age 48. b.1925 - d.21Mar1974, in Tacoma, WA. Son: Capt. Leslie A. Freeman, of Olympia, WA. Int. 8Nov1975, Space S-73-1. LBGFH. (w/John and Mary)

FREEMAN   John Henry. Age 89. b.14Jul1885 - d.17Oct1974. Daughter: Mrs. Mildred Alred, of Vancouver, WA. Chapel of Chimes, Portland, OR. Int. 21Oct1974, Space S-13-4. (w/Edna and Mary)

FREEMAN   Mary Ethel. Age 84. b.1891 - d.4Oct1975. Chapel of the Chimes, Portland, OR. Int. 9Oct1975, Space S13-3. (w/John and Edna)

FREEZOR   Hallie J. (Age 65. b.8May1919, Hartman, CO. - d.30Dec1984, Vancouver, WA. Wife of William W., at home. Service Wed., 2Jan1984, at Vancouver Funeral Chapel. Burial in MMP. Obit - The Columbian)

FRY   Hazel. Age 67. b.15Sep1909 - d.29Oct1976. Husband: Walter L. Fry. Son: Delvan Fry. Daughter: Patsy L. Fry (Wright). Evergreen F.C. Int. Space N-158-2.

FRY   Walter L. (Age 76. b.29Jun1909, Wichita, KS - d.20Jan1986, Vancouver, WA. Son: Delvin D. Fry, Portland, OR. Daughter: Patsy Wright, Vancouver, Brother: Harvey Fry, Burlington, WA. Graveside service Wed., 22Jan1986, at Memory Memorial Park. Evergreen Staples Funeral Chapel. Obit - The Columbian)

FULLER   Arlan D. Fuller. (Age 48. Heart failure. b.17Mar1939, Longview, WA. - d.30Mar1987, Vancouver, WA. Res: Battle Ground, WA. Widow: Mary, at home. Father: Donald Fuller, Phoenix, AZ. Mother: Wanda Wason, Vancouver, WA. Sons: Todd and Nathan, Battle Ground, WA. Brothers: Roger Fuller, Sedro Woolley, WA.; Steven Wason and Richy Wason, Vancouver, WA. Sisters: Elaine Kanooth, Vancouver, and Nancy Wason, Portland, OR. Funeral: Friday, 3Apr1987, Battle Ground Baptist Church. Burial: Memory Memorial Park. Layne's Battle Ground Funeral Home. Obit - The Columbian)

GAINES   Bennett Albert. "Brother". b.1898 - d.18Jan1962. Space N-5-1. VFC

GAINES   Orville C. "Father". Age 69. b.19May1905 - d.2Jul1974. Son: Franklin D. Gaines, of Auburn, Washington. Space N-5-2. VFC.

GARD   Arthur H. "Forever In Our Hears" 1895 - 1977. Space S-101-4. (w/Hazel)

GARD   Hazel D. Age 80. b.30Mar1897 - d.10Oct1977. Daughter: Mrs. Vtha Shannon, Battle Ground, WA. Son: Clifford E. Gard, Portland, OR. Int. 14Oct1977, Space S-101-3. LBGFH.

GARDNER   Absolem. Age 84. d. 5Jul1966. Daughter: Lola Hunter, Sutherlin, OR. Interred 7Jul1966. LBGFH.

GARDNER   Arthur R. Age 84. "Together Forever". b.1885 - d.8Jul1971. Stepson: Paul Roberts, Battle Ground, WA. Interred 13Jul1971, Space S-213-2. LBGFH. (w/Elvira)

GARDNER   Elvira Jane. Age 85. "Together Forever". b.1886 - d.10Dec1971. Stepson: Paul Roberts, Battle Ground, WA. Interred 14Dec1971. LBGFH. (w/Arthur)

GARNER   Tommy. Age 70. b.23Mar1917 - d.11May1983. Wife: Ruby Garner, Camas, WA. Straub's F.H., Camas. Int. 13May1983, Space S-239-2.

GERLOFF   Glenna E. (Age 54. Congestive heart failure. b.16Mar1933, Clear Lake, WI. - d.7Jun1987. Res: Vancouver, WA. Preceded in death by her mother, Gertrude Gerloff, in 1987. Graveside service Wed., 10June1987, at Memory Memorial Park Cemetery. VFC. Obit - The Columbian)

GERLOFF   Rufus W. PFC U.S. Army. b.27Mar1894 - d.28Feb1975. Wife: Gertrude Gerloff, Vancouver, WA. Layne's Battle Ground F.H. Space S-114-6.

GIAMATTEO   Charles J. "Father". 1911 - ____. (w/Venera)

GIAMATTEO   Venera A. "Mother". b.27Aug1913 - d.18Feb1979. VFC. Int. 21Feb1979. (w/Charles J.)

GINTER   Fred. b.4Jan1909 - d.27Aug1978. Wife: Sarah Ginter, Ridgefield, WA. LBGFH. Int. 31Aug1978, Space S-111-4.

GOFORTH   Mary Ann. Age 26. b.1Nov1955 - d.30Dec1981. Husband: Wade Goforth. Int. 2Jan1982, Space S-18-4.

GOMBOS   Stephen (Steve). Age 83. Cook, U.S. Army/WWI. b.8Sep1892 - d.27Mar1976. Wife: Margaret Gombos. Son: Warren Brown, Vancouver, WA. LBGFH. Int. Space S-36-6.

GOODRICH   Jesse R. "Together Forever". Age 79. b.7Apr1900 - d.8Jul1979. Wife: Mildred M. Goodrich, Vancouver, WA. VFC. Int. 12Jul1979, Space N-78-7. (w/Mildred)

GOODRICH   Mildred M. "Together Forever". b.30Jul1917 - d.27Mar1980. Son: Thomas Johnson. VFC. Int. 31Mar1980, Space N-78-8. (w/Jesse)

GRAF   Karl M. Charles. b.1891 - d.12May1964. Harold Graf, Militas, CA. VFC. Int. Space N-11-5.

GRAGG	Clarence E. "Together Forever". 1896 – ____. (w/Hazel)
GRAGG	Hazel M. "Together Forever". b.1898 – d.8Aug1978. Little Chapel of the Chimes, Portland, OR. Int. 11Aug.1978, Space S-220-7. (w/Clarence)
GRAHAM	Kenneth J. b.13Nov1900 – d.26Sep1974. Wife: Winnie Graham, Battle Ground, WA. Son: Kenneth Graham, Battle Ground. LBGFH. Int. 29Sep1977, Space N-114-4.
GRAHAM	Oma A. 19 Feb. 1909 – _____
GRAHAM	Wilo H. b.23Nov1906 – d. 1Dec1976. Wife: Oma Graham, Battle Ground, WA. LBGFH. Int. 6Dec1976, Space S-52-4.
GRAHAM	Winnie Fay. (Age 83. b.12Feb1901, Artesian, SD – d.18Jul1984, Vancouver, WA. Graveside service Sat., 21Jul1984, at MMP. Laynes Battle Ground Funeral Home. Obit – The Columbian) Int. Space N-114-5.
GRANT	Clio K. 1895 – 1968. Space N-4-6. (w/Kate M.)
GRANT	James C. (Age 80. b.25Feb1904, in Nebraska – d.3Aug1984, at home, Ridgefield, WA. Husband of Marie, at home. Memorial service Friday, 10Aug1984, at the Hazel Dell Jehovah's Witnesses. Burial at Memory Memorial Park. VFC. Obit – The Columbian) Lot 76-2, Christus.
GRANT	Kate M. 1900 – ____ (w/Clio K.)
GRAVES	Cecil Ralph. (Age 72. b.21Aug1913, Ellensburg, WA. – d.17Oct1985, Vancouver, WA. Res: Ridgefield, WA. Husband of Edna M., at home. Graveside service Tuesday, 22Oct1985, at Memory Memorial Park Cem. LBGFH. Obit – The Columbian)
GRAY	Herbert N. b.16Jan1915 – d.12Dec1974. Wife: Lucy A. E. Gray, Vancouver, WA. VFC. Cremains Int. Space N-145-7.
GRAY	Lucy A. E. b.17Apr1917 – d.10Dec1978. Memorial Gardens Funeral Chapel. Int. 13Dec1978, Space N-145-8.
GREEN	Thomas George. (Age 46. b.10Apr1937, Olympia, WA. – d. 21Sep1983, Philadelphia, PA. Res: North Wales, PA. (formerly resident of Vancouver, WA.) Husband of Barbara Green, North Wales. Funeral Monday, 26Sep1983, at Vancouver Funeral Chapel. Interment at MMP. Obit – The Columbian) Int. 26Sep1983, Space N-115-5 Vet.

HAATS
Albert. "Together Forever". b.2Sep1908 - d.25Feb1974. Wife: Grace Haats, Vancouver, WA. VFC. Interred Space N-93-1.

HABERSETZER
Theodore (Ted) J. b.17Aug1910 - d.30May1974. Wife: Viola Habersetzer, Battle Ground, WA. LBGFH. Int. Space N-78-1.

HAGGERTY
Freda Louise. b.9Jan1900 - d.9May1963. Husband: Leo Haggerty, Battle Ground, WA. VFC. Int. Space N-4-2.

HAGGERTY
Leo J. "Father". b.12Jan1896 - d.12Dec1971. Daughter: Mrs. Homer (Betty) Queen, Vancouver, WA. LBGFH. Int. Space N-4-1.

HAIR
Minnie O. (Age 84. b.31Oct1899, Shevlin, MN - d.11Feb1984, Vancouver, WA. Son: Stanley Hair. Services Tuesday, 14Feb1984, at Vancouver Funeral Chapel. Interment in MMP. Obit - The Columbian. Int. Space N-272-1.

HALSTEAD
Carl L. (Age 11. Fire. b.10Jul1974,, Vancouver, WA. - d.19Mar1986, Vancouver. Mother: Joyce Halstead, Battle Ground. Father: Everett L. Halstead, Vancouver. Brother: Robert Halstead, Battle Ground. Grandparents: Clayton Halvorson and Marceline Halstead, both of Vancouver; Ruby Halvorson, Long Beach, WA. Godfather, Bryan Brown, Vancouver. Godmother: Jeannie Halstead, Portland, OR. Mass of Christian Burial Sat., 22Mar1986, at St. John's Catholic Church. Interment: Memory Memorial Park. Hamilton-Mylan. Obit - The Columbian)

HALSTEAD
Lester E. "Loving Husband & Father". 1905 - 1976 Wife: Marraline Halstead. Int. Space S-57-3.

HAMILTON
Evelyn Lillian. (Age 70. Cancer. b.17Nov1916, Kennedy twp., ND - d. 17Mar1987, Vancouver, WA. Res: Vancouver. Mother: Lena Tews, Vancouver. Sons: Andrew and Thomas, both of Vancouver. Daughter: Sharon Conly, Vancouver. Brother: Clarence Tews, Reeder, ND. Funeral Friday, 20Mar1987, at Hamilton-Mylan Funeral Home. Burial MMP. Obit - The Columbian)

HAMILTON
Hester. b.31Aug1899 - d.25Jan1981. Daughter: Mrs. Reuben (Maxine) Patch, Vancouver, WA. Hamilton-Mylan F.H. Int. 28Jan1981, Space N-29-8.

HAMILTON
Hugh. b.22Jan1898 - d.17Mar1979. Wife: Hester Hamilton, Vancouver, WA. Hamilton-Mylan F.H. Int. 20Mar1979, Space N-29-7.

HANEY
Elenora L. b.24Nov1918 - d.26Jul1983. ESFH. Int. 28Jul1983, G.S. Maus. W. Tier 3, Crypt 7.

HANEY   Elza L. b.9Sep1904 - d.11Apr1977. Wife: Elenora
               Haney, Vancouver, WA. ESFH. Int. 13Apr1977, G.S.
               Maus. W. Tier 3, Crypt 7.

HANSEN   Lesetta J. "Together Forever" b.11Nov1900 -
               d.12Mar1976. Daughter: Donna Carpenter, Vancouver,
               WA. VFC. Int. 16Mar1976, Space N-150-2. (w/Wayland)

HANSEN   Wayland E. "Together Forever". b.1895 - d.20Oct1968.
               Wife: Lesetta J. Hanson, Vancouver, WA. VFC. Int.
               Space N-150-1. (w/Lesetta J.)

HARRINGTON   Marrianne. 1919 - ____   (w/Rodney)

HARRINGTON   Rodney G. "Together Forever". b.12Jul1914 -
               d.27Jul1981. Wife: Marianne, Vancouver, WA. VFC.
               Int. 31Jul1981, Space N-173-7 Vet.

HARRIS   George E. (Age 88. b.18Apr1896, Manor, WA. -
               d.27Feb1985, Portland, OR. Res: Vancouver, WA.
               Funeral Sat., 2Mar1985, at Layne's Funeral Home
               Chapel. Burial in Memory Memorial Park. Obit - The
               Columbian) Int. Space N-28-6.

HARRIS   Leonard I. WA. Cpl. U.S. Army/WWII. b.24Aug1916 -
               d.13Oct1973. Wife: Lida J. Harris, Ridgefield, WA.
               Hamilton-Mylan F.H. Int. Space S-89-8.

HARRIS   Orville M. WA. CM2 U.S. Navy/WWII. b.29Dec1918 -
               d.17Dec1970. Wife: Frances Harris, Ridgefield, WA.
               LBGFH. Int. 21Dec1970, Space S-149-2.

HARRIS   Ruby B. (Age 81. b.26Nov1902, Pawnee, OK. -
               d.28Oct1984, Vancouver, WA. Res: Brush Prairie, WA.
               Wife of William E., at home. Funeral Thursday,
               1Nov1984, at Layne's Battle Ground Funeral Home
               Chapel. Burial in Memory Memorial Park Cem. Obit -
               The Columbian)

HARRIS   William E. "Bill" (b.20Oct1901, Manor, WA. -
               d.18Sep1987, Vancouver, WA. Preceded in death by
               wife, Ruby, in 1984. Service Tues., 22Sep1987, at
               Layne's B.G. Funeral Home. Burial in MMP. Obit - The
               Columbian)

HARRISON   Jean C. b.25Jul1921 - d.20Oct1981. Daughter:
               Shirley Wills, Vancouver, WA. ESFH. Int. 23Oct1981.
               Space N-182-8. (Evergreen Staples Funeral Home
               Marker)

HARTER   Rene Lynn. "Together Forever". b.9May1917 -
               d.13May1969. Husband: Roy A. Harter, Ridgefield, WA.
               VFC. Int. Space S-50.

HARTER   Roy A. 1919 - ____

HASSELL   Frieda E.   Age 74.   (b.7Jan1912, Cheyenne, WY. –
               d.24Dec1986, Portland, OR.   Res: Battle Ground, WA.
               Daughter: Catherine Hassell, Battle Ground.
               Graveside service Wednesday, 31Dec1986, at MMP.   Obit
               – The Columbian)

HAYNES   Shirley A.   "I Thank My God Upon Every Remembrance of
               You" b.24Jan1938 – d.3Jan1978.   Husband: Roy Haynes,
               Brush Prairie, WA.   LBGFH.   Int. 6Jan1979, Space
               N-259-1.

HEBERER   Edward W.   "Father".   b.30Mar1894 – d.2Apr1964.   Wife:
               Melva Heberer, Vancouver, WA.   Hamilton-Mylan F.H.
               Int. Space N-11-1.

HEBERER   Melva Mae.   (d.5Nov1986.   Res: Clark County, WA.
               Preceded in death by husband, Edward, in 1964.
               Funeral Saturday, 8Nov1986, at Layne's B.G. Funeral
               Home.   Burial in MMP.   Obit – The Columbian)

HECK   John P.   QM2   U.S. Navy/WWII.   b.3Jul1900 –
               d.22Apr1976.   Wife: Maude Heck, Battle Ground, WA.
               LBGFH.   Int. 24Apr1976, Space S-3-4 Vet.

HEGG   Hedin M.   b. 1896 – d.12Dec1971.   Sister: Minnie O.
               Hair, Vancouver, WA.   VFC.   Int. 15Dec1971, Space
               N-272-2.

HENDERSON   Dallas M.   "Mother".   1910 – ____.   Space N-4-4.

HENDERSON   Harry L.   "Father".   1900 – 1967.   Space N-4-5.

HENDRICKSON   Ole Edwin.   U.S. Army/WWII.   (Age 69.   b.29Jun1915,
               New York Mills, MN. – d. 21Aug1984, Coeur D'Alene, ID.
               Res: Ridgefield, WA.   Husband of Anne M., at home,
               Funeral Friday, 24Aug1984, at Old Apostolic Lutheran
               Church.   Burial in MMP.   Layne's Battle Ground Funeral
               Home.   Obit – The Columbian)   Int. Space S-39-4.

HENRY   Alson Worth.   U.S. Army/WWII.   (Age 75.   b.8Jan1909,
               Manistee, MI. – d.19Aug.1984, Seattle, WA.   Res:
               Renton, WA.   Husband of Carol R. (Clay) Henry, at
               home.   Funeral Thurs., 23Aug1984, at VFC.   Interment
               in Memory Memorial Park.   Obit – The Columbian)

HENRY   David L.   b.26Jan1953 – d.31Aug1976.   Wife: Rebecca
               Henry, Vancouver, WA.   VFC.   Int. 3Sep1976, Space
               S-159-5.

HENRY   Dorothy.   b.23July1920 – d.8Mar1977.   Husband: Robert
               Henry, Washougal, WA.   Daughter: Mary Bennett.
               Memorial Gardens F.C.   Int. 11Mar1977, Space S-196-3.

HENRY   John C. b.28Jul1907 - d.31May1978. Wife: Robie L.
               Henry, Vancouver, WA. EFH. Int. 3Jun1978, Space
               S-12-4.

HENRY   Katherine Ann. U.S. Marine Corps/WWII. b.19Jan1923 -
               d.28Apr1978. Husband: Donald J. Henry, Vancouver,
               WA. Hamilton-Mylan F.H. Int. 3May1978, Space N-174-8
               Vet.

HENRY   Robert D. b.6Dec1913 - d.9Apr1980. Daughter: Betty
               Langlois, Spokane, WA. Brown's F.H., Camas, WA. Int
               12Apr1980, Space S-196-4.

HENRY   Robie L. (Age 86. b.21Nov1896, New Millport, PA. -
               d.25Jul1983, Vancouver, WA. Son: Lewis Hoover,
               Vancouver, WA. Funeral Friday, 29Jul1983, at
               Evergreen Staples Funeral Chapel. Interment in MMP.
               Obit - The Columbian)

HERIFORD   Oliva L. b.6Mar1925 - d.17Jan1980. Wiers Mortuary,
               Crescent City, CA. Son: Clyde Heriford, Brookings,
               OR. Brother: Clyde Webberly, Camas, WA. Interred
               2Feb1980, Maus. G.S. Tier 11, Niche 7.

HERMAN   Benjamin. b.20Jan1902 - d.28Aug1981. Brother:
               Theophil Herman, Shaw, OR. VFC. Int. 31Aug1981 -
               Space S-228-2.

HERRON   LeRoy. (Age 73. Cancer. b.16Apr1914, Newton Co.,
               MO. - d.16May1987. Res: Vancouver, WA. Widow:
               Erma, at home. Son: Denny Herron, of Vancouver.
               Daughters: Dixie Lund, Washougal, and Paula Herron,
               Vancouver. Brothers: Ray Herron, Placerville, CA.,
               and Edgar Herron, of San Diego. Graveside service
               Wednesday, 20May1987, at MMP. No funeral home listed.
               Obit - The Columbian)

HIATT   Bertha Jane "Our Beloved Mother" b.1919 -
               d.10Nov1973, Yakima, WA. Daughter: Elise Ginter,
               Ridgefield, WA. LBGFH. Int. MMP - Space S-51-8.

HIATT   Roland E. U.S. Navy. b.14Jul1914 - d.14Oct1978.
               Son: Roland Hiatt, Vancouver, WA. MGFC. Int.
               20Oct1978, Space S-125-8.

HILDENBRAND   Leila R. b.11Sep1897 - d.26May1977. Husband: L. A.
               Crocher, Portland, OR. Ross Hollywood Chapel,
               Portland, OR. Int. MMP - Space N-206-5.

HILDENBRAND   Truman A. b.1895 - d.29Aug1964. Wife: Vivian
               Hildenbrand, Portland, OR. Mikeworth F.H., Portland.
               Int. MMP - Space N-206-4

HILL	Dallas R. b.1Oct1896 - d.16Jul1972. Daughter: Audrie Christy, Brookings, OR. VFC. Int. MMP - Space N-39-5.
HILL	Sadie L. "Grammy" b.30Jul1901 - d.6Jun1975. Daughter: Nally Olson, Vancouver, WA. VFC. Int. Space S-29+30-8.
HITTLE	Henry C., Jr. "Together Forever" b.22May1922 - d.21Mar1979. Wife: Mary E. Hittle, Vancouver, WA. MGFH. Int. 24Mar1979 - Space S-222-2.
HITTLE	Mary E. 1921 - ____
HOLMES	Lela M. (Age 88. b.12May1898, Chelsea, OK - d.22May1986, Vancouver, WA. Niece: Mrs. Edward Chase, Vancouver, WA. Funeral Monday, 26May1986, at Vancouver Funeral Chapel. Interment at MMP. Obit - The Columbian)
HOLMES	Leo K. b.17Jul1888 - d.24Oct1981. Wife: Lela M. Holmes, Vancouver, WA. VFC. Int.28Oct1981 - Space S-95-5.
HOOD	Otto Vine. b.20Aug1914 - d.24Jan1967. Daughter: Mrs. Ronald Forsyth, Ridgefield, WA. Int. MMP - Space S-205-5.
HOUGH	Calvin R. b.4Dec1911 - d.2Dec1977. Husband of Jean R., Vancouver, WA. HMFH. Int. 6Dec1977 - Space S-25-3. (w/Jean R.)
HOUGH	Jean R. b.10Apr1920 - d.10Feb1981. Cancer. Son: Thomas C. Lund, Vancouver, WA. HMFH. Int. 12Feb1981 - Space S25-2. (w/Calvin)
HULL	Clarence E. "Father" b.4Feb1908 - d.9Jul1978. Wife: Marguerite Hull, Vancouver, WA. Int. 12Jul1978 - Space N-83-2. (w/Marguerite)
HULL	Marguerite "Top". "Mother" 1919 - ____ . (w/Clarence)
HUNNEL	John L. b.31Oct1909 - d.29Sep1977. Wife: Leona M. Hunnel, Camas, WA. Straub's F.H., Camas. Int. 20Oct1977, Maus. G.S. Tier 1 - Sp. 8.
HUNT	Amon Lee. Pvt. U.S. Army/Korea. b.8Apr1934 - d.22Sep1975. Wife: Helen Hunt, Vancouver, WA. Evergreen F.H. Int. Space S-53-6.
HUMPHREYS	Harold A. b.6Oct1906 - d.14Apr1982. Wife: Catherine Humphreys, Vancouver, WA. VFC. Int. 16Apr1982 - Space N31-5.

IRWIN | Rose E. b.12Mar1888 - d.26Oct1970. Son: Roy Irwin, Battle Ground, WA. HMFC. Int. MMP Space S-73-5.

IRWIN | Steve W. b.14May1956 - d.9May1982. Father: Roy Irwin, Portland, OR. VFC. Int. 22May1982 - Space S-73-4.

JAGGERS | Woodford P. WA. Pvt. 616 Fld. Arty. Bn. WWII. b.20Nov1915 - d.31Dec1972. Wife: Mary Jaggers. VFC. Int. Space S-92-6.

JAMISON | Edith M. b.18Oct1920 - d.2Jun1984. Husband: David W. Jameson, Vancouver, WA. MGFC. Interred 6Jun1984, Space S-49-8.

JARVIS | Blanche E. 1896 - _____

JARVIS | George C. "Together Forever" b.24Feb1893 - d.5Jul1979. Wife: Blanche Jarvis, Vancouver, WA. VFC. Int. 7Jul1979, Space N-53-3 Vet.

JASMER | Theodore. b.13Jul1919 - d.20Feb.1976. Wife: Margaret Jasmer, Battle Ground, WA. LBGFH. Interred 24Feb1976, Space N-18-1.

JASPER | Gene Francis. (Age 64. b.1Dec1919, Cottonwood, WA. - d.23Jun1984, Vancouver, WA. Funeral Wed., 27Jun1984, at Memorial Gardens Funeral Chapel. Interment at MMP. Obit - The Columbian) Space N-150-3.

JASPER | Velma E. b.7Oct1917 - d.24Nov1979. Husband: Gene Jasper, Vancouver, WA. VFC. Interred 28Nov1979, Space N-150-4.

JODZEWICZ | Adam P. b.11Jan1898 - d.17Jan1979. Wife: Catherine S. Jodzewicz, Vancouver, WA. Hamilton-Mylan F.H. Cremains Int. 23Jan1979, Maus. G.S. Tier 6, Niche 7.

JODZEWICZ | Catherine S. (Age 74. b20Oct1908, Walden, NY. - d.23May1983, Vancouver, WA. Funeral Thurs., 26May1983, at Hamilton-Mylan F.H. Entombment at MMP. Obit - The Columbian)

JOHANSON | Robert. b.7Jun1898 - d.28Jul1980. Wife: Martha Johanson, Vancouver, WA. ESFH. Int. 30Jul1980, Space S-191-4.

JOHNS | Glen M., Sr. b.1899 - d.4Feb1958. Wife: Grace Johns, Ridgefield, WA. HMFH. Int. MMP, Space S-130-1.

JOHNSON | Albert E.-WW2- b.17 Apr.1921,Brockett,S.D. wife,Marilyn, sons;Tim of Ridgefield,Carol of Brush Prairie,Wa. John of Marengo,Wi. stepsons;Joseph Pegoraro

256

of Arlington Heights, IL; James Pegoraro, of Yacolt, and Jeffrey Pegoraro, of Vancouver. Daughters: Starla Johnson, Yacolt; Tina Johnson, Redding, CA; Cora Kysat, of Hayti, SD; Sue Johnson, of Pahrump, NV; and Mona Kitto, of Astoria, OR. Brother: Benhart Johnson, Minneapolis. Sisters: Saima Acosta, Grand Forks, ND; Elma Sween, St. Louis Park, MN. Funeral Monday, 3Mar1986, at the Old Apostolic Lutheran Church, in Brush Prairie. Layne's Battle Ground Funeral Home Chapel. Burial in MMP. Obit - The Columbian.

JOHNSON	A. Ruth. 1906 - ____

JOHNSON — Alvin R. (Age 64. b.1May1919, Kulm, ND - d.14Feb1984, Vancouver, WA. Res: Ridgefield, WA. Husband of Edith J. Johnson, Ridgefield. Funeral Saturday, 18Feb1984, at Mt. View Christian Center, Ridgefield, WA. Interment at MMP. Obit - The Columbian) ESFH. Int. Lot 226-2, Devotion.

JOHNSON — Elmer J. "Takk For Alt" b.26Jun1901 - d.3Apr1974. Wife: Ruth Johnson. VFC. Int. Space S-134-2.

JOHNSON — Forrest H. SP3 U.S. Army. b.11Sep1933 - d.22Aug1974. Wife: Betty Johnson, Vancouver, WA. VFC. Int. Space S-133-2.

JOHNSON — Glen M. 1899 - 1958

JOHNSON — Grace E. 1899 - ____

JOHNSON — Wendy Melinda Edith. (Age 1-1/2. b.20Aug1982, Ridgefield, WA. - d.11Mar1984, Ridgefield, WA. Daughter of Wendall and Phyllis Johnson, Ridgefield. Funeral Wed., 14Mar1984, at Mt. View Christian Center. Interment at MMP. Evergreen Staples F.C. Obit - The Columbian) Space S-227-3.

JOHNSTON — Bradley F. b.16Nov1906 - d.19Feb1979. Father: Boyd F. Johnston, Anchorage, AK. Mother: Connie Tedder, Brush Prairie, WA. LBGFH. Interred 23Feb1979, Space N-43-5, Chimes.

JOHNSTON — Leland S. Age 12 Hours. b.8Sep1975 - d.8Sep1975. Mother: Nancy Johnston, Vancouver, WA. EFC. Int. Space S-60-5, Devotion.

KASKI — Esther Alexandria. (Age 78. b.27Jun1909, Clatskanie, OR. - d.15Oct1987. Res: Battle Ground, WA. Funeral Monday, 19Oct1987, at Old Apostolic Lutheran Church. Burial in Memory Memorial Park. LBGFH. Obit - The Columbian)

KATZENMEYER — John M. (Age 65. b.28Apr1918, Sanger, CA. - d.29Feb1984, Portland, OR. Res: Vancouver, WA. Husband of Delia, at home. Graveside service Monday,

5Mar1984, at MMP. Hamilton-Mylan F.H. Obit - The Columbian) Int. Space N-147-4 Ch.

KELLEY   William "Bill" Munroe. (Muroe?) (Age 77. d.29Dec1986. Res: Battle Ground, WA. Widow: Netti Kelley. Sons: John Kelley, Vancouver; Bill Kelley, Olympia, WA. Brother: Al Henderson, Overton, NV. Graveside Service Friday, 2Jan1987, at Memory Memoria Park. Layne's Battle Ground Funeral Home. Obits - The Reflector and The Columbian)

KELLY   Richard Guerrero Fulcher. (Age 20. b.4Feb1965, Tacoma, WA. - d. 27Oct1985, Sun City, CA. Formerly c Camas, Washougal area. Father and Step-mother: Richard and Joan Kelly, Vancouver; Mother and Step-father: Estella and Larry Fulcher, Sun City, CA Services Wed., 6Nov1985, at the Washougal Church of Christ. Interment at Memory Memorial Park. Brown's Funeral Home. Obit - The Columbian)

KENNEDY   Betty Ruth. b.24May1928 - d.23Feb1977. Next of Kin: James Wilson and John Wilson, both of Vancouver, WA. EFC. Int. 25Feb1977, MMP, Space N-95-3.

KING   Jimmy Dean. b.1957 - d.3Jun1972. Father: Truman King, Battle Ground, WA. LBGFH. Int. 8Jun1972, MMP, Space N-234-3.

KIRKPATRICK   Jeffrey Carr. b.1969 - d.14Jan1972. Father: George Carr Kirkpatrick, Vancouver, WA. VFC. Int. 19Jan1972, Space S-74-2, Christus.

KITTLESON   Ericka Sonja. "The Lord Is My Shepherd" b.28Aug1970 - d.18Jul1972. Father: Raymond Kittleson, Vancouver WA. VFC. Int. 20Jul1972, Space S-222-1, Devotion.

KITTLESON   Oscar S. b.1890 - d.9Jan1971. son: Raymond Kittleson, Vancouver, WA. VFC. Cremains Interred 12Jul1971, Space S-221-1.

KNAPP   Ana. b.17Aug1926 - d.10Oct1977. Husband: Daniel Knapp, Vancouver, WA. Dory, Mary and Sarah Knapp. Hamilton-Mylan F.H. Int. 5Oct1977, MMP, Space N-257-2, Chimes.

KNAUSS   Frank A. 1895 - 1968. Son: Ronald Knauss, Vancouver, WA. Interred 2Oct1968 - Memory Memorial Park, Space N-7-4, Chimes.

KNAUSS   Ruby M. b.2Dec1891 - d.8Mar1980. Son: Ronald Knauss. VFC. Int. 12Mar1980, MMP, Space N-67-1, Chimes.

KNIGHT Roscoe. b.1901 - d.15Jan1976. Wife: Stella Knight, Brush Prairie, WA. LBGFH. Int. 20Jan1976, MMP, Space N-137-7.

KNIGHT Stella. 1906 - 19__

KOSTMAN Carl A. "Together Forever" b.8Nov1916 - d.12Dec1980. Wife: Bernice, Vancouver, WA. VFC. Int. 16Dec1980, Space N-87-7. (w/Bernice)

KOSTMAN Bernice V. "Together Forever" 1916 - ____ (w/Carl A.)

KRAUCHE Martha F. b.1911 - d.10Nov1971. Husband: Rudolf Krauche, Battle Ground, WA. LBGFH. Int. 12Nov1971, Space S-170-6, Devotion.

KRAUCHE Rudolf. 1902 - ____

KRUEGER Marguerite D. (b.9Feb1901, Illinois - d.16Jul1986, Vancouver, WA. Funeral Friday, 18Jul1986, at Layne's Funeral Home Chapel. Entombment in Memory Memorial Park. Obit - The Columbian)

LA BRANCHE Arthur G. b.1902 - d.13Oct1975. Wife: Evelyn, Vancouver, WA. Int. MMP, Space S-19-6, Christus. (w/Evelyn)

LA BRANCHE Evelyn. b.21Nov1908 - d.13Sep1980. Son: Donald Calahan, Portland, OR. VFC. Int. 17Sep1980, Space S-19-5, Christus. (w/Arthur)

LAMKIN Glenn W. (Age 64. b.2Sep1919, Sheldon, IA. - d.23Jan1984, Port Elizabeth, South Africa. Res: Vancouver, WA. Husband of Dorothy P. Lamkin, at home. Services Wed., 8Feb1984, at Vancouver Funeral Chapel. Interment in Memory Memorial Park. Obit - The Columbian) Space N-33-7.

LAMPERT Andrew Clifford. "Our Baby" b.22May1978 - d.24Jan1979. Parents: Richard and Lisa Lampert. HMFH. Cremains Interred 2Feb1979, MMMP, Space S-138-6.

LARRABEE Elsie E. (Age 62. b.3Nov1920, Menominee, MI. - d.17Mar1983, Vancouver, WA. Son: Sidney Larrabee, LaCenter, WA. Mass of Christian Burial Monday, 21Mar1983, at St. James Catholic Church. Interment at MMP. Hamilton-Mylan F.H. Obit - The Columbian) Space S-75-1.

LARRABEE Sidney. b.15May1911 - d.14Sep1976. Wife: Elsie Larrabee. Int. 17Sep1976, Space S-75-2.

MEMORY MEMORIAL PARK

LESTER Jesse B. (Age 85. b.25Jul1898, Kingston, MO. -
d.27Apr1984, Vancouver, WA. Res: Clark County, WA
Husband of Sarah, at home. Funeral Tuesday, 1May198
at Faith Church of the Nazarene of Battle Ground.
Burial in Memory Memorial Park. Layne's Funeral Hor
Obit - The Columbian) Space N-90-1.

LEVANEN Luke Ovid. (Newborn ((Premature)) b.10Jun1984 -
d.10Jun1984, Portland, OR. Son of Paul and Karrie
Levanen, Kalispell, MT. Grandmother: Esther A.
Kaski, Vancouver, WA. Graveside services Wed.,
13Jun1984, at Memory Memorial Park. Layne's F.H.
Obit - The Columbian) Space S-39-5, at foot of Herr
Kaski.

LEWIS Bonolynn L. b.5Mar1903 - d.5Nov1974. Son: Lawrenc
Quina, Washougal, WA. Straub-Swank F.H., Camas, WA.
Int. Space N-54-5 Vet.

LEWIS Faye M. "Together Forever" b.22Sep1920 -
d.19Dec1980. Daughter: Marcia Clifton, Portland, C
ESFH. Int. 23Dec1980, Space N-195-2 (w/Perry)

LEWIS James P. b.26Sep1957 - d.28Mar1974, Portland, OR.
Father: James Patton Lewis. LBGFH. Space S-169-1.

LEWIS Leslie E. b.1898 - d.6Mar1973. Wife: Bonolyn Lewi
Vancouver, WA. VFC. Int. 10Mar1973, Space N-54-4
Vet.

LEWIS Perry C. "Together Forever" b.4Feb1907 -
d.27Nov1976. Wife: Faye M., Vancouver, WA. EFH.
Int. 30Nov1976, Space N-195-1 (w/Faye)

LILLY M. Louise. (Age 55. b.19Jul1931, Vancouver, WA -
d.6Jun1987, Vancouver, WA. Preceded in death by her
mother, Nell Albinson, in January, 1987. Widower:
George R. Lilly, at home. Son: Kevin Lilly, Fort
Devens, MA. Daughters: Georgeine Myers and Jeanine
Lilly, both of Vancouver. Grand-daughter: Shawna
Myers, Vancouver. Brother: James Albinson, Ocean
Park, WA. Interment in MMP. Vancouver F.C. Obit -
The Columbian)

LINCOLN Dorothy R. "Aho" b.21Nov1920 - d.25Oct1977. Sons:
James D. Lincoln, Camas, WA.; Jeffery Aho, Vancouver
WA. Daughters: Audrey Dukes Berry and Patricia
Lincoln, Vancouver. EFC. Int. 29Oct1977, Space
S-234-7.

LONG Oren G. (Age 50. Cancer. b.10Dec1936, Sheridan, W
- d.21May1987, Fort Lupton, CO. Res: Fort Lupton,
CO. Widow: Amelia, at home. Son: Paul Long, Fort
Lupton. Stepsons: Darrell Coles, Vancouver and Ran
Coles, San Antonio, TX. Daughter: Carol Long, Fort

Lupton, CO. Brother: Gerald, Fort Lupton. Sister: Mary Taylor, La Center, WA. Service: Wed., 27May1987, at Memorial Gardens F.C. Burial in Memory Memorial Park. Obit - The Columbian)

LONG   Thelma H. b.18Dec1907 - d.25Aug1987. Husband: Walter Long. Woodland F.H. Interred 27Aug1987, Maus. Tier 6, Crypt 13.

LONG   Walter O. (Age 81. b.6Jun1902, Green Castle, MO. - d. 10Oct1983, Vancouver, WA. Res: LaCenter, WA. Son: Orin Long, Woodland, WA. Cryptside service Tuesday, 11Oct1983, at Memory Memorial Park. MGM. Obit - The Columbian) Maus. Tier 6 - Crypt 12.

MADARA   Pauline R. b.9Oct1910 - _____ (w/Orien)

MADARA   Orien B. b.23Jul1909 - d.13Jan1977. Int. 17Jan1977. HMFH. Space S-148-2. (w/Pauline R.)

MAGNUSSON   Ruth S. "Beloved Mother & Sister" b.1905 - d.1Jul1969. Son: Joe Solbert, Yakima, WA. VFC. Int. 3Jul1969, Space N-83-6.

MAHAR   Catherine M. b.18Aug1903 - d.23Oct1983. Son: Robert Mericle, Vancouver, WA. ESFH. Int. 27Oct1983, Maus. Tier 11, Niche 14.

MANLEY   Henry. b.1882 - d.20Sep1958. Wife: Sylvia. VFC. Int. Space N-66-1. (w/Sylvia)

MANLEY   Sylvia. b.1893 - d.14Jul1972. Son: Henry Manley, Jr., Portland, OR. LBGFH. Int. 17Jul1972, Space N-66-2. (w/Henry)

MARCH   Lulu B. "Mother" b.1888 - d.24Jul1970. Daughter: Florence Frazier, Portland, OR. LBGFH. Int. 28Jul1907, Space N-84-1.

MARTIN   Alvina L. 1901 - _____

MARTIN   Daniel "Together Forever" b.1896 - d.24Aug1970 Wife: Alvina Martin, Battle Ground, WA. VFC. Int. Space S-96-6

MASHMEYER   Velma G. "Mother" In Loving Memory" Age 70. d.29Dec1970. Daughter: Mrs. Roland Fields, Vancouver, WA. EFC. Int. 31Dec1970, Space N-294-4. (w/Lola M. Meyer)

MASON   Jeannette Rae. b.3Oct1963 - d.5Mar1981. Mother: Sharon Mason, Vancouver, WA. ESFH. Int. 12Mar1981, Space N-38-5.

MATTOX Beverly N. "Mother" b.1926 - d.16Jul1964. Husband: LeRoy Mattox, Vancouver, WA. VFC. Int. 18Jul1964, Space S-71-2.

MAULDING Clyde W. TSgt U.S. Army/WWII. b.11Apr1898 - d.20Feb1976. Wife: Hazel, Vancouver, WA., Son: David, Battle Ground, WA. EFH. Int. Space N-47-1.

MAXWELL Glen LeRoy. b.12Jul1913 - d.16Aug1980. Brother: Vern Maxwell, Vancouver, WA. Brown's Stoller F.C., Camas, WA. Int. 20Aug1980, Space S-90-4.

MAXWELL Ruby R. (Age 69. b.4Mar1915, Hubbard, OR. - d.1Dec1984, Portland, OR. Res: Vancouver, WA. Wife of Vernie Maxwell, at home. Funeral Tuesday, 4Dec1984, at Zion Lutheran Church. Interment at Memory Memorial Park. Brown's Stoller Memorial Chapel. Obit - The Columbian)

MAYES Joseph W. "Father" b.1900 - d.8May1967. Brother: Frank Knauss. VFC. Int. Space N-7-1.

MAYES Lucille J. "Mother" b.1895 - d.25Feb1965. Brother: R. L. Gaines. VFC. Int. 27Feb1964, Space N-5-3.

MAYES Rose M. (Age 83. b.3Jan1901, Vancouver, WA. - d.2Apr1984,, at home, Vancouver. Daughter: Josephine "Jodi" Dilley. No funeral service. Interment in Memory Memorial Park. VFC. Obit - The Columbian)

MAYNE Arthur S. b.1898 - d.8Sep1960. Wife: Helen Mayne. Daughter: Joyce Baker. First buried in CA. then transferred to M.M. Cremaines. Int. Space S-36-8.

MAYNE Helen E. (Age 77. b.12Sep1908, Globe AZ. - d.3Mar1986, Napa, CA. Res: Vancouver, WA. Sons: Arthur, Los Alamos, NM; Robert of Lumas, CA. Daughters: Joyce Baker, Vancouver; Jean Barker, Napa, CA. Sister: Evelyn Ollson, Woodland, WA. Graveside service Friday, 7Mar1986 at Memory Memorial Park. LBGFH. Obit - The Columbian)

MC CLANAHAN Clifford M. U.S. Army/WWII. b.23Aug1906 - d.29Dec1978. Wife: Elaine McClanahan, Vancouver, WA. Layne's Battle Ground Funeral Home. Int. 17Jan1979, Cre. S-3-3.

MC CORD L. Joy 1927 - _____

MC CORD Roy M. b.3Mar1925 - d.15Oct1977. Wife: L. Joy McCord, Vancouver, WA. Son: Kevin McCord, Vancouver. HMFH. Int. 20Oct1977 - Space S-113-1. Cremains. (w/L. Joy)

MC DERMOTT Charles T., Jr. 1943 - 19679

MC DERMOTT	Charles, Jr. Age 26. d.20Nov1969. Wife: Linda McDermott. Father: Charles McDermott, Sr., Vancouver. VFC. Int. 25Nov1969 - Space S-115-8.
MC GEE	Shawn Marie. "Daughter - Sister - Our Eternal Love - The Lord Is My Shepherd" b.21Sep1964 - d.7Feb1976. Father: Richard McGee. VFC. Int. 10Feb1976 - Space N-92-1.
MC KINNEY	Howard C. b.27Apr1888 - d.9Mar1975. Wife: Leina E. McKinney. Step-Daughter: Mrs. Adam Bassel, LaCenter, WA. LBGFH. Int. - Space S-99-5.
MC KINNEY	Leina E. b20Jun1886 - d.11Nov1978. LBGFH. Int. 14Nov1978 - Space S-99-4.
MEISNER	Jack. b.2Aug1931 - d.4Nov1976. Parents: Mr. and Mrs. John Meisner, Centralia, WA. LBGFH. Maus. Row 3 - Crypt 9.
MEISNER	John David. (Age 77. Heart failure. b.4Jun1908, Kamaiah, ID - d.25Dec1985. Widow: Mae Meisner, at home, Vancouver, WA. Brothers: Bill and Ernest Meisner, Kamiah, ID; Fred Meisner, Creswell, OR. Sisters: Cann Day, Margaret Knight, Hillsboro, OR. Entombment at Memory Memorial Park. Funeral Sat., 28Dec1985, United Methodist Church, Battle Ground. Layne's F.H. Obit - The Reflector.)
METZENBERG	Violet F. (Age 67. b.15Mar1919, Northport, WA. - d.12Jun1986. Sons: Herb L. Kendrick and H. Ray Kendrick, both of Vancouver, WA. Brother: Dallas Johnson, of Spokane, WA. Graveside service Monday, 16Jun1986, at Memory Memorial Park. VFC. Obit - The Columbian)
MEYER	Lola M. b.13Jul1898 - d.29Oct1974. Niece - Mrs. Rae Fields, Vancouver, WA. EFC. Int. 1Nov1974, Space N-294-2. (w/Velma G. Mashmayer)
MILLER	Angela Louise. b.21Mar1979 - d.21Mar1979. Parents: Mr. and Mrs. David Miller, Vancouver, WA. Grandparents: Mr. and Mrs. Jerry Gaul, Vancouver. VFH. Int. 1May 1979, Maus. Tier 4, Niche 12.
MILLER	Clarence F., Sr. d. 11Aug1972. Son: Clarence, Jr., Vancouver, WA. VFC. Int. 15Aug1972, Space S-15-2.
MILLER	Edna 1901 - ____
MILLER	Gladys Lucille. (Age 68. b.30Nov1915, Parsons, KS. - d.10Jun1984, Vancouver, WA. Wife of Henry A., at home. No service. Entombment in Memory Memorial Park. Obit - The Columbian)

MILLER   Horace A.   d.6Oct1971. Wife: Edna Miller, Vancouver, WA. VFC. Int. 8Oct1971 - Space S-161-2.

MILLER   Luther G., Sr. d.11Mar1972. Wife: Lillian Miller, Vancouver, WA. VFC. Int. 15Mar1972 - Space N-132-8.

MILLER   Ruby C. d.17Oct1971. Husband: Clarence Miller, Vancouver. Son: Clarence Miller, Jr. VFC. Int. 2ØOct1971 - Space S-15-1.

MITCHAM   Kerry J. b.24Jan1956 - d.21Jun198Ø. Parents: Mr. and Mrs. Robert Mitcham, Vancouver, WA. VFC. Int. 25Jun198Ø - Space N-70-1.

MONDA   Charles L. d.16Jan1973. Wife: Nadine P. Monda, Vancouver, WA. VFC. Int. 19Jan1973 - Space S-135-2.

MONEN   John Herman. d.18Feb1966. Step-father: George Sellinger, Ridgefield, WA. VFC. Int. 24Feb1966 - Space N-5-4.

MOORE   Elmer C. b.14Apr1911 - d.27Aug1982. Daughter: Betty Ellis, Vancouver, WA. Int. 3ØAug1982 - Space N-58-8 Vet.

MOORE   Louise Amanda. (Age 47. b.18Dec1937, Braddock, ND - d.7Feb1985, Vancouver, WA. Wife of Bill Gene Moore, at home. Funeral Sat., 9Feb1985, at Old Apostolic Lutheran Church. Interment at MMP. VFC. Obit - The Columbian) Int. space N-94-8.

MOORIS   Goldie V. b.17Apr19Ø9 - d.28May198Ø. Son: James Mondabough, Polk City, IA. Straub's F.H., Camas, WA. Int. 31May198Ø - Space S-21Ø-1.

MOORMAN   Louise W. (Age 88. b.17Jul1898, Westpoint, NB - d.22Feb1987, Vancouver, WA. Res: Vancouver. Son: Lloyd Englebert, Vancouver. Daughters: Helen Borcherding and Doris Wilde, both of Vancouver. Brother: Les Willms, of Camas, WA. Sisters: Hanna Ruge and Mable Schweers, both of Vancouver. Burial Memory Memorial Park. Funeral service Wed., 25Feb1987, at VFC. Obit - The Columbian.)

MOORMAN   William F. d. 5Mar1967. Daughter: Mrs. Stanley Borcherding. VFC. Int. Space N-71-4.

MORGAN   Harriett Ann. (Age 57. Heart failure. b.21Apr193Ø, Champaign, IL. - d.6May1987, Vancouver, WA. Res: Vancouver. Widower: Jerry L. Morgan, at home. Mother: Grace Van Deventer, Champaign, IL. Sons: Bruce A. Swiger, Vancouver, and Steven R. Swiger, Scappoose, OR. Stepsons: Kevin Morgan, of Brush Prairie and John Morgan of Battle Ground. Daughter: Lisa Keller, Portland, OR. Stepdaughter, Lynne Fey of

Battle Ground. Brother: James Van Deventer, Champaign, IL. Sister: Mary Barker, Orlando, FL. Preceded in death by a daughter: Judy, in 1969. Funeral Sat., 9May1987 at VFC. Burial MMP. Obit - The Columbian)

MORRIS	Kathleen "Together Forever" 1902 - ____ Space N-94-8. (w/William Max)
MORRIS	William Max. b.17Sep1899 - d.16Sep1980 Wife: Cathleen M. Morris, Vancouver, WA. ESFC. Int. 20Sep1980 - Space 173-4.
MORROW	Bertha Mae LaVerne "Bert". (Age 62. b.26Jul1923, Vancouver, WA. - d.20Nov1985, Vancouver. Wife of James Edmund, at home. Graveside services Saturday, 23Nov1985, at MMP. VFC. Obit - The Columbian)
MOSBRUKER	Raphael J. (Age 68. b.18Jun1914, Glen Ullin, ND. - d.12May1983, Goldendale, WA. Res: Vancouver, WA. Husband of Lena K. Mosbrucker, at home. Mass of Christian Burial Wed., 18May1983, at Our Lady of Lourdes Church. Interment in MMP. Hamilton-Mylan F.H. Obit - The Columbian) Space S-67-4.
MOURTON	Mary Emma. b.29Jul1925 - d.18Jul1974. Daughter: Mata Mae Mourton, Battle Ground, WA. LBGFH. Space N-149-7.
MOURTON	Robert H. "For Everything You Have Missed, You Have Gained Something Else." b.19Jul1952 - d.11Nov1977. Wife: Ruth Mourton, Battle Ground, WA. Grandmother: Mrs. Meta Reick. LBGFH. Int. 15Nov1977, Space N-149-8.
MOYER	Gertrude E. (Age 67. b.26Aug1915, in Minnesota - d.9Jan1983, Vancouver, WA. Son: Elwood Moyer, Vancouver. Graveside service Wed., 12Jan1983, at Memory Memorial Park. VFC. Obit - The Columbian.Int. Space N-142-2.
MOYER	Leonard A. b.7Jan1903 - d.24May1982. Wife: Gertrude E. Moyer. VFC. Int. 27May1982 - Space N-142-1.
MULLEN	Clifford A. b.25Jun1921 - d.2Apr1983. Sister: Mrs. Herbert Paige (Lola), Vancouver, WA. ESFC. Int. 5Apr1983 - Space S-168-5.
MULLEN	Lola M. b.11Mar1899 - d.6Jan1974. Brother: Clifford A. Mullen, Vancouver, WA. EFH. Int. space S-168-6.
NAPPIER	Robert L. U.S. Army/WWII. b.28Oct1911 - d.16Nov1979. Wife: Irene Nappier, Vancouver, WA. VFC. Int. 19Nov1975 - Space N-118-1 Vets.

NATHO — Coral. b.24Mar1941 - d.24Oct1969. Parent: Clyde Wilhelm, Battle Ground, WA. LBGFH. Int. Space N-172-1

NELSON — Adelaide E. b.14Jul1903 - d.28Nov1981. Daughter: Earle O. Baird, Vancouver, WA. HMFH. Ashes Int. 22Dec1981 - Maus.Tier 17, Niche 13.

NELSON — Anna K. ____ - ____ (w/Chester D.)

NELSON — Benjamin M. b.1885 - d.13Nov1964. Wife: Elizabeth, Vancouver, WA. LBGFH. Int. Space N-11-3.

NELSON — Beverly Jo. "Wife & Mother - Psalm 49:15 - But God Will Redeem My Soul From the Power of the Grave, for He Shall Receive Me." b.20Jan1953 - d.19Mar1981. Husband: Edward R. Nelson, Vancouver, WA. Int. 23Mar1981 - Space S-82-3.

NELSON — Chester D. "Together Forever" b.1892 - d.23Mar1970. Wife: Anna K., Vancouver, WA. VFC. Int. 25Mar1970 - Space S-181-5.

NELSON — Denver C. b.22Jan1909 - d.15Oct1982. Brother: Charles Nelson, Battle Ground, WA. Chapel of Chimes, Portland, OR. Maus. Tier 6, Niche 14.

NELSON — Elizabeth M. b.25Aug1887 - d.13Nov1971. Son: Charles Nelson, Battle Ground, WA. LBGFH. Space N-11-4. (w/Benjamin)

NEWKIRK — Jesse L. "Pete". (Age 74. Cancer. b.16Nov1912, Giltedge, MT - d.18Jun1987. Res: Vancouver, WA. Husband of Irma, at home. Graveside service Tues., 23Jun1987, at MMP. ESFC. Obit - The Columbian)

NEWTON — Clayton Dale. d.1965 29Jan1969. Parent: Chester Newton. Int. Space N-184-7 - Babyland.

NEWTON — Clifford B. "Our Son" 3Jun1963. Father: Chester Newton, Battle Ground, WA. VFC.

NEWTON — James W. "Our Son - May You Find Peace And Rest" b.4Apr1958 - 1Jan1975. Parents: Mr. and Mrs. Robert S. Newton, Vancouver, WA. HMFH. Int. MMP - Space S-79-6.

NEWTON — Ima Sue Callahan. (Age 54. Cancer. b.8Apr1933, Washington, AR. - d.25Jul1987, Vancouver, WA. Res: Vancouver, WA. Service Tuesday, 28Jul1987, at Evergreen Staples Funeral Chapel. Burial in Memory Memorial Park. Obit - The Columbian)

NICELY

Hugh G. b.1Apr1908 - d.1Mar1977. Wife: Viola Nicely, Battle Ground, WA. LBGFH. Int. 4Mar1977 - Space N-98-5.

NICELY

Viola F. 1911 - ____

NOVARIA

Frieda F. b.11Dec1914 - d.29Apr1981. Husband: John B. Novaria, Underwood, WA. Gardner Funeral Home, White Salmon, WA. Int. 22May1981 - Cremains - Maus. G.S. Tier 11, Niche 11.

NOVOTNY

Danny N. b.21May1983 - d.21May1983. Mother: Rena Novotny, Camas, WA. Ashes Int. 27Jun1983, Maus. G.S. Tier 4, Niche 8.

OATES

Frank E. (Age 82. b.1Jan1903, Butte, MT. - d.22Mar1985, Vancouver, WA. Res: Battle Ground, WA. Service Tuesday, 26Mar1985, at Vancouver Funeral Chapel. Interment in Memory Memorial Park. Obit - The Columbian) Space N-7-4.

OATES

Marie M. b.25Oct1899 - d.24Oct1981. Husband: Frank E. Oates, Vancouver, WA. VFC. Int. 29Oct1981, Space N-73.

OSBAN

Ivy R. (Age 94. b.8Mar1891, Mildrum, KY. - d.28Nov1985, Battle Ground, WA. Res: Battle Ground. Funeral Tuesday, 3Dec1985, at Layne's Battle Ground Funeral Home Chapel. Interment in Memory Memorial Park. Obit - The Columbian) "Together Forever" (w/John K.)

OSBAN

John K. "Together Forever" b.1880 - d.3Feb1971. Wife: Ivy, Vancouver, WA. Son: Fred Osban. LBGFH. Int. Space N-169-7 Vet. (w/Ivy)

OSBORN

Lee B. "Together Forever" b.1895 - d.7Jun1970. Wife: Winnefred Osborn, Vancouver, WA. Daughter: Leona Stillman, Vancouver. VFC. Int. Space N-30-4.

OWENS

Ethel. b.21Feb1911 - d.10Jun1975. Husband: J. W. Owens, Woodland, WA. HMFH. Int. 13Jun1975 - Space S-176-3.

OWENS

J. W. "Bill" "Father" 1912 - ____ (w/Ethel)

PANTING

Frank L. b.13Nov.1900 - d.29Sep1982. Memorial Gardens F.C. Int. 2Oct1982 - Space N-174-2.

PAPENFUSE

Ola A. 1903 - ____

PAPENFUSE

William R. "Together Forever" b.1888 - d.15Jan1971. Wife: Ola Papenfuse. VFC. Int. 19Jan1971 - Space N-17-7.

PARKER   Marguarite E. b.17Jan1907 - d.8Jun1971. Husband: Sterling Parker, Vancouver, WA. VFC. Int. Space N-192-3.

PARKER   Ralph G. "In Memory Of" 1927 - 1959 (Not interred)

PARKER   Sterling M. "In Memory Of" 1929 - 1978 (Not interred)

PARKER   Sterling, Sr. (Age 80. b.20Dec1903, Fairmont, OK. - d.17Aug1984, Vancouver, WA. Memorial Service Tuesday, 21Aug1984, at VFC. Interment Memory Memorial Park. Obit - The Columbian) Cremains Int. 6Dec1984 at head of grave - Space N-192-2.

PAULEY   Arthur E. (Age 78. b.2Dec1905, in Maine - d.8Aug1984, Portland, OR. Res: Vancouver, WA. Husband of Oneta Pauley, Vancouver. Funeral Monday, 13Aug1984, at Evergreen Staples Funeral Chapel. Interment at Memory Memorial Park. Obit - The Columbian)

PETTERSON   Andrew. b.12Oct1908 - d.26Nov1976. Brother: Walter Anderson, Vancouver, WA. MGFC. Int. 30Nov1976 - Space S-196-2.

PETTERSON   Margaret A. (Age 89. Parkinson's disease. b.21Oct1897, Chicago, IL. - d.15Apr1987, Battle Ground, WA. Res: Battle Ground. Sons: Chester Snell, Wofford Heights, CA. and O. Robert Snell, Fair Oaks, CA. Daughter: Shirley Schey,, Vancouver. Sister: Sarah Huibregste, Omaha, NE. Funeral Saturday, 18Apr1987, at Layne's Funeral Home Chapel. Private entombment in Memory Memorial Park. Obit - The Columbian)

PETRIE   Laura Helen. 1908 - ____

PETRIE   William M. b.1894 - d.22Jul1971. Wife: Laura Petrie. Space N-267-1.

PHELPS   Ada S. (Age 82. b.22Sep1903, Andersonville, TN. - d.9Mar1986, Vancouver, WA. Res: Camas, WA. Sons: Ernest Warwick and Atlas Green, both of Camas, WA. Daughter: Karen Richaards, Washougal, WA. Brother: Sylvester Warwick, of Snohomish, WA. Sisters: Elzada Murray, of Camas, and Theresa Patrick, of Hinton, WV. Funeral Wed., 12Mar1986, at Brown's Funeral Home, Camas, WA. Burial in Memory Memorial Park. Obit - The Columbian)

PHELPS   Ada S. ____ - ____ (w/Augustus E.)

PHELPS   Augustus E. b.23Dec1909 - d.16Jul1980. Wife: Ada Phelps, Camas, WA. Brown's F.H., Camas. Int. 19Jul1980 - Space S-180-4.

PICKEN   Charles E. 1884 - 1936 (?)   Interred 26Feb1966, Space N-3-1. Mrs. Cecil Graves, Amboy, WA.

PICKEN   Ida M. b.1887 - d.18Feb1966. Layne's Battle Ground Funeral Home. Int. Space N-3-2. Mrs. Cecil Graves, Amboy, WA.

PIERCE   Doris H. "In Loving Memory Of My Wife" b.7Nov1934 - d.23Apr1978. Husband: Donald D. Pierce, Vancouver, WA. EFH. 6Apr1978 - Space S-172-1.

PIFER   Fred. b.14Oct1886 - d.24Apr1977. LBGFH. Int. 28Apr1977 - Space N-77-7.

PIFER   Vesta L. b.1894 - d.21Apr1973. Husband: Fred Pifer, Battle Ground, WA. LBGFH. Int. 24Apr1973 - Space N-77-8.

PORTER   Sgt. Dennis Lee. "In Memory Of - In Thee I Have Put My Trust" b.3Apr1958 - d.18Jan1980. Parents: Kenneth R. and Gladys M. Porter, Vancouver, WA. ESFH. Int. 22Jan1980 - Space S-214-3.

PRATHER   Randall Lee. b.5Dec1954 - d.18Jan1978. Wife: Deborah Prather, Yacolt, WA. Parents: Mr. and Mrs. Lee Prather, Yacolt. Int. 20Jan1978 - Space S-161-6.

PUNKO   Nellie M. (Also under Nellie M. BENEDICT) b.27May1903 - d.6May1977. Husband: John Punko, Vancouver, WA. LBGFH. Int. - Space N-82-2.

PURDY   Billie Agnus. 1904 - _____

PURDY   Stephen H. b.18Jun1898 - d.26Aug1964. Wife: Billie A. Purdy, Vancouver, WA. VFC. Int. - Space N-127-3.

QUIRK   Elsie B.   "Together Forever"   1911 - 19__ (w/J. Donald)

QUIRK   J. Donald. "Together Forever" b.8Jun1905 - d.14Jun1972. Wife: Elsie, Battle Ground, WA. LBGFH. Int. - Space S-117-8.

RANCORE   Harvey L. "Husband"   1914 - 1978

RANCORE   Mabel E.   1924 - _____

RANDOLPH   Magdalene F. 1916 - 1974

RAYMOND   Gloria M.   "Together Forever"   b.15Jan1921 - d.27Feb1981.   Husband: C. "Chuck" Russell, Vancouver, WA.   VFC.   Int. 3Mar1981 - Space N-152-4.

RAYMOND   C. Russell.   "Together Forever"   1917 - _____ (w/Gloria)

REAGER   Eileen Z.   1918 - _____   (w/Raymond)

REAGER   Raymond W.   b.9Sep1900 - d.29Apr1977.   Wife: Eileen Z., Vancouver, WA.   EFC.   Int. 2May1977 - Space N-210-3.

REEVES   Lester.   b.1Jun1913 - d.19Sep1982.   Daughter: Helen Hebblethwaite, LaCenter, WA.   VFC.   Int. 22Sep1982 - Space S-157-2.

REID   Anna V.   1904 - _____

REID   Melvin C.   "The Lord Is My Shepherd"   b.28Jun1902 - d.30Jul1972.   Anna Reid, Vancouver, WA.   VFC.   Int. Space S-163-3.

REMY   Charles A.   1875 - 1958.   VFC.   Int. 12Mar.1958 - Space N-71-1.   (w/Rose)

REMY   Clarence A.   b.1Jan1909 - d.16Sep1977.   Wife: Cara Remy, Battle Ground, WA.   LBGFH.   Int. 20Sep1977 - Space N-208-1.

REMY   Rose.   b.26Jul1884 - d.15Aug1978.   Daughter: Elva M. Johnson, Redwood City,, CA.   VFC.   Int. 19Aug1978 - Space N-71-2.   (w/Charles)

RICE   Griffin Solomon.   PFC.   U.S. Marine Corps. b.10Mar1909 - d.30Jul1976.   Daughter: Anna Mae Donnelly, Vancouver, WA.   VFC.   Int. 2Aug1976 - Space S-196-5.

RICHARDS   Hazel N.   "Together Forever"   1918 - _____ (w/Lawrence)

RICHARDS   Lawrence E.   "Together Forever"   b.22Nov1917 - d.24Nov1972.   Wife: Hazel M.   VFC.   Int. Space S-109-4

ROSE   Earl D.   b.1899 - d.13Feb1971.   Daughter: Mrs. Glen Lampkin.   Son: Earl E. Rose.   VFC.   Int. 17Feb1971 - Space N-34-7.

RUNGER   Leslie.   "Our Son Willis, WWII, Killed in Action" b.1898 - d.10Jan1976.   Wife: Velma Runger, Vancouver, WA.   VFC.   Vet's Garden.

RUNGER   Velma b.21Jan1897 - d.30Aug1981. Son: David Runger. VFC. Int. 3Sep1981 - Space N-44-2 Vet.

RUSSELL   Robert G. (Age 74. b.28Aug1911, Council Bluffs, IA. - d.21Oct1985, Vancouver, WA. Husband of Doris B. Russell, at home. Funeral Thursday, 24Oct1985, at Evergreen Staples Funeral Chapel. Interment Memory Memorial Park. Obit - The Columbian)

SAGE   Pearl A. "Mother" b.26Feb1878 - d.13Sep1967. Son: Gordon Sage, Vancouver, WA. LBGFH. Int. 16Sep1967 - Space N-199-5.

SANDERS   Gail. (Age 32. Car Accident. b.21Apr1954, Clarkston, WA. - d.16Jul1986, Portland, OR. Res: Vancouver, WA. Daughter of Mack and Dorothy Baker, Vancouver. Graveside service 18Jul1986 at Memory Memorial Park. VFC. Obit - The Columbian)

SALING   Ronald R. b.22Apr1925 - d.17Jan1980. Wife: Lois Saling, Battle Ground. LBGFH. Int. 21Jan1980 - Maus. E. Tier 6, Crypt 1.

SARGENT   Harvey L. South Dakota PFC Btry. B 383 FA BN/WWII. b.6Mar1909 - d.7Mar1968. Parents: Mr. and Mrs. Edson Sargent, Battle Ground. VFC. Int. 12Mar1968 - Space N-6-3.

SARGENT   Jess Morris. U.S. Army/WWII. b.29Jan1923 - d.26Feb1981. Wife: Genevieve Sargent, Molalla, OR. Brown's F.H., Camas, WA. Int. 3Mar1981 - Space N-178-6 Vets.

SARGENT   Martha. b.27Aug1889 - d.31Jan1969. Husband: Edson Sargent - Battle Ground, WA. VFC. Int. 5Feb1969 - Space N-67-2.

SCHEIWILLER   John J., Sr. "Together Forever" b.7Feb1904 - d.14Apr1980. Wife: Tillie Scheiwiller, Vancouver, WA. LBGFH. Int. 17Apr1980 - Space S-114-3.

SCHEIWILLER   Tillie ____ - ____

SCHOENBERG   Mary A. (Age 69. b.9Sep1916, North Prairie Twp., ND. - d.12May1986, at home. Res: This area. Widower: Irvin, at home. Sons: Gary and Edwin "Butch", both Vancouver, WA. Michael of Tacoma. Daughter: Audrey Williams, Bothell, WA. Brother: Kenneth Rolene, Gresham, OR. Sisters: Phyllis Blohm, Ruso, ND, and June Hystad and Jayne Scott, both Balta, ND. Preceded in death by son, Stephen Schoenberg. Funeral Friday, 16May1986, at Memorial Gardens Funeral Chapel. Burial in Memory Memorial Park. Obit - The Columbian)

SCHUBOTHE   Gerhaard "Gary". U.S. Air Force/WWII. (Age 74.
Heart attack. b.25Sep1912, Joseph, OR. - d.29Aug1987.
Res: Vancouver, WA. Husband of Shirley, at home.
Graveside service Wed., 2Sep1987, at Memory Memorial
Park VFC. Obit - The Columbian)

SCHUSTER   Edward. b.12Nov1885 - d.13Mar1961. Son: Albert
Schuster. VFC. Int. 16Mar1961 - Space N-193-4.

SCOTT   Raymond W. U.S. Navy. b.2Oct1909 - d.21Dec1977.
Wife: Virginia Scott, Vancouver, WA. Int. 27Dec1977
- Space S-55-4.

SCOTT   Virginia M. b.6Sep1903 - d.12Feb1982. VFC.
Int.15Feb1982 - Space S-55-3.

SEARS   Samuel George. b.11Oct1906 - 17Dec1978. Son: Walter
Sears, Vancouver, WA. EFC. Int. 23Dec1978 - Space
S-135-8.

SEAVERS   Barbara E. b.7Jun1904 - d.24Dec1965. Husband:
William J. Seavers, Vancouver, WA. EFC. Int.
29Dec1965 - Space S4-1.

SEAVERS   William J. b.25Jun1896 - d.24Nov1974. Son: William
R. Seavers, Kirkland, WA. Lacey F.H., Lacey, WA.
Int. Space S-4-2.

SECHLER   Earl D. b.5Jun1920 - d.22Jan1977. Wife: Ruth
Sechler, Battle Ground, WA. LBGFH. Int. 26Jan1977 -
Space N-207-4.

SECHLER   Ruth Marian. b.29Sep1913 - d.21Feb1982. Sister:
Marie Hanneford, Camas, WA. LBGFH. Int. 25Feb1982 -
Space N-207-5.

SELLINGER   George C. (Age 39. b.13Jul1947, Vancouver, WA. -
d.16Dec1987, Vancouver, WA. Cancer. Widow: Beverly,
at home. Mother: Lila Rose Sellinger, Battle Ground,
WA. Son: Edward, Seattle, WA. Daughter: Trela
Bargewell, Battle Ground. Funeral Sat., 20Dec1987, at
Layne's Funeral Home, Battle Ground. Burial Memory
Memorial Park. Obit - The Columbian)

SEMON   Vivian I. b.10Feb1895 - d.20Jul1970. Layne's Funeral
Home. Int.23Jul1970 - Space N-292-4.

SETERE   Richard T. 1916 - 1985 Space N-200-3.

SEVERS   Verna M. (Age 62. Cancer. b.13Jul1924, Pendleton,
OR. - d.13Apr1987, at home, Washougal, WA. Res:
Clark Co. Widower: Don, at home. Son: Joe Gesler,
Jr., Washougal. Daughters: Darlene Warner, Brush
Prairie, WA; Nona Stovner, Seattle, WA.; Linda White,
Washougal, and Gayle Baldwin, Camas, WA. Sisters:

Louise Taylor; Delphine Hermen; and Betty Queen, all of Vancouver, WA. Funeral Friday, 17Apr1987, at Brown's F.H., Camas. Burial in MMP. Obit - The Columbian)

SHAIBLE	Landis Clay. (Age 85. b.5Aug1899, Millersville, PA. - d.22Aug1984, Vancouver, WA. Husband of Eva, at home. Service Saturday, 25Aug1984, at ESFC. Burial in MMP. Obit - The Columbian) Space N-167-7 Vets.
SHIPMAN	Cora. b.11Apr1880 - d.27Dec1959. VFC. Int. 30Dec1959 - Space N-193-5.
SHROYER	Lyle C. b.27Apr1923 - d.21Mar1984. Wife: Carole Shroyer, Vancouver, WA. VFC. Int. 24Mar1984 - Space S-29-7.
SIMMONS	Clarence W. b.11Sep11896 - d.13Jan1979. Nephew: Fred D. McArthur, Washougal, WA. Straub's F.H., Camas, WA. Int. 17Jan1979, Space N-291-3.
SIMMONS	Martha P. b.5Oct1889 - d.18Aug1971. Husband: Clarence Simmons, Battle Ground. LBGFH. Int. 20Aug1971 - Space N-291-4.
SINGLETON	Florence R. b.20May1907 - d.20Mar1966. LBGFH. Int.22Mar1966 - Space N-123-3.
SINGLETON	George W. b.26Nov1899 - d.22Oct1965. Wife: Florence Singleton, Battle Ground. LBGFH. Int.26Oct1965 - Space N-123-2.
SMITH	Agnes R. Age 66. b.1Oct1918, in MN. - d.19Aug1985, Portland, OR. Res: Vancouver, WA. Wife of Ted. Service Thurs., 22Aug1985, at ESFC. Burial in MMP. Obit - The Columbian)
SMITH	Allison H. (Age 72. b.31May1913, Moora, MN. - d.11Apr1986, Vancouver, WA. Widow: Florence L., at home. Sons: Alvin, of Vancouver, and Daryl, of The Dalles, OR. Daughters: Phyllis Lackey and Norma Poasi, both of Vancouver. Brothers: Melvin, Vancouver; Howard, Little Rock, AK; Floyd, Woodburn, OR. Sisters: Neva Selleck, Idaho Falls, ID; Ruth Trunkhill, Burt, IA; Ethel Carlson, Florida. Service Monday, 14Apr1986, Memorial Gardens Funeral Chapel. Burial: Memory Memorial Park. Obit - The Columbian)
SMITH	Edward Emery. Washington PFS U.S. Army. b.17Aug1930 - d.19Mar1972. Mother: Genevieve Richardson, Vancouver, WA. VFC. Int. 22Mar1972 - Space N-138-4.
SMITH	Florence. 1911 - _____
SMITH	Gus R. b.29Apr1898 - d.22Jul1980. Wife: Velma Smith, Washougal, WA. Brown's F.H., Camas, WA. Int. 25Jul1980 - Space S-4-4.

SMITH   Howard W.   1909 - ____

SMITH   Ruth I. "Together Forever" b.10Jan1910 -
               d.20Dec1980. Husband: Howard Smith. Hamilton-My1
               F.H.   Int. 23Dec1980 - Space S-156-5.

SMITH   Roy D. b.2Aug1905 - d.11Mar1976. Wife: Florence
               Smith, Vancouver, WA. VFC. Int. 15Mar1976, Space
               N-203-7.

SMITH   Velma   1908 - ____

SNOBECK   Cleo A. Age 71. 1913 - 1984. Son-in-Law: Paul
               Duby. Gardner F.H., Stevenson, WA. Int. 22Mar1984
               Space N-12-7.

SPENCER   Michael L. (Age 36. Auto accident. b.12Dec1950,
               Vancouver, WA. - d.14Oct1987, Vancouver. Husband c
               Deborah, at home. Foster parents: Donald and Joyc
               Gillas, Vancouver, WA. MGM. Graveside service
               Tuesday, 20Oct1987, at Memory Memorial Park. Obit
               The Columbian)

SPERLING   Lois M. (Age 58. Cancer. b.24Sep1926, Arlington,
               - d.8Oct1984, Anchorage, AK. Res: Anchorage, AK.
               Wife of Adran D. Sperling, Brush Prairie, WA.
               Graveside memorial services, Sat., 19Jan1985, at
               Memory Memorial Park. Cremated. Witzelbem Funeral
               Home, Anchorage, AK. Obit - The Columbian)

SPERLING   Ronald Dean. Age 18. "Our Son-Brother" b.8Feb195
               d.13Nov1972. Parents: Mr. and Mrs. Adrian Sperlin
               HMFH. Int. Space N-148-7.

SPRENGER   Delores I. "Together Forever" 1929 - ____ (w/Les1

SPRENGER   Leslie E. Age 49.   "Together Forever" b.13Jul1929
               d.5Oct1978. Wife: Delores Sprenger, Battle Ground
               WA. LBGFH. Int. 8Oct1978 - Space N-253-1.
               (w/Delores)

SRONCE   Madge C. "Together Forever"   1914 - ____
               (w/Thomas)

SRONCE   Thomas L. "Together Forever" b.22Nov1910 -
               d.25Sep1979. Wife: Madge C. Sronce, Woodland, WA.
               Woodland Funeral Home. Int. 29Sep1979 - Space N-85

STALEY   Elva V. b.31Aug1895 - d.29Nov1971. Daughter: Lul
               Benedict, Ridgefield, WA. LBGFH. Int. 2Dec1971 -
               Space N-22-6.

STAMP   George M. "Father"   1904 - 19__

STAMP   Lucille M.   "Mother"   b.6Jun1906 - d.27May1973. Husband: George Stamp, Battle Ground, WA. LBGFH. Int. 29May1973 - Space N-143-4.

STARKEY   Patricia Ann.   PFC. U.S. Army.   b.25Oct1939 - d.14Aug1978.   Husband: Maurice Starkey, Camas, WA. (Divorced) LBGFH.   Int.17Aug1978 - Space S-52-8.

STEFFES   Albert P.   b.12Jan1907 - d.18Dec1976. Wife: Rachel Steffes, Dufur, OR. LBGFH.   Int. 22Dec1976, Space S-234-2.

STEFFERS   Rachel Rebecca. (Age 71.   b.22Jun1913, Fedora, SD - d.7Dec1984, Vancouver, WA.   Res: Brush Prairie, WA. Funeral, Tuesday, 11Dec1984, at Old Apostolic Lutheran Church.   Interment in MMP. LBGFH.   Obit - The Columbian)   Int. 11Dec1984 - Space S-234-1.

STEUDLER   Mike.   "Father"   b.11Aug1890 - d.22Sep1973. Wife: Rose E., Battle Ground, WA. LBGFH.   Int. 25Sep1973 - Space N-17-1.   (w/Rose E.)

STEUDLER   Rose E. (F.?)   "Mother"   1901 - ____   (w/Mike)

STOKER   Hans.   b.15Jul1914 - d.21Jan1972.   Wife: Hillie Stoker, Battle Ground, WA. LBGFH.   Int. 25Jan1972 - Space S-44-6.

STOWELL   Virginia E.   "In Loving Memory"   b.19Sep1916 - d.26Dec1975.   Son: Bud Sears, Vancouver, WA. VFC. Space S-135-3.

STRONG   Newton J. "Buck".   b.29Jan1941 - d.24Nov1977.   Wife: Lois Strong, Battle Ground, WA.   Int. 29Nov1977 - Space N-262-1.

SUMMERS   Joey B.   (Age 79.   b.29May1906, Anglin, WA. - d.5Sep1985, at home, Vancouver, WA.   Wife of Gerald Summers, at home.   Graveside service Saturday, 7Sep1985, at Memory Memorial Park.   Interment following. VFC.   Obit - The Columbian)

SUMRALL   James M.   (Age 57.   b.26Jan1927, Fort Worth, TX - d.7Jul1984, Vancouver, WA.   Daughter: Trudie A. Walters, Vancouver, WA.   Graveside service Friday, 13Jul1984, at Memory Memorial Park.   Hamilton-Mylan F.H.   Obit - The Columbian)

SURFACE   Delia E.   1912 - ____   (w/Dwight)

SURFACE   Dwight L.   b.16Nov1896 - d.9Feb1973.   Wife: Delia, Vancouver, WA. LBGFH.   Int. 12Feb1973 - Space S-42-8.

SYKES   Helen L.   b.28Dec1916 - d.6Mar1974.   Donald Sykes , Vancouver, WA. HMFH.   Int. 9Mar1974 - Space N54-8.

TAPLIN	Arnold Willis. (Age 59. Heart attack. b.1Apr1924, Presho, SD - d.4Nov1983, Placid Lake, WA. Res: Battle Ground, WA. Husband of Lila, at home. Funeral Tuesday, 8Nov1983, at LBGFH. Burial in MMP. Obit - The Columbian) N-48-1 Vet.
TAYLOR	David C. "Together Forever" b.2Oct1905 - d.30May1979. Wife: Rebecca, Vancouver, WA. LBGFH. Int. 2Jun1979 - Space N-81-1.
TAYLOR	Randel R. U.S. Air Force/WWII. Age 74. (b.11Oct1910, Galax, VA. - d.31Aug1985, Vancouver, WA. Husband of Sylvia Taylor, at home. Graveside service Wed., 4Sep1985, at Memory Memorial Park. Hamilton-Myland F.H. Obit - The Columbian)
TAYLOR	Rebecca M. b.18Mar1909 - d.4Oct1980. Son: David J. Taylor, Battle Ground, WA. LBGFH. Int. 8Oct1980 - Space N-81-2.
TERPENEY	Julia Agnes. (Age 86. b.12Feb1897, in Missouri - d.25Oct1983, Vancouver, WA. Res: Battle Ground, WA. Wife of Alva, at home. Funeral Friday, 28Oct1983, at Layne's Funeral Home Chapel. Burial in MMP. Obit - The Columbian) Int. Space S-236-3.
THRONE	Mildred. b.24Jun1901 - d.3May1978. Son: Norman Larry, Bellevue, WA. VFC. Int. 5May1978 - Space N-295-4.
TRAVINSKI	Frieda B. b.12Aug1915 - d.30Dec1968. Husband: Walter, Vancouver, WA. Int. 2Jan1969 - Space N-141-8.
TREDWAY	Wilbert DeLoss. (Age 71. Heart attack. b.7Jun1912, Chanute, KS - d.10May1984, Vancouver, WA. Husband of Helen, at home. Service Wed., 16May1984, at Evergreen Staples F.C. Burial MMP. Obit - The Columbian) S-43-8.
UELTSCHI	Arnold D. "Father" b.27Nov1898 - d.4Mar1969. Son: Floyd Ueltschi. Int. 6Mar1969 - Space N-19-1. (w/Elvina)
UELTSCHI	Elvina S. "Mother" b.12May1911 - d.25Sep1965. Son: Davis. VFC. Int. 29Sep1965 - Space N-19-4.
UELTSCHI	F. Alfred. "Together Forever - The Lord Is My Shepherd" b.21May1911 - d.4Aug1970. Wife: Flora M., Vancouver, WA. VFC. Int. 6Aug1970 - Space S-75-6.
UELTSCHI	Flora M. "Together Forever - The Lord Is My Shepherd" 1917 - ____ (w/F. Alfred)
URBAN	Edna P. "Mother" 1910 - ____ (w/Henry A.)

URBAN Henry A. "Father" b.1Jan1908 - d.6Jul1975. Wife: Edna P. Urban, Kallispel, MT. Daughter: Mrs. Darwin Spencer, Vancouver, WA. LBGFH. Int. 12Jul1975 - Space S-233-4. (w/Edna)

VAHL Donald P. b.5Nov1906 - d.4Sep1973. Wife: Lois E., Vancouver, WA. VFC. Int. 6Sep1973 - Space S-16-8.

VANDERMAST Gertrude Alma Goff. (Age 82. Cancer. b.7Aug1901, Doniphal, MO - d.16Oct1983, Vancouver, WA. Wife of Fred, at home. Funeral Wed., 19Oct1983, at Layne's Funeral Home Chapel. Entombment in Memory Memorial Park Mausoleum. (Obit - The Columbian) Tier 3, Crypt 2.

VAN METER Crystal Dawn. "Always Loving - Always Loved" b.2Mar1964 - d.27Jul1972. Parents: Mr. and Mrs. Lewis Van Meter, Vancouver, WA. VFC. Int. 31Jul1972 - Space N-19-3.

VAUGHN Clarence A. U.S. Army/WWII. b.26Apr1929 - d.20Jul1979. Parents, Mr. and Mrs. Ed Vaughn. VFC. Int. 24Jul1979 - Space N-178-5.

VEDAA Gene R., Jr. b.29Jul1971 - d.3Aug1971. Father: Gene R. Vedaa, Vancouver, WA. LBGFH. Int. Space N-156-3.

WAGNER Donald Fredrick. "Son & Brother - Friend" b.3Sep1969 - d.7Sep1979. Parents: Mr. and Mrs. Donald Wagner, Vancouver, WA. ESFH. Int. 13Sep1979 - Space S-49-5.

WALKER Carol Nadine "Mother" 1921 - ____

WALKER Rev. Flay V. "Father" b.24SSep1919 - d.10Oct1975. Wife: Carol N. Walker, Vancouver, WA. VFC. Int. Space S-162-2.

WALKER Harry E. b.10Jan1891 - d.12Jan1965. Son: Donald Walker, Portland, OR. Mikeworth Funeral Chapel, Portland, OR. Int. MMP, Space N-206-3.

WALLIS Edward E. b.16Jan1915 - d.28May1974. Wife: Estelle. EFC. Interred Space S-14-3.

WALLIS Edward Earl, Jr. (Age 27. Cancer. b.20Dec1957, Vancouver, WA - d.2May1985, Portland, OR. Res: Vancouver. Husband of Kandi, at home. Graveside service Monday, 6May1985, at MMP. ESFC. Obit - The Columbian) Space N-74-5.

WARREN Ernest J. "Eternally Together" 1924 - ____. (w/Faai' Uaso)

WARREN Faai' Uaso. "Eternally Together" b.1Jan1917 - d.20May1980. Husband: Ernest J. Warren, Vancouver,

WA. ESFH. Int. 24May1980, MMP Space S-20-1.
(w/Ernest)

WEBBERLY   Lara Diane. b.30Oct1970 - d.4Oct1970. Parents:
Ronald and Marsha Webberly, Washougal, WA. Brother:
Ty Webberly. Sister: Andrea Webberly. Maus. Col. Row
4, Niche 11. Disinterred 24Sep1975 from Portland Mem.
Cem.

WEGEN   Daisy Lilith. b.24Mar1906 - d.18Feb1983.
Int.4Mar1983 - Maus. Col. Tier 11 - Niche 9.

WEGEN   Walter G. (Age 81. b.17Mar1905, So. St. Paul, MN -
d.9May1986, Vancouver, WA. Son: Richard Wegen,
International Falls, MN. Daughter: Betty Hardy,
Ryderwood, WA. Sister: Doris Patton, North
Hollywood, CA. No service. Memory Memorial Park.
Memorial Gardens Funeral Chapel. Obit - The
Columbian)

WELLMAN   Tilda E. b.6Jun1904 - d.21Nov1978. Son: Raymond L.
Wellman, Vancouver, WA. HMFH. Int. 25Nov1978, Space
S-29-2. (w/Weldon B.)

WELLMAN   Weldon B. b.12Jul1891 - d.16Jul1973. HMFC. Space
S-29-3. (w/Tilda)

WELSH   Edna B. Age 90. b.1Sep1879 - d.1Sep1970. Son:
Lloyd Davie, Battle Ground, WA. VFC. Int. 3Sep1970,
Space S-56-8.

WERNER   Ivy. d. 17Sep1958. Body removed to Evergreen
Memorial 18Jan1973. Husband: William H. Werner.

WEST   Rose E. Age 76. (b.30Nov1908, Prairie Lake, MN -
d.28Dec1984, Vancouver, WA. Res: Battle Ground, WA.
Wife of Jesse, at home. Funeral Monday, 31Dec1984, at
the Old Apostolic Lutheran Church. Burial in MMP.
Obit - The Columbian) Space S-40-4.

WESTERGARD   Edward N. b.16Jul1900 - d.25May1979. VFC. Nephew:
Jim Larsen, Vancouver, WA. Int. 31May1980, Space
N-154-8.

WHITAKER   Gordon. b.9Jun1909 - d.17June1977. HMFH. Int.
20Jun1977, Space S-57-8.

WHITE   Agnes H. 1912 - _____

WHITE   Wesley B. "Together Forever" b.3May1897 -
d.21Jan1979. Wife: Agnes, Vancouver, WA. ESFH.
Int. 24Jan1979, Space N-149-3.

WICKSTROM   Alma C. b.13Feb1895 - d.22Aug1981. Son: Eldon
Wickstrom, Vancouver, WA. Layne's F.H. Int.
26Aug1981, Space N-39-4.

WICKSTROM

Carl. "Husband & Dad" d.3Aug1972. Son: Eldon, Battle Ground, WA. Layne's F.H. Space N-393

WILEY

Edith V. ____ - ____

WILEY

Ray. b.1891 - d. 11Oct1973. Wife: Edith V. VFC. Int. 26Oct1973, Space N-89-1.

WILKINSON

John C. U.S. Army/WWI. Age 94. b.30Oct1891, Winterset, IA - d.19Dec1985, Vancouver, WA. Husband of Alma K. Wilkinson, at home. Graveside service Saturday, 21Dec1985, at MMP. HMFH. Obit - The Columbian.

WILLIAMS

Blanche M. 1907 - ____

WILLIAMS

Earl J. C. "Together Forever" b.1900 - d.15Dec1969. Wife: Blanche, Heisson, WA. LBGFH. Int. 19Dec1969, space N-36-7.

WILSON

Adele Louise. b.6Feb1949 - d.22Oct1968. Parents: Mr. and Mrs. Ernest Wilson, Vancouver, WA. HMFH. Int. 25Oct1968, Space S-59-8.

WILSON

John Francis, Sr. WWI. Age 94. b.10Aug1891, Rimini, MT - d.4Mar1986. Res: Clark Co., WA. Sons: Ed, Battle Ground; Jack, Vancouver. Sisters: Marion Tucker, Vancouver and Dorothy Bradley, Encino, CA. Funeral Saturday, 8Mar1986, at LBGFH. Burial in MMP. Obit - The Columbian). (w/Veryl)

WILSON

Veryl L. b.1912 - d.16Feb1961. Husband: John F. Wilson, Sr. Int. 18Feb1961, Space N-74-2.

WILSON

William Milo. "In Loving Memory Of" b.1884 - d.16Dec.1961. Int. 21Dec1961, space S-70-5

WINTERSTEIN

Lester R. b.7Sep1910 - d.12Dec1981. Wife: Iona, Vancouver, WA. LBGFH. Int. 15Dec1981, space N-261-2

WISE

Colleen Rae. b.3Aug1953 - 29Apr1970. Grandmother: Maybelle Bray, Amboy, WA. VFC. Int. 2May1970, space N-62-1.

WULFF

Harold B. 1913 - ____ (w/Lily C.)

WULFF

Lily C. b.18Oct1918 - d.9Jun1977. Husband: Harold B., Vancouver, WA. VFC. Intr. 13Jun1977, Space N83-5.

YARNELL

Virgil Alfred. Washington S. Sgt./U.S. Army/WWII. b.11Feb1910 - d.16Oct1972. Wife: Georgia J., Battle Ground, WA. VFC. Int. 20Oct 1972, Space S-34-4 Vet.

YAW — Steven R. b.8Dec1951 - d.14Mar1981. Mother: LaVonne (Mrs. Don) Sandvig, Vancouver, WA. ESFH. Int. 17Mar1981, Space N-101-1.

YINGER — Ewald "Together Forever" b.17May1910 - 9Jul1981. ESFH. Int. 13Jul1981, Space S-115-3. (w/Helen)

YINGER — Helen M. "Together Forever" 1916 - ____. (w/Ewald)

YODER — Frances C. b.16Jan1895 - d. 20Oct1978. Son: Joseph Yoder, Vancouver, WA. LBGFH. Int. 23Oct1978, Space S-224-1.

YORK — Elias L. "Together Forever" b.1911 - d.1Apr1972. Son: Allen York, Vancouver, WA. VFC. Int. 6Apr1972, Space N-160-5. (w/Stella and Michael)

YORK — Michael L. "Together Forever" b.30Apr1950 - d.4Mar1980. Brother: David W. York, LaCenter, WA. Drowned in Columbia. Cremated - Ashes between parents. VFC. Int. 7May1980 - Space N160-5 & 6. (w/Elias and Stella)

YORK — Stella Mae. "Together Forever" b.1913 - d.19Dec1972. Son: Allen York. VFC. Int. 21Dec1972, Space N-160-6. (w/Elias and Michael)

ZESIGER — Floyd. Age 71. (b.7Jan1914, Tremonton, UT. - d.5Jun1985, Vancouver, WA. Husband of Helen Zesiger, at home. Daughter: Gail Moore. Funeral Friday, 7Jun1985, at VFC. Entombment at MMP Mausoleum. Obit - The Columbian) G.S. Maus. W. - Tier 6 - Crypt 5.

ZIMMERMAN — Evelyn Jean. Age 69. b.17Dec1913, Vancouver, WA. - d.15Jul1983, Vancouver. Wife of Wilmer Zimmerman, at home. Funeral Tuesday, July 1983 at VFC. Entombment at MMP Mausoleum. Obit - The Columbian) Maus. Good Shepherd - Tier 3 - Niche 3.

# # # # #

CRAWFORD CEMETERY

ALLWORTH

(Alice Allworth. Age 85, Mar 4, 1900, Portland, OR - Apr 5, 1985. Res: Battle Ground, WA. .... Funeral Tuesday, Apr 9, at Layne's Funeral Home Chapel. Burial at Crawford Cemetery. LFC. Obit - The Columbian).

BUMA

(Cody Allen Buma. Stillborn. March 21, 1987, Vancouver, WA. Parents: Dale & June Buma, Battle Ground. Sisters: Jessica Lorraine and Katy Ann, at home. Grandparents: Ed and Margaret Buma, Brush Prairie; Rosalee Sova of Tigard, OR; and Ted Webber, Vancouver. Great grandparents: Henry & Lorraine Arnold, Vancouver; and Henry & Lydia Manwell, Chelatchie Prairie; and Leonard & Cora DeHogg, Artesia, CA. Funeral Tuesday, Mar 24, 1987, at Layne's Funeral Home Chapel. Burial Crawford Cem. Layne's Funeral Home Chapel. Obit - The Columbian).

DUVALL

(Lester "Murph" Leo Duvall. Age 75. Oct 23, 1908 in Crawford, WA - Dec 26, 1983, Res: Battle Ground, WA. Husband of Goldie, at home. ----------- Funeral Friday, Dec 31, 1983, at Layne's Funeral Home Chapel. Burial in Crawford Cemetery. LFC. Obit - The Columbian).

HALVORSON

(Henry John Halvorson, Sr. Age 86. Mar 16, 1898, Chicago, IL - Nov 4, 1984, Vancouver, WA. Pes: Battle Ground, WA. ---------- Graveside services Wed, Nov 7, at Crawford. Cem. Layne's Funeral Home. Obit - The Columbian).

HANSEN

(Andrew "Andy" Hansen. Age 68. Oct 16, 1916, Battle Ground, WA - May 23, 1985, Vancouver, WA. Res: Battle Ground, WA. Husband of Ethel, at home. --------------- Graveside service Saturday, May 25, at Crawford Cem. in Battle Ground. Layne's Funeral Home. Obit - The Columbian). Coast Guard/WWII.

HATHAWAY

James E. Hathaway. Age 75. Oct 25, 1909, Mountain View, OK - Jan 30, 1985, Camas, WA. Res: Camas, WA. Husband of Georgia, at home. ------- Funeral Saturday, Feb 2, at Layne's Funeral Chapel. Interment at Crawford Cemetery, Battle Ground. LFC. Obit - The Columbian).

HEISEN

(Irene Ladine Heisen. Age 69. Feb 6, 1917, Heisseon, WA - June 13, 1986, Heisson, WA. Brother: "Mike" Heison, Heisson, WA. Sister: Lillian Linn, Battle Ground, WA. Funeral Wednesday, June 18, at Layne's Funeral Home. Interment in Crawford Cem. Layne's Funeral Home. Obit - The Columbian).

HIBBINX

(Billie "Galloway" Higgins. Age 62. Leukemia. Apr 26, 1921, Morris, MN - Jul 5, 1983, Vancouver, WA. Res: Battle Ground, WA. --------- Funeral Friday, Jul 8, at Layne's Funeral Home Chapel. Interment in Crawford Cemetery. LFC. Obit - The Columbian).

CRAWFORD CEMETERY

HILDEBRAND

(Marker was unreadable) Jesse Samuel Hildebrand. Husband of Bertha Jane. Date of birth Jan 23, 1886 - date of death May 24, 1935 Bonneville, Skamania (Co.) Son of Abraham Hildebrand. Burial Crawford Cemetery.

JENNINGS
MASLANKA
CLARK
SWOPE

(Jessie Mary Jennings Maslanka Clark Swope. Age 31. Truck accident. May 20, 1951, Portland, OR - Jan 12, 1983, LaCenter, WA. Res: La Center, WA. Dau of Bert Jennings, Seldovia, Alaska & Billie Higgins, Battle Ground, WA. ------- Funeral Monday, Jan 17, at Layne's Funeral Home Chapel. Interment at Crawford Cem. LFC. Obit - The Columbian).

OWENS

(Clarence E. Owens. Age 57. Oct 25, 1925, Monett, MO. - Aug 22, 1983, Battle Ground, WA. Cancer. Res: Battle Ground, WA. U. S. Navy/WW II. ------- Service Friday, Aug 26, at Layne's Funeral Home Chapel. Interment in Crawford Cemetery. Layne's Funeral Home. Obit - The Columbian).

SPENCE

(Ada J. Spence. Age 79. Apr 7, 1906, Kentucky - Feb 1, 1986. Res: Camas, WA. Son: Oscar Healea, Camas. Daughters: Mildred Mann, Washougal; Marguerite Brown, Camas and Sharon Ware, Milwaukie, OR. Brother: Guy Frazier, Salem, OR. Sisters: Lee Vega, El Paso, TX; Ruth Knapp, Illinois. Funeral Saturday, Feb 8, at Memorial Gardens Funeral Chapel. Burial in Crawford Cemetery in Battle Ground, WA. Obit - The Columbian).

CORRECTION:

THOM

Charles Thom died 1958 (not 1978).

FINN HILL CEMETERY

OSGOOD

(Vera L. Osgood. Age 79. Cancer. Mar 27, 1908, Watertown, SD - Apr 24, 1987, Vancouver, WA. Preceded in death by her husband, Elmer, in 1975. Son: Burdette Osgood, Battle Ground. Daughters: Jeannette Babbit, Mountlake Terrace; Bernetta Thompson, Everett; Lorraine Northrup, Battle Ground and Patricia Osgood, Vancouver. Sisters: Jessie Wallway, Ridgefield and Gracie Splinter and Sara Gertis, both of Watertown, SD. Service Tuesday, Apr 28, at the Apostolic Lutheran Church in Hockinson. Burial in Finn Hill Cem. Layne's Funeral Home. Obit - The Columbian).

TANDESKE

(Donny Tandeske. Age 78. Mar 25, 1906, Homnenspaag, Norway - Dec 4, 1984, Medford, OR. Wife of Vincent, at home. -------- Funeral Saturday, Dec 8, at the Apostolic Lutheran Church in Hockinson, WA. Interment in Finn Hill Cem. Layne's Funeral Home. Obit - The Columbian).

282

GRAVEL POINT CEMETERY

AXFORD

(Pearl Axford. Age 85. Feb 18, 1901, Hockinson, WA -
Mar 31, 1986, Vancouver, WA. Sister: Crystal I. Spencer,
Battle Ground, WA. Funeral: Wed, Apr 2, at Layne's Fune-
ral Home Chapel. Burial: Gravel Point Cem. Obit - The
Columbian).

BLYSTONE

(Margaret Jane Blystone. Age 92. Jan 7, 1891, Hockinson,
WA - Sep 8, 1983, Battle Ground, WA. Res: Battle Ground.
------- Graveside service Monday, Sep 12, at Gravel Point
Cemetery. Layne's Funeral Home. Obit - The Columbian).

MACKEY

(Esther Hilja Mackey. Age 74. May 29, 1910, Estelline,
SD - Jul 17, 1984. Res: Vancouver, WA. ------- Service
Saturday, Jul 21, at St. James Catholic Church. Burial
in Gravel Point Cem. Layne's Funeral Home. Obit - The
Columbian).

RIDGEFIELD CEMETERY

FRENCH

(Geraldine French. Services were held today (Thursday)
for Geraldine French at the Woodland Funeral Home. Final
interment was at Ridgefield Cemetery. Mrs. French, 63,
died Saturday in Vancouver. Born in Ridgefield December
29, 1912, Mrs. French lived in Woodland the past six years.
She is survived by a son, Everett Harrison of Salem, OR; a
brother, Glaze Ditmer of Vancouver, WA; and three sisters,
Mary Beebe of Woodland, Florine Chapman of Seaside, OR, and
Rosalie Davis of Lansing, IL.

SUNNYSIDE CEMETERY

GOODWIN

(Guy Goodwin. Age 88. Jul 20, 1896, Washougal, WA - Sep
24, 1984. Res: Camas, WA. -------- Graveside Service
Thursday, Sep 27, at Sunnyside Cemetery. Layne's Funeral
Home. Obit - The Columbian).

YACOLT CEMETERY

BAGGETT

(William Jennings Baggett. Age 86. Nov 20, 1897, Chickasha,
OK - Sep 18, 1984, Vancouver, WA. Res: Battle Ground, WA.
(previously Yacolt). ------- Service Saturday, Sep 22, at
Layne's Funeral Home Chapel. Burial in Yacolt Cem. LFC.
Obit - The Columbian). U. S. Navy/WW I.

CAHOON

(Larry D. Cahoon. Age 32. Apr 25, near Amboy in an auto
accident. Born Aug 13, 1947, Vancouver. Survived by widow,
Linda, at home; parents, Howard and Ella of Yacolt; sons,
Douglas, Darren, Dean and Devon, at home, and Duane Balvage
and Dean Balvage, at home; daughter, Darci; sister, Carol

CAHOON
(Larry D. Cahoon) cont. Boucher, Yacolt; grandfather, Cal Baggett, Yacolt; grandmother, Ruth Eubanks, Longview; great grandfather, Clarence of Snohomish. Interment at Yacolt Cemetery. Obit - The Columbian). May 14, 1980.

COLEMAN
(Mollie Coleman. Age 65. Aug 6, 1920, St. Louis, MO - Apr 23, 1986, Vancouver, WA. Res: Yacolt, WA. Preceded in death by her husband, George, in 1981. Son: Joseph Coleman, Yacolt. Burial: Yacolt Cem. Layne's Funeral Home. Obit - The Columbian).

FINNEGAN
(Darrel E. Finnegan. Age 55. Cancer. Jun 13, 1932, Jamestown, ND - Jul 24, 1987, at home, Yacolt, WA. Husband of Carol, at home. ------- Mass of Christian Burial Monday, Jul 27, at St. Joseph the Workman Catholic Church. Burial in Yacolt Cem. Obit - The Columbian. Layne's Funeral Home).

JACKSON
(James "Jack" Haynie Jackson. Age 65. Jun 16, 1918, Llano, TX - Apr 1, 1984, Vancouver, WA. Res: Yacolt, WA. Husb. of Betty Lou, at home. ------- Funeral Thursday, Apr 5, at Layne's Funeral Home Chapel. Burial in Yacolt Cem. LFC. Obit - The Columbian). U. S. Army/WW II

MINKLER
(Frank V. "Sam" Minkler. Age 52. Heart Failure. Jul 29, 1932, Kosmos, WA - Nov 17, 1984, Longview, WA. Res: Longview, WA. Husb. of Velma, at home. ------- Funeral Tues, Nov 20, at old Apostolic Lutheran Church, Brush Prairie. Interment - Yacolt Cemetery. Layne's Funeral Home. Obit - The Columbian). Korean War.

PATTERSON
(Perla K. Patterson. Age 89. Jul 14, 1894, Fordyce, Ark - Nov 6, 1983, Battle Ground, WA. Res: Battle Ground (previously res. Yacolt). ------- Graveside service Wednesday, Nov 9, at Yacolt Cemetery. Layne's Funeral Home. LFC. Obit - The Columbian).

POND
(Emily Pond. Age 78. Res: Yacolt area 35 years. Apr 21, 1898, Miles City, MT - Jun 17, 1976. Widower Jack at home. ------- Services Layne's Funeral Chapel, Battle Ground, Interment Yacolt Cem. Obit - The Columbian).

RAST
(Amelia W. Rast. Age 85. Aug 12, 1899, Hanover, Germany - Nov 21, 1984, Yacolt, WA. Res: Yacolt. ------- Funeral Monday, Nov 26, at the Yacolt Comm. Church. Burial in Yacolt Cemetery. Obit - The Columbian).

SHANNON
(Wayne W. Shannon. Age 48. Heart Attack. Feb 20, 1936, Bend, OR - Sep 6, 1984, Yacolt, WA. Res: Yacolt, WA. Husband of Virginia, in California. ------- Funeral Mon Sep 10, at Layne's Funeral Home Chapel. Burial in Yacolt Cem. LFC. Obit - The Columbian).

TAYLOR
(Iva May Taylor. Age 84. May 4, 1901, Smith County, KS - Aug 12, 1985, Vancouver. Res: Yacolt, WA. ------- Graveside service Fri, Aug 16, at Yacolt Cem. Layne's Funeral Home. Obit - The Columbian).

YACOLT CEMETERY

TEEL   (Herbert L. Teel. Age 75. Jan 15, 1911, Merna, NB - Dec 15, 1986, Vancouver, WA. Res: Yacolt, WA. Widow: Marian, at home. Daughters: Naomi Ferreira and Velma Minkler Cole, both of Yacolt. Brother: Carl Teel, White Salmon, WA. Graveside service Thurs, Dec 18, at Yacolt Cem. Layne's Funeral Home. Obit - The Columbian).

TOZIER   (Margaret B. Tozier. Age 87. Oct 20, 1898, Topeka, KS - Jul 13, 1986, Battle Ground, WA. Res: Yacolt, WA. ------- Graveside service Wed, Jul 16, at Yacolt Cem. Layne's Funeral Home. Obit - The Columbian).

VAN ALLEN   (Robert Warren Van Allen Sr. Age 55. Cancer. Sep 11, 1927, Williston, ND - Feb 15, 1983, Yacolt, WA. Husband of Dora Mae, at home. ------- Graveside service Sat, Feb 19, at Yacolt Cemetery. Obit - The Columbian).

CORRECTIONS:

OLD CITY CEMETERY

MORRIS   Page 115 WALT - name is incorrect. It should read MATHEW. Sec: NE, LOT 12. There is NO Walt.

DERR   Page 46 (Baby) correct Lot no. SEC: NE LOT: 126

MT. ZION CEMETERY

KARVONEN   Was: Joy Ann Karvonen. Should be infant twins Joy Karvonen and Jan Karvonen. Parents: Rudolph Leo and Aggie Karvonen. (He died age 64, Dec 1988 - heart attack, Portland, OR. Elim Luth. Ch. Blk 21, Isle 4 West.)

McFARLANE   Bill McFarlane. b. Jan 1, 1848, WI. Fa: Wallace of Scotland. Mo. Ellen McLay of Scotland. Mt. Zion Cem., LaCenter. d. Nov 21, 1930 Portland, OR. (No headstone - family records).

McFARLANE   Jennie (Halversen) McFarlane. (b. May 20, 1867, Valer, Solor, Norway - d. Jan 1911, Portland, Mult., OR. Father: Halvor Halversen. Mother: Karen "Carrie" Peder-datter). Headstone: 1867 - 1911

GREEN   Helena Green. Clark County Cemeteries, Volume 3 - page 187. Error in death year. Should read Oct 9, 1892.

MONUMENT HONORS 41 COUNTY
AREA VETS

Here are the names of residents from Clark, Skamania and Klickitat counties and Woodland among the 1,073 inscribed on the new Vietnam Veterans Memorial:

AMBOY: Raymond Earl Carpenter.

BINGEN: Terry Hugh Smith.

BRUSH PRAIRIE: Richard August Hostikka, Dale Raymond Lindberg, Timothy George Mattson.

CAMAS: Marvin Leo Hartman, Ronald Norman Koitzsch, Kenneth J. Krause, Robert Lee Miller, Gerald Ray Olmsted.

KLICKITAT: Randall Nave Arney, William Kenneth Austin.

SKAMANIA: Kenneth William Grubb.

VANCOUVER: Howard David Akehurst, Prentis Barney Boykin Jr., Robert Paul Degen, Steven Arthur Frink, Harley Hubert Hall, Harvey C. Harris, Roy F. Harbison, Paul Roger Jarvis, Patrick Dennis Kadow, Howard Lloyd Leroy Jr., Robert Arnold Mettert, Maurice Karl Mock, Stephen Edward Neas, John L. Peterson, Daniel Lloyd Poff, Hugh Leslie Sherburn, Charles J. Stohlmeyer, Donald Fredrick Thulin, Michael J. Wainwright, Daniel Guy Wessler.

WASHOUGAL: Gary Lynn Campen.

WHITE SALMON: Carl Frank Belding Jr., Lonnie Mark Wedrick.

WISHRAM: Lynn Dennis Anderson.

WOODLAND: Keith Noel Atchley.

YACOLT: Alvin Leroy Lowery.

*   *   *   *   *   *

A2 - The COLUMBIAN - Fri., May 29, 1987 - Vancouver, Wash.

RIDGEFIELD MEN LISTED ON VIETNAM WAR MEMORIAL

RIDGEFIELD - The names of two Ridgefield men were omitted last Friday when The COLUMBIAN published a list of residents from Clark, Skamania and Klickitat counties and Woodland whose names are inscribed on the new Vietnam Veterans Memorial in Olympia.

The names of Robert Lester Vaughan and David Wallace Baker, both of Ridgefield, are on the memorial, according to Sandra Martin, a clerk with the state Department of of Veterans Affairs.

BARNETT
George S. (Age 94, b. 1Ø Dec 1891, Clark County, WA – d. 1Ø Jan 1986, Vancouver, WA. Preceded in death by wife, Eva, in 196Ø. Dau: Mary Jagelski, Vancouver. Bro: Vern Barnett, Portland, OR. Sister: Lea Sharp, Vancouver. Service Tuesday, Jan. 4, at St. John's Catholic Church. Burial in St. John's Cemetery. Hamilton-Mylan Funeral Home. Obit – The Columbian)

BOYER
Veronica "Ronnie" M. (Age 71, b. 3Ø Sep 1915, Thief River Falls, MN – d. 3 Nov 1986. Res: Vancouver, WA. Wife of F. "Pat" Patrick Boyer, at home. Burial in St. John's Cemetery. HMFH. Obit – The Columbian)

BROSIUS
Edward H. U. S. Air Force/WWII (Age 63, b. 1 Sep 192Ø, Oakwood, ND – d. 16 Jul 1984, at home, Vancouver, WA. Husband of Olive Brosius, at home. Mass of Christian Burial Wed., July 18, at St. John's Catholic Church. Interment in St. John's Catholic Cem. VFC. Obit – The Columbian)

BUMP
George C. (Age 76, b. 23 Sep 19Ø9, Grant Co., MN – d. 24 Nov 1985, Vancouver, WA. Husband of Nora R. Bump at home. Mass of Christian Burial Friday, Nov. 29, at St. John's Catholic Church. Interment in St. John's Cem. Hamilton-Mylan Funeral Home. Obit – The Columbian)

CALDWELL
Helen Blanche. (Age 8Ø. Pneumonia. b. 11 Jul 19Ø6, Grand Forks, ND – d. ((no date. – Obit printed in Wed., 13 May 1987 Columbian.)) Died at Glisan Care Center, Portland, OR. Brothers: Leslie Caldwell, Vancouver, and Bill Caldwell, Sacramento, CA. Sisters: Frances Mickelsen, Carmichael, CA; Ruthe Caldwell, Vancouver, and Mary Lydon, Portland, OR. Niece & legal guardian: Barbara J. George, Portland, OR. Mass of Christian burial Friday, May 15, at St. John's Catholic Church. Interment in St. John's Cemetery. Corinthian Group Funeral Services of Portland, OR. in charge of arrangements. Obit – The Columbian)

CARROLL
Mary Irene. (Age 88, b. 4 Oct 1894, Saint John, WA – d. 1 Mar 1983 at home, Brush Prairie, WA. Mass of Christian Burial Saturday, Mar. 5, at St. John's Catholic Church. Interment in St. John's Catholic Cemetery. MGM. Obit – The Columbian)

COSSETTE
Judy Ann (Age 33, b. 2Ø Sep 1949, Fargo, ND – d. 6 Jun 1983, Vancouver, WA. Daughter of Roger and Eileen Cossette, Castle Rock, WA. Mass of Christian Burial Thurs., June 9, at St. John's Catholic Church. Burial in St. John's Cem. Hamilton-Mylan Funeral Home. Obit – The Columbian)

FOX	John L. (Age 87, b. 5 Jun 1887, Chicago, IL - d. 9 Feb 1985, Vancouver, WA. Husband of Mary M. Fox at the family home. Mass of Christian Burial Thurs., Feb. 14, at St. Joseph's Catholic Church. Private committal will follow at St. John's Cemetery. Hamillton-Mylan Funeral Home. Obit - The Columbian)
FRACKIEWICZ	Victor Cash. (Age 45, b. 27 Aug 1939, Warsaw, Poland d. 18 Mar 1985, Vancouver, WA. Husband of Judy Frackiewicz, at home. Mass of Christian Burial Frida Mar. 22, at St. John's Catholic Church. Interment in St. John's Catholic Cem. Evergreen Staples Funeral Chapel. Obit - The Columbian)
GRIFFITH	Jeremie Michael. (Age 2 Mos., b. 4 Nov 1982, Portland, OR - d. 7 Jan 1983, Vancouver, WA. Mother: Adele LeLonde Griffith, at home. Mass of the Angels Tues., Jan. 11, at St. John's Catholic Church. Interment in St. John's Cem. Baby Haven. Hamilton-Mylan Funeral Home. Obit - The Columbian)
MEYER	Vincent L. U. S. Navy/WWII. (Age 67. Cancer. b. 29 Feb 1920, New York City - d. 7 Jul 1987, at home Vancouver, WA. Husband of Amelia, at home. Service Friday, July 10 at St. John's Catholic Church. Buria will be in St. John's Catholic Cem. MGM. Obit - The Columbian)
MICHELS	Frances M. (Age 81, b. 2 Oct 1905, Detroit Lakes, MI d. 10 Jun 1987, Vancouver, WA. Sons: Donald of New Port Richey, FL; Roger of Utica, MI. Daughters: Claire Vigna, Vancouver and Betty Quirk, of Louisvill TN. Sisters: Rose Cronin, Minneapolis; Mary McPhail, Riverside, CA; Emmengarde Frederick and Margaret Tetrud, both of Tacoma. Graveside service Saturday, June 13, at St. John's Catholic Cemetery. Hamilton-Mylan Funeral Home. Obit - The Columbian)
NEHLER	Deal Edmund. U. S. Navy/WWII (Age 64, b. 9 Dec 1919, Greeley County, NE - d. 16 Mar 1985, Vancouver, WA. Husband of Leona K. Nehler, Vancouver. Mass of Christian Burial Thursday, Mar. 21, St. John's Catholi Church. Interment in St. John's Catholic Cemetery. Evergreen Staples Funeral Chapel. Obit-The Columbian)
QUIGG	Mabel M. "Pat" (Age 73, b. 18 Mar 1913 American Falls ID - d. 17 Sep 1986, Vancouver, WA. Preceded in death by husband, Thomas James Quigg, in 1969. Graveside service Tues., Sep. 23, at St. John's Catholic Cem. Hamilton-Mylan Funeral Home. Obit - The Columbian)
QUITUGUA	Enrique T. "Rick" (b. 12 Mar 1911, Guam - d. 17 Jan 1984, Brush Prairie, WA. Res: Vancouver, WA Mass of Christian Burial Saturday, January 28, at St. John's Catholic Church. Burial in St. John's Catholic Cemetery. Evergreen Staples Funeral Chapel. Obit - The Columbian)

THULIN   Arthur Henry. U. S. Army/WWII (Age 73, b. 31 Jul 1914,
                Turkey Ford, OK. - d. 16 Sep 1987 at home, Vancouver,
                WA. Husband of Mary Agnes. Graveside service Sat.,
                Sept. 19, at St. John's Catholic Cemetery. VFC.
                Obit - The Columbian)

VALENCIA   Rodrigo Elisea. (Age 31. Shot. B. March 1956,
                Aguilille, Michoacan, Mexico - d. 3 Oct 1987, Aloha,
                OR. Son of Maria Valencia Ochoa, Aguililla, Michoacan,
                Mexico. Mass of Christian burial Friday, Oct. 9, at
                St. John's Catholic Church. Burial in St. John's
                Catholic Cem. Hamilton-Mylan Funeral Home. Obit -
                The Columbian)

WOLF   Pauline G. (Age 58, b. 25 Jun 1927, Berwick ND -
                d. 8 Aug 1985, Vancouver, WA. Wife of Mathias Wolf,
                at home. Mass of Christian Burial Tuesday, Aug. 13,
                at St. John's Catholic Church. Interment in St. John's
                Cemetery. Hamilton-Mylan Funeral Home. Obit -
                The Columbian)

ALSTAD, Dagny L.	175	
ALTAMA, Mr.	60	
ALTIZER, Arnold	1	
, Ellen M.	1	
, Grace	1	
AMES, Arthur A.	93	
AMIS, Mike	7	
AMMETER, Bertha	74	
, Esther C. Godsil	74	
, Fred	74	
, Fritz	74	
, William	74	
ANDERSEN, Carroll G.	233, 234	
, Clara	234	
, Donald W.	234	
, Dorothy	233	
ANDERSON, Charles	93	
, Charles "Lucky"	121	
, Charles F.	1	
, Christina	176	
, Clara C.	74	
, David Charles	209	
, Elmer	121	
, Emil F.	1	
, Emil J.	93	
, Fern	209	
, Ferna/Fern A.	175, 176	
, Forny	176	
, Georgia A.	93	
, Hannah	121	
, Helen	93	
, John	93	
, John L.	175, 176	
, John S.	176	
, Lettie V.	1	
, Lydia J.	176	
, Lynn Dennis	286	
, Marie	176	
, Marie C.	1	
, Martin	176	
, Mary J.	176	
, May Belle	1	
, Myrtle Ming	234	
, N. P.	121	
, Natalie L.	234	
, Nels C.	74	
, Nels P.	122	
, Peter	60	
, Phillip	176	
, Ramus H.	176	
, Ray G.	1	
, Rosalie (Gertz)	234	
, Rosalie Irene	234	
, Thomas	176	
, Walter	268	
ANDRUS, Arthur G.	1	

ANFIN, Blanche	147	
, L. Ole	147	
ANHOLT, A. Loretta	122	
ANNIS, James R.	85	
ANTONELLI, Ann	220	
APRIMIS, Minerva	147	
APROZEAN, Alexandrea	1	
, Uasile	1	
ARMSTRONG, Baby	176	
, Daniel	122	
, David	122	
, Donna	222	
, George F.	93	
, George W.	176	
, Leroy A.	93	
, Margaret E.	122	
, Mary	93	
, Orpha C.	93	
, Ruth E.	122	
, Thomas S.	122	
ARNEY, Randall Nave	286	
ARNOLD, Henry	281	
, Lorraine	281	
ARRABEE, Elsie	234	
, Sidney	234	
ASHFORD, Helen I.	209	
ATCHLEY, Keith Noel	286	
ATKINS, Anna Lois	122	
, Bertie A.	122	
, Clyde A.	234	
, David	2	
, Elmer J.	1	
, Evangeline M.	122	
, Everette E.	1	
, Gary	2	
, John Everett	122	
, Lanelle	2	
, Lloyd E.	1	
, Lois Alberta	122	
, Mabel	122	
, Marian M.	122	
, Mollie S.	122	
, Muriel A.	2	
, Myrtle S.	2	
, Myrtle V.	234	
, William E.	122	
ATTEBERRY, Gladys	234	
, William B.	234	
ATTRIDGE, John J.	93	
ATTWELL, Bertha Alice	74	
, James Fremont	74	
AUGEE, Charles H.	176	
, Chalres Joe	176	
, Lilly Blanch	176	
, Millard	176	
AUGER, Albert W.	147	

HOFFMAN, Eva May	103	HONAN, Esta	104
, Nick	190	, Michael J.	104
HOFFMEISTER, Ralph M.	21	, Thomas J.	104
HOGAN, Juanita M.	217	HONGELL, Andrew	21
, Neil	153	, Andrew E.	21
, Ralph Leo	217	, Helena S.	21
HOGE, Oscar P.	21	, May T.	21
HOGUE, Louisa	190	HONKALA, Hilda	22
HOLBROOK, Jesse	21	HOOD, Flora E.	132
, W. H.	21	, Otto Vine	255
HOLDNER, Lonnin G.	21	, Walter F.	132
HOLLAND, Beverely June	190	HOOKER, Ella	191
, Gertrude	190	, Thomas A.	191
, James	190	HOOVER, Lewis	254
, James Farley	190	HOPKINS, Robert W.	132
, James W.	190	HORN, Martha	104
, Jessie (Welp)	190	, Mathias	104
HOLLENBECK, (Plot)	188	HORNE, Robert W.	191
, Mary	191	HORNOR, Charles W.	191
, Willard F.	191	, Emma B.	191
HOLLIN, Ruth Amanda	21	HOSENEY, Evelyn	22
HOLMES, Esther	228	, May R.	22
, Frank M.	132	, Otto W.	22
, Gertie Marks	132	HOSENEY, John R.	22
, John R.	132	HOSENY, James I.	22
, Lela M.	255	, Minnie B.	22
, Leo K.	255	HOSMER, Mr.	132
, Lester J.	132	HOSTIKKA, Richard August	286
, Vance D.	132	, Theodore	22
HOLMGREN, Al (M/M)	10	, Victoria E.	22
, Anna Helen	21	HOTTMAN, Tivis F.	22
, Brett	10	HOUGH, Calvin R.	255
, Brian	9	, Jean R.	255
, Peter	21	HOUSE, Clara E.	22
, Victor L.	21	, Lewis D.	22
HOLMGRENS, Baby	21	, Wesley	22
HOLSTINE, Fred	191	HOUSEMAN, Clara	22
, Jane	191	HOUSER, Ethel G.	104
HOLT, Baby Boy	21	, John H.	104
, Eugene D.	21	, Maude	104
, Dorothy	2	, May	104
, Eugene	2	HOUTER, Clarence	22
, Theresa S.	21	HOVER, George A.	22
HOLTER, Clarence	21	, Louisa W.	22
, Ruth M.	21	HOWARD, Adrain E.	22
HOLTMAN, John	103	, Anna M.	22
, John F.	103	, Barbara O.	132
, Minnie	103	, Bret R.	22
HOMAR, George A.	191	, Cecil Clyde	22
, Gustavis	191	, Frank J.	132
, Harry N.	191	, Nancy	22
, James G.	191	, Sarah E.	23
, John G.	191	HOWELL, Eugene O.	217
, Nellie	191	, Simon Peter	191
, Ruthie A.	191	, Vivian E.	217
HONAN, Emma	103	HOYES, Frederick R.	23

POTTER, Sgt. Dan'l 38
POWELL, Cathey 156
, Daisy B. 199
, Edgar C. 199
, Errett   A 38
, Ferdinand 110
, Franz 110
, Herbert Earl 38
, Irene 38
, John Lee 138
, Louise 110
, William 110
POWERS, Joel Jay 224
, Martha M. 38
PRAGER, James 156
, Kenneth 156
, Veronica T. 156
PRATHER, Deborah 269
, Lee 269
, Randall Lee 269
PRATT, Baby 79
, Daniel E. 79
, Fred Cotton 110
, M/M George 64
, Hallie 110
, Marvieen 79
, Myra Breed 110
PREST, Charles A. 38
, Ernest H. 38
, Ona Marie 38
PRESTON, Ethel R. 38
, Herbert T. 38
, Mary Manning 109
, Nelson H. 109
, Sarah A. 38
, Theodore 38
, Tony Lee 109
PREW, Arthur "Herb" Herbert 224
, Betty 224
PRICE, Baby 38, 110
, Birdella 38
, Elizabeth G. 110
, Horatio N. 110
, LeBaron W. 110
, Nancy 165
, Robert D. 110
, Robert Jeremy 224
PRIDEL, Dr. Phillip 39
PRIETZEL, Baby 138
, Thomas Leroy 138
PRINCE, David 138
PRITEL, Irene Clark 39
PROBESTEL, G. A. 110
, G. E. 111
, Henretta 110, 111
, Henry Oscar 111

PROBESTEL, John 111
, Leota May 111
, M. A. 111
, Rudolf 111
, Sarah 111
, Valentine 111
PROUDFIT, Cecil E. 39
, Dale E. 39
, Nora C. 39
PROUTY, Pearl 90
PRUETT, Charles L. 138
PRUTZMAN, Ella M. 199
, Flora G. 199
, Infant Son 199
, Mary A. 199
, William H. 199
PUCKETT, Ruth F. 224
PULFORD, Floyd 39
, Jane 39
, Ruth 39
PULLER, J. Elton 64
PUNKO, John 236, 269
, Nellie M. 236, 269
PURA, Anna 171
, Frank O. 171
, H. 172
, Henry 171
, Jennie E. 171
PURDY, Billie Agnus 269
, (Mrs.) S. H. 247
, Stephen H. 269

QUEEN, Betty 273
, Betty (Mrs. Homer) 251
QUESNELL, Tillie Ann 150
QUIGG, Mabel M. "Pat" 156, 288
, Patricia 156
, Thomas James 156, 288
QUIMBY, John L. 39
, Mildred I. 39
QUINA, Lawrence 260
QUIRK, Betty 288
, Elsie B. 269
, J. Donald 269
QUITUGUA, Enrique T. "Rick" 156, 288

RADENSLEBEN, Edna L. 34
RADFORD, Elmer V. 199
, Elva 98
, Myrtle I. 199
RAETZ, Annetta 138
, Frederick A. 138
RAHAJA, Emanuel 90
, Manuel 84
RAMBO, Harriet 39
, James 39